HELLO!

GOOD COOKING

HELLO!

GOOD COOKING

JILL COX

HEADLINE

The author would like to give special thanks to Dianne Curtin for her never-ending enthusiasm and invaluable help.

First published in 1993
by HEADLINE BOOK PUBLISHERS PLC

10 9 8 7 6 5 4 3 2 1

British Library Cataloguing in Publication Data

"Hello!" Magazine
"Hello!" Good Cooking
1. Title
641.5

ISBN 0-7472-0783-6 (Hardback)
ISBN 0 7472 7894 6 (Softback)

Designed by D&S Design, London

Colour reproduction by Koford, Singapore

Printed and bound in Great Britain by
Butler and Tanner Limited, Frome

HEADLINE BOOK PUBLISHING PLC
Headline House
79 Great Titchfield Street
London W1P 7FN

CONTENTS

COLOUR KEY

FRUIT AND NUTS

MEAT, POULTRY AND FISH

VEGETABLES AND PULSES

STORE CUPBOARD AND DAIRY

INTRODUCTION

Good Cooking Good Eating in Hello! has a unique format. Each week two pages are devoted to an item from the larder, store-cupboard, fridge or vegetable basket. It could be, for example, apple, chicken, prawns, nutmeg, among an unending list of others.

The history, nutritional details, what to look for when buying and how to store each ingredient, are accompanied by helpful tips and suggestions. Four exciting, original recipes are illustrated with excellent colour photographs.

In Hello! these pages are at the back of the magazine with cut-out-and-keep dotted edges for easy tearing out and collection. Over the past few years there has been a constant demand from readers who have missed issues, lost recipes or who would simply like to have a collection in a book for easy reference. This is the book.

There are over seventy subjects covered here from apples to tuna, Barbary duck to saffron. The vegetable pages include ordinary items such as mushrooms and tomatoes with delicious ideas for more unusual vegetables like asparagus and globe artichokes. Many of these recipes are suitable as accompaniments. For example, look up courgette for the recipe Courgette and Yellow Pepper Tagliatelle, and tomato for the Tomato Upside Down Potato Cake.

A range of fruit subjects includes among others raspberries, figs, bananas, pears and nectarines. These lend themselves to both fruity summer desserts when in season and many unexpected and unusual savory dishes like Pork with Nectarine and Onion Confit and Pheasant with Figs and Sherry.

Meats feature cuts like chuck steak with recipes for Beef and Orange Stew, Steak and Smoked Oyster Pies and Braised Beef with Olives. Fish dishes are centred on shellfish like crabs: Crab in Crackly Filo, Devilled Crab; langoustines: Seafood Risotto, or Langoustine Eclairs. Or seafish like cod, cooked in red wine, cobbled or curried. Tandoori Mackerel was a much requested recipe.

There is a host of other topics, including spices. For example, saffron, and paprika, are used in both new and specially adapted recipes. Saffron Thins are wonderful crisp, spicy and fragrant biscuits, Rabbit with Saffron is the most excellent mix of flavours. From the paprika pages try Marmite Marseillaise, a gutsy fish stew, and Paprika Scones with Tomato Butter.

Amongst other herbs, chives make a major contribution to

Green Risotto and Chilled Avocado and Chive Soup. Coriander is the herb in Salousa, Sea Bass en Papillotte and Coriander Roast Lamb. Basil flavours the most delectable clear, thin tomato soup, and comes into its own in the classic herb and cheese pasta sauce, pesto.

Cheeses such as Cheddar are used in Cheddar and Tuna Soufflé, and Cheese and Tomato Pie. A special pastry to top beef pies includes the king of English cheeses, Stilton.

Irresistible recipes from store-cupboard ingredients such as honey, mustard, olive oil and noodles are easy to look up and simple to follow.

Because of the nature of the weekly features which are headed by the name of the ingredient, the subjects in the book are arranged in alphabetical order under the same name. In addition, there is a compre-hensive index at the back where the recipes themselves are listed.

The approximate nutritional composition of each recipe is shown to give an idea of what it contains; preparation and cooking times are also given so enthusiastic cooks can plan their menus and fit them into busy schedules. The dishes range from simple, everyday ideas where most of the ingredients will be in the larder, to special occasion recipes, guaranteed to impress, where a bit of shopping may be involved. Main courses are sometimes quick and easy. Other times, when the subject lends itself, they may be smart and fancy – but still guaranteed achievable.

All the recipes in this book are easy to do – and more often than not are quick enough to make after a day's work. Stews and casseroles which take longer can be started the day before, then finished off when needed. This often improves the flavour, anyway.

And finally, what better to accompany good food than a well-chosen glass of wine? Choosing wines can sometimes be a bewildering task. At the back of the book there is a section on matching wines with food. This is in the form of a simple-to-follow chart using recipes from the book as examples. This section gives general advice on selecting wines which have a similar style to the dish in question and will therefore complement it well. Notes are included on how to serve wines and in which glasses. There are also thumbnail notes on wine-producing countries all over the world to encourage enthusiasts to try a wide variety.

Bon Appétit and Cheers!

Jill Cox
January 1993

HELLO!

GOOD COOKING

APPLES

Apples are thought to be the first fruit grown by man. In fact, carbonised apples from almost 15,000 years ago have been found in remains of prehistoric dwellings in Switzerland and Italy. Crab apples known as 'wildings' were eaten in ancient Britain before the Roman invasion. After this, Roman varieties were planted by monks in monastery gardens.

Henry VIII was responsible for the beginnings of the first apple orchards. Although he dissolved the monasteries where apples were established, he enjoyed the fruit and wanted more home-grown varieties. He sent his chief fruiterer, Richard Harris, over to France to learn about cultivation techniques and, on his return, he planted a large selection of cuttings in the first orchard at Teynham, Kent.

After this, fruit growing became a thriving industry and by the 18th century, apple growers were regarded as professional nurserymen.

Cox's Orange Pippin, one of the most popular apples today, was first grown in 1812 by Richard Cox in Colnbrook, Slough. The nine apple pips he planted in his garden grew into trees reputed to be crosses between Ribston Pippin and Blenheim Orange. The original 'Cox's' tree was lost in a gale in 1911.

Bramley's Seedlings were known in Southwell, Nottingham in 1812, and although popular with the locals, they were not exhibited until 1876. They prefer the UK climate and cannot be grown elsewhere.

Apples have many historical links with good health. King Arthur went specially to the island of Avalon, the ancient Elysium of Celtic heroes, which was covered with apple trees, to be healed of his war wounds. And in the 16th century, the herbalist Gerarde wrote about apples which were 'good for a hot stomach'.

Today, around 600 types of apple are grown in Britain but only a tenth of these are well known.

PORK WITH APPLES

Loin of pork cooked slowly in cider with mustard, garlic and apples. *Serves 6*

3 tbsp oil
3lb/1.4kg loin of pork, boned and rolled
1 onion, peeled and finely chopped
2 cloves garlic, peeled and crushed
12 shallots, peeled
³/₄pt/425ml dry cider
¹/₄pt/150ml stock
Salt and freshly ground black pepper
1oz/25g butter
2 apples, cored and in chunks
4oz/100g mushrooms, quartered
1 tbsp double cream
2 tsp Dijon mustard

Heat 1 tbsp oil in a large pan and seal and brown joint all over. Remove and place in an ovenproof dish. Add remaining oil and fry onion and garlic over low heat until soft. Scatter around pork. Brown shallots and add these, too. Pour cider and stock into frying pan and stir to scrape up sediment and juices. Bring to the boil and pour over pork. Season and cover with foil. Cook at Gas 4, 350F, 180C for 2 hours, or until pork is tender.

Melt butter in a pan and brown apples. Add these with the mushrooms to the pork 20 minutes before the end of cooking time. Remove foil at the same time to brown meat. Strain juices into a pan and boil until reduced by a third. Stir in cream and mustard, and check seasoning. Pour over joint before serving.

Preparation time: 30 minutes
Cooking time: 2¹/₂ hours

Approximate nutritional values per portion:	
475 calories	48g protein
45g fat	8g carbohydrate

NUTRITION

Apples are low in calories with only around 45 in an average-sized fruit. There are 11g of carbohydrate, but only a trace of protein and fat. They make a good snack for slimmers as they are filling but not fattening.

Apples contain some vitamin A and B. The most important contribution is C. An apple has 6mg which represents 20 per cent of the recommended daily amount for an adult. To make the most of this vitamin, apples should be eaten raw (heat destroys it) and unpeeled since this is where most of the fibre is found.

Vitamin C is essential for healthy bones, teeth, gums and blood vessels. It is also vital for the absorption of iron.

1 medium-sized apple contains:	
45 calories	trace of protein
trace of fat	11g carbohydrate

KNOW YOUR APPLES

Cox's Orange Pippin is one of the best-known in the UK. Red/yellow with a brush of russet, the flesh is crisp and juicy with a rich aromatic flavour.

Discovery is a medium-sized apple with a pale yellow colour heavily flushed with bright red. It is hard and crisp and tastes best when fully ripe. Eat lightly chilled.

Egremont Russet has a beautiful, golden russet appearance, hard, dry flesh and a nutty flavour.

Spartan when fully ripe turns a pretty purple maroon colour, and is crisp and juicy with a good fresh flavour.

Jonagold is large with greeny-yellow skin dappled with bright red. It has creamy white flesh with good crunch and plenty of juice.

Bramley's Seedling is the most famous and widely used cooking apple with pale yellow-green skin sometimes streaked with browny-red.

SAUSAGES AND APPLE JAM

A delicious fruity accompaniment to cooked Toulouse sausages. *Makes 12oz/350g jar*

- 2 tbsp oil
- 1 onion, peeled and finely chopped
- 2 cloves garlic, crushed
- 2 green peppers, de-seeded and finely chopped
- 2 apples, peeled, cored and finely chopped
- 1 tbsp sun-dried tomatoes in oil, drained and finely chopped
- 3 tbsp water
- 1 tbsp sugar
- 2 tbsp vinegar
- 1 tbsp dry sherry
- Freshly ground black pepper

Heat oil in a pan and fry onion and garlic gently to soften. Add green peppers and apples and cook for a further minute. Stir in the tomatoes and remaining ingredients. Bring to the boil and cook slowly until the liquid disappears. Cool and chill. Serve with grilled Toulouse sausages. Keep covered in the fridge and use within 3 days.

Preparation time: 20 minutes
Cooking time: 15 minutes

Approximate nutritional values per portion for apple jam:	
80 calories	nil protein
5g fat	10g carbohydrate

APPLE TIPS

● Use Bramley's Seedling cooking apples to make an apple and sage sauce for roast pork. Peel, core and chop 2 large Bramleys and sprinkle with lemon juice. Finely chop 4 shallots and fry in 1 tbsp oil with a clove of crushed garlic until softened. Add apples and stir to mix. Moisten with 1 tbsp port. Cover and cook gently until apples are mushy. Add a little water or more port if required. Stir in a few shredded sage leaves and season with salt and freshly ground black pepper. Serve with roast pork and crackling.

● Invest in an apple corer for easy preparation of apples. Push the corer through the centre of the apple from the stalk end to the base. Lift it out and it should contain a cylinder of flesh complete with pips and core. If there are any pips remaining, carefully scoop them out with a teaspoon.

● Home-made toffee apples are easy to make and hard to resist. Wash 8 Cox's Orange Pippins or other dessert apples and dry thoroughly. Push long wooden sticks into the stem end of each apple, making sure they are well pushed down. Melt 8oz/225g granulated sugar in ¹/₂pt/300ml water in a pan and bring to the boil. Boil rapidly until it begins to turn golden brown. Remove from heat before it becomes too dark. Carefully dip in apples one by one, turning so that toffee coats them completely. Place on oiled greaseproof with sticks pointing up and leave to set.

APPLE MUFFINS

Apple-flavoured and filled with garlic cream cheese and fresh apple purée. *Makes 10*

For the muffins:
- 4oz/100g plain flour
- Pinch of salt
- 1 tsp baking powder
- 1oz/25g butter
- 1oz/25g caster sugar
- 1 eating apple, cored, peeled and grated
- 2 tbsp milk (approx)
- 1 egg, beaten
- Caster sugar for sprinkling

For the filling:
- 4 eating apples, cored, peeled and very finely chopped
- A squeeze of lemon juice
- 6 tbsp water
- 2 tbsp runny honey
- 2oz/50g Boursin with garlic

Sift flour, salt and baking powder into a bowl. Rub in butter and stir in sugar and grated apple. Add enough milk to form a soft, but not sticky, dough. Turn out on to a lightly floured board and knead gently for 1 minute. Wrap in foil and chill for 15 minutes.

Roll out to ³/₄in/1.5cm thick. Cut into rounds with a 2in/5cm cutter. Place on a greased baking tray and brush with beaten egg. Cook in a pre-heated oven Gas 5, 375F, 190C for 15 minutes or until risen and firm. Remove and cool on a wire rack. Sprinkle with sugar.

Meanwhile, make the apple filling. Place apples, lemon juice, water and honey in a pan and cook until softened. Reserve and cool. Split muffins and spread base with cream cheese. Top with apple mix and sandwich together with lid.

Preparation time: 20 minutes
Cooking time: 20 minutes

Approximate nutritional values per muffin:	
115 calories	3g protein
6g fat	28g carbohydrate

CREPES NANETTE

Lacy pancakes filled with apple slices and flambéed with Calvados. *Serves 4*

For the pancakes:
- 4oz/100g plain flour
- Pinch of salt
- 1 egg, beaten
- ¹/₂pt/300ml milk
- Oil for frying

For the filling:
- 3oz/75g butter
- 2 apples, cored and in slices
- 2 pieces preserved stem ginger, sliced
- 4 tbsp Calvados
- Juice and zest of ¹/₂ lemon
- 2 tbsp juice from the ginger jar
- Lemon zest for decoration

First make the pancakes. Sift flour and salt into a bowl and make a well in the centre. Pour in beaten egg and a little milk. Beat in gradually until smooth, adding remaining milk, little by little. Heat oil in a pancake pan and add just enough batter to coat the base – swirl it around to cover. Cook until bubbles appear on the surface. Toss crêpes. Cook other side. Reserve.

Continue until all batter is used up.

For the filling, heat 1oz/25g butter and fry apple and ginger slices until apple is just soft. Fold pancakes into four to make a cone. Stuff with a little filling.

In another pan melt remaining butter and carefully add 2 or 3 filled pancakes – do this in batches. Add a little Calvados and tilt pan to ignite. Add lemon juice and zest and a little ginger syrup from the jar. Heat through.

Drizzle over the sauce to serve. Decorate with lemon zest.

Preparation time: 30 minutes
Cooking time: 20 minutes

Approximate nutritional values per portion:	
350 calories	7g protein
20g fat	32g carbohydrate

ASPARAGUS

The luxurious asparagus is a cousin of the lily. Much prized by the Ancient Egyptians for its exotic looks and taste, it was also popular with the Greeks and Romans. The Romans brought it to Britain, but after they left, it disappeared, too, and was not reintroduced until the 16th century.

Battersea, in south London owes some of its fame to asparagus. It was an area where the thin stems of asparagus grew in abundance and 'Battersea bundles' of 'sparrow grass' were much in demand.

This thin asparagus, or sprue, was preferred, well into the 19th century when England was the world's top producer.

It takes around three years before asparagus spears can be harvested and each one has to be hand-cut, which is why it is expensive.

May is the traditional month when English asparagus becomes readily available, but imported bundles are in the shops most of the year.

Continentals and Americans like the fat white stems, while home-grown is medium thickness with a deep green or purplish colour, and sprue is bright green and usually sold loose.

LUXURY ASPARAGUS OMELETTE

A light and delicate omelette filled with tender asparagus spears, excellent for a lunch treat.
Serves 1

4 spears of asparagus
2 eggs
Salt and freshly ground black pepper
¹/₂oz/15g butter
1 tbsp soured cream
Watercress sprigs to decorate

Trim asparagus and remove woody bases. Cut to equal lengths. Steam until tender. Reserve.

Beat eggs with seasoning. Melt butter in an omelette pan and pour in egg mixture. Over a high heat, stir egg mix around with a fork bringing the outside edge of mixture into the centre so that the uncooked mixture runs underneath. Do this until the mixture begins to set, then turn heat down low.

When it is firm and golden underneath but still soft on top, add the asparagus spears and a tbsp of soured cream. Make sure the tips are pointing the same way for pretty presentation.

Flip over the omelette on to a plate to enclose spears and cream and serve decorated with sprigs of watercress.

Preparation time: 10 minutes
Cooking time: 5 minutes

Approximate nutritional values per portion:	
305 calories	22g protein
23g fat	1g carbohydrate

ASPARAGUS TERRINE

Simplicity itself, this pretty terrine of asparagus set in homemade mayonnaise makes a stunning first course for a special dinner party. Guests are bound to be impressed! *Serves 6*

16 spears asparagus
1 sachet aspic
For the mayonnaise:
2 egg yolks
1 tsp herb mustard
Good squeeze lemon juice
¹/₂pt/300ml sunflower oil
Salt and freshly ground white pepper
Asparagus tips and sprigs of chervil for decoration

Trim asparagus to remove tough stalk bases and to make spears equal size. Rinse gently and pat dry. Cook in lightly salted boiling water until just tender, being careful not to overcook. Drain and refresh in cold water. Drain again and lay asparagus on a clean tea-towel to dry.

For the mayonnaise, whisk egg yolks in a bowl with mustard and lemon juice. Add oil drip by drip, whisking constantly, until mixture begins to thicken. Continue adding oil in a thin stream until all is incorporated. Season with salt and freshly ground white pepper and a squeeze of lemon juice to taste.

Make up the aspic according to instructions on the packet, but with ¹/₂pt/300ml boiling water instead of 1pt/600ml. Leave until cooled. Stir into mayonnaise and leave until syrupy and beginning to set – about 15 minutes.

Pour a thin layer in the base of a 1lb/450g terrine. Top with 4 sticks of asparagus, top to tail. Spoon over a layer of mayonnaise and smooth the surface. Repeat with a further 4 sticks of asparagus and mayonnaise. Continue layering in this way until asparagus and mayonnaise are used up, ending with a layer of mayonnaise. Smooth the surface. Chill until set. Turn out and serve in slices decorated with asparagus tips and sprigs of chervil. Use a serrated-edged knife to cut the slices, being gentle as you slice through the asparagus.

Preparation time: 30 minutes
Cooking time: 5 minutes approx

Approximate nutritional values per portion:	
300 calories	4g protein
35g fat	1g carbohydrate

BUYING AND STORING

May 1 heralds the start of the British asparagus season. This is the time when home-grown bundles of this delicious luxury vegetable flood into greengrocers and supermarkets.

During the season, English asparagus is reputedly the best. But at other times of the year, imported varieties from Spain, USA, and Australia, as well as other countries, are usually available.

Asparagus spears are nearly always sold tied neatly in bundles, but some are available 'loose', such as the thin sprue variety. Choose spears which are green and fresh looking with no sign of crushing, bruising or wilting. The buds at the tip should be tight and firm. Some asparagus is kept fresh by hydro-cooling after picking, so this sort may have a damp or moist appearance. Only the top-quality asparagus is processed in this way and the wetness should not be confused with moisture due to mould or rotting, so check carefully to ensure there are no signs of blemishes or deterioration on the stems.

Asparagus is best eaten on the day of purchase for maximum freshness and taste. It may be kept in a cool place or in the fridge for a day or so, but it is a luxury that should be enjoyed in the peak of condition, while crisp and firm.

Fresh asparagus can be frozen at home. For short-term keeping, freeze it unblanched. For longer storage, wash and blanch the trimmed stems for three minutes. Drain, refresh and dry before freezing loose or in bundles. Be warned, frozen asparagus is easily broken.

ASPARAGUS TIPS

● To prepare asparagus spears for cooking, first trim away the woody bases. If the spears are thick and the skin seems tough, pare away thinly to about a third up from the bottom. Leave the tips untouched. Cut the asparagus spears into equal lengths and tie in bundles before boiling or steaming.

● The best way to cook asparagus is by steaming. Place bundles, tips upwards, in an asparagus pan half-filled with simmering water. This pan is tall and narrow, just large enough to take a bundle standing up. The stalk ends are toughest, while the tips are delicate and tender. Simmer for 12 minutes, or until the ends of the stalks are tender. The tips get cooked at the same time.

● Hollandaise is the classic warm sauce to accompany hot asparagus – but sometimes this can be tricky to cook perfectly. This blender version is the answer. For 4: place 2 egg yolks in the goblet of the blender. Add a good squeeze of lemon juice, salt and freshly ground white pepper. Blend for 30 seconds. With the blender still running, gradually add 8oz/225g warm melted butter in a very thin stream until all is incorporated and the sauce is thick.

● Use older stems of asparagus for flavouring soup and making purées. You will need to sieve out the woody fibres after cooking.

PASTA PRINCESSE

A delightful dish of pasta shells with chicken shreds and asparagus in a white wine cream sauce. *Serves 4*

> *12oz/350g pasta shells*
> *2 tbsp oil*
> *4 shallots, peeled and finely chopped*
> *2 cloves garlic, crushed*
> *1 wine glass dry white wine*
> *4 tbsp double cream*
> *12oz/350g cooked chicken breast, in shreds*
> *8 spears cooked asparagus, cut into 2in/5cm lengths*
> *Salt and freshly ground black pepper*
> *1 hard-boiled egg, chopped for decoration*

Cook pasta shells in plenty of boiling salted water until just tender. Drain and keep hot.

Meanwhile, make the sauce. Heat oil in a pan and fry shallots and garlic until softened. Pour over white wine and bring to the boil. Add cream, then bubble to reduce slightly. Add chicken and continue bubbling for a further 3 minutes. Stir in asparagus and season.

Toss chicken and asparagus mix in pasta shells and pile into a serving dish. Sprinkle with chopped hard-boiled egg for decoration.

Preparation time: 20 minutes
Cooking time: 20 minutes approx

Approximate nutritional values per portion:	
550 calories	33g protein
15g fat	50g carbohydrate

PRAWN AND ASPARAGUS SALAD

A lovely mix of flavours and textures in this delicious salad of pearly prawns, sliced button mushrooms and asparagus, tossed in a herby vinaigrette. *Serves 4*

> *12 asparagus spears, trimmed*
> *8oz/225g button mushrooms, wiped and sliced*
> *12oz/350g peeled prawns*
> For the dressing:
> *4 tbsp sunflower oil*
> *1 tbsp white wine vinegar*
> *1 tsp Dijon mustard*
> *Salt and freshly ground black pepper*
> *1 tbsp finely chopped parsley and chervil, mixed*

Cook asparagus in lightly salted boiling water until just tender. Drain and refresh in cold water. Drain again. Pat dry gently and cut into short lengths.

Mix mushroom slices in a bowl with prawns. Shake dressing ingredients in a screw-top jar and pour over. Toss to coat. Add asparagus and toss again, carefully, to avoid breaking the asparagus tip. Leave in the fridge to marinate for 30 minutes or longer if possible. Pile into a pretty bowl to serve.

Preparation time: 15 minutes
Cooking time: 5 minutes approx

Approximate nutritional values per portion:	
150 calories	17g protein
6g fat	1g carbohydrate

NUTRITION

Asparagus is low in calories, with only 18 in 4oz/100g. Slimmers and the health-conscious can enjoy this wonderfully luxurious delicacy as a change from the run-of-the-mill salad stuffs, without any fear of piling on the pounds.

Asparagus makes a substantial contribution to the diet in the form of vitamin A, necessary for good vision. Traces of vitamins B1 and B2, to maintain the nervous system, are also present along with vitamin C for healthy skin and healing.

Asparagus also contains a good selection of minerals, calcium, for teeth and bones, iron for the blood, potassium for muscle tissue and phosphorus, for cells.

4oz/100g asparagus contain:	
18 calories	4g protein
nil fat	1g carbohydrate

AVOCADOS

Avocados originated in tropical South America where they were enjoyed by the Aztec and Inca Indians for centuries. Easy to digest, these creamy, buttery fruit were a plentiful staple. But the Indian women discovered another use for the avocado – as a beauty treatment.

Mashed avocados were included in facial preparations, and this practice still remains popular today. Women all over the world use moisturisers and face packs containing avocado to promote soft, smooth skin.

In this country, it took many years for avocados to become popular – and affordable. They were still considered a rare luxury up until around 20 years ago. However, at this time, large numbers began to be exported to the UK by Israel which meant that the price became more reasonable due to a more readily available supply.

These days, there are two main varieties. One has dark green knobbly skin and is sometimes referred to as the alligator pear because of its appearance. The other is the pale green smooth-skinned avocado.

Israel remains one of the main exporters of avocados, joined by the USA, Ivory Coast, Kenya and Canary Islands.

AVOCADO AND SUN-DRIED TOMATO SALAD WITH BACON AND MOZZARELLA

This dish is a superb main course salad packed with flavours. The tomatoes can be bought dried, and need soaking in water to soften before use, or in oil in a jar ready for use. Supermarkets stock them. *Serves 4*

> 6oz/175g back bacon, derinded and chopped
> 1 tbsp oil
> 4oz/100g sun-dried tomatoes in oil, drained
> 14oz/400g canned artichoke hearts
> 6oz/175g mozzarella
> 1 avocado
> Lemon juice
> For the dressing:
> 4 tbsp olive oil
> 1 tbsp white wine vinegar
> 1 clove garlic, crushed
> 1/2 tsp Dijon mustard
> Salt and freshly ground black pepper

Fry the bacon in a little oil until crisp. Drain on kitchen paper. Reserve. Cut sun-dried tomatoes into thick strips. Quarter artichoke hearts and cut mozzarella into thin slices. Place these in a bowl with the bacon and tomatoes.

Peel and coarsely chop the avocado. Drizzle with lemon juice, then add to bowl.

Shake all the dressing ingredients together in a screw-top jar then pour over contents of the bowl. Toss gently to avoid damaging the avocado. Serve immediately.

Preparation time: 20 minutes
Cooking time: 5 minutes

Approximate nutritional values per portion:	
600 calories	17g protein
50g fat	10g carbohydrate

NUTRITION

Avocados are high in fat, which explains the calorie content of 223g per 4oz/100g. On the plus side, though, even though they are fatty, it is vegetable fat and they contain no cholesterol.

A good source of other nutrients, avocados contain some protein, carbohydrate and vitamins A, B and C. Vitamin A is required for good sight, but in this hemisphere, deficiency is rare because the diet is usually well-balanced. Also, vitamin A is stored in the liver.

There are also good amounts of vitamin C in avocados. In fact, 4oz/100g of avocado flesh provides 30mg, the recommended daily requirement for a healthy adult.

There is a moderate amount of the mineral potassium in avocados, which makes up muscle tissue and works with protein to build and repair muscles.

4oz/100g avocado flesh contain:	
223 calories	4g protein
22g fat	1.8g carbohydrate

AVOCADO AND COURGETTE RISOTTO

Irresistible vegetable risotto. *Serves 4*

> 3 tbsp oil
> 1 onion, peeled and finely chopped
> 2 cloves garlic, peeled and crushed
> 2 courgettes, trimmed and diced
> 12oz/350g risotto rice
> 1 1/2 pt/850ml vegetable stock
> 2 tbsp chopped chives
> 1 tbsp fresh parsley, finely chopped
> Salt and freshly ground black pepper
> 1 avocado, peeled, stoned and finely diced
> Juice of 1/2 lemon

Heat oil in a pan and fry onion and garlic over gentle heat until soft but not brown. Add the courgettes and continue cooking for 5 minutes. Stir in rice and turn over to coat in the oniony mix.

Add stock gradually and simmer until each addition is absorbed and rice is tender. Sprinkle over chives and parsley. Season.

Meanwhile, prepare avocado and squeeze over lemon juice to keep it green. Just before risotto is cooked, stir in avocado. Heat through 2 minutes more.

Preparation time: 15 minutes
Cooking time: 30 minutes

Approximate nutritional values per portion:	
530 calories	4g protein
22g fat	25g carbohydrate

BUYING AND STORING

Avocados are picked when they are hard and unripened, and begin to mature after this. To test for ripeness, gently apply pressure with the thumbs – the avocado should yield slightly. But if it is very soft and the skin is discoloured, the flesh inside will probably be over-ripe with small black patches. This will be no use for salads or dips as the colour will turn into an unappetising brown and the flavour will be impaired. Do not use avocados which are in anything less than perfect condition.

Flesh should be buttermilk-coloured with a tinge of green, have a dense, creamy texture and fresh smell.

Always buy avocados firm, and ripen them at home, unless they are required for eating the same day. A good place for ripening is the fruit bowl, or to speed up the process, an airing cupboard, or in a paper bag with an apple.

To keep avocados hard for longer storage, refrigerate them in the salad drawer.

Eat ripe avocados within two days to avoid spoilage.

AVOCADO AND PRAWN SOUFFLE

Glamorous dinner party starter. *Serves 4*

1¹/₂oz/40g butter
1¹/₂oz/40g flour
¹/₂pt/300ml milk
2oz/50g Cheddar cheese, grated
4 eggs, separated
4oz/100g peeled prawns, chopped
Salt and freshly ground black pepper
2 avocados
Lemon juice
Peeled prawns and chive batons for garnish

Melt butter in a pan and stir in flour. Cook for one minute. Remove from the heat and add a little milk. Stir to make a smooth paste, then add a little more milk. Continue until all milk is incorporated. Return to heat and cook over gentle heat, stirring until sauce is thickened.

Stir in cheese until melted, then beat in egg yolks. Add chopped prawns. Season. At this stage you can leave the mix covered in the fridge until just before needed. Whisk egg whites stiff and fold in carefully.

Halve and stone avocados and sprinkle with lemon juice to avoid discoloration. Preheat oven to Gas 5, 375F, 190C. Spoon soufflé into avocado cavities.

Bake for about 20 minutes until risen and golden (it will not rise high). Serve immediately garnished with prawns and chive batons.
Preparation time: 20 minutes
Cooking time: 30 minutes approx

Approximate nutritional values per portion:	
522 calories	22g protein
42g fat	11g carbohydrate

GUACAMOLE

This famous Mexican dip is best made with ripe avocados which mash easily. *Serves 4*

2 avocados
Lemon juice
¹/₂ onion, peeled and grated
2 cloves garlic, peeled and crushed
1 red chilli, de-seeded and chopped
Juice of ¹/₂ lime
4 sprigs fresh coriander, chopped
Salt and freshly ground black pepper

Halve avocados and remove stones. Scoop out flesh, place in a bowl, drizzle with lemon juice and mash smooth. Add onion and garlic, chilli, lime juice, coriander and seasoning. Stir well and cover. Chill for 30 minutes before serving with tortilla chips or crudités.
Preparation time: 20 minutes
Cooking time: nil

Approximate nutritional values per portion:	
250 calories	3g protein
18g fat	2g carbohydrate

AVOCADO TIPS

● Prevent peeled avocado from discolouring by squeezing over a little lemon juice. Do this as soon as the avocado is peeled, and it will remain pale green until required.

● Avocados are simple to prepare. Cut from the stalk end along the length of the avocado to the rounded end with the point of the knife against the stone. Continue cutting over the rounded end and back along the length on the other side of the avocado to meet up with the original cut. The avocado will fall into two halves with the stone in one half. To remove the stone, carefully push the heel of the knife into it and twist it out. Rub the cut sides with lemon juice as in previous tip.

● Serve halved stoned avocados with a citrus vinaigrette for a quick first course. Peel and stone the avocados, allowing a half for each diner. Rub halves with lemon juice and carefully peel. Rub peeled sides with lemon juice. For a dressing to serve 4: mix 2 tsp Dijon mustard in a bowl with 2 tbsp white wine vinegar. Whisk in 8 tbsp sunflower oil and the juice and grated zest of ¹/₂ orange. Season to taste with salt and freshly ground black pepper. Drizzle over avocados.

● For impressive presentation for avocado vinaigrette, cut avocado halves into fan shapes. Place ¹/₂ peeled avocado on a chopping board, flat side down. Sprinkle with lemon juice. With a sharp knife, make cuts close together along the length of the avocado, without cutting right through the pointed end. Press down on the avocado with the fingers to open out into a fan shape. Arrange on plates and drizzle over vinaigrette to serve. Garnish with sprigs of dill.

● Avocado makes a wonderful creamy soup to serve chilled in summer. For 4: halve, peel and stone 2 ripe avocados. Cut into chunks and squeeze over lemon juice. Whizz in a blender with 1³/₄pt/1ltr vegetable stock, 1 clove crushed garlic and ¹/₂ onion, grated. Add 4 tbsp double cream and whizz again. Season with salt and freshly ground white pepper. Serve chilled, sprinkled with snipped chives.

● Avocado and prawns are the perfect combination for a simple first course salad to grace any dinner party table. Peel and chunk creamy, ripe avocados, allowing half for each person, and sprinkle with lemon juice. Mix with pearly pink peeled prawns and toss in a herb dressing. Pile into pretty dishes and decorate with finely sliced spring onions.

BANANAS

Native to the Caribbean, bananas are one of the most popular fruits eaten in the UK. It is thought that the first bananas came from South East Asia and that they were one of the earliest cultivated crops known to man.

As their popularity grew, bananas spread to India, where Alexander the Great saw them on his travels in the year 327BC. Eventually they were shipped to the Canary Islands in the 1400s and then on to the West Indies, where plantations of swaying banana palms are now a familiar sight.

It was not until the 19th century that bananas reached North America and Europe, when the advent of better transportation in refrigerated ships made the export of these tropical fruit much easier. At first, they were a luxury for the rich but demand increased and soon they became widely available.

Bananas grow on tall palm trees in large bunches or 'hands' with the fruit pointing upwards like fingers. They are normally harvested while still green and left to ripen on the way to their final destination.

BANANA MILK SHAKE

Creamy and sensuous tropical-flavoured shake, delicately spiced with nutmeg and cinnamon. As a special treat lace the milk shake with a dash of rum for grown-ups who like a taste of the Caribbean. *Makes 2 generous shakes or 4 small ones*

2 bananas, peeled
1pt/600ml chilled milk
4 scoops vanilla dairy ice cream
1/2 tsp ground cinnamon
Good grating of fresh nutmeg
1 tbsp white rum

Whizz bananas and milk in a processor. Add 2 scoops ice cream, cinnamon and nutmeg, rum (optional) and process again. Pour into glasses and top each with a scoop of ice cream. Serve with straws.

Preparation time: 10 minutes
Cooking time: nil

Approximate nutritional values per generous shake:	
430 calories	14g protein
16g fat	60g carbohydrate

NUTRITION

Bananas are instant-energy food, and this energy comes from natural sugars which make up 91 per cent of a fully ripe fruit. Naturally, calories are correspondingly high, with 94 in a medium-sized peeled banana.

Containing B vitamins and some minerals, bananas make a sound nutritional contribution to the diet. They are particularly good for children, because their ready-made and hygienic packaging makes them a convenient snack to be eaten any time in place of crisps or chocolate.

Bananas are a moderate source of vitamin C, necessary for iron absorption and rapid healing of cuts and sores. Some say large doses can ward off or even cure the common cold, although there is no convincing medical evidence to prove this.

4oz/100g bananas contain:	
80 calories	1g protein
0.3g fat	19g carbohydrate

BANANA MERINGUE PIE

Heavenly mix of bananas and homemade custard topped with a crisp, airy meringue. *Serves 6*

6oz/175g shortcrust pastry
For the custard:
4 egg yolks
2 tbsp sugar
2 tbsp cornflour
1pt/600ml milk
Few drops vanilla essence
3 bananas
For the topping:
4 egg whites
8oz/225g caster sugar

Roll out pastry on a lightly floured board and line a 7in/18cm fluted flan dish. Chill in the fridge for 20 minutes, then bake blind at Gas 6, 400F, 200C for 10 minutes. Remove from oven and cool.

Next make the custard. Beat yolks with sugar until light and fluffy. Mix cornflour with a little water to make a paste and add. Bring milk almost to boiling with vanilla and whisk on to yolk mixture. Return to a clean pan and stir over heat until thickened. Do not boil or the mixture will curdle. Remove from heat, cover surface with buttered greaseproof paper and cool.

Slice bananas and lay in pastry case. Pour over custard mix. Whisk egg whites stiff with a little sugar, then fold in remaining sugar, lightly. Pile on to banana filling. Bake in a pre-heated oven Gas 4, 350F, 180C for 25 minutes or until meringue topping is crisp and golden. Cool and chill before serving.

Preparation time: 20 minutes
Cooking time: 40 minutes

Approximate nutritional values per portion:	
450 calories	10g protein
14g fat	28g carbohydrate

BUYING AND STORING

Bananas should be eaten at the peak of freshness when they are fully ripe. When buying, check they will be ripe when you need them.

Bananas which are ready to eat will have yellow skin with a dappling of brown spots. Those with pale yellow skins tinged with green at each end are under-ripe and will not be edible for about three days.

Some supermarkets sell over-ripe bananas cheaply. These may have blackened peel, but if they feel firm, usually the flesh is still sweet and creamy and may be used immediately for eating or baking in loaves and teabreads. Avoid damaged ones though, or any with splits in the peel, as these will be mushy and probably past their best.

Under-ripe bananas may be kept in the fruit bowl at room temperature for a couple of days. Already ripe fruit should be stored in the fridge. Although this darkens the skin, the flesh inside will remain fresh and good to eat for up to 5 days.

BANANA TIPS

● Banana flesh is perfect in a creamy trifle – the combination of bananas and custard is a match made in heaven. For 8: break up 2 trifle sponges and pour over a little (or a lot) of white rum, enough to soak them. Pile in 4 sliced bananas. Pour over 1pt/600ml cold, preferably homemade, custard. Top with a layer of 1pt/600ml whipped cream. Leave to set in the fridge.

● A good source of energy, bananas are loved by children. Make banana and bacon sandwiches with crunchy lettuce for their school lunchboxes.

● Always sprinkle sliced bananas with lemon juice to avoid discoloration if prepared some time before eating.

● Bananas are a good addition to mild curries. Add just before serving.

● Use them in a banana raita as an accompaniment to curries. Chop 1 peeled banana, and add with 1 tbsp finely chopped mint, the zest and juice of $\frac{1}{2}$ lemon, $\frac{1}{2}$ tsp turmeric and 1 tsp sugar to $\frac{1}{4}$pt/150ml plain yogurt.

● Flambéed bananas make a quick and delicious mid-week pud. For 4: peel and halve 4 bananas and sprinkle with lemon juice. Melt 2oz/50g butter in a large pan. Add bananas, 1 tbsp dark brown sugar and 1 tbsp sultanas. Cook gently to soften slightly and coat in a sugary mix. Pour over 3 tbsp rum and tilt pan to ignite, standing well back. When flames have died down, serve immediately with whipped cream.

● Bananas are one of the best first solid foods for a baby. Simply purée a ripe banana.

● Bananas with their own hygienic covering make a great any time snack. Keep one in a handbag or pocket to satisfy between meals hunger pangs, instead of a chocolate bar.

● Make fruity banana lollies for young and old alike. Spike peeled bananas on lolly sticks and dip in melted chocolate to cover half way up. Coat in crushed nuts. Freeze.

TOFFEE BANANAS

Crackly toffee-coated banana chunks for a different kind of pudding and one that children simply love. *Serves 4*

> 4 bananas, peeled
> Juice of 2 limes
> 4oz/100g sugar
> $\frac{1}{2}$pt/300ml water

Cut bananas into chunks and sprinkle over lime juice to keep them white and prevent discoloration.

Pour sugar into water and dissolve over low heat, stirring gently. Bring to the boil and bubble rapidly until the colour turns golden, without stirring. Remove from heat.

Spike banana chunks on a fork and twirl around in caramel mixture to coat all over. Do this with great care – hot caramel is really very hot. Leave coated chunks on non-stick paper for toffee to become hard. Pile into a serving dish and 'spin' threads of remaining caramel over the top with the prongs of a fork.
Preparation time: 10 minutes
Cooking time: 20 minutes

Approximate nutritional values per portion:	
200 calories	1g protein
nil fat	28g carbohydrate

BANANA AND APRICOT TEABREAD

Moist and fruity bread, delicious spread with unsalted butter. A great tea-time treat. *Serves 10*

> 8oz/225g self-raising flour
> Pinch of salt
> 4oz/100g unsalted butter
> 4oz/100g caster sugar
> 2 bananas, peeled
> 4oz/100g dried no-soak apricots, chopped
> 2 eggs, beaten

Sift the self-raising flour and salt into a bowl. Rub in butter with fingers until the mixture reaches the breadcrumb stage. Stir in sugar. Mash bananas thoroughly and add to bowl with apricots and beaten eggs and mix to give a soft dropping consistency.

Spoon into a greased and lined 2lb/900g loaf tin and smooth over the top. Bake at Gas 5, 375F, 190C for 1 hour or until a skewer comes out clean.

Cool and remove the bread from tin before serving.
Preparation time: 20 minutes
Cooking time: 1 hour approx

Approximate nutritional values per thick slice:	
268 calories	5g protein
10g fat	20g carbohydrate

BARBARY DUCK

The history of the domestic duck goes back well over two thousand years. The Chinese were breeding them for consumption around the year 150BC. The present-day ducks used in Chinese dishes such as Peking Duck and Crispy Duck are descendants of these birds.

In Europe, evidence of the domesticated duck appears in engravings from the Middle Ages. By the 19th century, this bird had become part of the culinary tradition in most European countries.

The Barbary duck lives wild in Argentina and Brazil. It was introduced to France by Christopher Columbus, where, over the last 20 years, it has become the most popular bird for cooking, much prized for its characteristically tasty, tender dark meat. This bird is particularly good for the table since it has less obvious fat than other breeds. However, there is so much fat in the skin of the Barbary duck that there is no need to use more during roasting. Choose a Barbary duck for any Chinese dish as they are the nearest to the authentic breed. Or use for a change from chicken, lamb or beef for a traditional and delectable Sunday roast.

SHERRY AND OLIVE DUCK WITH ALMONDS

Lovely country dish of duck cooked with sherry in a sauce thickened with ground almonds. *Serves 4*

2 tbsp oil
1 onion peeled and finely chopped
2 cloves garlic, crushed
1 Barbary duck cut into 8 pieces
1 wine glass of fino sherry
1pt/600ml chicken or duck stock
1 tsp chopped thyme
4 tbsp ground almonds
2 tbsp double cream
8 large green olives
Salt and freshly ground black pepper
Squeeze of lemon juice
1 tbsp freshly chopped parsley

Heat oil in pan and fry onion and garlic until softened. Remove and transfer to a deep pan. Fry duck pieces to brown and add to pan. Pour in sherry and stock and bring to the boil. Add thyme. Cover and simmer for an hour or until duck is tender.

Stir in ground almonds, double cream and olives. Season with salt and freshly ground black pepper and add a squeeze of lemon juice. Sprinkle with chopped fresh parsley before serving.

Preparation time: 20 minutes
Cooking time: 1 hour 15 minutes

Approximate nutritional values per portion:	
550 calories	25g protein
30g fat	5g carbohydrate

NUTRITION

The calorie-count for duck can vary depending on the proportion of skin and fat to meat. However, Barbary duck has less than other breeds, because it has a thinner layer of fat. On average, a 4oz/100g portion of cooked Barbary duck meat and skin contains around 275 calories.

Fat intake can be reduced by removing the skin before eating, bringing the calories down to around 150 for a 4oz/100g portion, with only about 6g of fat.

Barbary duck is prized for its plump breast fillets and meaty legs. It is an excellent source of protein, necessary for normal growth, development and repair. 4oz/100g duck meat have 18g protein. There is no carbohydrate in duck.

Duck has a wealth of essential minerals, including calcium for healthy teeth and bones, potassium, for muscle tissue, and phosphorus, for cells. It also contains some magnesium which makes up bone tissue. There are also traces of the B vitamins in duck, which maintain the nervous system, and some folic acid, for healthy blood.

4oz/100g Barbary duck meat (no skin) contain:	
150 calories	18g protein
6g fat	nil carbohydrate

DUCK RISOTTO

Great blend of tastes in this dish, with duck and dried mushrooms in perfectly cooked rice. Leftover duck can be used for this recipe.
Serves 4

2oz/50g dried ceps
1/4pt/150ml water
2 tbsp oil
1 onion, finely chopped
3 peeled cloves garlic, crushed
8oz/225g Arborio rice
1pt/600ml duck or chicken stock
12oz/350g cooked shredded duck meat
Salt and freshly ground black pepper
Freshly grated Parmesan
Chopped parsley to decorate

Place mushrooms in a bowl and pour boiling water over. Leave to soak for 15 minutes. Heat oil in a pan and fry onion and garlic until soft but not brown. Add rice and stir, and coat in the onion and garlic mix. Do not let the rice brown.

Gradually add mushroom liquid and cook until absorbed. Add chopped mushrooms with a little of the stock, and continue cooking as before. Add duck, then remaining stock, little by little until the rice is tender. The amount of stock you need varies, so keep an eye on it. Season with salt and freshly ground pepper. Serve sprinkled with freshly grated Parmesan and a little chopped parsley.

Preparation time: 20 minutes
Cooking time: 45 minutes

Approximate nutritional values per portion:	
300 calories	12g protein
6g fat	35g carbohydrate

BUYING AND STORING

Barbary ducks are usually imported from France and arrive here pre-packed, oven-ready and chilled. Use them as soon as possible for the best results. They are available from speciality food shops, fishmongers who stock free-range chickens and game, and some supermarkets. They are extremely tasty birds with much less fat than the average duck, and well worth looking out for.

Preferably, buy the duck on the day you want to use it – or cook within three days. Keep it in its wrapping in the refrigerator. These ducks freeze perfectly well for cooking later. But make sure the duck is thoroughly defrosted before use. It is best to defrost it in the fridge overnight or in a cool larder.

TANDOORI DUCK

This makes an exotic change from the chicken version. *Serves 4*

> *1 Barbary duck, quartered*
> *Juice of 1 lemon*
> *2 tsp salt*
> *¼pt/150ml plain yogurt*
> *3 tbsp tandoori paste*
> *Oil for basting*
> *Lemon twist and mint sprig for decoration*

First skin the duck. This is a little tricky but easy once you lift a piece of skin which you can then use to pull. Don't worry about any left on the wings and knuckle bones.

Trim the skinned joints then prick them all over with a fork. Rub flesh with lemon juice and salt. Leave for 1 hour. Mix yogurt and tandoori paste and spread over duck joints. Place in a shallow dish, cover and leave to marinate in the fridge.

Remove from the fridge, paint lightly with oil, then cook at Gas 6, 400F, 200C for 35 minutes, or until crusty and cooked through. Paint with more oil just before serving to prevent it being too dry, then decorate with a lemon twist and mint sprig.

Preparation time: 20 minutes
Cooking time: 35 minutes

Approximate nutritional value per portion:	
275 calories	20g protein
10g fat	3g carbohydrate

CRISPY DUCK

Easy version of the popular Chinese favourite. Do take the trouble to prepare the skin first: although it takes several hours, this makes the result deliciously crisp. Serve shredded in pancakes with spring onions and cucumber strips. The pancakes can be bought from speciality delicatessens, but if you prefer they are easy to make. *Serves 4*

> *4lb/1.8kg Barbary duck*
> For the coating:
> *¼pt/150ml water*
> *2 tbsp dark brown sugar*
> *2 tbsp soy sauce*
> *1 tsp powdered lemon grass*
> *1 tsp ground ginger*
> *Juice of ½ lemon*
> For the pancakes:
> *8oz/225g plain flour*
> *¼pt/150ml boiling water*
> *Oil*
> *Hoisin sauce*
> *½ cucumber, cut into matchsticks*
> *Spring onions in strips*
> *Spring onion brushes to decorate*

Plunge the duck into boiling water for a few seconds. Remove and pat dry. Hang in a cold larder or in the fridge for several hours until completely dry.

Heat water and dissolve sugar over low heat. Add remaining ingredients and stir. Paint the duck with this. Leave to dry again (about four hours) with a dish underneath to catch any drips.

Paint again, then heat oven to Gas 7, 425F, 220C and roast for 30 minutes, then turn down to Gas 4, 350F, 180C and roast for another hour, or until duck is well cooked and skin crisp.

Meanwhile, make the pancakes. Sift flour into a bowl. Mix water with 1 tsp oil and gradually stir into the flour. Knead. Nip off walnut-sized lumps and flatten slightly. Brush one piece with oil and place another piece on top to make a sandwich. On a floured surface, roll out as thinly as possible. Heat a little oil in a pan and fry pancake sandwich on both sides. Peel apart gently.

To serve, shred duck flesh and skin. Spread each pancake with a little hoisin sauce. Place some skin and meat on top, plus some cucumber and spring onion strips, then roll up pancake. Decorate with spring onion brushes.

Preparation time: approx 8 hours minimum, which includes drying time
Cooking time: 1½ hours

Approximate nutritional values per portion:	
510 calories	26g protein
12g fat	46g carbohydrate

DUCK TIPS

● Barbary duck makes a great alternative spit roast for those whose barbecues are equipped with one. Mix up a baste in these proportions: 4 tbsp oil, 1 tbsp lime juice, 1 tbsp soy sauce, 2 tsp sugar, 1 tsp crushed anise seed, salt and lots of freshly ground black pepper. Spike the duck on the rotisserie and paint baste over it as it cooks. Season with more freshly ground pepper before serving.

● Fresh lime and onion marmalade is a good foil for roast duck. Heat 2 tbsp oil in a pan and gently fry 1 sliced Spanish onion and 2 crushed cloves of garlic over gentle heat until completely soft, but not brown. Sprinkle over 3 tsp sugar and continue cooking until this has dissolved and caramelised. Squeeze over the juice of a lime and sprinkle on the zest. Carry on cooking, still over gentle heat until all the liquid has disappeared. Season with salt and freshly ground black pepper.

● Duck stews work well with the addition of fruit. Try apricots, pears, prunes, cherries, or orange segments.

● Any leftover cold duck makes a good lunch salad. Skin and cut duck into strips. Toss in a bowl with baby spinach leaves, yellow pepper matchsticks, sliced spring onions and roughly torn iceberg lettuce. Pile into a salad bowl and dress with a mix of 4 tbsp olive oil, 1 tbsp dry white wine, a good squeeze of lemon juice, a dash of soy and freshly ground black pepper. Top with crumbled crisp fried bacon and croutons.

● Cook a Barbary duck on a trivet in the roasting pan so that it browns all over, and the fat runs off.

● Save the carcass from a roast Barbary duck to make a stock for use in risottos and soups.

● Roast duck on a bed of whole garlic cloves – about 20. They will soften during the cooking and the flavour will become subtle, refined and gentle.

BASIL

The name of this herb comes from the Greek, Basileus, meaning 'King'. The Ancient Greeks believed that only the king could cut basil leaves and then only with a gold sickle.

Another derivation of the name comes from a lizard-like creature in Greek mythology, the 'basilisk' who could kill his prey just by staring at it – such is the legendary power of this herb.

Basil is an annual plant with a square stem and fragrant, veined leaves. It has a unique and pungent perfume which is released as soon as a fresh leaf is squeezed.

The robust spiciness of this leafy plant lends itself to Malaysian and Thai curries and many South East Asian dishes. It is particularly appropriate in Italian cooking where the tomato reigns supreme. The famous Italian sauce, pesto from Liguria in north west Italy is based on basil, pine nuts, olive oil, garlic, Parmesan and Pecorino cheese. And indeed this herb is the mainstay of Ligurian cuisine.

When cooking vegetables use it with aubergines, artichokes, in ratatouille, and vegetable casseroles.

The flavour of basil with tomatoes is a marriage made in heaven. Always sprinkle basil over the tomato sauces of a pizza before adding the topping. Use it in a vinaigrette to finish off a tomato salad, and add it to a tomato sauce.

TOMATO AND BASIL SALAD

A tumbled salad of plum tomatoes, mozzarella, olives, slivers of anchovy and shredded lettuce tossed in a lime and onion vinaigrette. *Serves 4*

> 8 ripe plum tomatoes
> 4oz/100g mozzarella
> 12 stoned black olives
> 2 tbsp shredded basil
> 8 anchovy fillets, in slivers
> Basil sprig for decoration
> For the dressing:
> 1/2 onion, peeled
> 1 tsp Dijon mustard
> Zest and juice of 1 lime
> 4 tbsp olive oil
> Freshly ground black pepper

Slice tomatoes, mozzarella and olives thinly. Transfer to a bowl. Add basil and anchovies.

Grate onion into a jug making sure you keep all the juice. Add mustard, lime juice and zest, oil, and freshly ground black pepper. Whisk to blend.

Pour over salad in the bowl half an hour before serving and toss to coat. Pile on to salad plates and decorate with a sprig of basil.

Preparation time: 10 minutes
Cooking time: nil

Approximate nutritional values per portion:	
242 calories	9g protein
12g fat	6g carbohydrate

PENNE WITH PESTO

A quick pasta dish made with the basil, pine nuts and Parmesan paste, pesto. You can buy it ready made – but the homemade version is extra good and fresh-tasting. *Serves 4*

> 4 cloves garlic, peeled and crushed
> 2oz/50g pine nuts
> A little salt
> 2 large bunches basil, chopped
> 4 tbsp freshly grated Parmesan
> 1/4pt/150ml olive oil
> 2 tbsp ricotta
> Freshly ground black pepper
> 12oz/350g penne

Pound garlic with pine nuts in a pestle and mortar with a little salt. Add basil, little by little, all the time pounding with the pestle as you go.

Next, stir in the Parmesan cheese and mix well. Gradually add oil and the ricotta, then season with freshly ground black pepper.

An alternative method is to place the first eight ingredients in a processor and blend to a paste consistency – but the best results are by hand. Reserve.

Cook penne in lightly salted boiling water until al dente. Drain and toss pesto through.

Preparation time: 15 minutes
Cooking time: 12 minutes

Approximate nutritional values per portion:	
545 calories	18g protein
22g fat	70g carbohydrate

TOMATO SOUP WITH BASIL

This is a thin, almost clear soup, with a glowing colour and a delightful brush of basil. *Serves 4*

> 1 Spanish onion, peeled
> 1 clove garlic, peeled and crushed
> 1 tbsp oil
> 1 1/2lb/700g fresh tomatoes, roughly chopped
> 2 tbsp fresh basil, finely chopped
> 1 1/2pt/850ml vegetable stock
> Salt and freshly ground black pepper
> 2 fresh tomatoes peeled, de-seeded and in small dice
> Shredded basil for decoration

Roughly chop onion and place in a large pan with garlic and oil. Sweat over gentle heat, covered, for 3 minutes.

Add tomatoes and basil and stir gently. Add stock and bring to the boil. Turn heat down to a low simmer and cook for 30 minutes, topping up with extra stock if necessary. After 30 minutes all the taste from the vegetables and the colour from the tomato skin will be in the soup. Season with salt and freshly ground black pepper.

Carefully strain through a sieve, letting the liquid seep through on its own, making sure you do not push the vegetables through it – otherwise the soup will be cloudy.

Serve in soup bowl garnished with fresh tomato dice and shredded basil leaves.

Preparation time: 15 minutes
Cooking time: 35 minutes

Approximate nutritional values per portion:	
50 calories	2g protein
1g fat	7g carbohydrate

BUYING AND STORING

A perennial plant in warm countries, basil is treated as an annual in less temperate climes. Basil seeds can easily be propagated in a plant pot for fresh leaves all year round. Keep the pots in a warm, sunny place.

When the plant has become established, pinch out the centres to encourage bushy growth. Supermarkets and greengrocers sell the growing plant in a pot during the spring and summer months. But pre-packed fresh basil sprigs are available all year round. Choose bushy leaves with a good fresh smell. They will keep, wrapped, in the fridge for a day.

When there is no fresh basil, air-dried, or freeze-dried will do. The aroma and flavour of basil is pungent, and both these dried varieties retain this characteristic, only slightly reduced in potency. Freeze-dried will reconstitute in water. However, neither of these is suitable for use in salads.

Basil also freezes well. Shred basil and fill ice cube trays with it. Top up with water and freeze. Defrost when required for cooked dishes.

NUTRITION

Since basil is not consumed in any great quantity, its contribution to nutrition in the diet is negligible.

It is cultivated as a culinary herb, where it has a particular affinity with tomato, egg, and mushroom dishes. Using a herb in cooking adds flavour, and so increases the appetite. Like all green herbs, basil contains vitamin C and some calcium and potassium.

Herbs such as basil can be used instead of pepper and other spicy condiments where the digestion may not be able to cope.

Oil of basil can be used to treat mosquito bites and other insect stings.

CALVES' LIVER WITH BASIL

This dish of very thinly sliced liver tossed with onion rings and wilted basil leaves makes a deliciously aromatic combination of textures and flavours. *Serves 4*

4 tbsp oil
1 Spanish onion, peeled and thinly sliced
2 cloves garlic, peeled and crushed
1½lb/700g thinly sliced calves' liver,
  cut into strips
20 basil leaves
Salt and freshly ground black pepper

Heat 2 tbsp oil in a pan and gently fry onion rings and garlic until soft and slightly caramelised – not crispy. Remove from pan and keep warm.

Turn up heat and flash fry liver strips in the remaining oil for 2 minutes – until cooked, but still pink. Add whole basil leaves and toss around quickly with the liver until leaves are wilted.

Return onions and garlic to the pan and stir thoroughly. Season with salt and freshly ground black pepper.

Preparation time: 15 minutes
Cooking time: 15 minutes

Approximate nutritional values per portion:	
375 calories	26g protein
21g fat	7g carbohydrate

BASIL TIPS

● Fresh basil adds a real touch of Italy to pasta dishes. Use it on meat or vegetable lasagnes, fresh tomato sauces or Spaghetti Bolognese.

● Add basil leaves to a chicken curry for a Thai-style supper dish. For 4: heat 2 tbsp oil in a pan and fry 1 onion with 2 cloves garlic, 1 de-seeded and sliced red chilli and 1 tsp finely chopped fresh ginger root until softened. Remove with a slotted spoon and reserve. Add 4 chicken supremes, cut into strips, and stir-fry for 2 minutes to seal. Return onion mix and add 1 tsp turmeric, 1 tsp ground coriander and ½ tsp ground cumin, ¼pt/150ml chicken stock and bring to the boil. Simmer until chicken is cooked through. Stir in 2 tbsp creamed coconut and 12 whole basil leaves. Season.

● Deep fried basil leaves in crispy batter make a great garnish for grilled liver, roast lamb or barbecued king prawns. For the batter, sift 4oz/100g plain flour and a pinch of salt with 1½ tsp baking powder into a bowl. Add enough cold water to make a batter with the consistency of single cream. Dip basil leaves into flour, then into batter. Deep fry until crisp. Drain on kitchen paper.

● Roast slices of aubergine, chunks of courgette, thick pepper strips and wedges of onion in olive oil with shredded basil and freshly ground black pepper. Serve hot or cold as a first course dressed with a lemon vinaigrette.

● Add basil leaves to a salad of other pretty leaves like rocket, radicchio, lamb's tongue lettuce, escarole, and baby spinach and toss in a dressing of 3 tbsp sunflower oil, 1 tbsp hazelnut oil, 1 tbsp sherry vinegar, 1 tsp mild mustard and salt and freshly ground black pepper.

● Buy fresh basil in the pot from good supermarkets and greengrocers. This way it lasts longer and sprouts new shoots as you nip off sprigs. Keep it on a sunny windowsill and remember to water it.

● Flavour a good quality olive oil with basil leaves and peeled garlic cloves for use in dressings and for grilling chops, chicken or fish.

● Add diced peeled tomatoes and shredded basil leaves to beaten eggs and scramble lightly. Season and serve on crusty toast.

● Make a fresh tomato and basil sauce to serve with meat or pasta. Fry 1 onion and 2 cloves garlic in 2 tbsp oil until softened. Add 1lb/450g peeled, de-seeded and chopped tomatoes, 2 tbsp tomato purée and 1 wine glass red wine. Bring to the boil and reduce until thickened. Stir in 2 tbsp chopped basil leaves and seasoning.

● Dry an excess of fresh basil in bunches in a warm place out of sunlight. When the leaves are completely brittle, crumble them into an airtight storage jar.

BEANSPROUTS

PAGODA PANCAKES

These wafer-thin pancakes are filled with an Oriental-style mixture of sliced roast pork, strippy vegetables, beansprouts and flavoured with soy and chilli sauces. *Serves 4*

For the filling:
- 2 tbsp oil
- 2 cloves garlic, crushed
- 2 large carrots, peeled and in sticks
- 1 large courgette, in sticks
- 1 red pepper, de-seeded and in strips
- 4 spring onions, trimmed and in strips
- 4oz/100g cold roast pork, cut in strips
- 4oz/100g beansprouts
- 2 tbsp soy sauce
- Good dash of chilli sauce
- Freshly ground black pepper

For the pancakes:
- 4oz/100g plain flour
- Pinch of salt
- 1 egg, beaten
- 1/2pt/300ml milk
- Oil for frying

Heat the oil in a pan and fry together garlic, carrots, courgette, pepper and spring onions until slightly softened but still with bite. Stir in pork strips and beansprouts and cook for a further minute, until just heated through. Stir in soy and chilli sauce and season with plenty of black pepper.

For the pancakes, sift flour and salt into a bowl. Make a well in the centre and add the egg with half the milk. Gradually combine into the flour, beating until smooth. Stir in remaining milk. Heat a little oil in a non-stick pancake pan and add a spoonful of batter mix. Swirl mixture round to coat base of pan and cook until bottom sets, then flip over to cook other side.

Place on a warmed plate and fill with vegetable mix, rolling up as you go along. Keep hot under the grill or in the oven while cooking remaining batter and filling with the vegetables, then serve immediately.

Preparation time: 40 minutes
Cooking time: 30 minutes approx

Approximate nutritional values per portion:	
265 calories	6g protein
12g fat	33g carbohydrate

The familiar beansprout is the juicy white-green shoot of the mung bean, a small dark green pulse, known to the Chinese for around 4,000 years. Easy to sprout on a damp tea-towel (see tip 3), they produce around 6 times the volume of the beans, so only use a few tablespoons for a home harvest. But they are also readily available fresh, either pre-packed, or loose.

An important ingredient in Oriental cooking, they are usually stir-fried quickly in a little hot oil in a wok. But they are also added to noodle dishes and pancake rolls to give texture and crunch.

They are also vital in Chop Suey which is not, in fact, a proper Chinese dish. It was invented by a Chinese man who had emigrated to America.

As a Western vegetable, they are good steamed quickly and served tossed in butter or oil with a dash of orange juice and zest, a little salt and lots of freshly ground black pepper. Try this with chops or grills.

In salads, too, they make an interesting change from traditional leaves with their refreshing snappy texture, combining well with strippy peppers, slivers of spring onion, and raw mangetout.

BEANSPROUT TIPS

● Beansprouts add a refreshing crispness to sandwiches in place of lettuce for a crunchy change. Fry bacon slices crisp, then lightly toss beansprouts in the fat. Blot on kitchen paper. Layer them with tomato and toasted bread in a double decker BBT – bacon, beansprout and tomato – for a filling lunch snack.

● Make a flavourful Oriental omelette as a light supper dish or tea-time feast. For each omelette fry a chopped spring onion with ginger and garlic. Add 1 tbsp beansprouts and stir in. Add a dash of soy sauce. Beat 2 eggs and stir in over a high heat so bottom sets and top stays slightly runny. Fold over and serve immediately.

● Try sprouting your own beans. Chinese beansprouts are the shoots of the mung bean – a small dark green pulse. Soak beans for 24 hours. Dampen a clean tea-towel and lay on a chopping board. Spread soaked beans over this and cover with another clean damp tea-towel. Weigh this down with another board. Each day for 5 days wash beans and rinse tea-towels. Use resultant sprouts as needed.

● Look for tinned beansprouts in delicatessens when fresh are not available. Drain and use as fresh.

● Always cook beansprouts lightly either tossed in oil, quickly stir-fried, or gently steamed to retain texture and nutrients.

● Use beansprouts in an Oriental-style green salad. To serve 4: shred half a Chinese lettuce (bok choy) and place in a salad bowl. Add 4 sliced spring onions, 1/2 green pepper in strips, 1/2 cucumber in sticks and 4oz/100g beansprouts. Dress with a ginger and coriander vinaigrette. Blend 4 tbsp oil, 1 tbsp white wine vinegar, 1 clove garlic, crushed, 1 tsp grated fresh root ginger, a dash of soy sauce, 1/2 tsp Dijon mustard, 1 tbsp fresh coriander finely chopped, salt and freshly ground black pepper. Dress and toss just before serving.

● A valuable ingredient in a stir-fry, beansprouts add bulk and crispness to meat and vegetable dishes.

NUTRITION

Beansprouts are the shoots of the mung bean. Crisp and delicate-tasting, they give texture and bulk to many Oriental dishes and salads without loading up the calories – they contain only 35 per 4oz/100g.

It is interesting to note that as mung beans grow into beansprouts, so their nutritional composition changes. The carbohydrate is reduced to 6g per 4oz/100g, much less than beans, because it is turned into energy to aid growth. The most important vitamin contribution in beansprouts is vitamin C, needed for healing wounds. The amount of this vitamin increases with the changeover – 4oz/100g beansprouts contains up to 5 times more than the same weight of beans. And the water content leaps to almost 8 times that contained in beans.

There is a small amount of protein in beansprouts, 4g per 4oz/100g and some B vitamins. These vitamins play an important role in aiding the breakdown of carbohydrates and maintaining a healthy nervous system.

Minerals contained in beansprouts are iron, for healthy blood, and potassium, which forms part of muscle tissue. Beansprouts are also a source of dietary fibre.

4oz/100g beansprouts contain:	
35 calories	4g protein
trace of fat	6g carbohydrate

CHICKEN WITH CASHEWS AND BEANSPROUTS

A quick and delicious mix of tastes and textures.
Serves 4

2 tbsp oil
1 onion, finely chopped
2 cloves garlic, crushed
2 tsp ginger root, grated
3 chicken fillets in chunks
8oz/225g wild mushrooms, trimmed and torn
4oz/100g cashew nuts
$\frac{1}{2}$ wine glass dry sherry
2 tbsp soy sauce
Good dash chilli sauce
Salt and freshly ground black pepper
4oz/100g beansprouts
2 spring onions, sliced

Heat oil in a pan and cook onion, garlic and ginger until softened.

Add chicken chunks and cook quickly until stiffened. Stir in mushrooms, cashew nuts, and sherry and cook, covered, until chicken is cooked through. Add soy and chilli and season. Stir in beansprouts and spring onions and cook 2 minutes more, covered, so beansprouts are cooked, but retain a bite.
Preparation time: 20 minutes
Cooking time: 20 minutes

Approximate nutritional values per portion:	
320 calories	32g protein
18g fat	10g carbohydrate

NOODLES WITH PRAWNS AND BEANSPROUTS

Spicy egg noodles mixed with fresh vegetables and prawns. *Serves 4*

12oz/350g egg noodles
4 tbsp oil
1 medium onion, sliced
2 cloves garlic, crushed
1 fresh red chilli, de-seeded and chopped
$\frac{1}{2}$ green pepper, de-seeded and chopped
8oz/225g peeled prawns
2oz/50g beansprouts
Good dash of soy sauce
Freshly ground black pepper

Cook noodles in boiling salted water according to instructions. Drain and refresh in cold water. Drain again.

Heat oil in a pan and cook onion, garlic, chilli and green pepper over a low heat for 3 minutes. Add noodles, prawns and beansprouts and turn over in the mixture to coat. Season with soy and pepper. Heat through. Serve immediately.
Preparation time: 15 minutes
Cooking time: 15 minutes

Approximate nutritional values per portion:	
360 calories	13g protein
6g fat	20g carbohydrate

COLD MARINATED SALMON

An unusual way of preparing salmon steaks – poached, marinated in lime and ginger and then served with an endive and beansprout salad. *Serves 4*

4 salmon steaks
2 tbsp fish stock
For the marinade and dressing:
6 tbsp olive oil
Juice and zest of 1 lime
1 tsp Dijon mustard
1 tsp grated root ginger
Salt and freshly ground black pepper
For the salad:
2 heads endive, leaves separated
4oz/100g beansprouts
$\frac{1}{2}$ Spanish onion, finely chopped
3 tbsp fresh snipped chives

Poach salmon steaks, covered, in a little stock, or cook in the microwave. Reserve juices. Remove skin from steaks. Allow to cool completely. Transfer to a shallow dish in one layer.

Shake marinade ingredients together in a screw-top jar. Reserve 3 tbsp to dress the salad, pour rest over salmon with reserved juice or stock. Leave for 30 minutes.

Prepare and dress salad ingredients 15 minutes before serving. Using a slotted spoon, place salmon steaks on serving plates accompanied by salad.
Preparation time: 15 minutes
Cooking time: 10 minutes

Approximate nutritional values per portion:	
290 calories	23g protein
21g fat	2g carbohydrate

BUYING AND STORING

Beansprouts are a useful ingredient in Oriental cookery and mixed salads, adding both crispness and a delicate refreshing taste. Most good greengrocers and supermarkets sell fresh beansprouts. They are usually sold in plastic bags or small plastic boxes covered in cling film. But remember, they have a short fridge life.

Always ensure beansprouts are crisp and fresh before buying. Look for shoots that are sprightly and firm with a greeny tip and white stem. The tips should be moist but not wet – soggy sprouts are past their best and have lost vitamin C. Often, the shorter-stemmed, fatter beansprouts are more tender and sweeter tasting. Packaging may make it difficult to inspect them but it is wise to take a good look – there may be mushy sprouts in the middle of the bag that will rot the others.

Beansprouts should be eaten as soon as possible after buying to retain maximum nutritional value. They may last in the refrigerator, in a tied plastic bag, for 24 hours.

To prepare beansprouts, pick them over and discard any browned or soft ones, then rinse and drain them well. Eat them raw, lightly cooked in a little hot oil, or lightly steamed for the best results. Cooking should be done quickly and over a high heat.

BLACKBERRIES

Blackberries have been known as brumble-berries, brumble-kites or even lawyers, and references to them date back as far as the year 1000. Shakespeare even wrote about blackberries in *Henry IV* – 'If reasons were as plentiful as blackberries, I would give no man a reason upon compulsion'.

And according to legend, it is extremely unlucky to eat blackberries after Michaelmas Day, September 29, since the devil is thought to have trampled and squashed a blackberry bush when he was thrown out of heaven.

These shiny beautiful black fruits decorate the country hedgerows in the early autumn and it is a great tradition and pleasure to go blackberrying to collect them. Some 'pick your own' farms actually cultivate blackberries to make them easier for picking, and some growers are trying to extend the blackberry season, although the wet British climate does not help.

Cultivated blackberries are less pippy than wild, and are usually cleaner. Most shops do not indicate which variety is available, but if picking berries on a farm the best varieties are Bedford Giant, Himalaya or Ashton Cross.

BRUMBLE PUDDING

An old-fashioned name for blackberries which describes them well. This dish is based on a summer pudding – but which has autumn overtones. Alternatively mix blackberries together with cooked apple or even soaked dried fruits such as apricots. *Serves 4*

10 large slices white bread, crusts removed
Fruit filling:
2 punnets blackberries
1 punnet blueberries
1 punnet strawberries
2 tbsp sugar
1/4pt/150ml water
Blackberry leaves for decoration

Cut out a circle of bread to fit the base of a 2pt/1.1ltr bowl. Cut remaining bread into wedge-shaped slices and overlap around the sides of the bowl. Cut a lid of bread to fit the top.

For the fruit filling, rinse and drain blackberries and blueberries. Hull and wipe strawberries and cut into quarters. Place in a pan with sugar and water and cook until softened, but still retaining shape. Strain and reserve juice.

Spoon a little juice on to the base of the bread-lined basin. Pack in fruit, making sure to press it well down. Drizzle a little more juice on top and place bread lid on top. Reduce remaining reserved juices in a pan until they have become syrupy and pour from a jug over pudding. Cover with a saucer and then place a weight on top. Leave to chill in the fridge overnight.

Unmould the pudding on to a serving plate and decorate with blackberry leaves before finally serving.
Preparation time: 35 minutes approx
Cooking time: 3 minutes

Approximate nutritional values per portion:	
220 calories	5g protein
1g fat	40g carbohydrate

BLACKBERRY AND APPLE JAM

Family favourite conserve for a special tea.
Fills 2 jars

1lb/450g Bramley apples, weighed when peeled,
* cored and chopped*
2fl oz/50ml water
1lb/450g blackberries
1lb/450g preserving sugar

Place apples and water in a large heavy-based pan. Cook over a low heat until apples have softened. Mash lightly with a fork. Add blackberries and sugar, and stir over a low heat until sugar has dissolved. Bring to the boil for 10 minutes, stirring.

To test for setting point, spoon a little of the jam mixture on to a cold saucer. Cool slightly then push a finger across the surface. If the surface wrinkles the setting point has been reached.

Remove any scum that rises to the surface and pot into cleaned jars. Seal and label.
Preparation time: 15 minutes
Cooking time: 30 minutes approx

Approximate nutritional values per portion:	
50 calories	1g protein
1g fat	15g carbohydrate

LAMB NOISETTES WITH BLACKBERRY SAUCE

Choose small noisettes of lamb for this delicious and elegant dish with its unusual, deeply coloured blackberry sauce. *Serves 4*

12 lamb noisettes
Salt and freshly ground black pepper
1 tbsp oil
2oz/50g butter
12 shallots, peeled
3 tbsp ruby port
3/4pt/425ml lamb stock
1/2 punnet blackberries
1/2oz/15g chilled butter, diced
A few extra blackberries for decoration

Season lamb with salt and freshly ground pepper. Gently fry noisettes a few at a time both sides in oil and 1oz/25g butter until they are browned on the outside but still pink in the centre. Then remove with a slotted spoon and keep warm.

Add the shallots to pan with remaining butter and cook until they are caramel-coloured and softened. Remove with a slotted spoon and keep warm with the lamb noisettes.

Pour port into pan and bring to the boil. Add the lamb stock and then the blackberries. Bubble until the liquid has reduced and blackberries have become soft. Season and strain to remove seeds. Return to a clean pan. Whisk in butter and add the few extra blackberries for decoration. Arrange noisettes and shallots on four warmed serving plates and then pour over a little blackberry sauce and add a few poached blackberries in the centre of each plate. Finish with a tiny blackberry leaf.
Preparation time: 30 minutes
Cooking time: 30 minutes approx

Approximate nutritional values per portion:	
500 calories	45g protein
20g fat	5g carbohydrate

NUTRITION

Like all soft fruits, blackberries contain considerable amounts of vitamin C and also provide a natural source of dietary fibre. Fibre is found in the indigestible fibrous parts of the fruit like the skin and the pips, and consists of many thousands of glucose units. This is known as cellulose, and adds roughage to food as it passes along the digestive tract. Recent medical reports advise the intake of fibre should be at least 30g per day, alongside other essential nutrients. It is also recommended to drink plenty of fluids in a fibre-rich diet as it is extremely absorbent.

The vitamin C content of blackberries is high, which is why these fruits are used in cold remedies and energy-boosting drinks.

However, it must always be remembered that cooking and canning destroys some of the vitamin C, and these processes also let soluble B vitamins leak out.

Cooked blackberries are usually mushy after cooking as their skins collapse and their pectin, the natural setting agent essential for making jam, dissolves into the cooking juices. When making jam, blackberries are often partnered with apples, which have a high pectin content.

Blackberries contain no cholesterol, and are low in protein, fat and calories. They are relatively rich in potassium and calcium

4oz/100g blackberries contain:	
49 calories	1g protein
1g fat	12g carbohydrate

GOOD IDEA

Use damaged blackberries which are unsuitable for use in desserts to make a rich, fruity blackberry drink.

Liquidise 1lb/450g blackberries with a little sugar to taste. Sieve the purée into a bowl to remove all the pips. Add 1pt/600ml sweet cider and mix in some runny honey. Strain through muslin and pour into a clean bottle. Drink within 2 days, diluted with lemonade or soda, or add a dash of liqueur.

LACY PANCAKES WITH BLACKBERRY FILLING

A delightfully pretty dessert which is simplicity itself to make. *Serves 4*

For the pancakes:
4oz/100g plain flour
Pinch of salt
1 egg, beaten
½pt/300ml milk
½oz/15g melted butter
Blackberry filling:
2 punnets blackberries, rinsed
8 tbsp orange juice
1 tbsp sugar
1 tsp arrowroot

Sift flour and salt into a bowl. Make a well in the centre and add the egg and a little milk. Gradually work in the flour from around the edge of the bowl with a wooden spoon. Whisk in remaining milk with butter to a smooth batter. Leave to stand for 10 minutes.

Lightly oil a pancake pan and heat. Pour in just enough batter to coat the base of the pan. Swirl the mixture around and then fry until browned underneath. Flip over and brown the other side. Remove and repeat with remaining batter. Pile up with a piece of greaseproof paper in between and keep warm while making the filling.

For the filling, place blackberries in a pan. Pour over orange juice and sugar. Simmer gently until blackberries are soft but still whole. Mix arrowroot to a paste with a little water and stir into pan. Bring to the boil, gently stirring until slightly thickened. Remove from heat.

Fold pancakes into quarters and pile a little blackberry mixture into each. Arrange on plates and serve with whipped cream.
Preparation time: 30 minutes approx
Cooking time: 15 minutes approx

Approximate nutritional values per portion:	
350 calories	5g protein
15g fat	50g carbohydrate

BLACKBERRY TIPS

● Making blackberry jam? Add a few unripe red blackberries to the mixture to add extra flavour and to help the jam set. Blackberries do not contain much pectin so add fruit like apples or gooseberries which contain this natural setting agent.

● Make the most of the blackberry harvest by freezing some for later in the year. Open freeze on freezer trays leaving gaps in between. When the fruit is frozen, carefully place in layers in a rigid container, being careful not to overpack. When you defrost do so at room temperature for best results.

● Only wash blackberries if they are really dirty as it tends to soften and damage the fruit, and also dilutes the flavour and perfume.

● Check blackberries for ripeness before eating. Ripe fruit will be sweet and perfect for eating raw. Unripe berries can be slightly tart or sharp and should only be used for cooking with extra sugar to taste.

● For an unusual dessert try a blackberry clafoutis. This is a layer of sweetened blackberries topped with a sweet batter crust served hot with cream. First make the batter. Sift 4oz/100g self-raising flour into a bowl with 1 tsp baking powder and a pinch of salt. Beat 1 egg with 2oz/50g sugar and stir in 3 tbsp milk and 2oz/50g melted butter. Gradually stir into flour then beat to form a smooth batter.

Mix 1lb/450g blackberries with 4oz/100g sugar, a squeeze of orange juice and zest of ½ orange. Place in a shallow ovenproof dish and dot with a little butter. Pour over batter and smooth surface. Bake at Gas 4, 350F, 180C for 30 minutes or until topping is set. Serve hot with whipped cream.

BROCCOLI

Broccoli is a member of the cabbage family, alongside Brussels sprouts, cauliflower and kale. Together, these vegetables are known as brassicas.

The name of this delicate green vegetable is Italian, coming from the word broccolo which means cabbage sprout or head. Broccoli was well known by the Romans and the famous Roman cook Apicius talked of it in his book *De Re Coquinaria*.

Although Italy takes the credit for introducing broccoli to the rest of the world, its real place of origin is not exactly known. It was believed to be Catherine de Medici who brought it to France from Tuscany, and from there it spread throughout Europe. Eaten for its tender and tasty florets, its popularity soon grew.

The British began importing it in the late 1700s and sang the praises of this then unusual vegetable.

Today, Italy remains one of the largest producers. Now there are purple heads of broccoli available as well as the familiar dark green variety, plus a sprouting kind, though these are also grown elsewhere.

CHICKEN AND BROCCOLI GRATIN

A perfect marriage of tender broccoli florets, chicken breast, bacon strips and mushrooms cooked in cream, topped with melted cheese. *Serves 4*

8oz/225g broccoli, in florets
2 tbsp oil
4 rashers of back bacon, de-rinded and in strips
6oz/175g button mushrooms, wiped and halved
12oz/350g cooked chicken breast, in strips
½ glass dry white wine
Salt and freshly ground black pepper
¼pt/150ml double cream
2oz/50g Cheddar cheese, grated

Lightly cook broccoli in salted water or steam until just tender. Drain and reserve. Heat oil in a pan and fry bacon until crisp. Add mushrooms and toss around for 2 more minutes. Stir in broccoli, chicken and white wine. Season. Spoon into a flameproof dish and pour over cream. Top with cheese. Bake for 20 minutes at Gas 6, 400F, 200C until chicken is heated thoroughly and cheese has melted.

Preparation time: 20 minutes
Cooking time: 30 minutes approx

Approximate nutritional values per portion:	
405 calories	30g protein
30g fat	2g carbohydrate

PASTA WITH BROCCOLI AND PESTO

Tiny broccoli florets in the famous Italian pesto sauce, tossed through pasta ribbons and topped with Parmesan. *Serves 4*

12oz/350g pasta ribbons
12oz/350g broccoli, in tiny florets
3 tbsp ready-made pesto sauce
2 tbsp olive oil
Salt and freshly ground black pepper
2oz/50g Parmesan cheese, grated

Cook pasta in lightly salted boiling water until al dente. Drain and reserve, keeping hot.

Meanwhile, lightly steam broccoli until it's just tender but still has bite. This prevents the florets from breaking up.

Heat pesto in a pan with oil. Add broccoli florets and mix together carefully. Season. Toss through hot pasta and divide between 4 serving plates. Sprinkle with grated Parmesan before serving.

Preparation time: 15 minutes
Cooking time: 15 minutes approx

Approximate nutritional values per portion:	
464 calories	14g protein
27g fat	54g carbohydrate

BROCCOLI AND ALMOND SOUP

A creamy green soup of broccoli with the delicate flavour of ground almonds. *Serves 4*

2 heads of broccoli
2 tbsp oil
1 onion, peeled and finely chopped
2 pts/1.1ltr vegetable stock
2 tbsp ground almonds
4 tbsp double cream
Salt and freshly ground black pepper
Fresh grating of nutmeg
Extra double cream and toasted flaked almonds
 for decoration

Separate broccoli heads from stalks. Break heads into florets and peel and chop stalks. Rinse and drain. Heat oil in a pan and fry onion until softened, but not brown. Pour over vegetable stock and bring to the boil. Add broccoli and simmer, covered, until soft. Purée smooth in a blender. Return to the pan and stir in ground almonds. Bring back to bubbling and stir in cream, seasoning and nutmeg.

Pour into individual warmed bowls and decorate each with a swirl of cream and toasted almond flakes.

Preparation time: 15 minutes
Cooking time: 25 minutes approx

Approximate nutritional values per portion:	
195 calories	5g protein
17g fat	3g carbohydrate

BUYING AND STORING

Broccoli is available fresh all year round from greengrocers and supermarket vegetable counters. The usual variety is dark green in colour, but there are some speciality types now that have green stalks with beautiful purple heads. However, these turn green on cooking.

Look for sprightly fresh broccoli heads that have a good colour and tightly packed florets, avoiding those with soft or damaged stalks and wilting, or mushy leaves. Do not buy broccoli that has yellowing florets, as this indicates a lack of freshness, giving the cooked result a bitter taste.

Some supermarkets have broccoli heads packed in polythene in weights of 8oz/225g or 1lb/450g. Inspect these carefully for any signs of yellowing, rot or wetness caused by 'sweating' from the packaging.

Store broccoli in the refrigerator to maintain freshness after buying. But, as with all fresh vegetables, cook and eat it as soon as possible for the best results.

BROCCOLI TIPS

● Use broccoli cooking water in accompanying sauces or gravies to use the vitamins that leak out during cooking.

● Include raw broccoli florets in a selection of crudités with carrot and courgette sticks, cauliflower florets, button mushrooms and radishes. Serve with a cream cheese and onion dip. Mix 6oz/175g cream cheese with 3 tbsp double cream and 3 tbsp grated onion. Season with salt and pepper and stir in 1 tbsp snipped chives before serving surrounded with vegetables.

● Serve Broccoli Polonaise as a vegetable accompaniment to roasts or grills. For 4: lightly cook 12oz/350g broccoli florets in salted water until just tender. Drain and keep hot. Melt 2oz/50g butter in a pan and stir in 3 tbsp fresh white breadcrumbs, 1 finely chopped hard-boiled egg and 1 tbsp finely chopped parsley. Toss broccoli in this mixture and season with freshly ground black pepper. Serve immediately.

● Broccoli is a good vegetable to include in Oriental-style stir-fry dishes. The pretty florets add colour, texture and eye-appeal.

● Use broccoli stalks as a vegetable dish rather like a poor man's asparagus. Peel stalks before cooking in the usual way then serve hot or cold with vinaigrette or hot, simply drizzled with melted butter or accompanied by a hollandaise sauce.

● Dip broccoli florets in the lightest, crispiest batter to serve as a tempura-style dish of vegetable fritters. For the batter, mix 4oz/100g flour with a pinch of salt and ½ tsp baking powder. Gradually stir in enough water to give a batter with the coating consistency of single cream. Dip a selection of vegetables including broccoli in the batter and deep fry until crisp and golden. Drain on kitchen paper.

● Add broccoli florets to a creamy chicken pie for extra colour and taste.

TERRINE OF VEGETABLES

A three-layered terrine made from carrot, and thyme, broccoli and lemon and Boursin with herbs. *Serves 8*

> *1lb/450g carrots, peeled and sliced*
> *½ tsp thyme*
> *Salt and freshly ground black pepper*
> *1lb/450g broccoli, in florets*
> *Juice of ½ lime*
> *4 tbsp double cream*
> *4oz/100g Boursin with herbs*
> *1 tbsp grated onion*
> *1 tbsp chopped fresh dill*
> *3 sachets gelatine*
> *¼pt/150ml hot water*
> *Lime slices and a dill sprig to decorate*

Cook carrots in boiling salted water until soft enough to purée. Drain and whizz in a blender until smooth. Add thyme and seasoning to taste. Keep warm.

Cook broccoli as above. Drain and purée.

Add lime juice and season. Reserve in a separate bowl.

Beat double cream into Boursin to give a soft consistency. Stir in grated onion and dill. Season to taste. Reserve.

Dissolve gelatine in the water. Cool. Divide between the three bowls, stirring well to incorporate.

Grease a 2lb/900g non-stick loaf tin. Spread cheese mixture in a smooth layer over the base. Top with the broccoli mixture and smooth that over, then finish with the carrot layer. Smooth surface. Leave to chill and set in the fridge. Decorate with lime twists and a dill sprig and serve in slices.

Preparation time: 45 minutes
Cooking time: 20 minutes plus chilling

Approximate nutritional values per portion:	
108 calories	7g protein
9g fat	3g carbohydrate

NUTRITION

The best way to eat broccoli is raw, in salads and crudités, or lightly cooked by boiling or steaming. If broccoli is boiled, the cooking liquid should be used in an accompanying sauce or gravy to retain its valuable vitamins.

The major vitamin contributions in broccoli are the vitamins A and C. Vitamin A aids sight and is common in dark green vegetables. It is contained in the yellow carotenoids present under the chlorophyll layer which gives the plant its green colour. Vitamin C, which prevents skin diseases and

helps cuts and sores to heal, is also plentiful with 100mg in 4oz/100g raw broccoli.

Broccoli is also a good source of the mineral calcium, containing almost as much as milk, and potassium, an essential part of the body's muscle tissue.

4oz/100g raw broccoli contain:	
23 calories	3g protein
trace of fat	2g carbohydrate

CABBAGE

The earliest cabbages came from the southern hemisphere. But the varieties popular today came from the sea cabbage which grew wild around the coasts of Europe which can still be found on the south coast of England and the northern coasts of France.

The Romans liked cabbage – and in fact gave this member of the Brassica family its name. Cabbage derives from 'caput', Latin for head, which it resembles. Cato had a passion for cabbage. And it was the Romans who first introduced cabbage cultivation here.

The Greeks enjoyed it, and the Celts regarded it as a medicine, too.

Cabbage features in cookery all over the world. Even labourers working on the Great Wall of China in 300BC ate pickled cabbage.

By 1440, a horticultural plan had been worked out, planting cabbages in succession so that they would be available all year round. Today's popular varieties are usually classified by the season.

KNOW YOUR CABBAGE

Spring Greens are tender, leafy sprouts of cabbage that have no heart. Despite their name, they are grown year round and sometimes come pre-packed in 1lb/450g bags. These little cabbages are full of flavour and keep their dark green colour when they are cooked.

Summer Cabbage is green and has a firm and solid heart with crisp, fresh outer leaves. Some early summer cabbages have a pointed heart. These should be eaten soon after buying, as they wilt quickly.

Savoy Cabbage is a winter cabbage with a round pale green heart and dark green curled outer leaves. It has a distinctive crinkly texture and a less dense heart.

White Cabbage is a round, dense, closely packed, crisp cabbage – eat raw in salads.

Red Cabbage has burgundy colouring. This spicy-tasting cabbage is at its best in winter and accompanies goose, duck or pork well. It makes a great pickle.

NUTRITION

The best way to eat white cabbage is raw, in a crisp salad. This contains 22 calories per 4oz/100g and is a source of dietary fibre. Raw savoy has 26 calories.

The main nutritional contribution from cabbage is vitamin C. Necessary for healing and the prevention of excess bleeding, some also think that taking large supplements of vitamin C can stave off colds. It cannot be made or stored by the body and must be obtained from food daily, and a daily intake of 30mg is ample.

The colouring of the leaves of green cabbage, especially the dark green savoy, indicates a moderate source of vitamin A aiding vision in the dark and promoting healthy skin.

Cabbage contains some sodium and calcium, for strong bones and muscle maintenance.

4oz/100g raw cabbage contain:	
22 calories	3g protein
trace of fat	3g carbohydrate

WHOLE STUFFED CABBAGE

Substantial dish of tasty minced beef stuffed into green cabbage heart, served with a red pepper sauce. *Serves 4*

For the sauce:
1 tbsp oil
1 onion, peeled and finely chopped
1 clove garlic, crushed
1 carrot, peeled and finely chopped
1 large red pepper, de-seeded and finely chopped
2 glasses red wine
¼pt/150ml vegetable stock
3 tbsp tomato purée
Salt and freshly ground white pepper
Squeeze lemon juice

For the savoury mince:
1 tbsp oil
1 onion, peeled and finely chopped
2 cloves garlic, crushed
12oz/350g minced beef
2 tbsp tomato purée
½pt/300ml beef stock
½ tsp chopped fresh thyme
2oz/50g cooked white rice
1 whole seasonal green cabbage
Melted butter for brushing

For the sauce, heat oil in a pan and fry onion, garlic, carrot and pepper until soft. Pour over wine, stock and tomato purée. Bring to the boil and simmer until softened. Whizz in a processor and return to a clean pan. Season and add lemon juice.

Heat oil in a large pan. Fry onion and garlic until soft. Remove and reserve. Add mince and fry to brown.

Return onion mix and stir in tomato purée, stock and thyme. Season and bring to boil. Simmer for 20 minutes. Stir in rice.

Trim cabbage. Cook in salted water until just tender. Drain and cool slightly. Carefully unfurl leaves, folding them back. Stuff the centre with mince. Brush leaves with melted butter. Reheat at Gas 6, 400F, 200C. Serve with red pepper sauce.

Preparation time: 30 minutes
Cooking time: 45 minutes approx

Approximate nutritional values per portion:	
100 calories	7g protein
6g fat	7g carbohydrate

CABBAGE CHEESE

Tasty vegetarian main course or vegetable side dish. Quarters of just-cooked green cabbage with a melting, creamy cheese sauce. *Serves 4*

1oz/25g butter
1 tbsp flour
³/₄pt/425ml milk
4oz/100g Cheddar cheese, grated
½ onion, grated
Salt and freshly ground white pepper
2 tbsp double cream
1 whole seasonal green cabbage
Extra Cheddar, grated for sprinkling

Melt butter in a pan and stir in flour. Cook for 1 minute. Gradually add milk, stirring, and bring to the boil to thicken. Add cheese and onion. Season and stir in cream. Cover with buttered greaseproof to prevent a skin forming.

Trim stalk from cabbage and cut into quarters. Cut out the core, leaving the quarters still joined together at the stem. Blanch in slightly salted boiling water until just cooked. Drain. Place in a flameproof dish.

Pour over cheese sauce and sprinkle with extra grated cheese. Grill until browned and bubbling.

Preparation time: 10 minutes
Cooking time: 15 minutes

Approximate nutritional values per portion:	
265 calories	10g protein
16g fat	8g carbohydrate

SEAFOOD SLAW

Lovely mix of crisp shredded white cabbage with pearly cod flakes, prawns and mussels, tossed in a fresh dill vinaigrette. *Serves 4*

½ white cabbage, trimmed and stalk removed
12oz/350g cod fillet
¼pt/150ml fish stock
1 onion, peeled and grated
8oz/225g prawns, peeled
4oz/100g cooked mussels, shelled
For the dressing:
4 tbsp sunflower oil
1 tbsp white wine vinegar
½ tsp Dijon mustard
½ tbsp fresh dill, finely chopped
Salt and freshly ground black pepper
Extra chopped dill for decoration

Shred cabbage finely and rinse. Drain well. Poach cod in stock until cooked through. Drain, cool, skin and flake. Mix in a bowl together with cabbage, onion, prawns and mussels.

Shake dressing ingredients in a screw-top jar. Pour over salad and gently toss to coat.

Pile into serving dishes and then sprinkle with the extra chopped dill to decorate.

Preparation time: 15 minutes
Cooking time: 10 minutes

Approximate nutritional values per portion:	
150 calories	35g protein
7g fat	3g carbohydrate

CHOUCROUTE

Originally from Alsace, this country dish of pork knuckle, belly of pork and sausages is flavoured with juniper berries, white wine and the famous sauerkraut – salted shredded white cabbage. *Serves 4*

1 tbsp oil
1 onion, peeled and finely sliced
1 small pork knuckle, tied
4 thick strips belly pork
4 pork sausages
2 wine glasses dry white wine
8 juniper berries
1lb/450g jar sauerkraut
Freshly ground black pepper

Heat oil and fry onion until softened. Remove with a slotted spoon and transfer to a large saucepan. Add pork knuckle to frying pan and brown all over, then add to onion in saucepan. Brown belly pork and sausages in frying pan and then transfer these to saucepan.

Pour over white wine and top up with water to cover. Add juniper berries. Bring to the boil and simmer for 30 minutes. Drain and rinse sauerkraut. Add to pan and continue cooking for a further hour. Season with plenty of freshly ground black pepper.

Pile the sauerkraut into an earthenware pot and arrange pork knuckle, belly and sausages on top. Spoon over cooking juices and serve immediately with boiled potatoes.

Preparation time: 10 minutes
Cooking time: 1 hour 30 minutes approx

Approximate nutritional values per portion:	
750 calories	35g protein
50g fat	10g carbohydrate

CABBAGE TIPS

● Include green cabbage in a chunky fresh vegetable soup. For a Mediterranean taste and texture, add pasta and fresh tomato wedges and sprinkle with grated cheese to serve.

● Leafy spring greens are tender and tasty and grown all year round. Remove stalks, shred leaves and cook in a small amount of lightly salted water. Don't overcook – the leaves should still have bite. Serve simply seasoned with plenty of freshly ground black pepper and a knob of butter.

● The protective outer leaves of cabbage are usually tough and should be removed. The firm heart can then be halved and the hard centre core cut away before shredding or chopping. Wash cabbage and drain well before cooking.

● For best flavour and to avoid vitamins being lost, prepare cabbage and cook straight away. Do not over-boil in too much water. Simply cook in the smallest amount to achieve a crisp and tasty result.

● There are reputedly a number of ways to reduce the familiar tell-tale smell of cooking cabbage, caused by the sulphur content of the leaves. Some swear by a slice of bread added to the covered pan, while others favour leaving the lid off. Overcooking tends to make the smell linger.

● Add a few caraway seeds when cooking cabbage to give a slightly 'aniseed' flavour to the finished dish. Serve with melted butter.

● Choose fresh, firm, unblemished, white cabbage for the crispest coleslaw imaginable. Mix with shredded carrots, finely sliced onions, sticks of red skinned apple and few sultanas. Toss in homemade mayonnaise just before serving.

● Check the base of the cabbage stalk as an indication of freshness. It should be firm, clean and not slimy. The leaves should have a crisp healthy appearance and show no signs of insect or mould damage.

● Stir-fry finely shredded cabbage with garlic, ginger, beansprouts, spring onions and broccoli florets for a super Chinese-style vegetable dish. Moisten with stock or dry sherry and add a dash of soy sauce and freshly ground black pepper.

CHEDDAR

Cheddar, the favourite of all English cheeses, was first made in Somerset during the 16th century.

This flavoursome cheese took its name from the world-famous Cheddar Gorge, where the first Cheddars were traditionally matured.

The popularity of Cheddar cheese soon spread when west country farmers who emigrated to the USA, Canada, Australia and New Zealand took Cheddar recipes with them. These countries began making their own versions, but English Cheddar is the original and still remains the best cheese.

Cheddar can be mild, medium or mature. Mild Cheddar can be eaten in sandwiches, as it comes, with fruit, or in cooking. Medium Cheddar is good for rich cheese sauces. Strongly flavoured, mature Cheddar is an excellent choice for an after-dinner cheese.

CHEESE AND TOMATO PIE

A tasty tart packed with fresh and sun-dried tomatoes, olives and basil and topped with grated Cheddar. *Serves 4*

For the pastry:
>*6oz/175g plain flour*
>*Pinch of salt*
>*4oz/100g butter*
>*1 egg, beaten*

For the filling:
>*2 tbsp oil*
>*1 onion, peeled and finely chopped*
>*1 clove garlic, crushed*
>*1oz/25g sun-dried tomatoes, in strips*
>*Few basil leaves, shredded*
>*4 olives, chopped*
>*Salt and freshly ground black pepper*
>*1lb/450g tomatoes, skinned*
>*1 egg*
>*¼pt/150ml double cream*
>*4oz/100g grated Cheddar*
>*Tomato and olive slices, plus a few basil sprigs for decoration*

Sift flour and salt into a bowl and rub in butter to crumb stage. Add beaten egg, then work to form a dough. Knead lightly then wrap pastry and chill in the fridge for 30 minutes.

Heat oil in a pan and fry onion and garlic over a gentle heat until softened. Add sun-dried tomatoes, basil and chopped olives. Season with salt and freshly ground black pepper to taste.

Roll out pastry to fit an 8in/20cm fluted loose-bottomed flan tin. Bake blind at Gas 6, 400F, 200C for 10 minutes. Layer onion mix with sliced fresh tomatoes over pastry base. Beat egg and cream and add grated cheese. Pour over filling. Place tomato and olive slices on top for decoration. Bake at Gas 5, 375F, 190C for 30 minutes or until golden and set. Decorate with a sprig of basil.

Preparation time: 40 minutes
Cooking time: 30 minutes approx

BUYING AND STORING

Of all the English and Welsh cheeses, Cheddar is still the most popular, making up 60 per cent of cheese consumption here.

Cheddar can vary in flavour from mild to mature. The different strengths in taste come from the maturing time, which can be as little as three months for mild Cheddar to over 18 months for an extra mature cheese.

Apart from the mild, medium and mature Cheddars, there are also some speciality varieties, which are flavoured with beer, garlic, herbs or wine. There is also a red Cheddar, which has the natural vegetable dye annatto added to it.

Most types of Cheddar are available from supermarket cheese counters, specialist cheese shops and delicatessens.

Fresh Cheddar should have a close texture with a firm, moist consistency, and should not flake or crumble when cut. Check the cheese before buying to make sure there is no 'sweatiness' or cracked, dry patches.

Keep Cheddar well-wrapped in the fridge. This will keep it fresh for around three weeks, or longer.

NUTRITION

Cheddar cheese is a protein-packed high energy food, with 412 calories per 4oz/100g. It takes eight pints/five litres of milk to make 1lb of Cheddar, and the finished product preserves all the goodness of the milk from which it is made.

There is 25.5g protein in 4oz/100g Cheddar, containing all the essential amino acids required for normal growth and development. The same weight of Cheddar has 34g of fat. There is only a trace of carbohydrate in Cheddar.

Cheese is one of the richest sources of calcium, with 736mg in 4oz/100g of Cheddar. This mineral is particularly important in the diet of both the very young and very old. Growing children need calcium for the formation of strong bones and healthy teeth, while the elderly need it to maintain strong, healthy bones and to help any breakages heal quickly. Easy to digest, Cheddar is a well-balanced food perfect for the needs of any age group.

Useful amounts of vitamin A, together with some vitamin B2 and vitamin D, are found in Cheddar. It is interesting to note that its nutritional value does not alter during cooking.

4oz/100g Cheddar contain:	
412 calories	25.5g protein
34g fat	trace of carbohydrate

Approximate nutritional values per portion:	
430 calories	9g protein
26g fat	27g carbohydrate

SAUSAGE ROULEAUX

Sausage rolls with a difference. *Serves 4*

> *8 pork and herb sausages*
> *13oz/375g pack puff pastry*
> *4oz/100g mature Cheddar cheese, grated*
> *Beaten egg to glaze*

Cook sausages then cool.

Roll out pastry thinly. Sprinkle half with finely grated cheese. Fold unsprinkled half over to enclose, sealing the edges with water. Roll out again thinly and cut pastry into ½in/1cm strips.

Wrap strips around sausages with the pastry overlapping. Place on a baking sheet with the ends of the pastry underneath. Brush with egg.

Bake at Gas 6, 400F, 200C for 25 minutes, or until pastry is crisp and golden.

Preparation time: 20 minutes
Cooking time: 35 minutes

Approximate nutritional values per portion (2 rolls):	
745 calories	24g protein
55g fat	44g carbohydrate

CHEDDAR TIPS

● Choose mature cheddar for extra cheesy taste in a sauce to serve with fish or vegetables. Make a basic white sauce by melting 1oz/25g butter in a pan then stirring in 1oz/25g flour. Cook for 1 minute. Stir in 1 tsp English mustard. Gradually add ¾pt/425ml fresh milk over a low heat, stirring continuously. Bring to the boil and simmer until thickened, stirring constantly. Add 4oz/100g grated mature Cheddar and stir to melt. Season.

● Children love cheese and these kebabs will disappear fast. For 4: thread 4oz/100g cubed mild Cheddar on to kebab skewers with 1 red apple cut into 8 wedges (sprinkle it with lemon juice to prevent it discolouring), 4 cherry tomatoes and ½ cucumber cut into 4 rounds along the length. Serve immediately.

● For a quick cheese pastry, sprinkle grated Cheddar over rolled out ready-made shortcrust pastry. Fold pastry in half and roll out thinly again.

● Use strong, mature Cheddar for a fondue – the perfect way to entertain informally. For 8 diners, rub a fondue pot or flameproof casserole with a cut clove of peeled garlic and 1oz/25g butter. Place 1lb/450g cubed Cheddar into the pot with 1pt/600ml dry white wine and season to taste. Place over heat and stir until cheese melts. Mix 2 tsp cornflour with 4 tbsp kirsch to a thin paste and add to melted cheese. Continue stirring until thickened. Add a little freshly grated nutmeg and serve with vegetable crudités and French bread cubes for dipping.

● Mix 8oz/225g grated Cheddar with 2 tsp sherry, 1 tsp mild mustard, grated nutmeg and a pinch of cayenne pepper. Stir in 2oz/50g softened butter and pack into a small pot. Use as a sandwich filling or spread on to hot wholemeal toast.

CHEDDAR COBBLER

Cheese and herb scone topped pie filled with chunky vegetables in a mature Cheddar cheese and mustard sauce. *Serves 4*

> For the topping:
> *8oz/225g plain flour*
> *2½ tsp baking powder*
> *Salt*
> *2oz/50g butter*
> *4oz/100g mature Cheddar cheese, grated*
> *1 tbsp freshly chopped parsley*
> *¼pt/150ml milk*
> *Beaten egg to glaze*
> For the filling:
> *2 leeks, cleaned and chopped*
> *4 carrots, thickly sliced*
> *8oz/225g broccoli florets*
> *1 small cauliflower, in florets*
> *1oz/25g butter*
> *1oz/25g flour*
> *¾pt/425ml milk*
> *1 tsp made English mustard*
> *2oz/50g mature Cheddar cheese, grated*
> *Salt and ground black pepper*

First make the scone topping. Sift flour and baking powder into a bowl with salt. Rub in butter to breadcrumb stage. Stir in Cheddar and parsley. Add milk and gather dough together. Knead lightly, then wrap in film and chill for 30 minutes.

Blanch the vegetables in boiling salted water until just tender – do them separately.

For the sauce, melt butter in a pan and stir in flour. Cook for 1 minute then take off the heat. Add milk, stirring, then return to heat and bring slowly to the boil, stirring until thickened. Add mustard and cheese and stir until melted. Season. Add vegetables to the sauce, then pour into a pie dish.

Roll out scone mix on a lightly floured worktop to ¼in/0.5cm thick. Cut into 2in/5cm plain rounds. Arrange on top of vegetable mix around the edge of the pie dish. Glaze with beaten egg. Bake at Gas 5, 375F, 190C for 25 minutes, or until topping is risen and golden.

Preparation time: 45 minutes
Cooking time: 40 minutes

Approximate nutritional values per portion:	
600 calories	20g protein
32g fat	30g carbohydrate

CHEDDAR AND TUNA SOUFFLE

A light and airy soufflé with flaked tuna, capers and grated Cheddar. *Serves 4*

> *Melted butter and 2 tbsp freshly grated*
> * Parmesan for preparing mould*
> *1oz/25g butter*
> *1oz/25g flour*
> *¾pt/425ml milk*
> *4 eggs, separated plus 2 egg whites*
> *7oz/200g can tuna in oil, drained and flaked*
> *1 tbsp chopped capers*
> *3oz/75g grated mature Cheddar*
> *Salt and freshly ground black pepper*
> *Lemon juice*

Brush a 1½pt/900ml soufflé mould with melted butter and coat with fresh Parmesan. Reserve.

Melt butter in a pan and stir in flour. Cook for 1 minute. Gradually add milk, stirring continuously. Bring to the boil until thickened. Remove from heat and cool slightly. Beat in yolks. Add tuna, capers and Cheddar. Season with salt, pepper and a squeeze of lemon.

Whisk egg whites until stiff and carefully fold in. Check for seasoning. Pour mixture into a prepared soufflé mould and bake at Gas 5, 375F, 190C for 20 minutes or until risen, golden and just set.

Preparation time: 30 minutes
Cooking time: 30 minutes

Approximate nutritional values per portion:	
285 calories	18g protein
21g fat	6g carbohydrate

CHESTNUTS

A native of the Mediterranean, but related to the oak and beech, the edible chestnut grows inside a prickly shell. The wild husk contains two or three flat-sided nuts. But the nut known as 'marron' has only one. These should never be confused with horse chestnuts, or conkers, which are inedible.

Used in both sweet and savoury dishes, these versatile nuts are high in food values.

Chestnuts are often preserved. Drying produces nuts which need rehydrating before use. But dried nuts are also ground to make chestnut flour, sometimes used to make a kind of polenta, which has a sweetish taste.

Fresh chestnuts are mostly considered to be Christmas nuts since they are sold roasted on busy street corners during the weeks leading up to Christmas, and are rarely seen at any other time of the year.

Usually available from November to January, these nuts come from Spain, France and Italy, as well as from the home market.

CHESTNUT TIPS

● Chestnuts need to be cooked before being used in recipes. Otherwise choose canned, or vacuum-packed, ready-to-use nuts. These come as whole nuts, or sweet, or unsweetened purées, and have a more dense texture than fresh.

● Because of their sweetish and starchy nature, chestnuts make a good vegetable purée to serve with roast birds, or pork. Peel and cook the chestnuts and purée just before serving as it will become heavy if kept warm or re-heated.

● To roast chestnuts, first slit them with a knife, then roast at Gas 6, 400F, 200C for about 15 minutes, or until tender. The shell will be brittle enough to peel off, and the papery inner skin can be removed easily.

● For using in recipes, slit them, then simmer in boiling water for about 5 minutes. Peel while still hot. Cook for a further 45 minutes or until tender.

● Chestnut stuffing is traditional for turkey. Heat 1 tbsp oil in a pan and gently fry 1 chopped onion, 2 crushed cloves garlic and 4oz/100g sliced button mushrooms until soft. Transfer to a bowl and add 14oz/400g can chestnuts drained and finely chopped. Stir in 1 cored and grated apple, 3 tbsp fresh white breadcrumbs, 1 beaten egg, a good dash of Worcestershire sauce, 1 tbsp freshly chopped parsley and salt and freshly ground black pepper. Cool and stuff the neck end of the turkey. Secure skin with cocktail stick and roast in the usual way.

● Choose chestnuts which feel 'solid' in the shell. If it gives too much, the nut may have shrunk inside.

● When using fresh chestnuts in a stew, add them half an hour before the end of cooking time. Canned ones can be added 10 minutes before to avoid them breaking up.

CHESTNUT AND GINGER POTS

Rich and velvety smooth chestnut creams spiced with preserved ginger and topped with a swirl of whipped cream. *Serves 4*

14oz/400g fresh or canned chestnut purée
2 egg yolks
4oz/100g unsalted butter
2 tbsp caster sugar
6 small pieces preserved stem ginger,
 finely chopped
2 tbsp juice from ginger jar
¼pt/150ml whipping cream
Sliced stem ginger for decoration

Blend chestnut purée with egg yolks in a bowl until creamy. Melt butter and beat into mixture until incorporated. Stir in sugar, ginger and juice.

Whip cream until it stands in soft peaks. Reserve a little for the decoration and fold remainder into chestnut mixture. Spoon into small pots and then chill thoroughly until they are set firm. Serve decorated with swirls of the reserved whipped cream and top with slivers of stem ginger.

Preparation time: 30 minutes
Cooking time: nil

Approximate nutritional values per portion:	
480 calories	5g protein
35g fat	37g carbohydrate

FESTIVE CHESTNUT LOAF

This is a super vegetarian alternative to the Christmas turkey. *Serves 6*

6oz/175g wholemeal breadcrumbs
11oz/300g cooked chestnuts, finely chopped
1 onion, peeled and finely chopped
1 red apple, cored and chopped
Juice of 1 lime
2 sticks celery, finely chopped
2 cloves garlic, crushed
1 tsp grated fresh root ginger
2 tbsp tomato purée
Salt and freshly ground black pepper
1 tbsp finely chopped fresh parsley
3 floz/75ml vegetable stock
1 egg, beaten

Place crumbs in a bowl and mix in chestnuts. Add onion, apple, lime juice, celery, garlic and ginger. Stir in tomato purée, season and sprinkle in parsley. Add stock and egg to bind. Press mixture into an oiled loaf tin. Bake at Gas 6, 400F, 200C for about 40 minutes or until firm and set.

Preparation time: 30 minutes
Cooking time: 40 minutes approx

Approximate nutritional values per portion:	
185 calories	5g protein
3g fat	30g carbohydrate

SPROUTS WITH CHESTNUTS

Traditional Christmas vegetable dish of young Brussels sprouts tossed in butter with crispy bacon strips and chestnuts. *Serves 4*

2lb/900g baby Brussels sprouts
2 rashers back bacon, de-rinded and chopped
1oz/25g butter
8oz/225g cooked, peeled chestnuts
Freshly ground black pepper

First prepare the sprouts. Trim off base of stalk and make a small cross in the centre. Boil in lightly salted water until just tender. Drain.

Fry bacon brown in a pan. Remove with a slotted spoon and reserve. Melt butter in the pan and add drained sprouts. Toss around to coat. Add chestnuts and season with black pepper. Transfer to a warmed serving dish. Sprinkle over bacon before serving.

Preparation time: 15 minutes
Cooking time: 10 minutes approx

Approximate nutritional values per portion:	
225 calories	10g protein
10g fat	22g carbohydrate

NUTRITION

Chestnuts have fewer calories than most other nuts with only 170 per 4oz/100g. This is good news for weight-watching nut lovers who can enjoy them freshly roasted and peeled instead of walnuts, brazils or peanuts.

There is a small amount of protein in chestnuts, 2g per 4oz/100g, but this protein is not complete in essential amino acids. For vegetarians, nuts should be eaten with beans which supply the remaining amino acids necessary for a healthy diet.

One of the main nutritional contributions from chestnuts is carbohydrate, with 36g in 4oz/100g cooked peeled chestnuts.

Unlike other nuts, chestnuts are extremely low in fat, with only 3g per 4oz/100g, and most of this fat is unsaturated. Also on the plus side, chestnuts have no cholesterol.

Vitamins present in chestnuts include vitamin E for healthy, glowing skin, and some of the B vitamins along with good supplies of the minerals potassium, phosphorus and calcium.

4oz/100g cooked peeled chestnuts contain:	
170 calories	2g protein
3g fat	36g carbohydrate

POULET DE BOIS

Winter stew of chicken joints with chestnuts cooked in red wine with onion quarters and oyster mushrooms, topped with crisp golden croutons and crisp pork lardons. It's as delicious as it sounds. *Serves 4*

3lb/1.4kg fresh chicken, jointed into 8 pieces
Seasoned flour
6 tbsp oil
4 small onions, peeled and quartered
2 cloves garlic, crushed
1 wine glass red wine
1/2pt/300ml chicken stock
4oz/100g oyster mushrooms, torn
6oz/175g cooked chestnuts,
* (or use canned and drained)*
Salt and freshly ground black pepper
1 tbsp fresh parsley, finely chopped
1 thick strip skinless belly of pork, chopped
2 slices bread, crusts removed and cubed
Oil for frying

Dip chicken in seasoned flour and shake off excess. Heat half the oil in a pan and fry onions and garlic for 2 minutes. Then remove them with a slotted spoon and transfer to an ovenproof casserole.

Add remaining oil to pan and fry chicken to brown. Transfer to casserole with onion mix. Pour wine and stock into frying pan and stir to scrape up any sediment. Bring to the boil and pour over chicken. Cover with a lid and cook at Gas 5, 375F, 190C for 1 hour or until chicken is tender.

Add mushrooms and chestnuts to casserole 10 minutes before end of cooking time. Season with salt and freshly ground black pepper and sprinkle in parsley.

Fry pork lardons until crisp and browned. Remove with a slotted spoon and drain on kitchen paper. Add a little extra oil to pan and fry bread cubes golden. Scatter lardons and croutons over chicken before serving.

Preparation time: 30 minutes
Cooking time: 1 hour 20 minutes approx

Approximate nutritional values per portion:	
525 calories	35g protein
28g fat	29g carbohydrate

GOOD IDEA

The most famous chestnut dessert, Meringue Mont Blanc, is an impressive pudding, and perfect for a festive Christmas dinner.

To serve 4: whisk 2 egg whites stiff and beat in 2 tbsp sugar. Gently fold in 2 more tbsp. Using a star nozzle, pipe a 7in/18cm circular round of meringue on a piece of buttered greaseproof paper on a baking sheet. Pipe another ring of meringue 1in/2.5cm wide to make a border on a separate sheet. Pipe rosettes with the remaining meringue on to another sheet of greaseproof. Bake at Gas 1, 275F, 140C for 1 hour or until crisp, dry and buff-coloured. Peel off greaseproof and cool meringue shapes on a wire rack.

Beat 8oz/225g sweetened chestnut purée with 2oz/50g softened butter. Press through a ricer and heap on to meringue base, or carefully spread it over. Place ring of meringue on top. Spread a little whipped cream on to base of rosettes and stick them on top of ring border like a crown. Top chestnut purée with extra whipped cream. Chill before serving.

CHICKEN LIVERS

The chicken is one of the oldest domesticated birds. Today's chickens probably originated from the wild jungle fowls of India – where historical records give evidence of domestication before 3200BC.

The livers have always been a delicacy. In frozen birds these may be packed with the rest of the giblets in a polythene bag which is tucked into the cavity. However, some frozen birds are sold without giblets – which means the livers can be bought separately. This is good news since they are delicate, tasty – and very cheap.

They can be used in sautés and stir fries, and make a good substitute in meat sauces instead of mince. They are excellent cooked with the Mediterranean flavours of tomatoes, peppers and garlic, and are well complemented by hot seasonings like chilli, or Worcestershire sauce.

For lovers of the traditional British cooked breakfast, they make an excellent luxury extra – whether as part of the eggs and bacon dish, or stirred into scrambled eggs.

LUXURY CHICKEN LIVER PATE

This is a really excellent smooth pâté with a hint of garlic and a brush of brandy. *Serves 8*

> *11oz/300g unsalted butter, slightly softened*
> *¹/₂ Spanish onion, peeled and grated,*
> * or very finely chopped*
> *2 fat cloves garlic, crushed*
> *1lb/450g chicken livers, picked over,*
> * washed and dried*
> *4 tbsp brandy (or to taste)*
> *Bay leaves and green peppercorns for decoration*

Melt 1oz butter in a pan and gently fry onion and garlic over gentle heat until soft. Transfer to the processor.

Turn up the heat and add chicken livers in batches. Fry very quickly to brown and do not crowd the pan. Add cooked livers to onion mix.

Add brandy to pan, bring to the boil and scrape up any sediment. Transfer liquor and 8oz/225g butter to processor and season well. Whizz smooth.

Transfer pâté to an earthenware or other attractive serving pot, and smooth over the top. Leave to set covered in the fridge. When cold, melt remaining butter and pour over the top to seal. Then decorate the top with a couple of bay leaves and a few green peppercorns. Serve with crusty French bread.

Preparation time: 15 minutes
Cooking time: 10 minutes

Approximate nutritional values per portion:	
332 calories	10g protein
24g fat	2g carbohydrate

CHICKEN LIVER SAUTE

A fast and tasty and nourishing supper dish. Delicious served piping hot ether with rice or on toast. *Serves 4*

> *2 tbsp oil*
> *1 medium onion, peeled and finely chopped*
> *2 cloves garlic, peeled and crushed*
> *8oz/225g chicken livers, prepared*
> *¹/₂ wine glass dry sherry*
> *1 tbsp tomato purée*
> *1 tbsp fresh parsley, finely chopped*
> *Salt and freshly ground black pepper*
> *4 tomatoes*

Heat oil in a pan and fry onion and garlic until softened. Add chicken livers to pan and quickly turn about over high heat to stiffen – about 2 minutes. Add sherry, tomato purée and parsley. Season with salt and freshly ground black pepper. Turn down heat and simmer for 5 minutes. Add tomatoes and cook on low heat for 5 minutes more. Serve hot with basmati rice or spread on thick slices of toast.

Preparation time: 10 minutes
Cooking time: 15 minutes

Approximate nutritional values per portion:	
150 calories	10g protein
5g fat	3g carbohydrate

NUTRITION

Liver is a valuable food, rich in 'complete' proteins (which supply all the essential amino acids). Chicken livers contain 18.7g in 4oz/100g. They are not as high in fat as other livers (pig, lambs) with only 6.4g in the same weight.

Dieters should toss them around in a non-stick pan with only a smear of oil for the least fattening way of cooking this useful source of protein.

The most important vitamins present are A, and a group of B vitamins. Vitamin A is essential for healthy teeth, bones and development. It keeps both the skin, and the linings of the mouth, nose and throat healthy. It also helps protect the digestive and urinary systems against infection. Vitamin B12 is also present in liver: this is vital for the growth of the genetic material in cells and it also helps with the formation of red blood cells and with the maintenance of the nervous system.

4oz/100g chicken livers contain:	
133 calories	18.7g protein
6.4g fat	nil carbohydrate

BUYING AND STORING

Free range chickens usually have the giblets included. There will only be one liver in each of these so wash and cover in the fridge until needed and use within 24 hours.

Mostly chicken livers are sold in 8oz/225g tubs, generally frozen. These should always be defrosted before use so they can be picked over and relieved of any membranes, fibrous material, or gall bladders. These are peanut-sized and dark green. Also discard any of the liver tainted green as it will taste bitter. Never try to prise the livers apart – they are delicate and the flesh easily tears. Do not refreeze.

For immediate use, defrost in the tub at room temperature, then cook straight away. Cooked chicken liver pâté or terrines will keep for three to four days covered in the fridge.

CHICKEN LIVER TIPS

● A chicken liver salad makes an inexpensive dinner party first course. Mix some unusual pretty salad leaves in a bowl. Add sliced spring onions, sliced button mushrooms. Cook 8oz/225g chicken livers with garlic and onion in an equal mix of oil and butter. Sprinkle over freshly chopped parsley. Toss this, plus 1 tbsp tiny croutons and 1 tbsp crumbled crisp bacon into the leaves.

● Use chicken livers for a deliciously tasty risotto. For 4: heat 4 tbsp oil in a pan and gently fry 1 finely chopped onion and 3 cloves garlic until soft. Remove with a slotted spoon and reserve. Add 8oz/225g prepared, sliced chicken livers to the pan and cook over high heat, very quickly, to brown – less than a minute. Return onion mix to pan. Turn down heat and add 8oz/225g risotto rice. Turn over to coat in the tasty juices in the pan. Add about ¼pt/150ml chicken stock, 1 tbsp freshly chopped parsley and lots of freshly ground black pepper. Add a further ¾pt/425ml stock little by little, cooking over a low heat until rice is tender and all the liquid is absorbed. Check seasoning before serving.

● Try Devilled Chicken Livers on toast for a weekend breakfast. Grill 4 halved tomatoes sprinkled with Parmesan cheese. Reserve. Very quickly fry 8oz/225g prepared chicken livers. Season with a good dash of Worcester sauce, salt and lots of freshly ground black pepper. Lightly butter 4 slices toast and spread thinly with Dijon mustard. Top with chicken livers and serve with tomatoes on the side.

● How do you test if uncooked pâté mix has enough seasoning? Heat a little oil in a pan and fry 1 tsp. Taste it, then adjust seasoning if necessary.

● Use chicken livers for a quick spaghetti sauce made in the microwave. To serve 4: start cooking the pasta. Then prepare 8oz/225g chicken livers. Mix 2 tbsp tomato purée, good dash Worcestershire sauce, 1 tbsp grated onion, 2 tbsp red wine in a bowl. Add livers and stir to coat. Cover and cook in the microwave on high for 2 minutes. Add 4oz/100g sliced button mushrooms and stir. Cook on high 1 minute more. Leave to stand. Drain pasta and stir through sauce. Serve with freshly chopped parsley sprinkled over.

WARM CHICKEN LIVER SALAD

These warm salads are rather fashionable. This one is attractively colourful and packed with flavour. *Serves 4*

> *4 rashers streaky bacon, de-rinded and chopped*
> *1 red and 1 yellow pepper, de-seeded and in strips*
> *8 whole cloves garlic, sautéed*
> *1 Spanish onion, peeled and in rings*
> *1lb/450g chicken livers, prepared*
> *1 tbsp balsamic vinegar*
> *Salt and ground black pepper*
> *Watercress sprigs for decoration*

Fry bacon until crisp. Remove and reserve. Fry peppers, garlic and onions slowly in remaining oil until soft. Remove and reserve.

Add chicken livers to pan and fry them quickly to brown on the outside while still pink inside. Pour over vinegar and season.

Toss livers and vegetables and arrange in a serving dish. Sprinkle over crispy bacon bits and decorate with watercress before serving. Serve warm.

Preparation time: 15 minutes
Cooking time: 15 minutes

Approximate nutritional values per portion:	
320 calories	27g protein
10g fat	5g carbohydrate

HAM AND CHICKEN LIVER LASAGNE

The chunky chopped ham and chicken livers make a deliciously different filling for this popular dish. *Serves 4*

For the sauce:
> *2oz/50g butter*
> *2oz/50g plain flour*
> *1pt/600ml milk*
> *2 tsp Dijon mustard*
> *2oz/50g Cheddar cheese, grated*

For the filling:
> *2 tbsp oil*
> *1 onion, peeled and finely chopped*
> *2 cloves garlic, crushed*
> *12oz/350g chicken livers, prepared and roughly chopped*
> *2 thick slices ham, finely chopped*
> *14oz/400g can chopped tomatoes*
> *¼pt/150ml red wine*
> *Salt and freshly ground black pepper*
> *1 tbsp fresh oregano or parsley*
> *6 sheets no pre-cook lasagne*

First make the sauce. Heat butter in a pan and stir in flour. Cook for 1 minute. Take off the heat and gradually add milk. Return to heat and cook over a medium flame, stirring all the time until sauce is thickened. Add mustard and cheese and continue simmering until cheese has melted. Push a piece of greaseproof paper on to the top of the sauce to stop a skin forming.

Next prepare the filling. Heat oil in a pan and fry onion and garlic over a low heat until soft. Add chicken livers to pan and turn over quickly to stiffen and brown. Add ham, tomatoes and red wine. Season. Sprinkle in freshly chopped oregano. Turn down and simmer for about 10 minutes, or until slightly reduced and thickened.

Grease a lasagne dish. Layer lasagne sheets over the bottom. Top with half the chicken liver mix. Add another layer of lasagne and spread over remaining mixture. Top with cheese and mustard sauce. Bake in a pre-heated oven Gas 5, 375F, 190C for 45 minutes approx until top is bubbling and golden.

Preparation time: 20 minutes
Cooking time: 1 hour

Approximate nutritional values per portion:	
650 calories	44g protein
34g fat	38g carbohydrate

CHICKEN SUPREMES

The first chickens known to man were probably domesticated from the wild jungle fowl of India, thousands of years ago. In the year 3200BC, chickens were mentioned in records from India and China.

The Romans farmed chickens, not only for eating, but for medicinal purposes too. The dung was used by Roman doctors as a cure for gout, and the fat was melted for medicines and potions.

In the UK, chickens are one of the oldest domesticated fowl. In fact before the second world war most town households and country small-holdings kept runs.

These days, free-range farming methods produce plump 'table birds' with plenty of white breast meat. Chicken suprêmes are taken from the breast, skinned and boned except for the small wing bone which is left intact. Their low fat content is a boon for the health- and diet-conscious.

CHINA CHICKEN

Spicy chicken suprêmes served with a hot parsley and garlic butter and egg noodles. *Serves 4*

For the marinade:
> *4 tbsp soy sauce*
> *4 tbsp sunflower oil*
> *2 tbsp lemon juice*
> *Freshly ground black pepper*
> *4 chicken suprêmes*

For the dressing:
> *2oz/50g butter*
> *2 cloves garlic, chopped*
> *1 tbsp fresh parsley, finely chopped*
> *Juice of ¹/₂ lemon*

Make the marinade first. Mix together soy sauce, oil, lemon juice and freshly ground black pepper.

Make cross cuts into the flesh of the suprêmes and brush with marinade. Leave for 10 minutes.

Preheat the grill then cook suprêmes, basting with remaining marinade. Cook for about 8 minutes one each side, basting all the time.

Meanwhile, heat butter in a pan and add garlic, parsley and lemon juice. Cook gently for 1 minute. Pour over cooked chicken just before serving with noodles.

Preparation time: 15 minutes
Cooking time: 20 minutes

Approximate nutritional values per portion:	
422 calories	41g protein
15g fat	nil carbohydrate

NUTRITION

Chicken suprêmes come from the breast of the chicken, with the skin removed. Because most of the fat in chicken is in the skin, they are very low in calories. One suprême weighing 6oz/175g has around 180 calories, 6g of fat, and no carbohydrate.

These days, white meat like chicken is recommended for a healthy diet because of the trend away from red meat and its link with high cholesterol. However, though most of the fat in chicken is unsaturated, cooked chicken contains about the same amount of cholesterol as in the same weight of cooked lean beef.

Suprêmes are high in protein, containing 20g per 6oz/175g of suprême. They are also a good source of B vitamins, necessary for a healthy nervous system.

Chicken suprêmes contain the mineral zinc, which plays many vital roles in body functions. It helps in the production of proteins, aids utilisation of carbohydrate and maintains normal growth. This mineral also speeds healing of wounds and burns and is often included in creams to treat nappy rash in babies.

There is a useful amount of iron in chicken, necessary for the formation of red blood cells.

6oz/175g chicken suprême contain:	
180 calories	30g protein
6g fat	nil carbohydrate

CHICKEN AND TARRAGON KIEV

Based on a classic dish originating in Russia, this is a suprême of chicken stuffed with garlic and tarragon butter. *Serves 4*

> *4oz/100g butter*
> *Juice and zest of ¹/₂ lemon*
> *4 cloves garlic, crushed*
> *2 tbsp fresh tarragon, finely chopped*
> *Salt and freshly ground black pepper*
> *4 chicken suprêmes*
> *Seasoned flour*
> *1 egg, beaten*
> *4 tbsp fresh white breadcrumbs*

First make the garlic and tarragon butter. Mash butter smooth, then beat in lemon juice and zest, garlic, tarragon and seasoning. Roll into a sausage shape, then wrap in film or foil and chill.

Beat the suprêmes lightly with a rolling pin to flatten them evenly. Cut the butter into 4 equal sized pieces and place in the middle of each suprême, lengthways. Roll up securely, making sure butter is completely enclosed. Secure with cocktail sticks.

Dip each suprême in seasoned flour, then in egg, then in fresh breadcrumbs. Chill for 30 minutes.

Heat oil in a frying pan and shallow fry suprêmes seams side down. Turn over and cook the other side. This takes about 15 minutes. The chicken should be firm to the touch. Do not test it with a knife – or the butter will escape. Blot dry on kitchen paper and remove cocktail sticks before serving.

Preparation time: 40 minutes
Cooking time: 20 minutes approx

Approximate nutritional values per portion:	
460 calories	33g protein
26g fat	10g carbohydrate

BUYING AND STORING

Most butchers sell chicken suprêmes ready done, or will prepare them to order. This is useful when only one is needed, supermarkets usually only sell packs of two or four, and sometimes economy packs of eight.

Because suprêmes are made from the breast of the chicken and need preparation, they cost a little more than ordinary chicken breast portions. However, there is no excess fat and absolutely no waste.

Choose chicken suprêmes which are well trimmed and have a good shape, with the wing bone attached and not broken. The flesh should be pink and unblemished, with no sign of damage or bruising. It should also have a fresh, appealing smell.

CHICKEN SUPREME TIPS

● Serve cold poached chicken suprêmes glazed in a tarragon-flavoured aspic as part of a cold buffet selection. Poach suprêmes in stock. Drain and cool. Mix up aspic according to packet instructions and add sprigs of fresh tarragon to infuse flavour. When aspic is syrupy and ready for use, discard tarragon. Place suprêmes on a wire rack and brush with a thin layer of aspic. Decorate each one with thin halved lemon slices and a tarragon sprig. Leave to set, then spoon over another layer. Chill until required.

● Make a filling and healthy salad of chicken and red apple. For 2: slice 1 large cold poached suprême into strips, discarding wing bone. Mix in a bowl with 2 cored and sliced red apples, and 4 trimmed spring onions, cut into 2in/5cm lengths. Mix dressing of 1 tbsp mayonnaise and 2 tbsp thick natural yogurt with seasoning. Toss through salad and chill. Serve with wholemeal bread rolls.

● To roast a suprême without drying out the delicate flesh, wrap it in bacon rashers. Season it with freshly ground black pepper first. Stretch 2 rashers of streaky bacon with the back of a knife. Halve rashers and lay them over the suprême in a roasting tray. Drizzle over a little oil and roast in the oven for about 20 minutes or until cooked through. Remove rashers about 5 minutes before end of cooking to allow chicken to brown slightly. Make a gravy from the pan juices.

● For a great all-in-one salad, slice cold cooked chicken suprêmes and add to cooked long grain rice with chopped yellow peppers, spring onions, flaked cooked cod, peeled prawns and cooked mussels. Toss in homemade mayonnaise mixed in equal proportions with soured cream.

● Use chicken suprêmes to make a quick version of Coq au Vin. For 4: heat 3 tbsp oil in a large pan and fry 12 baby onions with 2 cloves garlic until softened and golden. Remove and reserve. Dip 4 suprêmes in seasoned flour and add to pan to brown. Return onions and garlic and pour over ½pt/300ml red wine and ¼pt/150ml chicken stock. Bring to the boil and simmer until chicken is cooked through – about 20 minutes. After 10 minutes, add halved button mushrooms. Season. Serve sprinkled with crisp croutons and chopped parsley.

CHICKEN FARAH WITH COUS COUS

Chunky chicken kebabs served on a bed of cous cous salad. *Serves 4*

For the salad:
    8oz/225g fine cous cous
    4 tbsp oil
    1 tbsp white wine vinegar
    3 cloves garlic, peeled and crushed
    Salt and freshly ground black pepper
    4 spring onions, trimmed and sliced
For the marinade:
    Juice of 1 lemon
    2 tbsp soy sauce
    2 tbsp tomato purée
    1 clove garlic, crushed
    Good dash Worcestershire sauce
    Good dash chilli sauce
    2 tbsp oil
    Freshly ground black pepper
    4 chicken suprêmes, bone discarded,
        then cut into chunks
    1 red and 1 green pepper de-seeded and
        cut into squares

First prepare salad. Place cous cous in a bowl and just cover with water. Leave for 30 minutes or until all the water is absorbed and the cous cous is tender. Shake oil, vinegar, garlic and seasoning in a screw-top jar and pour over cous cous. Add spring onions and toss. Reserve.

Make the marinade by mixing lemon juice, soy sauce, tomato purée, garlic, Worcestershire sauce, chilli sauce, oil. Season.

Marinade chicken for 1 hour, turning. Thread kebab skewers with chicken and pepper chunks.

Grill for 10 minutes, turning and brushing with marinade, or until chicken is cooked through. Sprinkle kebabs with coriander and serve on a bed of cous cous salad.

Preparation time: 20 minutes
Cooking time: 15 minutes approx

Approximate nutritional values per portion:	
250 calories	37g protein
2g fat	2g carbohydrate

GREEN AND WHITE SALAD

Refreshing crunchy salad in a piquant dressing. *Serves 4*

    2 large chicken suprêmes, poached or microwaved
    1 green pepper
    ½ cucumber
    8 spring onions
    Chive batons to decorate
For the dressing:
    4 tbsp olive oil
    1 tbsp white wine vinegar
    1 tsp wholegrain mustard
    Good dash of soy sauce
    Salt and freshly ground black pepper

Discard bone from suprêmes and cut flesh into even slices.

Slice green pepper into matchsticks. Cut cucumber into 3in/7.5cm lengths and then into strips. Trim and chop spring onions.

Place all ingredients in a salad bowl. Shake dressing ingredients in a screw-top jar and pour over salad about 15 minutes before serving. Toss and serve decorated with chive batons.

Preparation time: 15 minutes
Cooking time: nil

Approximate nutritional values per portion:	
186 calories	20g protein
11g fat	5g carbohydrate

CHIVES

The chive plant is the baby sister of the onion family with its slender tapering tubular stalks and dainty purple pom-pom flowers.

A cultivated plant, it is not often found in the wild, but when it is, it will be growing along the banks of streams, by ponds or woods.

Unlike other herbs, it has no medicinal uses – it is a culinary herb. Its delicate onion taste enhances dishes like cold soups, grilled fish and salads. And, of course, it is a delightful decorative herb when the leaves are used snipped, finely chopped or in batons, or the flowers just as they are.

Chives thrive on continual use. Snip them to decorate a soup and they will soon grow up again for future use. Although the flowers make pretty decorations for salads and summer meals, the best way to make this plant sturdy is to pinch out the flowers when they appear so the leaves grow stronger.

In the garden, chives grow enthusiastically. Once a patch is established it is best to split the roots each year and replant them so they do not overcrowd themselves.

As a plus, they make a lovely garden border during the summer months. In the winter, transplant a root to a pot and keep it on a windowsill in the kitchen. It will keep the cook in the family in garnish and fresh flavouring for several months.

GREEN RISOTTO

This tasty dish of rice flavoured with courgette, onion and chives is a perfect accompaniment or a vegetarian main course. *Serves 4*

2 tbsp oil
1 onion, peeled and finely chopped
2 cloves garlic, crushed
1 large courgette, washed and diced
8oz/225g risotto rice
1½pt/850ml vegetable stock
3 tbsp fresh snipped chives
2oz/50g freshly grated Parmesan
Salt and freshly ground black pepper

Heat oil and fry onion and garlic until softened. Stir in courgette and cook for 2 minutes. Add rice and mix in. Add the stock, little by little. Wait until each addition has been absorbed before adding more stock if necessary.

Stir in chives, Parmesan and finally the seasoning, and serve immediately.
Preparation time: 15 minutes
Cooking time: 45 minutes approx

Approximate nutritional values per portion:	
200 calories	2g protein
4g fat	15g carbohydrate

NUTRITION

Since chives are used as a flavouring and garnish and not in any appreciable quantity as a main recipe ingredient, they make little contribution to a nutritionally healthy diet.

However, the essential oil in chives contains a useful amount of sulphur, similar to that in onion and garlic. This has reputed antibiotic properties which can sometimes retard the growth of some bacteria.

GOOD IDEA

Chives are not easy to dry except on a commercial scale. But during the summer freeze them for a constant year-round supply. They react well to freezing, re-constitute well and retain their flavour.

Snip and wash the stalks, then chop finely or cut into lengths. Freeze chopped chives in an ice cube tray with water or flat freeze chive lengths on a tray, then transfer to a sealed polythene bag. Defrost, use as fresh.

Hello! Good Cooking

HAKE STEAKS WITH CHIVE BUTTER

Meaty steaks of juicy hake barbecued or grilled and served oozing with chive butter. *Serves 4*

> *4 thick hake steaks*
> *Salt and freshly ground black pepper*
> For the chive butter:
> *4oz/100g unsalted butter, softened*
> *4 tbsp fresh snipped chives*
> *Good squeeze lemon juice*

For the chive butter, mix all of the ingredients together in a bowl. Pile on to cling film and roll into a cylinder. Chill until set.

Wipe hake steaks and season with salt and pepper. Spread them with a little of the chive butter and then grill or barbecue until cooked through, about 5 minutes each side.

Serve the steaks topped with extra chive butter, new potatoes and a rocket salad.

Preparation time: 15 minutes
Cooking time: 10 minutes approx

Approximate nutritional values per portion:	
350 calories	30g protein
14g fat	nil carbohydrate

CHIVE TIPS

● Sprinkle a few snipped chives into a vinaigrette dressing for pretty leaves like rocket, oakleaf, lollo rosso and watercress for a piquant oniony flavour.

● Delicate batons of chives are a pretty, colourful decoration floating on top of the classic French cold leek and potato summer soup, Vichyssoise.

● Add a couple of tablespoons of chopped chives to a mixture for posh chicken burgers. Mix minced chicken breast fillet, garlic, grated onion, salt and a pinch of cayenne. Stir in a good squeeze of lemon juice and chives then bind with an egg. Shape into burgers then grill and serve in soft wholemeal rolls with lettuce, tomatoes and mayonnaise.

● Spice up the old favourite mix of vodka and tomato juice – Bloody Mary – with Worcestershire sauce, lemon juice, tabasco and snipped chives. Pour into a tall glass of ice with a celery stick for stirring. Sprinkle over a few extra chives and a grinding of black pepper before serving.

● Make a marinade for barbecued fresh sardines. Mix together olive oil, lime juice, garlic, chilli sauce, snipped chives and salt and freshly ground black pepper. Soak sardines for 30 minutes before barbecuing to allow flavours to penetrate. Cook for 5 minutes each side and serve with lime wedges for sprinkling.

● Top a simple dish of fresh tagliatelle with an oyster mushroom and chive sauce. Gently tear mushrooms and fry in butter with shallots and garlic until softened. Add a dash of white wine and a little double cream then stir in 2 tbsp snipped chives, salt and freshly ground black pepper. Toss through pasta and serve with Parmesan for sprinkling.

CHICKEN GOUJONS WITH LIME AND CHIVES

Strips of chicken fillet marinated in lime and garlic then dipped in egg, deep fried and rolled in fresh snipped chives. *Serves 4*

> *4 chicken breast fillets, skinned and*
> *   lightly flattened*
> *Salt and freshly ground black pepper*
> *Juice of 1 lime*
> *2 cloves garlic, crushed*
> *Flour for dipping*
> *1 egg, beaten*
> *Oil for frying*
> *6 tbsp fresh chopped chives*
> *Lime twists for garnish*

Cut chicken breasts into strips. Place in a bowl and season with salt and pepper. Sprinkle over lime juice and garlic. Leave to marinate for 30 minutes.

Dip chicken in flour and shake off excess. Dip into egg, then fry in hot oil until cooked through and golden. Roll in chopped chives. Garnish with lime twists to serve.

Preparation time: 10 minutes
Cooking time: 5 minutes approx

Approximate nutritional values per portion:	
220 calories	35g protein
8g fat	3g carbohydrate

CHILLED AVOCADO AND CHIVE SOUP

Pretty eau-de-nil coloured chilled summer soup of avocado with the piquancy of fresh snipped chives. Making this soup is simplicity itself. *Serves 4*

> *2 ripe avocados*
> *Juice of ½ lemon*
> *1½pt/850ml chicken stock*
> *1 tbsp grated onion*
> *2 tbsp double cream*
> *Salt and freshly ground white pepper*
> *3 tbsp fresh snipped chives*
> *Avocado slices and chive batons for garnish*

Cut avocados in half and remove stones. Carefully peel, chop and sprinkle with the lemon juice to prevent discoloration. Purée in a blender with chicken stock and onion. Then, whizz in cream and seasoning. Transfer to a bowl. Stir in chives. Chill.

Pour into soup bowls and decorate with avocado slices and chive batons before serving.

Preparation time: 10 minutes
Cooking time: nil

Approximate nutritional values per portion:	
220 calories	3g protein
20g fat	1g carbohydrate

CHUCK STEAK

Beef has been known to man for many centuries. As early as the year 2400BC, it was mentioned in the records of the Palace of Sumer. And beef joints were buried with the bodies of ancient Egyptians in their tombs, so they wouldn't go hungry on their journey to the other world.

In medieval Britain, beef was salted to preserve it, so the winter supply would be plentiful. Elizabethan sailors also ate salt beef on long voyages.

Another way of preserving beef was by potting, and this was topped with a thick suet seal to keep the meat fresh for long periods. Potted beef is still available today, covered with a layer of melted butter – much tastier than its original counterpart.

By the 1800s, boiled beef was a regular feature on the menu in men's clubs, and was served as a breakfast dish to riders setting off for a day's hunting. Around this time, the song *Boiled Beef And Carrots* was made famous because of the popularity of this dish with the less well-off.

Today, beef herds are bred small-boned with plenty of meat, unlike their predecessors of old. This gives much tastier and more tender cuts, like chuck steak, and at reasonable prices.

Chuck steak comes from the fore quarter of the animal, around the shoulder area. It is lean and flavoursome, but the muscle tissue needs to be broken down with long, slow, moist cooking. For this reason it makes the best choice for stewing, braising or casseroles.

BEEF AND ORANGE STEW

A robust beef stew with a surprisingly successful mix of tastes. *Serves 4*

4 tbsp oil
1 onion, peeled and chopped
2 cloves garlic, peeled and crushed
2lb/900g chuck steak, cubed
Seasoned flour
7oz/200g can chopped tomatoes
3/4pt/425ml beef stock
1 tsp chopped thyme
Juice of 2 oranges
Zest of 1/2 orange
1 peeled orange, in segments
Salt and black pepper
Chopped parsley

Heat half the oil in a pan and fry onion and garlic until softened. Remove and reserve. Dip chuck steak in seasoned flour and shake off excess.

Add remaining oil to pan and fry steak in batches to brown. Transfer to a large flameproof casserole with onion mix. Add tomatoes, stock and thyme, plus the juice of one orange.

Bring to the boil. Cover and simmer for 2 hours, or until meat is tender. Stir in remaining orange juice, zest and segments. Season and serve decorated with parsley and orange zest.

Preparation time: 20 minutes
Cooking time: 2¹/₂ hours approx

Approximate nutritional values per portion:	
370 calories	40g protein
19g fat	8g carbohydrate

BUYING AND STORING

Chuck steak is available from butchers' shops and at supermarket meat counters.

Butchers will trim chuck steak and slice it to order, or chop it for casseroles and pies. This way, even the smallest amount can be bought – just one thin slice for braising or 8oz/225g cubed for a single portion of stew.

Choose chuck steak with a fresh red colour and an appealing smell. The flesh should be moist, firm and lean with a faint marbling of fat. Supermarkets without meat counters sell chuck steak pre-packed. It is harder to check freshness, but always look at the sell-by date.

Remove chuck steak from its wrapping as soon as possible after purchase. Place it in a shallow dish or bowl to catch any drips. Cover with non-PVC film or foil. Store in the fridge and cook as soon as possible for maximum freshness and taste.

NUTRITION

Chuck steak has fewer calories than other fattier cuts of stewing beef, with 153 per 4oz/100g weight. It has 7g fat and no carbohydrate.

The biggest nutritional contribution from chuck steak is protein – it is an excellent source, with 20g in a 4oz/100g portion. This protein is 'complete', that is, all the essential amino acids needed for a healthy diet are present.

The B vitamins are abundant in beef, especially B6 and B12, and B3 nicotinic acid. These are necessary to maintain the nervous system, and vitamin B6 in particular is sometimes useful to women during menstruation. It is thought to help relieve the tension and headache that may occur at this time.

Chuck steak provides a good amount of iron in its organic form. This type, called heme iron, is more useful to the body than the inorganic iron found in vegetables. Iron is needed for healthy blood and prevention of anaemia.

Other major minerals found in chuck steak are potassium, for muscle tissue, phosphorus, for bone formation, and zinc, to aid healing. Blood levels of zinc may decrease in pregnancy and old age.

4oz/100g chuck steak contain:	
135 calories	20g protein
7g fat	nil carbohydrate

BRAISED BEEF WITH OLIVES

Slices of chuck steak cooked with onions, mushrooms and black olives with olive paste and red wine. *Serves 4*

> 4 tbsp oil
> 1 onion, peeled and finely sliced
> 2 cloves garlic, crushed
> 8 small, thin slices chuck steak
> Seasoned flour
> ¹/₄pt/150ml red wine
> ¹/₄pt/150ml beef stock
> 1 tbsp tomato purée
> 1 tbsp black olive paste
> 4oz/100g button mushrooms, wiped and sliced
> 8 stoned black olives
> Salt and freshly ground black pepper

Heat 2 tbsp oil and fry onion and garlic gently until softened. Remove. Dip steak in seasoned flour and shake off excess. Add to the pan with remaining oil and fry to seal and brown. Return the onion mix to pan and pour over wine and stock. Stir in tomato purée and olive paste and bring to the boil.

Transfer steak and onions to an ovenproof dish. Spoon sauce over. Cover and braise at Gas 3, 325F, 160C for 2 hours or until meat is tender. Add mushrooms and olives 15 minutes before finish. Season.

Preparation time: 15 minutes
Cooking time: 2 hours approx

Approximate nutritional values per portion:	
360 calories	30g protein
16g fat	4g carbohydrate

BEEF TIPS

● Calculate 6oz/175g to 8oz/225g of chuck steak per person when buying to allow for shrinkage during cooking.

● Chuck steak is the perfect choice for a steak and kidney pie, topped with golden puff pastry. For the filling, fry 1 peeled and finely chopped onion with 2 cloves garlic in 2 tbsp oil until softened. Remove with a slotted spoon and reserve. Dip 2lb/900g chuck steak cubes into seasoned flour and shake off excess. Fry in batches in a little more oil until well browned all over.

Transfer to a large pan with onion mix. Fry 8oz/225g chopped kidney and add to pan. Pour over 1pt/600ml beef stock and add 1 tbsp tomato purée. Stir in 1 tsp chopped thyme and a bay leaf. Bring to the boil, cover and simmer, for 2 hours or until meat is tender. Spoon into a pie dish and cool. Top with rolled out ready made puff pastry and brush with beaten egg to glaze. Bake at Gas 6, 400F, 200C for 30 minutes or until pastry is golden.

● Chunky chuck steak stews can be enhanced by the subtle addition of fruit. Add a few chopped dried apricots, or orange segments and zest for a tasty change.

MOUSSAKA

An old Greek favourite made with fresh chuck steak mince layered with aubergines and courgette slices and topped with a creamy cheese sauce. *Serves 4*

> 3 tbsp oil
> 1 onion, peeled and finely chopped
> 2 cloves garlic, crushed
> 1¹/₂lb/700g chuck steak, minced
> 14oz/400g tin chopped tomatoes
> Few sage leaves, shredded
> 1 bay leaf
> 1 tbsp chopped parsley
> Salt and freshly ground black pepper
> 2 aubergines, sliced
> 2 courgettes, sliced
> For the sauce:
> 2oz/50g butter
> 2oz/50g flour
> 1pt/600ml milk
> 2oz/50g grated Cheddar
> Tomato slices for decoration
> 1oz/25g grated Parmesan

For the filling, heat 2 tbsp oil and fry onion and garlic until softened. Remove with a slotted spoon and reserve. Add mince to pan and fry to brown. Return onion mix and add chopped tomatoes, sage, bay leaf and parsley. Season with salt and freshly ground black pepper. Cover and simmer gently until the mince is tender.

Meanwhile heat remaining oil in a pan and fry aubergine and courgette slices until slightly brown. Drain on kitchen paper. Then layer in an ovenproof dish with mince.

For the cheese sauce, melt butter in a pan and stir in flour. Cook for 1 minute. Gradually add milk stirring constantly. Bring to the boil, stirring continuously to prevent lumps or until sauce has thickened. Add cheese, stirring until it melts. Season and spoon sauce over moussaka. Top with tomato slices and sprinkle with Parmesan. Bake at Gas 6, 400F, 200C for 20 minutes or until filling is hot and top is browned.

Preparation time: 25 minutes
Cooking time: 45 minutes approx

Approximate nutritional values per portion:	
600 calories	41g protein
35g fat	26g carbohydrate

STEAK AND SMOKED OYSTER PIES

A lovely combination of chuck steak with smoked oysters. *Serves 4*

> 4 tbsp oil
> 1 onion, peeled and chopped
> 2 cloves garlic, crushed
> 4 thick slices chuck steak, cubed
> Seasoned flour
> 2 glasses red wine
> 1pt/600ml beef stock
> 1 fresh bouquet garni
> 1 tbsp tomato purée
> 1 tbsp red wine vinegar
> Salt and freshly ground black pepper
> 3oz/75g tin smoked oysters
> 13oz/375g pack puff pastry
> Beaten egg for glazing

Heat oil in a large pan and fry the onion and garlic until soft. Remove and reserve. Dip steak in flour and dust off excess. Fry to brown. Return onion mix to pan. Pour over wine and stock.

Bring to boil and add bouquet garni. Stir in tomato purée and vinegar. Cover and simmer for 2 hours. Season. Stir in oysters 5 minutes before end.

Meanwhile, roll out pastry to make 4 individual oval pie lids. Use trimmings to decorate. Chill lids and decorations. When filling is cooked, spoon into pie dishes and cool slightly. Attach lids and decorations. Brush with egg.

Bake pies at Gas 6, 400F, 200C for 25 minutes. Cover with foil if pastry becomes too brown.

Preparation time: 30 minutes
Cooking time: 2¹/₂ hours approx

Approximate nutritional values per portion:	
470 calories	44g protein
22g fat	8g carbohydrate

COD

One of Britain's most popular fish, cod also features in most other countries' cuisine. The firm flesh and good flavour lends itself to many styles of cooking.

Caught in the waters around Britain, cod is also found further afield in the North Atlantic and North Pacific. They vary in size, and can grow to a massive 6ft/2m, though their average length is 3ft/1m, weighing around 10lb/4.5kg – although smaller ones are also sold.

Cod has a delicate grey-green tone to the skin, a distinctive, pale grey lateral line, and a flush of darker coloured spots almost like freckles which run along the length of the fish. However, most cod are cut into fillets or steaks on the fishmonger's slab so the beauty and appeal of the whole fish is lost.

Although in the UK cod is almost always eaten fresh, it is popular in Europe, and especially Portugal, in the form of dried salt cod – bacalhau in Portuguese. The Portuguese have 365 recipes for cooking this type of cod, one for every single day of the year.

The roe of the female cod is sold in most fishmongers, either fresh, smoked or salted. And the liver of this fish is an excellent source of vitamins, taken in the form of cod liver oil capsules.

BUYING AND STORING

Cod is available fresh and frozen in the form of steaks or fillets.

Fresh cod fillet should have a white, pearly, moist appearance with no signs of dryness. The smell is also important. All fresh fish should have an appealing scent of the sea with no bitter or sour odours.

Check the packaging of frozen cod for any damage. It should be tightly sealed and the fillets inside neatly packed. Staining could indicate something has spilt on to the package, and leaked on to the fish. An excess of ice crystais may mean that the fish has defrosted and been refrozen.

Keep fresh cod in the refrigerator for up to a day. Remove it from its wrapping and place on a clean plate covered with greaseproof or foil. This will stop the fishy smell tainting other foods and prevent drips falling from or on to the fish.

Defrost frozen cod thoroughly before cooking and do not refreeze any that has defrosted.

COBBLED COD

Rustic dish of pearly cod chunks, prawns and eggs in a creamy onion and parsley sauce, finished with the lightest cheese scone topping. *Serves 4*

1½lb/700g cod fillet, skinned and in chunks
6 tbsp fish stock
4oz/100g peeled prawns
2 hard-boiled eggs, quartered
Salt and freshly ground black pepper
For the scone topping:
8oz/225g self-raising flour
1 tsp baking powder
Pinch of salt
2oz/50g butter
2oz/50g finely grated Cheddar cheese
Pinch of dry mustard
6 tbsp milk
1 egg, beaten
For the sauce:
1½oz/40g butter
1½oz/40g flour
14fl oz/400ml milk
2 tbsp fresh parsley, finely chopped
½ onion, grated

Make the cobbler topping of cheese scones first. Sift flour, baking powder and salt into a bowl and rub in butter to breadcrumb stage. Add the cheese and mustard. Gradually add milk and work in to form a soft dough. Wrap in film and leave in the fridge for 30 minutes.

For the sauce, melt butter in a pan and add flour. Cook one minute over gentle heat. Gradually add milk, stirring all the time until thickened. Add parsley and onion. Remove from heat, cover surface with buttered greaseproof, and reserve.

Poach cod in fish stock in a covered pan, or microwave, until cooked through. Stir gently into sauce with 2 tbsp cooking juices, prawns and eggs. Season the mixture with salt and freshly ground black pepper. Transfer to an ovenproof dish.

Roll out scone dough to ½in/1cm thick. Cut out rounds with a plain 2in/5cm cutter. Arrange overlapping around the edge of the dish. Brush with beaten egg to glaze.

Bake at Gas 5, 375F, 190C for 25 minutes, or until topping is risen and golden and filling is hot.
Preparation time: 20 minutes
Cooking time: 45 minutes

Approximate nutritional values per portion:	
670 calories	45g protein
30g fat	60g carbohydrate

COD IN RED WINE

Cod cooked in red wine is given a delicious subtle flavour. *Serves 4*

4 tbsp oil
4 rashers bacon, de-rinded and in strips
1 onion, finely chopped
2 cloves garlic, crushed
1½lb/700g thick cod fillet, in chunks
Seasoned flour
4oz/100g button mushrooms, wiped
2 wine glasses red wine
1 tbsp finely chopped fresh parsley
Salt and freshly ground black pepper
2 slices white bread, crusts removed
Extra chopped fresh parsley

Heat 2 tbsp oil and cook bacon until brown. Add onion and garlic and continue cooking over a gentle heat until soft but not brown. Transfer to a flameproof dish.

Toss cod chunks in seasoned flour and fry gently in remaining oil to seal. Add to dish with mushrooms. Pour over wine and sprinkle over parsley. Season.

Bring to the boil then simmer gently for approximately 10 minutes – or until cod is cooked through.

Meanwhile, make croutons. Cut the bread diagonally into triangles. Shallow fry in hot oil until golden on both sides. Dip edges in chopped parsley. Serve with stew.
Preparation time: 15 minutes
Cooking time: 15 minutes

Approximate nutritional values per portion:	
425 calories	33g protein
25g fat	15g carbohydrate

CREAMY COD CURRY

Mild South East Asian-style curry with cod chunks cooked with ginger and chilli in a creamy coconut sauce. *Serves 4*

> 3 tbsp oil
> 1 onion, peeled and sliced
> 2 cloves garlic, crushed
> 1 tsp root ginger, finely chopped
> ½ large chilli, de-seeded and chopped
> 1 tsp turmeric
> ½ tsp ground cumin
> 2 tsp mild curry paste
> 1oz/25g creamed coconut
> ½pt/300ml chicken stock
> 1½lb/700g cod fillet in chunks
> 1 tbsp fresh mint, chopped
> Salt and freshly ground black pepper

Heat oil and gently fry onion, garlic, ginger and chilli until softened. Add turmeric and cumin. Stir in curry paste. Cook for 3 minutes. Add creamed coconut and pour over stock. Bring to the boil until coconut has blended. Add cod and mint and stir – *carefully* so the fish doesn't break up.

Simmer over a medium heat until cod is just cooked. Season with salt and freshly ground black pepper and serve immediately.

Preparation time: 15 minutes
Cooking time: 12 minutes

Approximate nutritional values per portion:	
250 calories	25g protein
15g fat	2g carbohydrate

COD AU POIVRE

Glamorous dinner party dish of cod steaks served with a green pepper sauce. *Serves 4*

> 4 cod steaks
> Oil for brushing
> 2 tbsp green peppercorns in brine, drained
> Lamb's lettuce to decorate

For the sauce:
> 2 tbsp oil
> 1 medium onion, finely chopped
> 2 green peppers, de-seeded and chopped
> ¼pt/150ml vegetable stock
> Salt and freshly ground black pepper

First make the sauce. Heat oil in a pan and fry onion and green peppers over a low heat until softened. Pour over stock and season. Bring to the boil and simmer for 5 minutes. Whizz in a blender until smooth.

Brush cod steaks with oil. Crush green peppercorns and press into both sides of cod steaks. Sprinkle with a little salt. Fry, turning once until cod is cooked through.

Transfer to warmed plates and add a little warm sauce around one side. Decorate with lamb's lettuce.

Preparation time: 10 minutes
Cooking time: 15 minutes

Approximate nutritional values per portion:	
200 calories	16g protein
12g fat	5g carbohydrate

NUTRITION

Cod is a low-fat white fish with only 82 calories per 4oz/100g. It is an excellent source of 'complete' protein, with 18g for the same weight of fish. This protein contains all the essential amino acids required for a healthy diet. There is only a small trace of fat in cod, 1g per 4oz/100g, and no carbohydrate.

One of the most essential nutrients in fish is the Omega-3 fatty acids, contained in the fish oils. Although cod is not an oily fish, Omega-3 is still present in small amounts. These acids can reduce the levels of molecules that carry cholesterol into the bloodstream and increase the levels of the molecules that carry it away. This can ultimately reduce the risk of blood clots, heart attacks and strokes.

Moderate amounts of the B vitamins, particularly B3 or nicotinic acid, are present in cod. Vitamin B3 can be made by the body from high protein foods but fish provides it naturally.

Cod liver is of special nutritive value because of its oil and is usually taken in the form of cod liver oil capsules or mixed with malt in a jar of malt and cod liver oil. It is a rich natural source of vitamin A in the form of retinol. This vitamin aids vision in dim light though deficiency is rare because it is stored in the liver. However, these stores may occasionally become depleted, particularly in old people.

4oz/100g raw cod fillet contain:	
82 calories	18g protein
1g fat	nil carbohydrate

COD TIPS

● Make your own fish fingers – they won't be regular sizes, but will taste good. To serve 4: cut 1lb/450g thick cod fillet into 1in/2.5cm wide slices. Dip in flour seasoned with salt, pepper, paprika and a pinch of powdered mustard. Coat with beaten egg and shallow fry for about 3 minutes, turning once, or until fish is cooked through.

● Try this light, crisp batter for the traditional Great British fish and chips. Sift 4oz/100g plain flour into a bowl with ½ tsp salt and 1½ tsp baking powder. Beat in enough water to give the coating consistency of single cream. Dip pieces of cod in flour, then the batter and deep fry.

● Cod steaks make filling and substantial meals. Ask your fishmonger to cut them thickly. Grill on one side, then turn over to grill other side until almost cooked through. Top with a mixture of 2 tbsp fresh white breadcrumbs mixed with 1oz/25g finely grated cheese, a good pinch of mixed herbs, juice and grated rind of half a lemon, salt and black pepper and 3 tbsp oil. Continue grilling until topping is browned and steaks are thoroughly cooked.

● Baking cod steaks in foil in the oven keeps the flesh moist and tasty. Place cod steaks on a square of foil big enough to enclose them in a single layer. Sprinkle over a little thinly sliced spring onion (sliced vertically into shreds), a few sliced mushrooms, a good squeeze of lemon juice and a dash of soy sauce. Seal foil into a parcel and bake for 10 minutes at Gas 5, 375F, 190C.

● Wheedle cod skin and bones from your fishmonger to make fish stock. If heads are used, wash away any blood and remove eyes first as these can taint the flavour. Cover cod scraps and bones with water, add the chopped white of a leek, 2 chopped celery sticks and a few sprigs of parsley. Bring to boil then simmer for 20 minutes only – after this the stock may sour. Strain and discard fish and vegetables. Return stock to the pan and reduce. Never season stock for general use – do it when you complete the finished dish.

CORIANDER

Coriander is a herb and spice in the same plant.

An annual, easy to grow from seeds sown in the spring or autumn, it can reach a height of about three feet, with attractive fronds of delicate leaves floating from central stalks. These leaves are used as a fresh and distinctive herbal flavouring.

Tear them up to add to salads or sprinkle in vegetable soups such as cauliflower, broccoli, fennel or leek. In summer, pale purple flowers appear which mature into the seeds. These are prized as a pungent spice and essential for curries and Far Eastern or Oriental specialities.

But the ground seeds are used in other parts of the world, too. Crush them in a pestle and mortar and add to rich country pâtés, Mediterranean stews, light vegetable soups or even in fruit teabreads for a subtle spicy character.

Coriander as a herb or spice complements rich meats such as pork, duck, lamb or liver, contributing a personality of its own to any sauces made from the meat juices.

And the herb, used sparingly because it has an unmistakable taste, enhances cheese and eggs – in soufflés, cheese omelettes, or baked eggs with cream. Try it sprinkled on scrambled eggs, too.

ORIENTAL BEEF AND PRAWNS

An unusual, but delicious combination of tender strips of beef and peeled prawns tossed in oyster sauce. *Serves 4*

> 3 tbsp oil
> 1 onion, halved and sliced
> 1 tsp finely chopped root ginger
> 2 cloves garlic, crushed
> 1 red and 1 green pepper, de-seeded and
>   cut in strips
> 2 thin slices rump steak, in strips
> 4oz/100g peeled prawns
> 2 tbsp dry sherry
> 2 tbsp soy sauce
> 1 tbsp oyster sauce
> 1 tbsp finely chopped fresh coriander
> Salt and freshly ground black pepper

Heat 2 tbsp oil in a large pan or wok and fry onion, ginger and garlic over gentle heat until softened but not browned. Add pepper strips and stir-fry for 2 more minutes until just cooked but still crunchy, tossing around while they cook. Remove with a slotted spoon and keep warm.

Add remaining oil to pan and stir-fry beef quickly over a high heat to brown and seal the meat. Stir in prawns and reserved vegetables. Pour over sherry, soy and oyster sauce and sprinkle in coriander. Season and bring to the boil. Simmer covered for 1 minute and serve.

Preparation time: 20 minutes
Cooking time: 10 minutes approx

Approximate nutritional values per portion:	
245 calories	21g protein
38g fat	2g carbohydrate

SEA BASS EN PAPILLOTTE

Fragrant dish of a whole small sea bass stuffed with strips of ginger, spring onion and sliced garlic cooked in a parcel, then served drizzled with soy, lime and coriander. *Serves 4*

> 1in/2.5cm piece of root ginger,
>   peeled and in matchsticks
> 2 cloves garlic, peeled and sliced
> 3 spring onions, trimmed and in matchsticks
> 2 tbsp oil
> 1 small sea bass, de-scaled and gutted
> Greaseproof paper for wrapping
> For the dressing:
> 2 tbsp sunflower oil
> ½ tbsp soy sauce
> Juice of ½ lime
> 1 tbsp chopped coriander

Fry ginger, garlic and spring onions in oil until soft. Cool and stuff cavity of sea bass. Season. Wrap it in an oiled, greaseproof parcel to enclose completely. Bake at Gas 5, 375F, 190C for 20 minutes or until cooked through.

Transfer the fish to a serving platter while still wrapped. For the dressing: heat oil in a pan over a low heat and add soy sauce and lime juice. Stir in coriander over heat. Unwrap paper at the table and pour dressing along the length of fish. The liquid mixes with the fish juices to make a delectable sauce.

Preparation time: 15 minutes
Cooking time: 25 minutes approx

Approximate nutritional values per portion:	
220 calories	18g protein
14g fat	2g carbohydrate

NUTRITION

Coriander is used merely as a flavouring and as such, makes no nutritional contribution to the diet. This herb has been known in Oriental and Middle Eastern cuisine for centuries. The Chinese in particular were quick to see its potential, not only for culinary purposes, but also for medicinal use.

Coriander leaves contain a volatile oil which acts as a stimulant, and helps to cure flatulence. In fact, this herb is often included in a herbal gripe water for young babies suffering from colic.

Because it does not play a substantial part in the diet the nutritional values of coriander are irrelevant.

BUYING AND STORING

Coriander is best bought and used fresh. Keep it sprightly in a jug of cold water. However, this herb is seasonal and is not always available. There are several other ways to keep coriander ready for use.

1 Dried, available in tubs or sachets or home-dried when there is a glut of the fresh herb.

2 Frozen in small ice cubes. Finely chop coriander and fill ice-cube moulds. Top with water and freeze until the coriander is needed. Add frozen to stews and casseroles.

3 Seeds. These are the spice part of the plant. They are used whole or ground.

CORIANDER TIPS

● Buy coriander fresh from most good greengrocers or supermarkets. Keep it sprightly at home by placing it in a jug of cold water in a cool place until ready to use.

● Chop coriander just before using, not too far in advance. All herbs release the natural oils which flavour them on chopping. But chopped herbs soon begin to deteriorate, losing freshness and taste.

● Use fresh coriander to flavour homemade fishcakes for an Oriental taste. For 4: mix 8oz/225g mashed potato with 1lb/450g poached, skinned and flaked cod. Season with salt, freshly ground black pepper, a dash of chilli sauce and 1 tbsp freshly chopped coriander. Stir in 2 tbsp grated onion and mould into 4 fish cakes. Fry in hot oil until golden on both sides and heated through. Serve with a bowl of soy sauce mixed with lime juice for dipping.

● Revitalise wilted small sprigs of coriander to use for decoration by placing them in a ramekin with a sprinkling of cold water. Cover the ramekin tightly with cling film and refrigerate for an hour. The sprigs should spring back to life!

● Coriander has its own definite taste which tends to overpower other more delicate herbs. For the best results, use it alone to appreciate the distinctive flavour and aroma.

● Marinate cod fillets in lime juice mixed with oil, garlic, ginger and coriander before grilling or frying.

● Add coriander to a creamy chicken curry for a pretty, speckly effect and spicy taste. To make a quick curry for 4: heat 3 tbsp oil in a pan and fry 1 finely chopped onion with 2 cloves crushed garlic and 1 de-seeded and finely chopped chilli pepper. Remove with a slotted spoon and reserve. Add 4 skinned and cubed chicken breast fillets to the pan and stir to seal. Return onion mix and stir in 2 tbsp mild curry paste. Pour over ¼pt/150ml chicken stock and bring to the boil. Cover and simmer until chicken is cooked through. Stir in 4 tbsp double cream and 2 tbsp ground almonds. Add 1 tbsp finely chopped coriander and season to taste. Serve with rice.

● Coriander is often used in Oriental-style stir-fry dishes. Use the best ingredients including strips of beef or chicken fillet mixed with evenly sliced crisp vegetables. Flavour with freshly chopped coriander.

CORIANDER ROAST LAMB

A lovely dish of roast lamb lightly spiced with coriander, lemon, garlic and ginger. *Serves 4*

> *Juice of 1 lemon*
> *2 fat garlic cloves, crushed*
> *½ tbsp crushed fresh root ginger*
> *4 tbsp oil*
> *2 tbsp soy sauce*
> *1 tbsp dark brown sugar*
> *2 tbsp finely chopped coriander*
> *2lb/900g leg of lamb (fillet end)*
> *Salt and freshly ground black pepper*
> *8oz/225g mixed wild and brown rice*

First make the marinade. Mix together lemon juice, garlic, ginger, oil, soy, sugar and coriander. Spoon over lamb and leave for at least an hour in the refrigerator. Season with salt and freshly ground black pepper.

Place joint on a trivet in a roasting tray. Roast at Gas 5, 375F, 190C for 20 minutes per pound plus 20 minutes, or until cooked to preference. Baste with any remaining marinade throughout cooking.

Serve with mixed wild and long grain brown rice. This is available ready mixed in packets. Wash rice in plenty of cold water and drain well. Place in a pan, then cover with cold salted water. Cover with a lid and bring to the boil. Turn down heat and simmer for 45 minutes or until tender. Test occasionally as this rice takes quite a long time to soften. Drain, then fluff up with a fork before serving. Place lamb and rice on a serving dish and pour over cooking juices from the roasting pan.

Preparation time: 10 minutes
Cooking time: 1 hour approx

Approximate nutritional values per portion:	
375 calories	28g protein
30g fat	1g carbohydrate

SALOUSA

A rough-textured, garlicky chickpea, tahini and coriander dip, served with strips of pitta bread. Good as a first course or light lunch. *Serves 8*

> *14oz/400g can chickpeas, drained*
> *2 tbsp tahini paste*
> *2 cloves garlic, crushed*
> *1 tbsp finely chopped coriander*
> *6 tbsp olive oil*
> *2 tbsp lemon juice or to taste*
> *Salt and freshly ground black pepper*
> *Pitta bread to serve*

Whizz chickpeas in a blender with tahini paste and garlic for a few seconds until roughly blended. Stir in coriander and mix in oil. Thin mixture to a dipping consistency with lemon juice to taste. Season with salt and freshly ground black pepper. Spoon into a small pot and serve with warm strips of pitta bread.

This dip is also good with crudités – raw strips of crunchy vegetables. Choose from peppers, carrots, cucumber, celery, courgettes or spring onions and arrange in groups around the dipping pot.

Preparation time: 15 minutes
Cooking time: nil

Approximate nutritional values per portion:	
206 calories	6g protein
15g fat	11g carbohydrate

COURGETTES

Courgettes – or zucchini – are members of the squash family, alongside marrows, cucumbers, gherkins, pumpkins and melons.

Originating in Italy, they arrived here and in America in the mid-Forties.

Nowadays they are relatively commonplace and available all year round. But you may need to give your greengrocer a day's notice for the finger-sized ones complete with their elegant yellow flowers. They are easy to grow at home, too, which means they can be harvested very young and tender. In fact, they need to be, as courgettes can grow very big, very quickly.

A versatile vegetable, the flesh is firm, but dainty. Courgettes need not be peeled before cooking, as the skin is quite edible – and contains vitamins.

Small ones can be cooked whole or even eaten raw in salads. Larger courgettes still taste delicate, but need to be sliced into rings or cut into sticks before use.

COURGETTE PIZZAS

These individual pizzas topped with homemade tomato sauce, mozzarella cheese and courgette rings are firm favourites with children and grown-ups. *Serves 4*

> *1 pizza dough mix*
> *¹/₂ onion, peeled and finely chopped*
> *1 clove garlic, crushed*
> *4 tbsp oil*
> *7oz/200g tin chopped tomatoes*
> *1 tbsp tomato purée*
> *Salt and freshly ground black pepper*
> *¹/₂ tbsp finely chopped fresh marjoram*
> *¹/₂ tbsp finely chopped fresh basil*
> *4oz/100g mozzarella cheese, thinly sliced*
> *2 courgettes, trimmed and sliced*
> *Extra chopped herbs for sprinkling*
> *Flat parsley sprigs for garnish*

Make up dough base according to instructions and leave to rise in a warm place until doubled in size (approx 1 hour). Cover with a damp tea-towel.

While dough is rising, make the tomato sauce. Fry onion and garlic in 2 tbsp of the oil until softened. Add chopped tomatoes and tomato purée and bring to the boil. Simmer until slightly reduced. Season with salt and freshly ground black pepper and add marjoram and basil. Reserve.

Knead risen dough on a lightly floured board and divide into 4. Roll out 4 circles about the size of a tea plate. Place on a greased baking sheet. Spread each circle with tomato sauce and layer with cheese slices. Lightly fry courgette rings in 1 tbsp oil to brown slightly and top pizzas with these.

Brush with remaining oil and sprinkle with extra chopped herbs and a good grinding of black pepper. Bake at Gas 6, 400F, 200C for 20 minutes or until dough is firm and pizzas are golden. Serve garnished with flat parsley sprigs.

Preparation time: 35 minutes plus rising time
Cooking time: 30 minutes approx

Approximate nutritional values per portion:	
350 calories	11g protein
10g fat	26g carbohydrate

COURGETTE AND YELLOW PEPPER TAGLIATELLE

A lovely mix of tagliatelle, courgette and yellow pepper strips, tossed in cream and parsley. *Serves 4*

> *4 thin courgettes, washed*
> *1 large yellow pepper, de-seeded*
> *12oz/350g green tagliatelle*
> *2 tbsp oil*
> *¹/₂ large onion, peeled and finely chopped*
> *2 peeled cloves garlic, crushed*
> *1 tbsp fresh parsley, chopped*
> *4 tbsp cream*
> *1 tbsp olive oil*
> *Salt and freshly ground black pepper*
> *Extra chopped parsley to garnish*

Cut courgettes into thin strips lengthways with a potato peeler. Blanch in boiling salted water until al dente. Drain, refresh and drain again. Reserve. Cut pepper into matchstick strips.

Cook tagliatelle in boiling salted water until al dente. Drain and reserve.

Heat oil in a pan and fry onion and garlic until softened. Remove with a slotted spoon and reserve. Add pepper strips to pan and cook till soft without browning. Return onion mix to pan and add courgette strips and parsley. Cook 2 minutes more or just enough to heat courgettes through. Add to tagliatelle with cream and olive oil. Season. Toss gently to mix. Serve garnished with a little extra chopped parsley.

Preparation time: 30 minutes
Cooking time: 20 minutes approx

Approximate nutritional values per portion:	
400 calories	14g protein
16g fat	77g carbohydrate

BUYING AND STORING

Choose dark green slim courgettes with thin unbroken skin. The best courgettes are about 6in/15cm long and ¹/₂in/1cm in diameter. Do not accept ones which are limp or rubbery. They will be past their best.

Courgettes have tender skin so they should be handled carefully to avoid bruising. They can often be bought pre-packed, in which case, check there is no 'sweating' on the plastic wrap – and no sign of mould.

Best cooked on the day of purchase, courgettes should be kept in the fridge salad drawer to keep them in good fresh condition. Use within a few days. A glut of home-grown courgettes can be frozen. Use for cooked dishes once defrosted.

NUTRITION

A perfect vegetable for weight watchers, the calorie content is low – around 20 in 4oz/100g. There is 1g protein, 4g of carbohydrate and only a trace of fat in the same weight.

Like all green vegetables, courgettes are a good source of vitamin C – 4oz/100g contains 5mg – about 15 per cent of the recommended daily amount.

Vitamin C is essential to maintain healthy skin tissue, to help the body ward off infection and promote healthy bone growth, and keep gums and teeth in good condition.

However, vitamin C is destroyed by cooking, both by heat itself and also by the vitamin being thrown away in the cooking water. This is why steaming or using the microwave to cook courgettes is preferable to boiling them. But keep cooking water to use as stock.

The main mineral contribution is potassium with 202mg in 4oz/100g. This works with sodium to regulate the water balance of the body.

4oz/100g courgettes contain:	
20 calories	1g protein
trace of fat	4g carbohydrate

COURGETTE TIPS

● For a really stunning dinner party presentation, buy baby courgettes with the flowers still attached. You may have to ask your greengrocer to order them – but they are available. For 4: heat 2 tbsp oil in a pan and fry ½ onion with 2 cloves crushed garlic until just soft. Add 8oz/225g finely chopped mushrooms and fry for a further 2 minutes. Stir in 1 tbsp fresh white breadcrumbs, 1 tbsp finely chopped fresh parsley and season. Remove from heat and cool slightly. Stuff the flowers of 12 courgettes with this mixture and twist the petals to enclose. Brush with melted butter and season. Steam or bake until just tender. Serve on individual plates with a homemade tomato sauce.

● To preserve all the flavour and nutrients in courgettes, cook them by lightly steaming or use the microwave. Slice and place in a steamer or microwave-proof bowl. Sprinkle with a little salt and cook until just tender – about 10 minutes by steaming or 4 minutes in the microwave on full power. Serve tossed in butter with chopped mint and freshly ground black pepper.

● Serve puréed as a vegetable dish to go with roast lamb. To 12oz/350g of puréed courgette stir in 1 tbsp double cream, and add a dash of tabasco sauce, 1 tbsp freshly grated onion, 1 tbsp snipped chives and seasoning.

● Cook large courgettes until soft and mash with butter and cheese, then add to an equal quantity of mashed potatoes for a colourful vegetable accompaniment or topping for a fish or shepherd's pie.

● Make a quick stir-fry ratatouille with matchsticks of courgette, aubergine, green and red peppers, and chopped tomato cooked with finely chopped onion and crushed garlic. Cook in sunflower oil and season with salt and freshly ground black pepper and a good sprinkling of freshly chopped mint before serving.

COURGETTE AND LEEK SOUP

A beautiful pale green soup delicately flavoured with chervil. *Serves 4*

> 2 tbsp oil
> 1 onion, peeled and finely chopped
> 2 cloves garlic, crushed
> 3 small leeks, washed, trimmed and sliced
> 3 courgettes, washed and chopped
> 2pt/1.1ltr vegetable stock
> 1 potato, peeled and chopped
> 2 large slices white bread, crusts removed
> Oil for frying
> 2 tbsp finely chopped fresh chervil
> Salt and freshly ground black pepper
> 2 tbsp double cream
> Chervil sprigs for garnish

Heat oil in a pan and fry onion and garlic until softened, but not browned. Add leeks and courgettes and cook for a further 2 minutes. Pour over stock and add potato. Bring to the boil, then turn down heat and simmer, covered, until vegetables are soft.

Meanwhile, prepare the croutons. Cut bread into tiny cubes and fry in hot oil until crisp. Drain on kitchen paper and reserve.

Purée soup in a blender. Stir in chopped chervil. Reheat gently and season. Serve sprinkled with croutons and garnished with cream and chervil sprigs.

Preparation time: 20 minutes
Cooking time: 30 minutes approx

Approximate nutritional values per portion:	
155 calories	2g protein
10g fat	20g carbohydrate

STUFFED COURGETTES

A veritable vegetarian feast. *Serves 4*

> 4 large courgettes
> 3 tbsp oil
> 1 onion, peeled and finely chopped
> 2 cloves garlic, crushed
> 12oz/350g mixed flat and button mushrooms, finely chopped
> 2oz/50g sun-dried tomatoes in oil, drained and finely chopped
> 1 tbsp mushroom ketchup
> Salt and freshly ground black pepper
> Squeeze of lemon juice
> 3oz/75g grated Cheddar cheese
> Lemon twists

Wipe courgettes and cut off a thin slice lengthways from one side. With a teaspoon, scoop out seeds and a little flesh to make a hollow for the stuffing.

Blanch courgettes in boiling salted water until just beginning to tenderise. Drain and reserve with hollow facing down.

For the stuffing, heat oil in a pan and fry onion and garlic until softened. Add mushrooms and cook for a further 5 minutes. Stir in tomatoes and add mushroom ketchup. Continue cooking until the liquid disappears. Taste, then season. Add a squeeze of lemon juice. Stuff courgette cavities. Brush with oil and place on a baking sheet. Bake at Gas 5, 375F, 190C for 15 minutes. Sprinkle with cheese and return to oven to melt. Serve immediately garnished with lemon twists.

Preparation time: 30 minutes
Cooking time: 30 minutes approx

Approximate nutritional values per portion:	
195 calories	8g protein
20g fat	10g carbohydrate

CRAB

There are over 4,000 types of crab worldwide – and most of these are edible. The crab most often found in Great Britain is the Common or Brown Crab. This familiar crustacean is a dull brown colour when alive, but changes to a reddish brown after cooking.

Crabs fall into two categories. Some have large bodies where most of the meat is concentrated. The others are long-legged crabs, which have most meat in the legs and the claws.

The Common Crab is found in Western and Northern Europe, and occasionally in the Western Mediterranean. Body size can be as large as 10in/25cm, and weight up to 11lb/5kg. White meat comes from the claws and bony inner body only, and the brown meat – the liver – is contained in the outer carapace. From a cook's point of view, the yield of meat will be $\frac{1}{3}$ its weight, of which $\frac{1}{2}$ will be brown meat.

Cromer is famous for its small meaty crabs – so plentiful they can be picked up from the beach. These are much smaller than those from the west of England or Scotland.

Other types of crab include the North American Blue Crab, the Florida Stone and Australian Mud Crab, where only the claws are eaten. Because of this, the claws are broken off and then the crab is thrown back into the ocean where it will eventually grow new claws. The Spider Crab usually has a small body and the meat is in the long, thin legs.

The Hermit Crab, which lives in other shellfish's shells, is also a delicacy although this is not sold commercially. The smallest edible crabs of all are the Pea or Oyster Crabs which live inside oyster shells, and offer a crunchy contrast to the softness of the oyster flesh.

Crabs are in season year round in warm waters, and elsewhere in late spring through to autumn.

POTTED CRAB

Super first course or luxury snack, this crab paste is quite delicious served with brown toast or with crusty bread. *Serves 4*

3 tbsp white crabmeat
3 tbsp brown crabmeat
3 tbsp curd cheese
1 tbsp grated onion
2 tsp Tabasco sauce
Salt and freshly ground black pepper
4oz/100g butter
Dill sprigs for garnish

Mix together the white and brown crabmeat to a smooth paste. Stir in the curd cheese, onion and the Tabasco sauce. Then season the mixture well.

Spoon the mixture into four ramekin dishes. Melt the butter in a saucepan, and slowly pour over the crab mixture.

Garnish each with a small sprig of dill and serve with toast or crusty bread.

Preparation time: 15 minutes
Cooking time: 2 minutes

Approximate nutritional values per portion:	
280 calories	15g protein
12g fat	0.5g carbohydrate

DEVILLED CRAB

Scrumptious hot and savoury crab dish which is best served in a crab shell. *Serves 1*

4oz/100g white crabmeat
4oz/100g brown crabmeat
1 tsp French mustard
Good dash of Tabasco sauce
Juice of $\frac{1}{2}$ lemon
2 tbsp double cream
Salt and freshly ground black pepper
1 tbsp white breadcrumbs
1 tbsp grated Cheddar cheese

Mix together the crabmeats, mustard, Tabasco sauce, lemon juice and double cream. Season well with salt and freshly ground black pepper.

Heat gently for a few minutes in a saucepan, then transfer into the crab shell.

Top with breadcrumbs and grated cheese. Brown under the grill until the cheese starts to bubble. Serve immediately.

Preparation time: 15 minutes
Cooking time: 15 minutes

Approximate nutritional values per portion:	
550 calories	50g protein
25g fat	20g carbohydrate

GOOD IDEA

Crab soup takes a bit of preparation but is worth the effort. You need a whole really fresh crab because the shell and empty claws are needed for the stock. First pick out all the white and brown meat and reserve. Make the stock by simmering shells with $1\frac{1}{2}$pt/850ml water with 2 generous wine glasses white wine, a small quartered onion, 2 sprigs parsley, fresh tarragon and dill for 40 minutes. Strain and reserve.

Sauté a chopped onion with 2 crushed cloves garlic until softened, not brown. Add 6 medium, peeled, de-seeded and quartered tomatoes and 1 carrot, finely sliced. Cook gently for 5 minutes. Add stock and simmer for 20 minutes, then stir in crabmeat. Blend smooth in a processor. Season. Stir in a measure of brandy and 3 tbsp single cream.

CRAB TIPS

● Crab is usually bought cooked from the fishmonger. Separating the brown meat from the white meat and picking all the shreds from the body and claws can be a painstaking task. A job for the dedicated, perhaps, but fresh (not frozen) white or brown meat can be found in some fishmongers and supermarkets. Frozen crabmeat is also available which will do.

● Fresh crab eaten with claw crackers and crab picks with the nuggets of crabmeat dipped in homemade mayonnaise is a great treat. But you must prepare the crab first. Lay the crab underside up. First twist off the big claws and the legs and retain. Remove the tail and discard. Next, press down on the shell at the mouth. The undershell will crack. Pull away the undercarriage which contains all the body meat – keep this. Where you pressed down pull away the mouth and stomach and any other odd looking bits and pieces. Finally remove the lungs – pointed spongy organs around the bony body. Break the bony inner body in half. Arrange this with the legs, claws and carapace full of brown meat on a platter. Serve with mayonnaise – and a selection of picks and crackers for extracting every last shred.

● This starter of poached egg and crabmeat is unusually delicious. Poach 4 eggs and keep them in warm water. Make 8fl oz/250ml hollandaise sauce, and keep warm in a bain marie. Sauté 1lb/450g white crabmeat, preferably in chunks, in a pan with 3oz/75g butter. Season with salt, freshly ground black pepper and a dash of brandy. Place some of the crabmeat on a plate, then top with an egg. Pour over some sauce, and sprinkle with paprika.

● It is handy to keep a few already cleaned shells for dressed crab or even a crab soufflé which can be cooked and served in the shell.

● To dress a crab, finely chop the white meat and season with salt, freshly ground black pepper, cayenne and a few drops of white wine vinegar. Mix the brown meat with a little mayonnaise, 2 tbsp fresh white breadcrumbs, and a little lemon juice. Place this mixture in the centre of the shell, with the white meat on either side. Top with finely chopped egg white on the brown meat and sieved yolk on the white. Garnish with chopped parsley.

CRAB AND PASTA SALAD

Salad of pasta shells with nuggets of crabmeat and diced peppers. *Serves 4*

> *8oz/225g pasta shells*
> For the mayonnaise:
> *1 egg yolk*
> *1 tsp Dijon mustard*
> *¹/₂ tsp salt*
> *¹/₂ tsp pepper*
> *¹/₂ tsp sugar*
> *1 tbsp white wine vinegar*
> *¹/₄pt/150ml oil*
> *8oz/225g white crabmeat*
> *1 green, 1 red, 1 yellow pepper, de-seeded and diced*
> *1 tomato, skinned and diced*
> *¹/₂ onion, sliced into thin rings*
> *Salt and freshly ground black pepper*

Cook the pasta until al dente. Drain and leave to cool.

Put the egg yolk into a bowl with the mustard, seasoning, sugar and 1 tsp vinegar. Mix thoroughly, then add the oil drop by drop, whisking continuously until the mixture is thick and smooth. When all the oil has been added, mix in the remaining vinegar.

Put the pasta, crabmeat, mayonnaise, peppers, tomato and onion into a salad bowl. Season well and toss.

Preparation time: 15 minutes
Cooking time: 10 minutes approx

Approximate nutritional values per portion:	
195 calories	10g protein
10g fat	15g carbohydrate

CRAB IN CRACKLY FILO

Fantastic crackly filo pastry parcels of crabmeat – the most delicious appetisers imaginable. *Makes 8*

> *3 tbsp white meat*
> *3 tbsp brown meat*
> *1 tbsp finely chopped parsley*
> *Salt and freshly ground black pepper*
> *4 sheets filo pastry*
> *Melted butter*

Mix together the crabmeats and parsley, and season well.

Cut a sheet of filo pastry in half to make two strips. Brush each strip with melted butter. Place a spoonful of the crab mixture at the end of one strip, and then fold up the pastry flag fashion to make a triangle.

Brush top with melted butter, and place on greased baking tray. Repeat this process until all crab mix is used.

Bake at Gas 6, 400F, 200C, for about 10 minutes, or until golden brown.

Preparation time: 15 minutes
Cooking time: 10 minutes

Approximate nutritional values per portion:	
165 calories	10g protein
8g fat	10g carbohydrate

CREAM

Cream is made from fresh milk by skimming off the visible fatty layer which rises from the surface or by spinning in a separator.

The composition of cream varies with the butterfat content. Half and single cream have the least. The minimum fat contents are specified in government regulations. Calorie content varies depending on the amount of fat.

The fat content determines its richness and how it may be used. A tablespoon or two of fresh dairy cream turns many simple dishes into luxuries. A wonderful illustration of a little of what you fancy does you good. Casseroles and curries are enriched, cakes leap into the spectacular class topped with whipped cream, and sauces and soups take on a velvety smoothness.

However, synthetic substitutes for the real thing have been introduced in the past couple of years packed in the same type of pot which look very similar. This makes it quite difficult for the shopper to tell the difference.

Daisy, the Leaping Cow, is the eye-catching blue symbol to look for, or the words 'Fresh Cream'. This guarantees the tub contains only pure and natural, fresh dairy cream.

CREAM TIPS

● Add cream to a smooth vegetable soup for a luxurious velvety finish. Stir in after processing and gently reheat before serving. For a pretty decoration on each bowl of soup, drizzle a little cream into the centre and draw into a swirl with a cocktail stick.

● Double cream withstands high temperatures – perfect for adding to sauces and gravy for pan-fried meats and flambé dishes.

● For a light, crumbly-textured shortcrust pastry, add a little soured cream to the mixture. Use 4 tbsp soured cream for 8oz/225g pastry and mix in before adding water to bind. Chill, then roll out and use in the usual way.

● Make a lightly spiced hot chocolate drink for a delicious relaxing nightcap. Heat milk until it just reaches boiling point and add a pinch of ground cinnamon and nutmeg. Stir into hot chocolate powder and top with some whipped cream.

● Never over-whip cream for piping. Just whip it into soft peaks and spoon into a piping bag. The cream will thicken more as it is forced through the nozzle.

● Pipe left over whipped cream in swirls on to a sheet of greaseproof paper and freeze to be used at a later date.

● Add the last spoonful of cream in the pot to mashed potatoes along with a knob of butter, seasoning and a sprinkling of fresh snipped chives.

● No soured cream? Make your own by adding 1 tbsp lemon juice to ½pt/300ml single cream. Leave to stand for 4 hours in the fridge before using.

CREAMY CHICKEN CURRY WITH ALMONDS

Tender chunks of chicken breast in a mildly spiced, creamy curry sauce flavoured with almonds. *Serves 4*

4 tbsp oil
1 onion, peeled and finely chopped
2 cloves garlic, crushed
1 tsp ground coriander
1 tsp turmeric
½ tsp ground cumin
Pinch chilli powder
4 chicken supremes, cut into chunks
¼pt/150ml chicken stock
3 tbsp ground almonds
Salt and freshly ground black pepper
5 tbsp double cream
Sprigs of parsley to decorate

Heat oil in a pan and fry onion and garlic until softened but not browned. Add spices and cook for a further minute. Add spices and cook for a further minute. Add chicken to pan and stir to coat in spicy mix. Stir to seal. Pour over stock and bring to boil. Cover and gently simmer until chicken is cooked through (approx 10-15 minutes). Stir in almonds, seasoning and cream and reheat to bubbling. Decorate with sprigs of parsley to serve.

Preparation time: 20 minutes
Cooking time: 30 minutes approx

Approximate nutritional values per portion:	
285 calories	9g protein
42g fat	2g carbohydrate

Although cream contains a large proportion of fat, and therefore calories, it is usually only eaten as an accompaniment, or an enhancer of dishes, and does not as a rule form an appreciable part of the diet on a daily basis.

Cream is rich in several minerals. A 4oz/100g carton of cream has 50mg calcium, 0.2mg iron, 0.15mg zinc, 79mg potassium and 27mg sodium.

Vitamins are also present. 4oz/100g double cream contains 0.8mg Vitamin C, and small amounts of A, D, E, B2 and B12.

4oz/100g single cream contain:	
200 calories	2.5g protein
20g fat	3g carbohydrate

4oz/100g double cream contain:	
450 calories	2.5g protein
48g fat	2g carbohydrate

4oz/100g whipping cream contain:	
360 calories	2.1g protein
38g fat	3g carbohydrate

KNOW YOUR CREAM

Single Cream is the traditional pouring cream to serve over fruits and desserts, and perfect for using in soups, sauces and casseroles. Unsuitable for freezing as it comes, single cream will however freeze when incorporated in a cooked dish such as quiche. Single cream does not whip. It contains a minimum of 18 per cent fat and is easily recognised by the red banding on the pot.

Double Cream is the most versatile and can be used in all types of cookery. Use it to top liqueur coffees, whip it to fill cream cakes, eclairs and tarts, spoon it straight from the pot on to hot fruit pies, or add it to sauces for meats and flambé dishes. It withstands high temperatures and can be boiled without curdling. It freezes well, either whipped or unwhipped, but should be defrosted thoroughly before use. This cream contains about 48 per cent fat. Identify it by the blue banding on the pot.

Whipping Cream is an economical way to fill and decorate cakes and pastries as it doubles in volume once whipped. Other uses include floating on coffees or soups or adding to mousses and dips to give a luxurious taste with a light, airy consistency. This cream pipes perfectly and can be frozen piped in swirls on a sheet of greaseproof paper. Recognise it by the green banding on the pot.

Soured Cream is made from single cream which is soured by the addition of a natural culture. This gives a refreshingly tangy flavour with the same consistency of double cream. Use it in dips or as a filling with herbs for jacket potatoes. It also lends itself beautifully to sweet dishes such as cheesecakes. It will not freeze or whip. The pot will usually have purple banding.

Clotted Cream is the thick, golden cream served with scones and jam for a typically English tea-time treat. It can be frozen, but should not be used in cooking as it separates when heated. Clotted cream contains 55 per cent fat and comes in an orange banded pot.

Half Cream is a light cream rather like the top-of-the-milk, which adds a drop of luxury to a cup of coffee, enhances scrambled eggs and perks up quick midweek desserts. It is not suitable for whipping or freezing. This cream is the weight-watcher's friend, containing only 12 per cent fat.

PATATAS MALAGA

Slices of potato layered with anchovy fillets in a creamy savoury egg custard. *Serves 6*

2lb/900g potatoes, peeled
1oz/25g butter, softened
8 anchovy fillets, cut into slivers
4 eggs
1/2pt/300ml double cream
Freshly ground black pepper
1oz/25g grated Cheddar cheese

Cook potatoes in boiling salted water until just tender. Drain and pat dry. Slice thinly.

Butter an ovenproof dish. Layer potato slices with anchovies, finishing with a neat layer of potatoes in an overlapping roof tile pattern.

Mix eggs with cream and seasoning. Pour over potatoes and sprinkle the cheese over. Bake at Gas 5, 375F, 190C for 45 minutes or until golden.
Preparation time: 35 minutes
Cooking time: 1 hour 15 minutes approx

Approximate nutritional values per portion:	
450 calories	10g protein
30g fat	20g carbohydrate

HUNGARIAN RED PEPPER SOUP

Hot and tasty red pepper soup served with a swirl of soured cream. *Serves 4*

2 tbsp oil
1 onion, peeled and finely chopped
1 clove garlic, crushed
4 red peppers, de-seeded and diced
1 carrot, peeled and diced
Pinch of cayenne pepper
1/2 tsp paprika
2pt/1.1ltr vegetable stock
Salt
4 tbsp soured cream

Heat oil in a pan and fry onion, garlic, peppers and carrot until soft but not browned. Stir in spices and cook for 1 minute. Pour over stock, season and bring to the boil. Simmer until vegetables are tender. Whizz soup in a processor until smooth. Sieve into a clean pan and reheat to bubbling. Serve in warmed bowls with 1 tbsp soured cream swirled on top of each serving.
Preparation time: 20 minutes
Cooking time: 20 minutes approx

Approximate nutritional values per portion:	
85 calories	1g protein
8g fat	3g carbohydrate

MOULES A LA CREME

A steaming bowl of fresh mussels cooked in a white wine sauce with cream. *Serves 4*

2lb/900g fresh mussels
2 tbsp oil
1 onion, peeled and finely chopped
1 clove garlic, crushed
1 wine glass dry white wine
6 tbsp double cream
1 tbsp finely chopped fresh parsley
Freshly ground black pepper

Wash mussels in several changes of cold water and remove beards. Discard any that do not close when tapped with a knife. Heat oil in a pan and fry onion and garlic until soft. Add mussels and pour over wine. Cover and bring to the boil. Simmer until mussels open.

Remove mussels with a slotted spoon and place in a bowl. Pick out any that have not opened and discard. Cover and keep hot. Reduce cooking liquid and stir in cream, parsley and pepper. Pour over mussels just before serving.
Preparation time: 30 minutes
Cooking time: 15 minutes approx

Approximate nutritional values per portion:	
235 calories	16g protein
18g fat	5g carbohydrate

CUCUMBER

One of the oldest vegetables, first cultivated over 4,000 years ago, the cucumber is a member of the gourd family.

It was so revered by a Mesopotamian horticulturalist, Ur-Nammu, who had the world's first vegetable garden, that he built a temple to the god Nanna in gratitude.

Cucumbers are thought to have originated in India. They were introduced to China two centuries before the birth of Christ and were also grown by the Ancient Greeks, who knew them as 'sikuous'.

They were introduced to England in the 16th century and known as cow-cumber for around 300 years.

The Victorians had a choice of white, yellow, bronze or blue cucumbers, in addition to the usual green-skinned type.

There are two kinds of cucumber. Most widely known is the long, thin green hot-house cucumber. This variety can only survive under glass in Britain and other similar climates.

The second variety is shorter, thicker and with a rough skin. This is called the ridge variety, because it used to be grown on raised banks of soil. It can be grown outside easily. Gherkins are a type of ridge cucumber, which are grown and picked small for pickling.

CUCUMBER AND SALMON EGG CANAPES

Crunchy cucumber slices scooped out and filled with taramasalata and topped with salmon eggs (available from delicatessens, food halls and some supermarkets). *Serves 4 (makes 8)*

> 1 cucumber
> 2oz/50g smoked salmon pieces
> 2oz/50g taramasalata
> 1oz/25g jar salmon eggs

Cut the cucumber into 1in/2.5cm deep rounds. Score the sides vertically with a canelle knife.

Scoop out the centres with a melon baller, being careful not to cut out the bottom.

Line the base of each cucumber round with a piece of smoked salmon, then pipe taramasalata on top in a swirl.

Top with a few salmon eggs.

Preparation time: 15 minutes
Cooking time: nil

Approximate nutritional values per portion:	
115 calories	9g protein
8g fat	2.5g carbohydrate

NUTRITION

Cucumbers are the slimmer's dream, containing only 10 calories per 4oz/100g. This is because they are about 96 per cent water.

Eaten with their skin on, they are an excellent source of dietary fibre.

Cucumbers provide substantial amounts of vitamin C – good for the healthy growth and maintenance of bones, teeth and ligaments. Some potassium is present which helps to control the body's water balance. Small amounts of iron and folic acid can also be found.

Peeling and slicing a cucumber tears its cell walls, releasing an enzyme that destroys the vitamin C content, so try not to slice it until just before serving.

4oz/100g cucumber contain:	
10 calories	0.6g protein
0.1g fat	1.8g carbohydrate

CUCUMBER AND GORGONZOLA SALAD WITH CROUTONS

Chunky salad of cucumber, croutons, Gorgonzola and tomatoes dressed with vinaigrette. *Serves 4*

> 4 slices of bread
> A little oil
> 1 cucumber, diced
> 5 tomatoes, skinned and diced
> 4oz/100g Gorgonzola, diced
> For the dressing:
> 2 tbsp white wine vinegar
> 2 tsp Dijon mustard
> Salt and freshly ground pepper
> 6 tbsp oil

Slice the crusts off the bread, and then cut into equal-sized cubes. Heat some oil in a frying pan, and when hot, drop in the cubes. Fry until golden brown and crisp. Drain on kitchen paper.

Shake dressing ingredients together in a screw-top jar.

Toss all salad ingredients together and pour on the dressing. Toss lightly before serving.

Preparation time: 15 minutes
Cooking time: 3 minutes

Approximate nutritional values per portion:	
350 calories	10g protein
24g fat	24g carbohydrate

BUYING AND STORING

Look for straight, firm cucumbers, with an even colour and no sign of wilting. Yellowing skin means they are old. The freshest cucumbers will still have a withered flower at one end.

Bendy or misshapen cucumbers are often much cheaper. The taste and texture is rarely affected, but still check the freshness points. One way to do this is to pick the cucumber up and shake it. It should be stiff – any bendiness or rubberiness indicates old age.

Supermarkets stock shrink-wrapped cucumbers which keeps them fresh longer by reducing moisture loss.

Keep shrink-wrapped cucumbers in their wrapping until you want to use them.

Store unwrapped cucumbers in the salad box of the fridge or in a tall jug with the stalk end soaking in a little water. Use as soon as possible.

CHICKEN AND CUCUMBER SKILLET

Light and tasty supper dish of chicken fillets cooked with cucumber and dill in white wine.
Serves 4

1 onion, peeled and finely chopped
2 garlic cloves, peeled and crushed
2 tbsp oil
4 chicken supremes (breast fillets)
1 cucumber, cut into chunks
1 wine glass white wine
¹/₂pt/300ml chicken stock
Salt and freshly ground pepper
1 bunch dill, broken into sprigs

Fry the onion and garlic in 1 tbsp oil until soft. Remove with a slotted spoon and reserve. Cut the chicken into chunks, and fry in remaining oil until golden.

Return onion mix to the pan. Add the cucumber, wine, stock, and seasoning. Simmer for about 15 minutes or until chicken is tender. Add the dill, adjust the seasoning and serve immediately.

Preparation time: 20 minutes
Cooking time: 20 minutes

Approximate nutritional values per portion:	
324 calories	34g protein
7g fat	7g carbohydrate

CUCUMBER AND MINT SOUP

Deliciously delicate soup which is very low in calories. For a luxury creamy version stir ¹/₄pt/150ml double cream at the end and heat.
Serves 4

1 onion, finely chopped
1 tbsp oil
1¹/₂ cucumbers
1¹/₂pt/850ml vegetable or chicken stock
Salt and freshly ground white pepper
Juice of ¹/₂ lemon
Few sprigs fresh mint

Fry the onion in some oil until soft. Chop the cucumbers into cubes leaving the skin on. Put the onion, stock, cucumber and seasoning into a pan, bring to the boil, then simmer for 30 minutes.

Add the lemon juice, and then whizz the mixture in a blender until smooth.

Leave to cool, and then add the mint. Whizz again.

Preparation time: 15 minutes
Cooking time: 30 minutes

Approximate nutritional values per portion:	
30 calories	nil protein
2g fat	4g carbohydrate

CUCUMBER TIPS

● Cucumbers can be used to garnish a dish – as borders, fans, boats, twists etc, to add a special finishing touch.

● This cucumber and strawberry mixture is an unusual but delicious salad to serve with cold chicken or salmon. Peel and slice 1 cucumber thinly. Hull and slice about 12 strawberries. Arrange the slices alternately, overlapping slightly, on a plate, then season with salt and pepper. Sprinkle 2 tbsp dry white wine or white vine vinegar over the salad and chill for at least one hour.

● Pickling cucumbers is an excellent way of bringing out their full flavour. Wash and thinly slice 3 cucumbers. Peel and slice 4 onions. Mix both together in a bowl and sprinkle with 4 tbsp coarse salt. Leave for 2 hours, then rinse and drain. Bring 1pt/600ml white wine vinegar, 6oz/175g sugar, 1 tsp celery seeds, and 1 tsp mustard seeds to the boil and simmer for 3 minutes. Fill sterilised jars with the cucumber and onion, then cover with the spiced vinegar and seal immediately.

● Try serving cucumber as a hot vegetable. Peel 4 cucumbers and then scoop out their flesh with a melon baller, or cut into large dice. Blanch cucumber for 5 minutes. Drain. Melt 4oz/100g butter in a frying pan, add the cucumber and season. Cover and cook gently for 20 minutes. Stir 4 tbsp of single cream into pan and heat gently for 2 minutes and serve.

● If you need to keep a cucumber fresh, but have no room in the fridge, stand it stalk down in a tall jug with a little water in the bottom.

● An ideal dip to serve with crunchy crudités at a buffet, this cucumber dip is also delicious served with smoked salmon rolls. Peel, de-seed and roughly chop 2 cucumbers. Whizz with ¹/₂pt/300ml sour cream, 3 tbsp white wine vinegar, 2 tsp chopped chives and ¹/₂ tsp Tabasco in a food processor. Pour into a bowl and chill.

DRIED APRICOTS

The kings of Egypt revered dried fruit and small amounts were always included with other foods in their tombs to ease the passage through to the afterlife. This is not surprising, as preserved fruit had a long 'pyramid life'.

Fruit was originally dried in the sun, and in some cases still is. One modern method uses heat-controlled hot-air cabinets after the apricots have been cleaned and prepared. This process slowly removes all the moisture from the fruit, without cooking it.

The drying process also increases the proportionate amount of dietary fibre. Fresh apricots contain 2 per cent fibre and dried have 25 per cent because of the removal of water.

Today, it is more acceptable and healthy to choose dried apricots rather than tinned, which are often in sugary syrups containing additives.

GOOD IDEA

This unusual velvety apricot soup is delicious as a first course or as a dessert.

To serve 4: soak 8oz/225g dried apricots in 4 tbsp boiling water then pour over half a bottle of medium dry white wine. Leave overnight to infuse. Whizz in the blender with the juice of half an orange. Cool then stir in enough single cream to give a pouring consistency. Then chill. Serve decorated with a mint sprig.

WINTER FRUIT SALAD

Delicious healthy breakfast dish – or a dessert served either hot or cold with cream. *Serves 4*

> 12 no-soak dried apricots
> 8 dried apple rings
> 4 dried pear slices
> 8 pitted dried no-soak prunes
> 8 dried figs
> 12 dates
> 1 orange
> 1/2pt/300ml fresh orange juice
> 1 wine glass sweet white wine
> 2 bananas, peeled and sliced
> Lemon juice

Place dried fruit and dates in a large bowl. Peel orange and remove pith with a sharp knife. Cut into small chunks, catching juices over a bowl. Add to dried fruit mixture and pour over orange juice, reserved juice and wine. Stir well and leave for at least 30 minutes.

Pile into a pretty glass bowl. Peel and thinly slice banana and drizzle over a little lemon juice to prevent browning. Add just before serving.
Preparation time: 10 minutes
Cooking time: nil

Approximate nutritional values per portion:	
270 calories	5g protein
1g fat	50g carbohydrate

LAMB WITH APRICOTS AND OKRA

Fragrant lamb stew flavoured with garlic and coriander and spiked with apricots and okra.
Serves 4

> 2 tbsp oil
> 1 onion, peeled and sliced
> 2 cloves garlic, crushed
> 2lb/900g lean lamb, cut into cubes
> Seasoned flour
> 1 tbsp tomato purée
> 1 wine glass red wine
> 1pt/600ml lamb stock
> 8 dried apricots
> Salt and freshly ground black pepper
> 4oz/100g okra, wiped and trimmed
> 1 tbsp fresh coriander, finely chopped

Heat oil in a large pan and fry onion and garlic until softened. Transfer to a flameproof casserole.

Dip lamb in seasoned flour and shake off excess. Add to pan in batches and fry to brown and seal. Place in the casserole.

Add tomato purée, wine and stock to frying pan. Stir well to incorporate all the cooking juices. Pour over lamb and add apricots and seasoning. Bring to the boil. Cover and cook at Gas 4, 350F, 180C for 2 hours or until the lamb is tender.

Add okra and coriander 30 minutes before end of cooking time. Serve with a sprinkling of coriander.
Preparation time: 20 minutes
Cooking time: 2 1/2 hours approx

Approximate nutritional values per portion:	
600 calories	50g protein
65g fat	2g carbohydrate

NUTRITION

The process of drying fruit has always been an important method of preservation for the months when fresh apricots are not available. It not only increases the shelf life of the fruit, but also intensifies the flavour, giving a sweeter-tasting fruit.

Apricots are rich in carotene. This is the natural deep yellow or orange pigment found in certain foods which the body converts into vitamin A. Dried apricots are also high in iron – 4oz/100g contains one third of the recommended daily requirement for a female.

Ounce for ounce, dried apricots are richer in fibre and nutrients than fresh ones. But they are also higher in calories because of the concentration of the sugar. One fresh apricot contains about 20 calories, the equivalent weight of dried, about 170. During the process of drying or cooking, the nutrients are not affected to any significant degree.

4oz/100g dried apricots contain:	
170 calories	5g protein
nil fat	40g carbohydrate

APRICOT TIPS

● Marinate dried apricots in white wine, brandy or gin before chopping to use in stuffings or cakes.

● Brighten up muesli with extra chunks of chopped dried no-soak apricots and fresh apple or pear.

● For jam tarts with a difference, put a half soaked dried apricot in the base of each tartlet case and top with apricot jam before baking.

● Make an apricot pickle to serve with duck. Finely chop 2oz/50g dried apricots. Add to a bowl with 3in/7.5cm peeled, de-seeded and diced cucumber, ½ yellow pepper, de-seeded and chopped, a small peeled and grated onion, 2 crushed cloves garlic, 1 tbsp fresh chopped chives, 1 tsp sugar and 3 tbsp spiced white wine vinegar, salt and black pepper. Leave to marinate overnight.

● Ever tried a Netherlands pudding? This is a kind of toad-in-the-hole made with a sweet batter and filled with dried apricots. Soak 4oz/100g dried apricots in 4 tbsp sweet white wine. Sift 4oz/100g flour into a bowl with a pinch of salt. Make a well in the centre and add 2 beaten eggs and a dash of milk from ½pt/300ml. Beat to combine well. Gradually whisk in the rest of the milk.

Heat 1oz/25g butter with 1 tbsp oil in an 8in/20cm solid-bottomed cake tin. Place apricots in the base. Pour over batter mix. Sprinkle top with a little soft brown sugar. Bake at Gas 6, 400F, 200C for 30-35 minutes. Serve with cream.

● Stir chopped dried apricots, glacé cherries and angelica into heated tinned rice pudding for an instant jewelled pud and serve with flaked toasted almonds.

● Substitute chopped dried apricots for crystallised peel in fruit cakes for a less bitter and more tangy fruit flavour.

APRICOT UPSIDE-DOWN CAKE

A glamorous and fruity sponge pudding, delicious hot or cold with cream. *Serves 8*

For the apricot topping:
    4oz/100g no-soak dried apricots
    2 tbsp orange juice
    Good dash of white wine
    1 tbsp soft dark brown sugar
    2 tbsp apricot jam, sieved
    Squeeze of lemon juice
For the cake:
    4oz/100g butter, softened
    4oz/100g caster sugar
    2 eggs, beaten
    4oz/100g self-raising flour, sifted
    Zest and juice of ½ orange

Place apricots in a bowl and add orange juice and white wine. Leave for 30 minutes.

Sprinkle sugar in the base of a lightly buttered or non-stick 8in/20cm sandwich tin. Mix the apricot jam with the lemon juice and spoon the mixture into the base. Arrange apricots on top.

Cream butter and sugar until light and fluffy. Gradually beat in the egg then a little flour, alternately, beating well between each addition. Beat in zest and orange juice. Spoon over apricots and smooth surface.

Bake at Gas 5, 375F, 190C for 20 minutes or until the pudding is firm to the touch. Cool slightly then turn out on to a cake plate. Serve hot or cold with cream.
Preparation time: 15 minutes
Cooking time: 20 minutes

Approximate nutritional values per portion:	
230 calories	2g protein
15g fat	30g carbohydrate

CHICKEN WITH APRICOT STUFFING

One of the tastiest stuffings for chicken; the apricots add a fruity piquancy. *Serves 6*

    4lb/1.8kg fresh oven-ready chicken
For the stuffing:
    1 tbsp oil
    2 shallots, peeled and finely chopped
    1 clove garlic, crushed
    3oz/75g dried apricots, snipped into small pieces
    4 tbsp dry white wine
    4 slices fresh white bread, crusts removed
    2 large sprigs of parsley, stalks removed
    1 egg, beaten
    Salt and freshly ground black pepper
    Watercress sprigs

Heat oil in a pan and fry shallots and garlic until softened. Add the apricots and stir over a low heat for 1 minute. Stir in wine and transfer to a bowl.

Whizz bread in a processor with parsley to crumb stage and add to the bowl. Mix in egg and seasoning and bind together. Cool the mixture completely.

Wipe chicken inside and out and season. Stuff neck end with cooled apricot stuffing and secure skin with a cocktail stick.

Roast at Gas 6, 400F, 200C for 1 hour 40 minutes or until the juices run clear when pierced in the thickest part of the thigh with a metal skewer. Serve on a warmed platter decorated with watercress sprigs.
Preparation time: 20 minutes
Cooking time: 2 hours approx

Approximate nutritional values per portion:	
800 calories	80g protein
50g fat	15g carbohydrate

EGGS

Eggs have played a large part in the diet of man for thousands of years, even before the domestication of chickens. In ancient times, hunters would steal eggs from the nests of wild birds to sustain their families.

In 1400BC the Chinese ate eggs and discovered ways of preserving them. Also at this time, the people of South East Asia began keeping chickens, which are seen in Egyptian wall drawings.

The Romans loved eggs and when they invaded Britain, they found that domesticated chickens were well established here. These were kept for both their meat and the eggs they laid.

Eggs have always had religious associations. At one time it was forbidden to eat them during Lent, so eggs were used up on Shrove Tuesday before the fast. Then, after Lent, coloured and decorated eggs at Easter time linked eggs with spring celebrations.

POACHED EGG TARTS

Jumbo vol au vents. *Serves 4*

> *13oz/375g puff pastry*
> *1 egg, beaten*
> *2 tbsp oil*
> *1 small onion, peeled and finely chopped*
> *2 cloves garlic, peeled and crushed*
> *4oz/100g mushrooms, chopped*
> *4 rashers bacon, de-rinded and fried*
> *4 tbsp fresh parsley, chopped*
> *Dash of soy sauce*
> *Freshly ground black pepper*
> *4 eggs*
> For the sauce:
> *1oz/25g butter*
> *1oz/25g flour*
> *1/2pt/300ml milk*
> *1oz/25g mature English Cheddar, grated*
> *Salt*

Roll out pastry to 1/4in/0.5cm thick. Cut four 3in/7.5cm circles with a cutter. Using next smallest cutter, press a cut inside each circle without forcing right through, to make rims. Chill for 30 minutes. Glaze with egg and bake at Gas 6, 400F, 200C for 15 minutes, or until risen and golden. Carefully prise off lids made by inner cuts.

Heat oil and gently fry onion, garlic and mushrooms soft. Add bacon, parsley, soy and pepper.

Melt butter and stir in flour. Gradually stir in milk off heat. Bring to boil, stirring, until thickened. Melt in cheese and season.

Poach eggs soft. Spoon some mushroom filling in each case and top with eggs. Coat with sauce and brown under grill.

Preparation time: 20 minutes
Cooking time: 20 minutes

Approximate nutritional values per portion:	
725 calories	19g protein
62g fat	45g carbohydrate

BUYING AND STORING

Eggs are sized and graded by weight for selling and these range from nought to seven. Grades one to four are the most popular on the supermarket shelves. The remaining grades, four to seven, decrease in weight with size, seven weighing under 45g.

You can test how fresh an egg is by immersing it in water. If it floats on its side it is very fresh, but if it floats vertically with the rounded end pointing up it could be up to three weeks old.

Contrary to popular belief, the colour of the shell bears no significance to the quality or taste of an egg. Eggs should be stored in a very cold place or in the fridge. The best way to store them is pointed end down so the yolk is in the centre of the egg. Like this, fresh eggs will keep for up to three weeks.

If eggs have been separated and only the yolks remain, keep them moistened with water, cover and refrigerate for up to two days. Whites will keep for up to two weeks, covered.

NUTRITION

Eggs are an excellent source of protein, and vitamins A and D are present in egg yolk. Vitamin A is required for good vision. Vitamin D is necessary for the formation of healthy bones. Eggs are one of the few natural sources of this vitamin. Egg white contains vitamin B2, which is involved in the breakdown and utilisation of carbohydrates, fats and proteins.

Eggs are fairly low in calories with around 80 in an average egg but high in cholesterol, which has been linked with heart disease – containing about 1,260mg in one egg. In the past this was the reasoning behind lowering egg intake, although new information has now come to light.

There are two types of cholesterol: blood cholesterol and dietary cholesterol. Blood cholesterol is the amount in the blood stream produced naturally by the liver. Some cholesterol is essential for bodily functions and without it the body could not work. Dietary cholesterol is consumed in food. Whilst it should not be ignored, it is not the

most influential factor in producing high levels of cholesterol in the blood stream.

It is now known that it is a high intake of saturated fat – in which eggs are low – that encourages the liver to produce excess cholesterol, which is absorbed into the blood stream, rather than the intake of dietary cholesterol present in food.

In other words, it is not the amount of cholesterol that is eaten, but the amount of fat, which is most significant in raising levels of cholesterol in the blood.

So a sensible healthy person eating a low-fat, high-fibre diet can eat seven eggs a week without the worry of raising blood cholesterol levels.

Eggs contain the minerals calcium, for healthy bones, iron for the blood and useful amounts of potassium and phosphorus.

1 egg contains:	
80 calories	6g protein
6g fat	nil carbohydrate

PRAWN OMELETTE

A flat open omelette packed with prawns, spring onions and mangetout with ginger and soy.
Serves 2

> *2oz/50g mangetout, topped and tailed*
> *3 spring onions, sliced*
> *3 eggs*
> *1 tsp grated root ginger*
> *2 tsp grated onion*
> *Good dash soy sauce*
> *Freshly ground black pepper*
> *1oz/25g butter*
> *¹/₂ tbsp oil*
> *3oz/75g peeled prawns*

First blanch the mangetout and spring onions for 1 minute.

Beat eggs with ginger, onions and soy. Season with black pepper.

Melt butter in a pan with oil over high heat. Pour the egg mix in and stir rapidly dragging the uncooked mixture underneath and the cooked egg to the top. Turn down heat and add prawns, mangetout and spring onions. Continue cooking over reduced heat until omelette is just set – still a little runny on top. If necessary, quickly flash it under the grill to finish off, then slide on to a serving plate. Or serve as it is in the pan.

Preparation time: 15 minutes
Cooking time: 7 minutes

Approximate nutritional values per portion:	
120 calories	8g protein
8g fat	3g carbohydrate

EGG TIPS

● The secret of scrambled eggs is to cook them over a low heat then remove from the pan before they set. They carry on cooking on their own. Allow two eggs per person and beat in a bowl with salt and freshly ground black pepper. Melt a little butter in a pan and then turn down to gentle heat. Add eggs and stir continuously until almost set but still a little runny.

● Serve little scrambled egg and smoked salmon canapés with drinks. These are tasty and economical if they are made with salmon trimmings, available from delicatessens. Scramble eggs soft and stir in finely diced smoked salmon. Pile spoonfuls on to small circles of brown toast. Decorate canapés with a few salmon eggs and a sprinkling of finely snipped chives.

● Omelette-lovers will find it's worth investing in a special omelette pan. The pan should be 'seasoned' before use, to ensure perfect results every time. Cover the base of the pan with about ¹/₂in/1cm oil and a liberal sprinkling of coarse sea salt. Leave overnight then heat gently until the oil is almost smoking. Cool until just tepid then tip out the oil and salt mixture and wipe dry with kitchen paper. Once the pan is seasoned, it need never be washed after use. Simply wipe it with a cloth while still warm.

● Add quartered hard-boiled eggs to a homemade fish pie and top with creamy mashed potato before baking.

EGG AND LEMON SOUP

This is quite delicious, best made with homemade chicken broth, which is easy. The strained broth is enriched with eggs beaten with the juice of two lemons. *Serves 4*

> *2 eggs*
> *Juice of 1 lemon*
> *Freshly chopped parsley for decoration*
> *Salt and freshly ground black pepper*
> For the broth:
> *2 chicken leg joints (plus any wings you can prise out of the butcher)*
> *1 onion, quartered (skin on to give a golden colour)*
> *2 sticks celery, chopped*
> *1 large carrot, chopped*
> *Handful of parsley, roughly chopped*

Place the broth ingredients in a pan and cover with water. Bring to the boil and simmer, uncovered, for about 1¹/₂ hours, topping up with more water if the level gets low. Strain and discard flavourings.

Return broth to the pan and bring to the boil until reduced to 1³/₄pt/1ltr. Season with salt and freshly ground black pepper. Cool a little.

Beat eggs with lemon juice and add a little broth. Return this mixture to the pan and heat without boiling (otherwise the egg will curdle). Ladle into soup bowls and sprinkle with parsley before serving with crusty French bread.

Preparation time: 30 minutes
Cooking time: 1¹/₂ hours

Approximate nutritional values per portion:	
95 calories	3g protein
3g fat	1g carbohydrate

LEMON AND LIME PIE

Irresistible version of an old favourite. *Serves 6*

> *8oz/225g pack shortcrust pastry*
> For the filling:
> *Juice and zest of 1 large lemon and 1 large lime*
> *¹/₂pt/300ml water*
> *3oz/75g sugar (or to taste)*
> *2oz/50g cornflour*
> *2 egg yolks*
> For the topping:
> *2 egg whites*
> *4 tbsp sugar*

Roll out pastry to line an 8in/20cm greased flan dish or tin. Bake blind for 10 minutes, lined with greaseproof and filled with baking beans, at Gas 6, 400F, 200C. Remove beans and paper, and bake 5 minutes more to set base.

Mix half lemon and lime juice, add zest, water and sugar in a pan. Mix cornflour with remaining juice. Bring water and juice mix to boil, add 1 tbsp to cornflour mix, then tip this into pan. Boil stirring, until thickened. Cool slightly. Beat in egg yolks gradually. Pour into base.

Whisk whites stiff, whisking in 1 tbsp sugar. Carefully fold in remaining sugar with a metal spoon.

Bake at Gas 3, 325F, 160C for 30 minutes, or until meringue is risen, firm and browned.

Preparation time: 35 minutes
Cooking time: 40 minutes

Approximate nutritional values per portion:	
125 calories	7g protein
28g fat	30g carbohydrate

FENNEL

Fennel is a fibrous bulb vegetable with a crisp texture and refreshing aniseed flavour. Also known as Florence fennel or finocchio, bulb fennel is often confused with the herb fennel. Although they are relatives, they are not from the same plant. Bulb fennel is a cultivated form of the herb, which grows happily in the wild.

The ancient Egyptians and Romans were fennel lovers and used it both medicinally and in the kitchen. Fennel also plays a part in Greek history. When the Battle of Marathon was fought in a field of fennel, a messenger ran all the way to Athens with the news – hence the name marathon given to a long run. More recently, in the 1600s, fennel was thought to improve the eyesight and aid slimming.

In the 1820s Thomas Jefferson, a former President of the United States, grew fennel from seeds sent to him from Italy. He had many new varieties of vegetable growing in his Virginia gardens, and fennel fast became a favourite.

As its name suggests, fennel plays a large part in the cuisine of Italy. In fact, it is sometimes offered at Italian tables as part of an after-dinner fruit selection, as well as being included in numerous salads, fish and pasta dishes. Most of the fennel eaten in the UK is Italian, but attempts to grow it here have been more successful in the past few years.

Since the Stuarts first introduced this unusual vegetable to Great Britain, it has risen in popularity and now appears in the shops almost all year round. Its unique taste adds interest to many recipes, and it teams excellently with fish, chicken, tomatoes and Parmesan cheese.

COD AND FENNEL PIE

Chunks of cod cooked with fennel in a creamy white wine sauce topped with a delicious frilly filo pastry crust. *Serves 4*

2 tbsp oil
1oz/25g butter
1 onion, peeled and finely chopped
2 cloves garlic, peeled and crushed
1 bulb fennel, trimmed and chopped
1 tbsp flour
1 glass dry white wine
¼pt/150ml fish stock
2lb/900g cod fillet, skinned and in chunks
2 tbsp Pernod
2 tbsp double cream
1 tbsp fresh dill, chopped
Salt and freshly ground black pepper
4 sheets filo pastry
Melted butter for brushing

Heat oil and butter in a pan and cook onion and garlic over a gentle heat until soft. Add fennel and cook gently for a further 5 minutes.

Stir in flour and cook for 1 minute more. Gradually add white wine and fish stock, stirring constantly. Bring to the boil and cook until sauce is thickened.

Add cod and cook for 3 minutes. Turn cod over in the sauce carefully to avoid breaking.

Add Pernod, cream and dill. Season and gently reheat, stirring constantly. Transfer fish mixture to a pie dish.

Cover with 2 sheets of filo, brushing with melted butter in between. Cut remaining filo pastry into 2in/5cm strips. Drape in a ripply pattern over the top, buttering the pastry as you go.

Cook at Gas 6, 400F, 200C for 20 minutes, or until filo topping is crisp and brown.
Preparation time: 20 minutes
Cooking time: 35 minutes approx

Approximate nutritional values per portion:	
445 calories	42g protein
15g fat	18g carbohydrate

BUYING AND STORING

Fennel has become more easily available in recent years as the demand for this unique-tasting vegetable has grown. Most greengrocers and supermarket vegetable counters sell fennel, sometimes pre-packed in plastic but more often loose.

Fresh fennel should be pale green shading to almost white with green stalks which sprout feathery, frond-like leaves. Look for fennel with a fresh, crisp look and no sign of withering or wilting. There may be a little browning on the tough outer bulb case, but bulbs that are excessively battered should be avoided.

Check pre-packed fennel for any rot caused by 'sweating' or bruising. Store fresh fennel in a refrigerator salad box until required.

To prepare a bulb of fennel, trim off the coarse base and discard. Remove the outer bulb case and cut off stalks together with any feathery leaves. Keep the trimmings for use in stock and the leaves for decoration. Larger bulbs of fennel may be cooked in quarters whilst small ones are left whole. If the fennel is to be included raw in salad, slice it thinly or chop roughly, rinse and dry it on kitchen paper.

NUTRITION

Fennel adds aroma and crisp crunch to salads, and eating it raw is the best way to retain its nutrients. Low in calories, it contains only 16 per 4oz/100g. A perfect aid for slimmers, a piece of raw fennel dipped in cottage cheese is a healthy, filling and low-calorie way to keep hunger pangs at bay.

As with all fresh vegetables, one of its most important contributions to the diet is to provide fibre. Eating more fibre helps constipation sufferers and is thought to reduce the risk of bowel cancer and heart disease.

4oz/100g raw fennel contain:	
16 calories	1g protein
nil fat	4g carbohydrate

SCORCHED FENNEL SALAD

A colourful mix of char-grilled slices of fennel, peppers and aubergines brushed with an olive oil, lemon, rosemary and garlic dressing. A perfect snack lunch or first course, served with crusty bread. *Serves 4*

1 red and 1 green pepper
1 large bulb fennel
1 aubergine
Olive oil for brushing
Salt and freshly ground black pepper
For the dressing:
4 tbsp olive oil
Juice of ½ lemon
2 cloves garlic, peeled and crushed
2 sprigs fresh rosemary, chopped

Remove seeds from peppers and trim fennel. Slice fennel and peppers vertically. Wipe and slice aubergine. Brush all vegetables with olive oil and season with salt and pepper. Place slices on hot barbecue coals or grill in the conventional way. Cook until vegetables are soft but still have bite and are slightly charred.

Combine olive oil, lemon juice, garlic and rosemary. Arrange vegetables on a platter and drizzle over dressing before serving.

Preparation time: 15 minutes
Cooking time: 10 minutes approx

Approximate nutritional values per portion:	
105 calories	2g protein
8g fat	7g carbohydrate

FENNEL AND CARROTS WITH ORANGE

An unusual dish of fennel and carrots braised in stock and orange juice. The carrots take on a delicious hint of the fennel flavour. *Serves 4*

2 small fennel bulbs
4 carrots
1pt/600ml vegetable stock
Juice and zest of 1 orange
1 tsp sugar
Salt and freshly ground black pepper

Trim the fennel and cut into quarters. Peel and halve carrots vertically.

Layer vegetables in a shallow pan and pour over stock and orange juice. Sprinkle over orange zest and sugar. Season with salt and freshly ground black pepper.

Cover and bring to the boil. Turn down to simmer and cook for 15 minutes or until vegetables are tender.

Transfer vegetables to a serving dish and keep hot. Bring braising liquid to the boil and reduce slightly. Pour over vegetables just before serving.

Preparation time: 15 minutes
Cooking time: 20 minutes

Approximate nutritional values per portion:	
30 calories	1g protein
trace of fat	6g carbohydrate

FENNEL AND TOMATO SOUP

A chunky main course soup of fennel cooked with ripe tomatoes, onions, celery, potatoes and garlic, topped up with a melted cheese crouton. *Serves 4*

2 tbsp oil
1oz/25g butter
1 onion, peeled and chopped
2 cloves garlic, peeled and crushed
1 large bulb fennel, trimmed and chopped
2 sticks celery, washed and chopped
2pt/1.1ltr vegetable stock
1 tbsp tomato purée
1 fresh bouquet garni
1 large potato, peeled and cut into chunks
Salt and freshly ground black pepper
4 thick slices French bread
Oil for frying
2 tbsp grated Cheddar cheese
1 tbsp fresh parsley, finely chopped

Heat oil in a pan and fry onion, garlic, fennel and celery until softened. Pour over stock and stir in tomato purée. Add bouquet garni. Bring to the boil and add potato. Simmer until vegetables are just tender. Remove bouquet garni. Season with salt and freshly ground black pepper to taste.

Meanwhile, fry bread in hot oil until golden. Sprinkle over cheese. Ladle soup into warmed bowls and set aside.

Grill cheese over croutons until it has started to melt. Then top each bowl of warm soup with a crouton and sprinkle with a little chopped parsley to decorate. Serve immediately.

Preparation time: 15 minutes
Cooking time: 20 minutes approx

Approximate nutritional values per portion:	
222 calories	8g protein
8g fat	26g carbohydrate

FENNEL TIPS

● The aniseed flavour of fennel is a perfect complement to fish. Use it as a base for a creamy sauce to go with grilled fish or include it in fish pies and stews.

● Add chopped raw fennel to a mixed salad for refreshing crispness and crunch and a different flavour sensation.

● Wash and keep the trimmings and feathery fronds from a bulb of fennel to use with celery, leeks and onions in a simple fish, chicken or vegetable stock.

● Sprinkle braised fennel with freshly grated Parmesan cheese and grill until bubbling and brown. Serve as an unusual vegetable accompaniment to rich meat dishes.

● Make a creamy fennel soup for a wonderfully sensuous first course. For 4 servings: fry 1 peeled and finely chopped onion, 2 cloves crushed garlic, 2 trimmed and chopped bulbs of fennel and 2 sticks celery until softened. Pour over 2pt/1.1ltr vegetable stock and bring to the boil. Add 1 large potato, peeled and in chunks and simmer until tender. Liquidise until smooth, then return to a clean pan. Stir in 4 tbsp double cream and season with salt and freshly ground white pepper. Serve in warmed bowls.

● Include thin slices of fresh, raw fennel in a selection of crudités with carrot strips, spring onion sticks, celery stalks, broccoli florets, whole button mushrooms and cucumber sticks. Serve with a garlic mayonnaise for dipping.

● Use the feathery fronds on top of a bulb of fennel for a pretty decoration for fennel dishes.

● A dash of Pernod, Ricard or Greek Ouzo added to fennel recipes enhances the fresh aniseed flavour.

FIGS

Figs are one of the oldest fruits known to man. They are mentioned in the Bible – Adam and Eve dressed discreetly with fig leaves to hide their embarrassment in the Garden of Eden – giving figs an association with love that still remains.

Figs were highly prized by the ancient Greeks and Romans, eaten not just for their delicious succulence but to give strength and fertility – hence their reputation as an aphrodisiac.

Figs were first grown in Asia Minor, but their cultivation soon spread. The plant thrives in warm climates and today figs are grown all over the Mediterranean. But it is the Turkish Smyrna fig that is reputed to be the best in the world.

Other varieties include the Calimyrna – a species of Smyrna fig which has been grown in California since the 1800s, and the Greek greeny-yellow Kodota fig. The purple Mission fig is the one most often used for drying. Dried figs are mostly used in dried fruit compôtes, as a Christmas delicacy and in substantial hot winter desserts, like figgy pudding.

BUYING AND STORING

Fresh figs are a wonderful luxury in the peak of season – around September to December.

Look for plump figs that have a sweet, ripe smell. The skin should be smooth and velvety with no blemishes and can be green, brown or purple depending on the variety.

During ripening, figs become soft. Over-ripe figs shrink and the skin becomes shrivelled. Any figs that smell sour are spoiled because the natural sugars in the flesh have fermented.

These fruits perish quickly, so always refrigerate until required for eating or cooking.

In this way, they may be kept for up to two days, but are best eaten as soon as possible after purchase.

FIG TART

A wonderful pud with a taste of the Mediterranean. Sliced fresh figs with sweet pastry cream in a crisp shortcrust case. *Serves 6*

> 6oz/175g shortcrust pastry
> 4 eggs
> 1 tbsp caster sugar
> 2 tsp cornflour, sifted
> 1/2pt/300ml milk
> 4 ripe figs, halved and sliced
> 1 tbsp runny honey

Roll out pastry on a lightly floured board. Line a 7in/18.5cm fluted flan dish with pastry and prick the base. Chill for 30 minutes. Bake blind at Gas 6, 400F, 200C for 15 minutes or until the pastry is crisp and set. Leave to cool.

For the pastry cream, whisk eggs in a bowl with the sugar and cornflour. Bring milk to the boil and whisk into egg mixture. Return to a clean pan and continue cooking over medium heat, whisking continuously until thickened. Cover surface with buttered greaseproof paper and leave to cool.

Spread pastry cream in the bottom of the pastry case. Arrange sliced figs in a circular pattern on top. Glaze with honey. Chill before serving.

Preparation time: 45 minutes
Cooking time: 20 minutes approx

Approximate nutritional values per portion:	
255 calories	8g protein
13g fat	25g carbohydrate

SPICED FIGS IN SWEET WHITE WINE

Simple and delicious dessert of fresh figs, lightly poached in sweet white wine with cinnamon and freshly grated nutmeg. *Serves 4*

> 8 fresh ripe figs
> 1/2pt/300ml sweet white wine
> 1 cinnamon stick
> Good grating of fresh nutmeg

Wipe and quarter figs and place in a large shallow pan in one layer. Pour over white wine and then add the cinnamon and nutmeg.

Bring to the boil and simmer gently for 2 minutes, until just beginning to soften. Spoon into a pretty bowl and pour cooking juices over the top. Leave to cool and chill before serving.

Preparation time: 5 minutes
Cooking time: 2 minutes approx

Approximate nutritional values per portion:	
150 calories	trace of protein
trace of fat	22g carbohydrate

NUTRITION

The exotic fig is a slimmer's treat at only 74 calories per 4oz/100g – the approximate weight of two.

Low in protein and fat, at only 0.8g and 0.4g respectively, figs are quite high in carbohydrate to provide energy with 19g per 4oz/100g of fruit. Figs also contain calcium for healthy teeth and bones. Potassium is also present which acts with sodium to control the body's nerve impulses and helps maintain normal heart rhythm.

Some iron is found and there is a small quantity of B group vitamins.

4oz/100g figs contain:	
74 calories	0.8g protein
0.4g fat	19g carbohydrate

FIG TIPS

● Make the most of fresh figs when they are in peak season – from September to December – by using them raw or cooked in sweet and savoury dishes.

● Serve fresh, ripe figs as a fruity accompaniment to salty cheeses such as Chèvre, Feta, Stilton or Cambazola.

● Include sliced fresh figs in an exotic fruit salad with sliced mango, guava, banana and pineapple. Soak in orange juice laced with sherry before serving chilled with softly whipped cream.

● Lightly prick the skins of figs before cooking them whole, in order to allow cooking liquid and flavourings to be absorbed.

● To peel the skin from fresh figs before eating, simply pull away from the flesh with a sharp knife. It should come away easily.

● Figs make a super, simple dessert, flambéed in Cognac. For 4: halve 8 ripe figs. Gently cook in 2oz/50g butter and 1 tbsp sugar for 2 minutes to soften. Pour over the juice of 1 orange and stir. Add 4 tbsp Cognac and tilt pan to ignite. Stand well back from the flames. When the flames have died down, spoon figs into pretty bowls and serve with cream or ice cream.

● Serve figs sautéed with onions and garlic to accompany rich meats like duck, pheasant, and venison. Gently fry 1 peeled and sliced onion with 2 cloves garlic until softened. Add 8 ripe figs, in quarters. Toss around in the pan for 3 minutes, or until just tender. Season with salt, freshly ground black pepper and serve while still warm.

● Whole spiced figs make a wonderful treat to eat with cold meats and curries. Place 2lb/900g wiped figs, skins pricked, in a bowl and pour over 2pt/1.1ltr water mixed with 2oz/50g salt. Leave overnight then rinse the figs, drain and pat dry. Dissolve 1lb/450g sugar in ½pt/300ml spiced vinegar and add 1 cinnamon stick, 10 cloves and a good grating of fresh nutmeg with the grated rind of 1 lemon and ½ orange. Bring to the boil and simmer for a few minutes, then strain and discard spices. Place figs in a sterilised jar then top up with cooking juices to fill. Leave to cool then seal and label.

PHEASANT WITH FIGS AND SHERRY

Warming winter dish of pot-roasted pheasant cooked with sherry and fresh figs. *Serves 4*

> 3 tbsp oil
> 1 onion, peeled and finely chopped
> 2 cloves garlic, peeled and crushed
> Salt and freshly ground black pepper
> 1 oven-ready pheasant
> 1 wine glass dry sherry
> ½pt/300ml chicken or game stock
> 8 fresh figs, quartered

Heat oil in a large pan and fry onion and garlic until softened. Remove with a slotted spoon and place in an earthenware casserole. Season pheasant and add to pan to brown and seal all over. Pour over sherry and tilt pan to ignite. Stand well back from the flames. When they have died down, add pheasant to casserole. Pour stock into frying pan and bring to the boil. Pour over pheasant and surround with the quartered figs. Cover with foil and place in the oven at Gas 4, 350F, 180C for 1½ hours or until bird is tender.
Preparation time: 20 minutes
Cooking time: 1 hour 45 minutes approx

Approximate nutritional values per portion:	
290 calories	30g protein
9g fat	23g carbohydrate

FIGS WITH PARMA HAM

A lovely first course of ripe figs wrapped with pieces of very finely sliced Parma ham. Serve this with soured cream and chives for refreshing piquancy. *Serves 4*

> 4 ripe fresh figs
> 8 wafer-thin slices Parma ham
> For the dressing:
> ¼pt/150ml soured cream
> 1 tbsp fresh chives, snipped
> Salt and freshly ground black pepper

Wipe figs and cut a slit in the top of each one, without cutting right through. Gently squash each fig between thumb and index finger to open them up slightly.

Wrap two slices of ham around each fig, arranging it so that the edges curl over like the petals of a rose.

For the dressing, mix soured cream with chives and seasoning. Spoon mixture into a small pot and serve separately.
Preparation time: 15 minutes
Cooking time: nil

Approximate nutritional values per portion:	
130 calories	3g protein
6g fat	11g carbohydrate

FILLET STEAK

B eef has been consumed for thousands of years. The ancient Egyptians even buried beef ribs with the dead so they would not go hungry on the long journey to the other world.

In medieval Britain, beef was salted, dried and smoked, in order to keep it throughout the winter. Elizabethan ships' cooks salted and potted beef, to ensure a supply of meat throughout months at sea.

For centuries, though, roasting beef was one of the most popular cooking methods, usually by spit-roasting it. In the 19th century, oven roasting became common.

Until the 18th century, beef came from cattle that were small and tough. Then, cattle farmer Robert Bakewell improved his herds by breeding to produce small-boned, heavily-fleshed animals. His work made British beef world famous.

Research is now looking to improve the eating quality of beef and to determine which are the best cooking methods and temperatures for different cuts.

The leanest cuts are rump and fillet steak. Brisket and chuck have the most fat and they contain muscles used for movement, which makes them tougher, too.

Fillet of beef is the most luxurious cut, an unused and therefore extremely tender muscle situated underneath the sirloin. Sometimes this is included in a joint of sirloin.

BROCHETTES BURLINGTON

Cubes of fillet steak skewered with little rolls of Parma ham and halved artichoke hearts. *Serves 4*

> *12oz/350g fillet tail*
> *14oz/400g can artichoke hearts*
> *4 slices Parma ham*
> For the baste:
> *4 tbsp sunflower oil*
> *Good squeeze of lemon juice*
> *2 tsp grated onion*
> *Freshly ground black pepper*
> *1 tbsp chopped fresh herbs*

Cut fillet steak into cubes. Drain and halve artichoke hearts. Slice Parma ham into 1¼in/3cm lengths and roll up.

Spike on skewers. Mix baste ingredients together and brush over before grilling to preference. This takes 6 minutes for rare or longer if you prefer it well cooked.

Preparation time: 20 minutes
Cooking time: 6 minutes

Approximate nutritional values per brochette:	
190 calories	16g protein
14g fat	1g carbohydrate

FILLET STEAK WITH ROQUEFORT

Richly flavoured steak dish with Roquefort oozing over the top. *Serves 4*

> *1lb/450g baby new potatoes*
> *4 fillet steaks*
> *Freshly ground black pepper*
> *A little oil*
> *4oz/100g Roquefort*
> *Sea salt*
> *12oz/350g thin French beans, topped and tailed*

Scrub the new potatoes and bake at Gas 5, 375F, 190C for about 35 minutes.

Meanwhile season the steaks with freshly ground black pepper and cook to preference in a little oil over high heat. Top each steak with a round of Roquefort cheese the same size as the steak. Grill until bubbling. Serve with French beans cooked until just tender, and potatoes lightly tossed in oil and sea salt.

Preparation time: 10 minutes
Cooking time: 40 minutes

Approximate nutritional values per portion, excluding potatoes:	
330 calories	47g protein
22g fat	nil carbohydrate

GREEN PEPPERCORN STEAK

Crushed green peppercorns are embedded in this steak served with a cream and brandy sauce. *Serves 4*

> *2 tbsp green peppercorns*
> *2 tsp coriander seeds*
> *4 fillet steaks*
> *4 tbsp oil*
> *4 shallots, finely chopped*
> *2 tbsp brandy*
> *¼pt/150ml double cream*
> *Sliced courgettes to serve*

Press green peppercorns and crushed coriander seeds in both sides of each steak.

Heat 2 tbsp oil in a pan and fry steaks on both sides until cooked to preference. Transfer to a serving platter and keep warm.

In another pan, gently fry shallots in remaining oil until soft but not brown. Add brandy and tilt pan to ignite. When flames have died down add cream to pan and stir well. Pour into steak pan and stir to incorporate cooking juice and sediment. Add a few more green peppercorns to the pan and bring to the boil. Pour over steak and serve with sliced steamed courgettes.

Preparation time: 10 minutes
Cooking time: 15 minutes

Approximate nutritional values per portion:	
550 calories	55g protein
38g fat	15g carbohydrate

BUYING AND STORING

The colour of beef is no indication of eating quality – it darkens after cutting. And colour differences disappear during cooking.

Always look for a fresh, moist appearance with smooth-textured meat, and a small amount of fine marbling.

Refrigerate raw steak as soon as possible, wrapping it in greaseproof paper. Best eaten as soon as possible after purchase, wrapped steaks will keep in the refrigerator for three days.

Hello! Good Cooking

FILLET STEAK TIPS

● The classic sauce to serve with steak is Sauce Bearnaise. Boil 2 tbsp white wine vinegar, 2 tbsp white wine, 3 peeled and chopped shallots, 10 crushed peppercorns and 1 tbsp chopped fresh tarragon until reduced by two thirds. Strain and transfer liquid to a blender. Whizz in 3 egg yolks with a pinch of salt and freshly ground black pepper. While motor is running add 6oz/175g hot, melted unsalted butter in a slow stream until mix is thick and creamy. Stir in 1 tbsp freshly chopped tarragon.

● Make luxury Saturday lunch sandwiches with thin slices of cooked fillet steak. Slice granary bread and spread lightly with butter and wholegrain mustard. Flash fry fillet and fill sandwich with this, tomato and some crisp lettuce.

● The perfect meat for a stir-fry – fillet of beef cooks quickly and is always tender. Toss strips of fillet in a wok with a little oil, some grated root ginger, chopped garlic and sliced spring onions. Add matchsticks of green and red peppers, courgettes, whole thin green beans and a few beanshoots. Pour over a little sherry and a good dash of soy sauce and serve immediately.

● Creamed horseradish is the traditional accompaniment to plain grilled steaks. Make your own by beating ½pt/300ml soured cream in a bowl until smooth. Stir in 2 tbsp grated horseradish. Season with salt and freshly ground black pepper with a dash of lemon juice.

● Steak tartare is a classic dish of minced raw fillet seasoned with salt and freshly ground black pepper. For 4: use 1lb/450g fillet and shape into 4 rounds after mincing. Make a dent in the top of each and pour a raw egg yolk into this. Garnish with chopped onion, capers, green and red pepper, Dijon mustard and Tabasco sauce.

● For a quick, chic supper, fry some chopped onion and garlic in a pan, cook fillet steak to preference, then add a good dash of Sercial Madeira, bring to the boil and stir in enough double cream to make a velvety sauce. Season.

● Always keep a selection of flavoured mustards in the larder to serve with steaks. Choose from wholegrain, herb mustard, horseradish mustard, Dijon and English.

● As a general cooking guide, a 1in/2.5cm steak needs 6 minutes for rare, 10 minutes for medium rare and 15 minutes for well done (total cooking time).

● Roast a whole fillet spread with wholegrain mustard and crushed black peppercorns quickly, so the outside is crusty and the inside pink. Cool and serve in slices.

FILET DE BOEUF EN CROUTE

Luxury dinner party dish of fillet steak with mustard and chopped mushrooms, wrapped in glazed puff pastry. *Serves 8*

> *2lb/900g fillet of beef*
> *4 tbsp oil*
> *14oz/400g puff pastry*
> *4oz/100g flat mushrooms*
> *2 cloves garlic, peeled and crushed*
> *1 tbsp lemon juice*
> *Freshly ground black pepper*
> *2 tsp English mustard*
> *1 egg, beaten*

Trim fillet and fry quickly in 2 tbsp oil over high heat until browned all over and sealed. Cool.

Chop mushrooms and fry with garlic in remaining oil until soft. Add lemon juice and lots of black pepper. Cool.

Roll out pastry on a lightly floured board or worktop to ¼in/0.5cm thick. Spread half the mushroom mixture in the centre of pastry and place beef on top. Spread mustard over beef. Add remaining mushroom mixture.

Fold pastry over to enclose meat and seal edges with beaten egg. Decorate the top with pastry strips and leaves and brush with beaten egg to glaze.

Cook in a pre-heated oven Gas 6, 400F, 200C for 25 minutes or until pastry is golden and crisp.
Preparation time: 20 minutes
Cooking time: 35 minutes

Approximate nutritional values per portion:	
400 calories	26g protein
32g fat	20g carbohydrate

NUTRITION

Fillet of beef is relatively low in calories since it contains little fat. A 4oz/100g steak, for example, contains around 160 calories and 4.6g fat. All beef is high in protein, containing approximately 18.9g in the same weight.

There is no fibre or carbohydrate in beef. Beef is a high source of B vitamins including nicotinic acid, B1, B2, B6 and B12. And the major mineral contribution is organic iron, considerably more useful to the body than inorganic iron found in plants. Iron plays a vital part in the formation of red blood cells and is a main component of haemoglobin, which acts as the oxygen carrier in the blood.

4oz/100g fillet steak contain:	
160 calories	18.9g protein
4.6g fat	nil carbohydrate

GARLIC

Since ancient times, strings of garlic were worn around the neck to ward off evil spirits and protect against infection. In fact its medicinal properties were originally more important than its flavouring qualities. Culpeper reported that garlic was good for asthma and many breathing disorders.

It was the Romans who first brought garlic to Britain. The name garlic comes from the Anglo Saxon gar, meaning spear, and leac, meaning leek. Garlic is a member of both the onion and leek families.

During World War I, juice was extracted from bulbs of garlic and used as an antiseptic, when conventional preparations were in short supply. It has also been used to relieve cramp and colds.

Garlic is available in white, pink or purple skins, with the cloves varying in size. However, cloves must not be confused with bulbs. A bulb is the whole garlic made up of several cloves. These are broken off separately and can be squeezed with a garlic press, sliced or finely chopped. It is used for flavouring so many savoury dishes that a cook would find it difficult to manage without it.

GOOD IDEA

Garlic is quite easy to grow. It needs a rich soil and a sunny position. Plant garlic cloves in a pot or garden, about 2in/5cm deep and 6in/15cm apart, in early spring. Water well, and when the tops have died down, pull bulbs out and leave to dry.

GARLIC SOUP

A treat for garlic fans. This is a creamy soup flavoured with garlic and thickened with almonds.
Serves 4

---

4 tbsp whole blanched almonds
4 fat cloves garlic, peeled
1 egg
8oz/225g white bread, crusts removed
2pt/1.1ltr homemade vegetable stock
6 fl oz/175ml olive oil
4fl oz/100ml dry sherry
Juice of ½ lemon
Salt and freshly ground white pepper
Toasted flaked almonds to decorate

Place whole almonds in a processor and whizz until smooth. Add garlic and egg and continue whizzing to a smooth paste.

Soak bread in stock. Drain and reserve liquid. Squeeze bread to extract excess stock then add to the processor. Whizz. Whisk oil, sherry and lemon juice and pour into processor in a thin stream with motor running. Thin to soup consistency with reserved stock. Season and chill before serving. Decorate with flaked almonds.
Preparation time: 20 minutes
Cooking time: nil

Approximate nutritional values per portion:	
395 calories	5g protein
15g fat	15g carbohydrate

GARLIC TIPS

● One way of getting rid of the smell of garlic and freshening the breath is to chew fresh parsley sprigs. Rinse mouth afterwards.

● Every cook needs a garlic crusher, one of the most useful time-savers in the kitchen. Remember to peel the cloves first before crushing.

● For the daintiest hint of garlic in a salad, rub the inside of the bowl with a cut clove of garlic before filling with clean salad ingredients. Make a plain vinaigrette with no extra garlic and toss lightly.

● Garlic fans will love Italian garlic crostini, usually served as an appetiser. Mash peeled garlic well with a little salt. Spread onto bite-sized toasted slices of crusty bread and drizzle with olive oil. Serve with drinks.

● Garlic is sold as a ready made purée in jars or tubes. This saves time and is a good substitute for fresh garlic.

● For a tasty garlicky vegetable dip, remove the stalk from a whole aubergine and roast until tender. Carefully peel off the skin. Mash the flesh with 2 fat cloves of crushed garlic and salt and freshly ground black pepper. Whisk in enough olive oil to form a smooth dipping consistency. Sprinkle in plenty of chopped parsley and add a good squeeze of lemon juice. Serve with hot pitta bread.

● Garlic cloves can be roasted or deep fried whole and unpeeled. This gives them a mild sweet flavour and is an unusual decoration for meat or whole fish dishes.

● Remember to always wash the chopping board thoroughly after chopping garlic as the juice can transmit the smell to other foods.

● Insert slivers of finely sliced garlic under the skin of a chicken or into a joint of meat to infuse a delicate flavour during cooking. A joint of lamb studded with garlic and rosemary is sure to delight your Sunday lunch guests.

● Store garlic bulbs in a special terracotta garlic pot. This has holes to allow air to circulate and keep the garlic fresh.

GARLIC MEDITERRANEAN PRAWNS

Delicious plump Mediterranean prawns cooked in a skillet with garlic and shallots and served with a herby cream dip. *Serves 4*

4 tbsp olive oil
1oz/25g butter
2 shallots, peeled and finely chopped
12 Mediterranean prawns
4 cloves garlic, peeled and thinly sliced
Good squeeze of lemon juice
Zest of ½ lemon
Freshly ground black pepper
1 tbsp parsley, finely chopped
For the herby dip:
¼pt/150ml soured cream
4 tbsp mayonnaise
1 tsp finely snipped chives
1 tbsp finely chopped coriander

Remove heads from prawns. Heat the oil and the butter together in a pan and fry shallots and garlic until softened. Add prawns and fry quickly. Sprinkle with the lemon juice and the zest. Season with pepper and sprinkle over parsley. Finally, stir, and coat in garlicky oil.

For the dip, mix all ingredients together with a wooden spoon until well combined and spoon into a serving pot. Keep in the fridge until ready to serve.

Preparation time: 10 minutes
Cooking time: 15 minutes approx

Approximate nutritional values per portion:	
150 calories	8g protein
10g fat	9g carbohydrate

GARLIC BREAD

Aromatic crunchy French bread, oozing with garlic butter. *Makes 2 loaves, serves 4*

8oz/225g salted butter, softened
6 plump garlic cloves, crushed
1 tbsp finely chopped parsley
1 tbsp snipped fresh chives
Freshly ground black pepper
Squeeze lemon juice
2 short crusty French loaves

Mash butter with garlic, parsley, chives, pepper and lemon.

Cut bread into diagonal slices three-quarters down to the crust without cutting through.

Spread buttery mix between each slice. Wrap in foil and bake in a pre-heated oven at Gas 6, 400F, 200C for 15 minutes then remove from foil and cook for a further 5 minutes to crisp.

Preparation time: 10 minutes
Cooking time: 20 minutes

Approximate nutritional values per portion:	
550 calories	10g protein
30g fat	35g carbohydrate

CHICKEN WITH 40 CLOVES OF GARLIC

A speciality of Provence, this sounds like an adventurous way to cook chicken, but in fact it is simple and delicious. Don't be scared by the number of garlic cloves that are used in this recipe as it actually becomes much milder during cooking. *Serves 4*

3½lb/1.6kg fresh chicken
Sprig of thyme, parsley, bay leaf tied together
Olive oil for brushing
Salt and freshly ground black pepper
Squeeze of lemon juice
40 cloves of garlic
Parsley sprigs to decorate

Wipe chicken inside and out and insert the herbs in the cavity. Truss chicken to retain shape during roasting. Brush with olive oil, season and drizzle over the lemon juice.

Remove papery skins from garlic, but do not peel. Place the trussed chicken in an ovenproof dish and pack the garlic tightly around the bird.

Roast at Gas 6, 400F, 200C for 1½ hours or until juices run clear when chicken is pricked.

Serve the chicken surrounded with the garlic and decorate with parsley sprigs. Lightly steamed vegetables, for example mangetout or beans, or a crisp salad go well with this dish.

Preparation time: 10 minutes
Cooking time: 1½ hours approx

Approximate nutritional values per portion:	
420 calories	30g protein
20g fat	2g carbohydrate

NUTRITION

Although originally used for 'folk' medicine before it became popular as a culinary flavouring, garlic was considered by some to help lethargy and ulcers and cure skin blemishes. It was also given to the workers on the pyramids to maintain their vitality and strength.

Today, garlic is thought to have antiseptic qualities if the juice is diluted with water and applied direct to the wound. Others believe it may cause a healthy drop in blood pressure if taken in the right quantities.

1 clove of garlic contains:	
5 calories	0.17g protein
0.01g fat	1.3g carbohydrate

GLOBE ARTICHOKES

Globe artichokes are members of the thistle family. Originally believed to have come from North Africa, they have been known and enjoyed in Europe for centuries.

The Romans loved globe artichokes because they were thought to have aphrodisiac powers. And it was from Italy that they were introduced to France, by Catherine de Medici. In fact, she liked them so much that she shocked French courtiers when she greedily ate almost all of the globe artichokes provided at a special feast. At that time, this odd vegetable was firstly thought to stimulate the sexual appetite, and secondly, to cure any unwanted diseases which might occur as a result. Either way, it was considered better for a girl not to be seen eating them.

In this country, globe artichokes were, and still are, thought of as an expensive delicacy. In Europe, where they are plentiful, they often appear in salads and are eaten on their own as a first course served with vinaigrette or hollandaise sauce.

Attractive in appearance, globe artichokes have tightly packed, rounded heads of coarse leaves which grow upwards into a point. These heads are supported on long stalks. Inside, in the centre of an artichoke head, is the hairy 'choke', which must be removed before eating. The stalks must also be taken off. Only the soft heart of older artichokes is edible, but baby artichokes may be eaten whole.

Today, although globe artichokes are imported from France and the USA, Italy is still the main supplier.

STUFFED ARTICHOKE HEARTS

Great as a garnish for roast meats or as a vegetable dish, these artichoke hearts have a savoury stuffing flavoured with bacon and mushrooms. *Serves 4*

4 young artichokes
Lemon juice
For the stuffing:
2 tbsp oil
4 rashers back bacon, de-rinded and in strips
1 onion, finely chopped
2 cloves garlic, crushed
6oz/175g button mushrooms, wiped and finely chopped
4 slices brown bread, crusts removed and crumbed
3 tbsp dry white wine
Salt and freshly ground black pepper

First prepare the artichokes as in the first tip, cutting leaves off down to the base.

Then cook artichokes in boiling salted water with lemon juice added until tender, about 30 minutes or so. Drain.

Meanwhile, make the stuffing. Heat oil in a pan and fry bacon until crisp. Remove with a slotted spoon and reserve. Add onion and garlic to pan and fry to soften. Stir mushrooms into the mixture and cook for 2 more minutes. Stir in breadcrumbs and add white wine gradually to moisten. Remove from heat, return bacon to pan and stir to mix. Season. Stuff each artichoke heart with a spoonful of mixture and place in a flameproof dish. Cover with foil and bake at Gas 6, 400F, 200C for 10 minutes, or until heated through.

Preparation time: 45 minutes
Cooking time: 40 minutes approx

Approximate nutritional values per portion:	
270 calories	9g protein
17g fat	15g carbohydrate

NUTRITION

Globe artichokes are low in calories, with only 7 in 4oz/100g cooked weight. This is an advantage for slimmers, who can enjoy them as a first course or in a salad. But in either case, make sure you choose a low-fat dressing, as a hollandaise or vinaigrette piles on the calories.

Globe artichokes have some vitamin C, necessary for healthy skin and rapid healing. A 4oz/100g serving of artichoke contains 10 per cent of the recommended daily intake of vitamin C for a healthy adult.

4oz/100g artichoke contain:	
7 calories	0.5g protein
trace of fat	1.2g carbohydrate

BUYING AND STORING

Globe artichokes reach their peak during the spring and autumn, and although they are plentiful at this time, they are still quite expensive. These attractive vegetables can be eaten alone or included in salads for a stylish taste and texture and to add a touch of luxury to many dishes.

Choose globe artichokes with tightly packed leaves, making sure there are no dark patches or dryness. In large, older artichokes, the diameter of the base is an indication of the size of the bottom, or heart, which is the edible part. These are best for serving as a first course, when the leaves are pulled out and the flesh at the base nibbled off.

Young or baby artichokes have much longer, narrower heads. After trimming the outside leaves and the top, all of the rest can be eaten. Baby artichokes are the ones most often used in continental salad recipes.

Fresh globe artichokes will keep in a vegetable basket for a day. For longer storage, wrap in plastic bags and keep them in the salad drawer of the refrigerator. They will keep well like this for up to four days. Always wash and drain before cooking in boiling salted water.

When fresh artichokes are out of season, small hearts and whole baby artichokes are available canned. Artichoke bottoms ready to use as a vegetable or for stuffing are also available frozen. These do not need to be defrosted before cooking.

CRAB AND ARTICHOKE QUICHE

Sensual and sophisticated quiche with flaked crab meat and young artichokes, perfect for a special buffet party or light lunch. *Serves 4*

> *7oz/200g shortcrust pastry*
> *2 eggs*
> *4fl oz/100ml double cream*
> *2fl oz/50ml milk*
> *Salt and freshly ground black pepper*
> *3oz/75g flaked crabmeat*
> *4 young whole artichokes, cooked (fresh or*
> *frozen, bottled or tinned)*

Roll out pastry to fit a 7in/18cm fluted loose-bottomed flan tin. Chill for 30 minutes. Bake blind for 10 minutes at Gas 6, 400F, 200C. Remove from oven and cool slightly.

Next make the filling. Whisk eggs with cream and milk and season with salt and pepper. Sprinkle crab into base of pastry case. Quarter 3 artichokes, reserving one whole for the centre. Arrange quarters on top of crabmeat and place remaining whole one in the centre. Pour over egg mixture.

Return to oven for a further 30 minutes, or until pastry is crisp and quiche is set and golden.

Preparation time: 20 minutes
Cooking time: 40 minutes plus chilling

Approximate nutritional values per portion:	
400 calories	15g protein
30g fat	25g carbohydrate

GLOBE ARTICHOKE TIPS

● A globe artichoke needs a bit of preparation before cooking and serving whole. First place it on a chopping board and snap off the stalk by pressing down on it with the heel of the hand. This pulls out any tough fibres. Next, trim away the points of all the leaves to about half way up with kitchen scissors. Cut off the central point of the artichoke with a sharp knife.

Rub the cut edges of the leaves and the underneath base with a halved lemon to prevent discoloration. Keep the prepared artichokes in water with lemon juice until needed for cooking.

Drain and place in a large pan of boiling salted water with a squeeze of lemon juice. Weigh down with a heatproof plate so the artichokes remain under the surface, cover and simmer for 35 minutes or until tender. Drain.

Take out the flimsy central leaves in one piece by gently twisting and tugging. Underneath is the hairy 'choke'. Remove this by scraping it out with a spoon, being careful not to dig out the tender heart.

● After cooking, artichokes can be eaten hot or cold. To eat them, simply pull out the leaves one by one and dip into a sauce such as hollandaise, vinaigrette, etc. Nibble off the soft nugget of flesh at the end of each leaf, then discard the rest. When all the leaves have been removed, there will be the tender heart of the artichoke left. Eat this with a knife and fork.

ARTICHOKES WITH TOMATO HOLLANDAISE

A stylish first course of whole cooked artichokes, served with a rich hollandaise sauce flavoured with fresh tomatoes. *Serves 4*

> *4 globe artichokes, prepared for cooking*
> *as in tip 1*
> *Lemon juice*
> For the hollandaise:
> *3 egg yolks*
> *Juice of ½ lemon*
> *3 tbsp water*
> *6oz/175g unsalted butter, melted*
> *Salt and freshly ground white pepper*
> *2 large tomatoes, peeled, de-seeded and diced*

Cook artichokes in boiling salted water with lemon juice added for 35 minutes or until tender. Drain upside down and keep hot.

While they are cooking, make the hollandaise sauce. This quick version is made in the blender. Place egg yolks in the blender with lemon juice and water. Whizz until light and frothy. Gradually add melted butter drip by drip, with the motor running, until mixture starts to thicken. Continue adding butter in a thin stream until all of it is incorporated.

Spoon sauce into a bowl, add seasoning and diced tomato. Keep warm until ready to serve, then spoon a little sauce into the centre of each artichoke.

Preparation time: 30 minutes
Cooking time: 40 minutes approx

Approximate nutritional values per portion:	
412 calories	2.5g protein
36g fat	1.2g carbohydrate

ARTICHOKE FRITTERS

Light, crispy artichoke fritters, with a piquant dipping sauce. *Serves 4*

> For the batter:
> *4oz/100g plain flour*
> *Pinch of salt*
> *1 tsp baking powder*
> *Cold water*
> For the sauce:
> *2 tbsp oil*
> *½ onion, finely chopped*
> *1 small red chilli pepper, de-seeded and*
> *finely chopped*
> *1 clove garlic, crushed*
> *1 red pepper, de-seeded and chopped*
> *2 tbsp chopped tomatoes from a tin*
> *12 cooked baby artichokes, halved*
> *Seasoned flour*

First make the batter. Sift flour, salt and baking powder into a bowl. Make a well in the centre and gradually add water, until batter has the coating consistency of single cream. Reserve.

For the sauce, heat oil in a pan and fry onion, garlic and chilli until softened. Add pepper and cook for 2 more minutes. Stir in tomatoes and bring to the boil. Simmer, covered, until pepper is tender. Blend, season, and keep warm.

Dip artichokes in flour and then in batter. Fry in hot oil until crisp and golden. Sprinkle sauce with chopped parsley before serving.

Preparation time: 25 minutes
Cooking time: 20 minutes

Approximate nutritional values per portion:	
150 calories	3g protein
8g fat	30g carbohydrate

GRAPEFRUIT

Grapefruit are members of the citrus family. They are one of the largest citrus fruits, with juicy flesh that has a zesty, sharp flavour. The white-fleshed varieties are slightly more acidic in taste than sweeter pink grapefruit, which have few pips and more juice.

The true reason behind the name of this refreshing fruit is not known, but it is thought to be because grapefruit grow in clusters, rather like grapes, on an evergreen tree. However, records from the early 19th century refer to grapefruit as having the taste of grapes, and bearing their name for this very reason.

Grapefruit are thought to have originated in Jamaica. In this country, they were written about in the *Daily Chronicle* in 1904, when it was reported that 'the grapefruit is gradually growing in popularity in England'. At this time, writers were never sure whether to hyphenate the name or to leave it as one word.

By 1938, grapefruit were well known and the famous London store Fortnum & Mason advertised special knives to prepare them, for sale at 3 shillings each.

Juicy and refreshing, grapefruit are usually eaten as they come, for a zesty start to the day. But they are versatile, too, and can be included in savoury dishes, salads or sweet recipes. The juice squeezed over poultry or fish adds a citrussy flavour, and can be used in an accompanying sauce or vinaigrette dressing.

GRAPEFRUIT CHEESE

A delightful grapefruit-flavoured spread to serve on bread as a tea-time treat. Also use it as a base when making grapefruit meringue pie. Use a medium-sized grapefruit – the pink ones tend to have a lot of juice. *Makes 1lb/450g jar*

1 pink grapefruit
8oz/225g caster sugar
4oz/100g butter
3 eggs

Wash grapefruit and pat dry. Grate zest finely into a bowl. Squeeze juice, add to zest and leave to infuse for about 30 minutes; then strain and discard zest.

Pour juice into a clean bowl and add sugar and butter. Heat over a pan of simmering water. When the butter is melted, beat in eggs. Stir continuously over heat until the mixture thickens and coats the back of a wooden spoon.

Pour the thickened mix into the prepared jar, seal and label.

Preparation time: 30 minutes
Cooking time: 15 minutes

Approximate nutritional values per portion:	
70 calories	3g protein
5g fat	15g carbohydrate

NUTRITION

Grapefruit are low in calories, with around 30 in an average-sized fruit. They contain about 1g of protein, no fat and 8g of carbohydrates.

Vitamin C is the major nutritional contribution of grapefruit, with 64mg in one fruit. This vitamin is needed for healthy skin and assists with the healing process.

There are traces of vitamins B1, B2 and B3, too,

necessary for maintaining the nervous system. Some vitamin E is also present.

Grapefruit contain the mineral folic acid, for prevention of anaemia, especially in pregnancy.

1 average-sized grapefruit contains:	
30 calories	1g protein
nil fat	8g carbohydrate

BUYING AND STORING

Although they are available most of the year, grapefruit are at their best and most plentiful in the month of July. There are several varieties, each with their own special characteristics.

Marsh grapefruit have very thin skins with white flesh and only a few pips. They are exceedingly juicy with a tangy flavour. Available from May to October.

Rose grapefruit have yellow skin with a pretty pink blush. The juicy flesh is tinged pink, too. They have a refreshing flavour with a hint of sweetness. Available from May to September.

Ruby grapefruit have, as their name suggests, red peel with ruby coloured flesh. They are much sweeter than the other varieties and are practically seedless. These grapefruit are excellent for children, who prefer the milder flavour. Use them in sweet and savoury recipes, too. Available from May to August.

Choose firm grapefruit, with bright, shiny skin. The pores in the skin should be small, and the fruit should feel heavy in relation to the size. This indicates plenty of juicy flesh. Store at room temperature for 4-5 days. They will keep longer in the fridge. Remove them about an hour before serving to get rid of the chill. Or on a hot day, eat straight from the fridge for a refreshing treat. Remove any grapefruit with signs of mould from the fruit bowl or they will cause the rest to rot.

GRAPEFRUIT SORBET

A cool summer pudding. *Serves 4*

12oz/350g granulated sugar
¹/₂pt/300ml water
²/₃ large juicy grapefruit
Juice of 1 lime
1 egg white
Grated citrus zest for decoration

Dissolve sugar in water in a pan over a low heat. Bring to the boil then remove from heat. Squeeze juice from grapefruit and stir into sugar mix, add lime juice.

Pour mixture into a freezer-proof container and freeze. When it is half frozen (after approx 2 hours), turn out into a mixing bowl. Whisk egg white until stiff and fold into mixture. Return to freezer and half freeze again. Remove and whisk. Freeze until firm. Serve in scoops.

Preparation time: 15 minutes
Cooking time: 5 minutes

Approximate nutritional values per portion:	
360 calories	1g protein
1g fat	20g carbohydrate

GRAPEFRUIT TIPS

● Serve a bowl of chilled ruby grapefruit segments topped with a spoonful of natural yogurt as a refreshing start to the day.

● Chill grapefruit and serve straight from the fridge as a thirst-quenching summer fruit with a burst of citrus flavour.

● Grapefruit are not as sharp as lemons, but more so than oranges. The pink varieties are sweeter and these are good to introduce to children's diets. They prefer the milder taste and tangy juiciness.

● Squeeze the juice of a grapefruit over a fillet of white fish like cod or monkfish with a few drops of lemon juice, salt and freshly ground black pepper and some finely chopped fresh herbs like parsley, chives and chervil. Grill or barbecue for a simple supper.

● Serve melon balls and grapefruit segments spiked with vodka as a refreshing pud for a balmy evening. Pile the mix into melon shells for pretty presentation. For 4: halve 2 Charentais melons and remove seeds. Scoop out flesh with a melon baller and place in a bowl. Scrape out shells to neaten them and reserve. Peel and segment 2 ruby grapefruit, reserving juice. Add to bowl with reserved juice, 2 tbsp vodka and 2 tbsp mint syrup. Mix together and pile into melon shells. Chill and decorate with mint sprigs before serving.

● Stuff grapefruit slices under the skin on the breast of a roasting chicken and baste all over with a mixture of orange, lemon and grapefruit juice. Stuff the cavity with garlic cloves. Brush with butter and season. Roast in the usual way, basting with the citrus juices as it cooks. When the chicken is cooked, remove from roasting tin. Pour off excess fat and add ¹/₄pt/150ml chicken stock and any remaining fruit juice. Bring to the boil and season. Serve poured over chicken.

SCALLOP AND GRAPEFRUIT SALAD

A lovely salad combination of tastes and textures tossed in a citrus vinaigrette. *Serves 4*

12 fresh scallops, with corals
¹/₂ head frisée, trimmed and washed
4 rashers back bacon, de-rinded and in strips
1 tbsp oil
2 slices white bread, crusts removed and in small cubes
1 pink grapefruit, segmented and chopped
2 tomatoes, peeled, de-seeded and diced
Croutons to serve
For the dressing:
4 tbsp sunflower oil
1 tsp Dijon mustard
Juice of ¹/₂ grapefruit
Squeeze of lemon juice
Salt and freshly ground black pepper

First make the dressing. Shake all ingredients in a screw-top jar, reserve. Slice scallops if large, halve if small. Leave corals whole.

Tear frisée into small pieces and place in a salad bowl. Fry bacon in a pan until browned and crisp. Remove with a slotted spoon and drain. Keep warm.

Add oil to bacon frying pan and cook bread cubes until browned. Remove and drain on kitchen paper. Next, add scallops and corals to pan and fry for 30 seconds each side until just cooked. Mix with frisée, bacon, grapefruit segments and diced tomato. Pour over dressing and toss. Pile on to a platter and scatter over croutons to serve.

Preparation time: 15 minutes
Cooking time: 15 minutes

Approximate nutritional values per portion:	
260 calories	17g protein
16g fat	13g carbohydrate

SPICY CITRUS CHICKEN

The sauce in this lightly curried chicken dish is subtly spiked with grapefruit, and thickened with avocado. *Serves 4*

3 tbsp oil
1 onion, peeled and finely chopped
2 large cloves garlic, crushed
1 tsp finely chopped fresh root ginger
4 chicken suprêmes, cut into chunks
¹/₂ tsp chilli powder
1 tsp ground cumin
1 tsp ground coriander
¹/₄pt/150ml chicken stock
1 small avocado, peeled and stoned
Lemon juice
Juice of 1 grapefruit
Salt and freshly ground black pepper
¹/₂ avocado, sprinkled with lemon juice
Segments of 1 grapefruit
Chopped coriander for decoration

Heat oil in pan and fry onion, garlic and ginger until softened. Remove with a slotted spoon and reserve. Add chicken to pan and seal. Return onion mix and stir in spices. Cook for 1 minute.

Pour over stock. Mash whole avocado and sprinkle with lemon juice. Stir into chicken mix with grapefruit juice. Bring to the boil and cover. Simmer gently for 15 minutes or until chicken is cooked through. Season. At the end of cooking time, peel and slice remaining half avocado, then stir in with grapefruit segments. Heat through. Decorate with chopped coriander.

Preparation time: 20 minutes
Cooking time: 25 minutes approx

Approximate nutritional values per portion:	
365 calories	36g protein
21g fat	5g carbohydrate

GRAPES

Grapes are one of the oldest known fruits in the world. Grape seeds have been found in the tombs of the Pharaohs, and also in excavated remains from the bronze age dating back over 5,000 years.

Though Noah is credited with planting the first vineyard, vine-growing goes back much further than this. The wild vine grew in the Caucasus and it was here that it was first cultivated.

Wine was not made until pottery containers were invented, and only became an accepted drink in the first millennium BC.

Though the main use for grapes was wine, they were also dried by Mediterranean countries in the Middle Ages for export to northern Europe. These dried fruits retain all the nutrition of fresh grapes, but weigh a quarter as much. They also keep almost indefinitely. In Britain, they supplemented winter diets when stored apples and pears were scarce, and before fridges were invented.

There are hundreds of different varieties of grape available for making wine, but only about a dozen are specially grown for table use. They complement fish and poultry dishes particularly well.

CHICKEN WITH GRAPES AND CALVADOS

Country stew of chicken portions cooked in Calvados and white wine with white seedless grapes. *Serves 4*

2 tbsp oil
1 onion, peeled and finely chopped
2 cloves garlic, crushed
3lb/1.4kg oven-ready chicken, cut into 8 portions
Seasoned flour
4 tbsp Calvados
1 wine glass white wine
1 pt/600ml chicken stock
2 sprigs thyme
6oz/175g white seedless grapes
4 tbsp double cream
Salt and freshly ground black pepper
1 tbsp snipped chives

Heat oil in a large pan and cook onion and garlic until softened. Remove with a slotted spoon and reserve. Dip chicken in seasoned flour and shake off excess. Add to pan and fry to brown all over and seal. Pour over the Calvados and flame. When flames have died down, stir in wine and chicken stock. Add thyme and bring to the boil. Cover and simmer gently for 1 hour or until chicken is tender.

Remove chicken and keep hot. Bring cooking liquid to the boil and reduce by one third. Then, stir in the grapes and cream. Season to taste and stir in snipped chives. Return chicken and gently reheat to bubbling point.

Preparation time: 15 minutes
Cooking time: 1 hour approx

Approximate nutritional values per portion:	
475 calories	30g protein
30g fat	8g carbohydrate

DUCK BREAST AND BLACK GRAPE SALAD

Luxurious salad dressed in a walnut oil vinaigrette. *Serves 4*

2 tbsp oil
2 large duck breasts
6oz/175g lamb's tongue lettuce
2oz/50g walnut halves
6oz/175g black grapes, de-pipped and halved
For the dressing:
3 tbsp sunflower oil
1 tbsp walnut oil
1 tbsp red wine vinegar
1/2 tsp mild mustard
Salt and freshly ground black pepper

Fry duck breasts, skin side first, for 5 minutes each side or until cooked to preference. Remove and keep warm.

Shake dressing ingredients in a screw-top jar.

Trim excess fat from duck breasts and cut into strips. Toss in a bowl with lamb's tongue lettuce, walnut halves and grapes. Pour over dressing and toss again to coat. Arrange the salad on a pretty plate and serve immediately.

Preparation time: 15 minutes
Cooking time: 10 minutes

Approximate nutritional values per portion:	
390 calories	32g protein
26g fat	15g carbohydrate

NUTRITION

Though delicious, grapes are relatively low in nutritional value.

A bunch of grapes has few calories, a little fibre, a useful amount of carbohydrate in the form of sugars, hardly any protein and just a trace of fat.

However, grapes also contain B vitamins, essential for cell division and the metabolism of amino acids, plus vitamin C for healthy connective tissue. The phosphorus and potassium, found in all cells, have a special role in balancing body fluids, are present in small quantities.

Grape skins, seeds and pips contain tannins, the astringent chemicals. Hence peeled and de-pipped grapes are more palatable.

4oz/100g grapes contain:	
50 calories	trace of protein
trace of fat	13g carbohydrate

BUYING AND STORING

All grapes are excellent dessert fruit, and it is only a question of taste as to what you choose.

Varieties available include the large juicy hothouse black grapes with pips, the smaller red grapes, plump white, sweet Muscatels and small white Californian seedless.

Grapes may be bought all year round, but there are peaks in the season for both white and black varieties. Black grapes are at their best from late summer to winter while white reach perfection from summer to autumn.

Look for firm fruit that has no sign of blemish or withering. Each grape in the bunch should be firmly attached to the stalk and the skins may have a 'bloom' – a white coating made from natural yeasts which protect the fruit. This is often more noticeable on black grapes and indicates the bunches have been recently picked.

Black grapes should have no green tinge, as this may mean they are not yet ripe. In fact, it is always wise to try grapes before buying. Smell them too, they ought to have a fresh, sweet aroma.

Grapes can be kept refrigerated in a plastic bag for up to two weeks.

GRAPE TIPS

● Arrange frosted bunches of black and white grapes in a pedestal fruit bowl for a stunning table centrepiece. Wipe grapes and brush with egg white. Sprinkle or dip into caster sugar and leave to set. Dust again and arrange in the bowl with vine leaves for an elegant finishing touch.

● Soft cheeses such as Brie and Camembert go very well with fresh grapes. Arrange grapes in a basket to serve with the cheese board, and offer scissors so that guests can snip off small bunches.

● Choose white seedless grapes for the simple, classic dish of Sole Veronique. Poach sole fillets in fish stock, with onion rings, herbs and bay leaves. Remove and keep hot. Strain cooking liquid into a pan and add dry white wine. Reduce slightly then stir in double cream and halved white seedless grapes. Season and pour over sole.

● Include juicy black grapes in a fresh fruit salad with chunks of crunchy apple, banana slices, kiwi fruit, orange segments, melon pieces, strawberries, and fresh pineapple chunks. Pour over a mixture of white wine, orange juice and Cointreau and leave to chill before serving with double cream for pouring.

● Some supermarkets sell cartons of grape juice – great for serving chilled at summer buffet parties for the non-alcohol-drinking guests. Pour juice into a large jug and float some de-seeded grape halves and ice cubes on top.

● De-seed black or white grapes for fruit salads using the curved end of a new hair grip. Simply push into the fruit and hook the pips out disturbing the flesh as little as possible.

● Stir halved seedless white grapes into a lime jelly for a quick and easy children's party treat.

● Halve large black seedless grapes and fill with cream cheese mashed with a little Roquefort. Sandwich back together and arrange in a pile on a pretty plate. Serve as appetizers with pre-dinner drinks.

CHAMPAGNE SORBET

Refreshing champagne-flavoured sorbet with white grapes. *Serves 4*

> 4oz/100g sugar
> 1/2pt/300ml water
> 1/2pt/300ml champagne or sparkling wine
> Squeeze of lemon juice
> 2 egg whites
> 4oz/100g white seedless grapes, chopped
> Mint sprigs for decoration

Heat sugar and water in a pan over a low heat to dissolve. Bring to the boil and simmer for 10 minutes. Remove from heat. Cool slightly and stir in champagne and lemon juice. Place in a freezer container and freeze for 2 hours or until mushy.

Whisk egg whites to stiff peaks, fold into champagne mixture with grapes. Return to freezer and freeze until firm. Serve with mint sprigs.

Preparation time: 10 minutes
Cooking time: 10 minutes approx

Approximate nutritional values per portion:	
235 calories	3g protein
trace of fat	5g carbohydrate

GREEN AND BLACK GRAPE TART

Pretty stripy grape tart with a crisp puff pastry case. *Serves 4*

> 8oz/225g puff pastry
> 1 egg, beaten
> 1/4pt/150ml double cream
> 4 tbsp sweet white wine
> 3oz/75g each black and green grapes,
>   halved and de-pipped
> For the glaze:
> 2oz/50g caster sugar
> 1/4pt/150ml water

Roll out pastry on a lightly floured board to a 7in/18cm square. Cut a border 1in/2.5cm wide from the edge. Roll out remaining pastry to 7in/18cm square again. Attach border to the top with beaten egg. Score a criss-cross pattern on the border with a sharp knife. Chill for 30 minutes. Prick base of case and bake at Gas 6, 400F, 200C for 15 minutes or until risen and golden. Cool.

Whip cream with wine to a soft peak consistency. Spread around base of pastry case. Arrange grapes on top of the cream.

Boil sugar and water until syrup begins to turn golden. Remove from heat and brush over grapes. Leave to set and then serve immediately.

Preparation time: 30 minutes
Cooking time: 15 minutes

Approximate nutritional values per portion:	
350 calories	5g protein
20g fat	30g carbohydrate

HAM

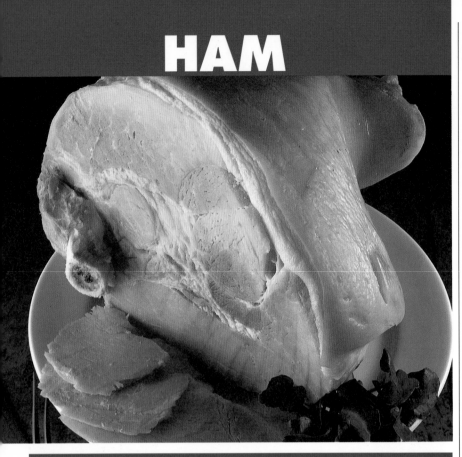

Domesticated pigs have been reared for over 5,000 years. The Romans preserved wild pigs by salting them as a means of providing winter protein.

And in Britain, pigs used to be kept on common ground, such as the village green, during the summer months, then moved to woods in the autumn, where they ate acorns and beechnuts to fatten them up. During the winter, they were kept in sties and those not needed for breeding were slaughtered and cured.

A side of bacon usually hung in every country home. In fact, in the Middle Ages, cured pork was so popular that in Shakespeare's time, peasants were often referred to as 'bacons'.

York ham became famous during the building of York Minster. York hams are dry cured, then salted, then hung for weeks to mature. Home-cooked hams can never resemble this.

But slow simmer a gammon and allow it to cool, peel off the skin if you like, then press breadcrumbs into the fat, and you have a wonderful, inexpensive cut and come again meaty joint for a celebration, to feed a crowd at a buffet, or simply to last over a weekend or holiday.

Ham also makes great sandwich or roll fillings, and forms the basis of many tasty and delicious dishes, from pizzas and pastas to burgers. The moist and flavourful character of home-cooked ham makes it the perfect meat to liven up recipes using leftovers.

HAM AND EGGS FLORENTINE

A filling lunch dish of buttered spinach topped with ham slices, soft poached eggs and a creamy cheese sauce, then browned under the grill.
Serves 4

1oz/25g butter
1oz/25g flour
¹/₂pt/300ml milk
2oz/50g mature Cheddar, grated
1 tsp made mustard
Salt and freshly ground black pepper
4 eggs
1lb/450g pack frozen leaf spinach
Walnut-sized knob of butter
Lots of freshly grated nutmeg
4 slices cooked ham
Paprika

Melt butter in a pan and stir in flour. Cook for 1 minute. Gradually add milk, stirring. Bring to the boil to thicken, stir in cheese, mustard and seasoning. Cover top with buttered greaseproof and reserve.

Soft poach eggs in a poacher or in simmering water with a little vinegar added. Remove and drain. Meanwhile, cook spinach according to instructions and add butter, nutmeg and seasoning.

Transfer spinach to a flameproof dish and cover with ham. Arrange poached eggs on top and pour over cheese sauce. Grill to brown, then serve sprinkled with paprika.

Preparation time: 20 minutes
Cooking time: 20 minutes

Approximate nutritional values per portion:	
300 calories	17g protein
17g fat	8g carbohydrate

HOT HAM SALAD

A satisfying lunch or supper dish of ham mixed with new potatoes, French beans, and broccoli.
Serves 4

4 thick slices cold ham
8oz/225g new potatoes, scrubbed
8oz/225g French beans, topped and tailed
1 head broccoli, in florets
2 tbsp oil
¹/₂ large onion, peeled and sliced
For the dressing:
4 tbsp oil
1 tbsp white wine vinegar
2 tsp wholegrain mustard
Salt and freshly ground black pepper

Cut ham into strips. Cook potatoes in boiling salted water until tender. Drain and keep hot. Cook beans and broccoli in separate pans until just tender. Drain and reserve.

Heat oil in a pan and gently fry onion until soft. Add ham and stir until heated through. Add vegetables to the pan and gently turn over. Transfer to a warmed serving dish. Shake dressing ingredients together in a screw-top jar and pour over salad just before serving.

Preparation time: 10 minutes
Cooking time: 20 minutes

Approximate nutritional values per portion:	
208 calories	8g protein
13g fat	18g carbohydrate

NUTRITION

The energy values of ham depend on the way it is cooked. Lean boiled gammon probably contains the least number of calories at 140 for 4oz/100g.

Ham is a valuable source of protein with 18g in the same weight. 5g of fat is present but there is no carbohydrate.

Ham is particularly rich in thiamin. A 4oz/100g portion of ham contains more than a third of the recommended daily amount required by an adult. Thiamin, or vitamin B1, is essential for healthy nerves and muscles and normal heart functioning.

Ham also contains some iron to help in the formation of red blood corpuscles, and potassium which acts with sodium to control the water balance of the body.

4oz/100g lean home-cooked ham contain:	
140 calories	18g protein
5g fat	nil carbohydrate

CHICKEN AND HAMBURGERS

A tasty combination of coarsely minced tender chicken breast and chopped cooked ham made into burgers and served in a bun with a gherkin and cucumber salad. *Serves 4*

For the salad:
  ½ cucumber, peeled and thinly sliced
  4 gherkins, sliced
  2 tbsp oil
  ½ tbsp white wine vinegar
  Salt and freshly ground black pepper
  Dill sprigs
For the burgers:
  2 chicken breast fillets, skinned
  4oz/100g finely chopped ham
  1 tbsp grated onion
  1 tbsp parsley, finely chopped
  Salt and freshly ground black pepper
  1 egg
  Oil for frying
  4 wholemeal buns
  Frisée
  Tomato and onion slices
  Mayonnaise (optional)

For the salad, mix cucumber and gherkin slices in a bowl. Sprinkle over oil and vinegar and season. Add dill sprigs. Leave to stand.

Mince chicken or whizz in a processor. Mix with ham in a bowl and add onion, parsley and seasoning. Bind with egg and form into 4 burgers.

Fry burgers in hot oil until cooked through. Serve in wholemeal buns with lettuce, tomato and onion slices and mayonnaise. Serve with the salad.

Preparation time: 30 minutes
Cooking time: 20 minutes approx

Approximate nutritional values per portion:	
300 calories	25g protein
12g fat	32g carbohydrate

BUYING AND STORING

Cooked ham, boned or on the bone, is available from supermarkets, butchers and delicatessens.

Ham can be smoked or plain depending on the 'cure'. Look for firm flesh which is not too dry although again the cure is important here – some hams are not as moist as others. Excess moisture may indicate that water has been injected during the processing of cheaper hams.

In general, ham should be fresh-looking with an appetising smell. It is usually thinly sliced, but most butchers or supermarket cooked meat counters will cut it to any thickness on request.

Supermarkets also sell ready-sliced ham in pre-weighed packs. Check sell-by dates on these and also that the ham is not 'sweating' inside. Look for lean slices with only a thin layer of fat around the edge.

For home cooking, buy a gammon joint. Once cooked and cooled, this becomes ham. Gammon comes from the hindquarters of the pig and the flesh should be fresh and pink. It can be smoked or 'green'. It is cooked by gentle simmering sometimes with flavourings, then left to cool before serving.

HAM AND CABBAGE PIES

Crisp puff pastry vol au vent cases filled with a great mix of country tastes and textures. *Serves 4*

  13oz/375g pack frozen puff pastry, defrosted
  1 egg, beaten
  *12oz/350g spring greens, brussel tops, or
    cabbage, trimmed and finely shredded*
  Salt and freshly ground black pepper
  1½oz/40g butter
  1oz/25g flour
  ½pt/300ml milk
  1 tbsp herb mustard
  1 tsp cayenne pepper
  2 thick slices ham, finely diced
  Good squeeze lemon juice
  Watercress for decoration

Roll out the pastry on lightly floured worktop ¼in/0.5cm thick. Cut out 4 rounds 3in/7.5cm across. Using the next size down cutter, press a circle inside the edge of the rounds, half way through the pastry to mark a border. Brush tops with beaten egg, then bake in a pre-heated oven at Gas 6, 400F, 200C for 15 minutes, or until risen and golden. Transfer to a wire rack, lift out the lids, and reserve them.

Meanwhile make the filling. First blanch the greens. Drain, season and stir in ½oz/15g butter. Melt remaining butter in a pan and stir in flour. Cook 1 minute. Remove from heat then gradually add milk. Return to gentle heat and stir until thickened. Stir in herb mustard, salt and cayenne. Mix in diced ham, cabbage and lemon juice. Pile into vol au vent cases and top with lids. Serve warm or hot, decorated with watercress.

Preparation time: 25 minutes
Cooking time: 30 minutes approx

Approximate nutritional values per portion:	
485 calories	8g protein
40g fat	50g carbohydrate

HAM TIPS

● Before ham is cooked and cooled it is known as gammon. It is easy to cook at home – once in the pan it practically looks after itself, with just the occasional skim to clear any scum from the surface. Ask the butcher if he recommends soaking the meat to remove excess salt. A large joint should be soaked for about 24 hours. Overnight will be enough for smaller joints.

● To cook a soaked joint of gammon, first drain off the soaking water and rinse. Place in a pan and cover with fresh, cold water. Bring to the boil and drain. Cover with more cold water and bring back to the boil. Skim off any scum from the surface and add flavourings like an onion studded with cloves, bay leaves and thyme. Cook for 25 minutes per pound plus 25 minutes, skimming every now and then. Cool completely before serving.

● Always save the ham bone after eating all the meat. It makes a good stock base for soups and casseroles.

● For a special occasion, when a cold ham is to be served as part of a buffet, invest in a ham stand. This enables even the largest joint to be displayed whole, and carved as required from a firm base.

● Ham should be carved thinly. To carve a large ham with the bone like the one pictured opposite, hold the narrow shank end with a carving fork or clean cloth and cut slices.

● Fry thin strips of ham to crisp and brown and drain on kitchen paper. Use to sprinkle over winter soups and stews for extra taste.

● For a speedy supper, toss strips of cooked ham, diced, peeled tomatoes and Parmesan cheese through a pan of hot, drained spaghetti. Stir to heat through and season with plenty of freshly ground black pepper and a sprinkling of chopped parsley.

● Leftover cooked ham is a good flavouring for meat casseroles. Add it at the beginning when frying the onions and garlic for a tasty and savoury end result.

HONEY

Honey was one of the first known natural sweeteners and was highly regarded as a valuable and nourishing food.

It is an ancient food, too, found buried in the tombs of the Pharaohs in Egyptian pyramids. This was to ensure a source of 'eternal food to nourish them in the afterlife'.

The ancient Greeks were also fond of honey which they regarded as essential to a healthy diet. 'Ambrosia' was a mixture of milk and honey and 'nectar', fermented honey with spices, a kind of mead.

It takes around 200 bees one month to make 1lb/450g honey. This processed form of nectar is collected by bees who can carry their own weight in nectar.

It is stored in a honey sac and mixed with enzymes. The bee can dip into this sac to fuel his own energy requirements while he collects a full load of nectar. Pollen is gathered in the leg sacs. At the hive an indoor worker accepts the nectar which is then transferred to another worker. This digestive process reduces the moisture content and makes the sought-after substance, honey.

Naturally the bee stores this rich food in wax combs in the hive. But today reusable, man-made combs are used for a more pure end product. Nevertheless, there are enough essences and oils remaining to give honey the distinctive taste of its origins of flowers and blossoms.

Man has never been able to reproduce this complicated natural process, although attempts have repeatedly been made.

Known as 'the nectar of the gods', honey's magical qualities have mystified man for centuries.

The word 'honeymoon' comes from an ancient English custom whereby the bride and groom ate only honey and drank only mead for the first month of marriage.

SPICED HONEY DRUMSTICKS

Lovely sweet and sour coating for drumsticks for a truly delicious difference. This baste works excellently with spare ribs, too. *Makes 8*

1 tbsp Acacia honey, or blended clear
2 tsp mustard powder
1 tsp paprika
1 tbsp tomato purée
2 tbsp Worcestershire sauce
1 tbsp white wine vinegar
2 tbsp lemon juice
1/4pt/150ml water
Salt and freshly ground black pepper
1 onion, peeled and finely chopped
2 cloves garlic, peeled and crushed
1 tbsp oil
8 chicken drumsticks

Mix honey, mustard powder, paprika, tomato purée, Worcestershire sauce, white wine vinegar, lemon juice, water and seasoning together in a bowl.

Gently fry onion and garlic in oil until softened. Remove with a slotted spoon and reserve.

Fry drumsticks quickly to brown. Return onion mix to pan and pour over sauce. Cook at Gas 5, 375F, 190C for 45 minutes, basting three or four times until chicken is cooked through and baste has reduced to an aromatic sauce.

Preparation time: 15 minutes
Cooking time: 50 minutes

Approximate nutritional values per drumstick:	
130 calories	15g protein
5g fat	3g carbohydrate

NUTRITION

Honey is one of nature's miracles. Approximately 70 per cent fructose and the rest water, it is an instant energy boost.

It is made by bees who change the natural nectar collected from flowers into the well-known sweet substance, which has enormous appeal to young and old alike.

Honey is a natural product which cannot be reproduced by man – although there have been many attempts.

It contains a trace of protein, is quite high in carbohydrate, has little fat and a trace of minerals. The B2 vitamin, Riboflavin, is present in small quantities.

One of the oldest aids to beauty, honey's ability to retain moisture means it is often used in skin and hair preparations.

4oz/100g honey contain:	
285 calories	0.5g protein
trace of fat	76g carbohydrate

PEACH AND HAM SALAD

Unusual mix of tastes and textures for a refreshing and flavourful salad with a honey vinaigrette. *Serves 4*

2 heads chicory, cleaned
8oz/225g Parma ham
2 peaches, halved and stoned
For the dressing:
4 tbsp olive oil
1 tbsp white wine vinegar
1 tsp mild French mustard
2 tsp clear citrus honey, or blended clear
Salt and freshly ground black pepper

Separate chicory leaves and place them in a bowl. Cut the ham into strips and thinly slice peaches. Add to bowl.

Shake dressing ingredients in a screw-top jar and drizzle over salad just before serving, tossing gently.

Preparation time: 20 minutes
Cooking time: nil

Approximate nutritional values per portion:	
180 calories	14g protein
12g fat	6g carbohydrate

HONEY TIPS

● Make a delicious hot toddy to bring warmth to winter days. Pour 2 tbsp whisky into a mug and add juice of ¹/₂ lemon with 2 lemon slices. Pour over boiling water and add 1 tsp honey. Stir well and drink while still hot.

● Honey adds a distinct aroma and richness to many desserts and cakes. Remember it is sweeter than sugar so less is needed.

● Prevent crystallisation of honey by storing in a cupboard rather than a cold fridge or larder. Alternatively, heat the jar in hot water before use to make the honey more liquid.

● Glaze a joint of home-cooked ham with a sherry and honey baste. Remove the rind from ham while still hot and score a criss-cross pattern into the thin fat layer. Baste with ¹/₂ wine glass of sherry mixed with 1 tsp honey and a dash of soy sauce. Roast at Gas 6, 400F, 200C, basting continually until browned. Serve hot or cold.

● Poach pears in white wine, honey and cinnamon for a quick midweek dessert served with cream. Peel 4 ripe pears, leaving stalks intact. Place in a large pan and pour over a glass of white wine. Add 1 tsp honey and a cinnamon stick. Bring to the boil, cover and simmer until pears are tender. Eat hot or cold with the cooking juices poured over, topped with double cream.

● Make a refreshing honey and avocado face pack to leave skin feeling soft and silky. Peel ¹/₂ ripe avocado and mash with 2 tsp honey to a smooth purée. Spread over face and neck and leave for 10 minutes. Gently rinse away with warm water and dab dry with a soft towel.

● Set honey often has a frosted appearance. It can be one-flavour or a blend.

KNOW YOUR HONEY

Bluebell: Clear honey with an aroma of woodland flowers. Sweet and grapey taste.

Acacia: Pale and clear, this honey has a sophisticated aroma and is light-flavoured with a touch of herbs in the taste.

Lime Blossom: Set, golden honey with a tangy citrus fragrance and zesty lime zing.

Orange Blossom: Can be set or clear, a pale honey with a mild orange flavour.

Mexican: Set, blended honey with a smooth and fruity taste.

Australian: Dark set or clear blended honey with a rich toffee flavour.

Tasmanian Leatherwood: A connoisseur's set honey with a full rich and distinctive flavour and a kiss of herbs.

Blended Clear or Set: Economical blends of honey from many sources, usually sold as a supermarket own label or cheap brand.

HONEY MANGO SYLLABUB

Ambrosial pud of thick Greek yogurt with puréed mango sweetened with Bluebell honey. Simple and irresistible! *Serves 4*

2 large mangoes, peeled and stoned
500g tub thick Greek yogurt
4 tbsp Bluebell honey, or clear blended
Dessert biscuits for serving

Purée mango flesh smooth. Place in a bowl with yogurt. Fold in lightly to give a marbled effect. Spoon into glasses and swirl honey over the top.

Chill before serving.

Preparation time: 10 minutes
Cooking time: nil

Approximate nutritional values per portion:	
275 calories	8g protein
12g fat	35g carbohydrate

HONEY PORK TWIZZLES

Strips of pork fillet twirled around wooden kebab skewers and marinated with lime, honey, soy sauce and garlic, and served with a peanut dip. *Serves 4*

1 pork fillet
Watercress sprigs to garnish
For the marinade:
2 tbsp oil
1 clove garlic, peeled and crushed
Juice of 2 limes
Zest of 1 lime
¹/₂ tsp cayenne
2 tsp warmed lime blossom honey, or blended set
For the sauce:
3 tbsp crunchy peanut butter
1 tbsp soy sauce
Good dash chilli sauce
2 cloves garlic, peeled and crushed

Lay pork fillet on a board and carefully cut through one long side leaving the other long side intact – so it opens out like a long book. Open out and place between 2 sheets greaseproof paper. Flatten out using a rolling pin or meat mallet. Remove from greaseproof paper and cut into long strips about ¹/₂in/1cm wide.

Secure one end of each strip on to a kebab stick and wind around. Secure other end.

Mix marinade ingredients. Lay kebabs in a shallow dish and brush with marinade. Leave for 30 minutes.

Meanwhile, make the sauce by mixing peanut butter with soy, chilli sauce and garlic. Warm gently, stirring, and spoon into a small pot. Keep warm.

Grill kebabs turning and basting with marinade for 10 minutes, or until cooked through. Serve with watercress, accompanied with peanut dip.

Preparation time: 30 minutes, plus marinading
Cooking time: 10 minutes approx

Approximate nutritional values per portion:	
285 calories	19g protein
13g fat	4g carbohydrate

KIDNEY BEANS

Kidney beans are legumes or pulses and there are many types, differing in colour and size – but most of them are related to the well-known red kidney bean.

These beans with their colour ranging from deep mahogany to dusty pink, their rather mealy texture and slightly sweet flavour, are popular in stews and casseroles where they richly complement beef and lamb. They are an essential ingredient of many Mexican dishes, one of which is the world famous chilli con carne.

Pulses are an important source of food – especially for vegetarians, since the high protein content means they can replace meat. But they make delicious, inexpensive dishes in their own right, too.

Most pulses need a long soaking and cooking time. Red kidney beans benefit from an overnight soak, and need to be simmered for an hour. They must also be boiled rapidly for 15 minutes before they are simmered to eliminate all toxins. But there are good quality canned beans available, which keep their shape in stews – and these make a reliable time-saving substitute.

CHILLI CON CARNE

A world famous Mexican mix of mince cooked with red kidney beans and chillies. *Serves 4*

> 3 tbsp oil
> 1 large onion, peeled and chopped
> 3 cloves garlic, crushed
> 1½lb/700g very best mince
> 14oz/400g can chopped tomatoes
> 1 tbsp tomato purée
> 1 tsp cumin
> 1 tsp chilli powder
> 1 fresh red chilli, de-seeded and finely chopped
> 2 tsp pickled Jalapeño chillies, chopped
> ¼pt/150ml beef stock
> 14oz/400g can red kidney beans
> Salt and freshly ground black pepper
> Sliced spring onions to decorate

Heat oil in a pan and fry onion and garlic over gentle heat until soft. Remove with a slotted spoon and reserve. Add mince to the pan and fry in batches until browned. Return all mince to the pan with the onion mix. Pour over tomatoes and add tomato purée, cumin, chilli powder, fresh chilli and pickled Jalapeño chillies. Stir. Add beef stock and drained red kidney beans.

Bring to the boil and then simmer for 15 minutes. Season. Decorate with chopped spring onions and serve with tacos, or rice.

Preparation time: 30 minutes
Cooking time: 30 minutes

Approximate nutritional values per portion:	
440 calories	23g protein
20g fat	29g carbohydrate

BUYING AND STORING

Even though they are preserved by drying, pulses do deteriorate over a period of time so it is wise to buy them from shops which have a high turnover, and to use them quickly. They become even drier with age which means they may break up during cooking and will neither look nor taste as good.

Dried red kidney beans should have a bright, attractive colour, look shiny and plump. Avoid any wrinkled, dull or damaged specimens. Pre-packed dried red beans are usually of high quality – but check the sell-by date.

It is a temptation to store pulses in glass jars – they look so pretty on a kitchen shelf – but this is not a good idea if you intend to eat them. Sunlight destroys the flavour and more importantly, some nutrients. The best place to keep them (once the packet is opened) is in an airtight plastic container or a stone jar in a cool cupboard.

NUTRITION

Like all pulses, red kidney beans are an important source of nutrition. In 4oz/100g dried beans (which swell up to 12oz/350g when cooked) there are 300 calories. Though this may sound high, 12oz/350g is a lot of beans – so this is quite moderate really – 4oz/100g of *cooked* kidney beans work out at only 100 calories.

Red kidney beans are packed with protein, too, which makes them a useful addition to the diet of vegetarians. But even in a meat eater's diet beans can be substituted for meat. In 4oz/100g, there is 25g protein, half the daily recommended amount.

Red kidney beans are also rich in carbohydrate for energy with 50g in 4oz/100g. There is a trace of fat, a useful amount of fibre, and no cholesterol. The reason pulses produce 'gas' in the human intestine is due to certain indigestible complex sugars, which simply ferment.

The most important vitamin in kidney beans is niacin. There is around 6mg in 4oz/100g. Niacin plays an important part in assisting enzymes. It is essential for maintaining healthy digestive and nervous systems, and good skin. It also helps in the formation of sex hormones.

4oz/100g red kidney beans contain:	
300 calories	25g protein
trace of fat	50g carbohydrate

MEAN BEANS

An irresistible salad of mixed beans to make in a big pot and keep covered in the fridge. *Serves 8*

14oz/400g can kidney beans, drained
7oz/200g can canellini beans, drained
7oz/200g can borlotti beans, drained
7oz/200g can butter beans, drained
11oz/300g can broad beans (or cooked frozen)
8 stoned black olives, chopped
1 medium onion, peeled and finely chopped
4 anchovies, thinly slivered (optional)
1 tbsp fresh parsley, finely chopped
For the vinaigrette:
4 tbsp white wine vinegar
2 cloves garlic, peeled and crushed
1 tsp Dijon mustard
Salt and freshly ground black pepper

In a large bowl mix kidney, canellini, borlotti, butter and broad beans together. Add the olives, onion, slivered anchovies and parsley.

Shake dressing ingredients together in a screw-top jar. Pour over bean mixture and toss gently so beans do not break up.

Preparation time: 10 minutes
Cooking time: nil

Approximate nutritional values per portion:	
156 calories	12g protein
7g fat	28g carbohydrate

TACOS WITH CHILLI LAMB

Taco shells stuffed with chopped lamb flavoured with chilli and herbs. *Serves 4*

3 tbsp oil
1 onion, peeled and in rings
1 green chilli, de-seeded and sliced
2 cloves garlic, peeled and crushed
1lb/450g lean lamb, trimmed of fat and hand chopped (not minced)
8 small tomatoes, quartered
14oz/400g can red kidney beans, drained
1 tbsp tomato purée
3 tbsp stock or red wine
1 tbsp fresh parsley, finely chopped
Salt and freshly ground black pepper
4 taco shells
2oz/50g grated Cheddar cheese

Heat oil in a pan and fry onion rings gently until soft. Add chilli and garlic and continue cooking over a low heat for a few more minutes. Remove from pan and reserve.

Add chopped lamb to the pan in batches and fry over high heat to brown. Add tomato quarters, kidney beans, tomato purée, stock and parsley and return onion mix. Season. Cook for about 15 minutes. Pile into taco shells and top with grated cheese.

Preparation time: 15 minutes
Cooking time: 20 minutes

Approximate nutritional values per portion:	
338 calories	20g protein
21g fat	27g carbohydrate

BEANBURGERS

Sensational burgers made with chopped red kidney beans. *Serves 4*

14oz/400g can red kidney beans, drained
1½lb/700g best mince
½ Spanish onion, grated
2 cloves garlic, peeled and crushed
Salt and ground black pepper
Good dash Tabasco sauce
Heaped tbsp chopped parsley
Buns, lettuce and tomato slices to serve

Coarsely chop red kidney beans or whizz for about 15 seconds in a processor. You do not want a purée – just rough them up a bit. Break up the mince with your hands and add it to the bowl.

Grate the onion directly on top so you don't lose any juice. Crush in the garlic the same way. Season and add a good dash of Tabasco sauce. Add 1 heaped tbsp freshly chopped parsley.

Work all this together with your hands. Shape into burger-shaped rounds about 1in/2.5cm thick.

Fry in a little oil slowly until the outside is crusty and brown and the inside cooked.

Serve in a bun with lettuce and tomato slices.

Preparation time: 15 minutes
Cooking time: 12 minutes approx

Approximate nutritional values per burger without bun:	
390 calories	22g protein
12g fat	27g carbohydrate

BEAN TIPS

● Dried kidney beans need soaking before cooking, preferably overnight. Use a large bowl as the beans swell up during soaking.

● For safe cooking, all pulses should first be brought to the boil, then boiled rapidly for 15 minutes to eliminate toxins. After this, turn down the heat and simmer for approximately an hour or until cooked. Test by eating a bean. The skin may be firm, but the inside *must* be soft.

● Add salt *after* the beans have been cooked – it tends to toughen them if added during cooking.

● All pulses are a rich source of inexpensive protein. Red kidney beans are difficult to resist in a dish such as this. For 4: soak 1lb/450g red kidney beans overnight, then cook as in the second tip. Parboil 2 large potatoes. Heat 3 tbsp oil in a pan and fry 8 de-rinded chopped rashers of streaky bacon until the fat runs and bacon starts to crisp. Add 1 large sliced onion, 2 cleaned and thinly sliced leeks and 2 crushed cloves garlic to the pan and cook over a low heat until they soften. Add the potatoes cut into large dice. Drain the cooked beans and add to the pan with ¼pt/150ml chicken stock. Cook over gentle heat until potatoes are soft and beans heated through. Taste, then season.

● Refried Beans (Frijoles Refritos) is a delicious Mexican snack dish. Use canned for this – it's quicker. Drain a 14oz/400g can red kidney beans, mash roughly. Heat 4 tbsp oil in a pan and add a little mashed beans, cooking until any liquid disappears. Add more beans, plus more oil if necessary. Continue cooking until you have a thick paste. Season to taste. Divide between 4 shallow earthenware serving dishes. Sprinkle with lots of freshly grated Cheddar cheese. Grill until bubbling.

● Use drained canned red kidney beans for a quick sausage supper. For 4: drain 2 x 14oz/400g cans and empty into a shallow ovenproof dish. Fry 8 sausages until browned and cooked. Bury them in the beans. Sprinkle over 4 fried chopped streaky bacon rashers. Pour over 14oz/400g can chopped tomatoes mixed with 2 tbsp tomato purée. Sprinkle over a good shaking of Worcestershire sauce, a dash of Tabasco, the juice of a lemon, salt and masses of freshly ground black pepper. Bake at Gas 5, 375F, 190C for 20 minutes. Either sprinkle with grated Cheddar and grill to melt before serving or top with slices of leftover or parboiled potatoes and sprinkle them with grated cheese.

LAMB CHOPS

The wild sheep was probably first tamed around 8920BC in Iraq. And evidence has been found to prove sheep were in existence in India around 5500BC.

The Ancient Greeks always adored lamb, particularly roast or baked – as indeed the present day nation still does. In classical Greece, rich farmers kept small flocks of sheep on hillsides not simply for the meat, but for wool and milk too. The poor at that time saw little meat at all.

In the eighth century, by order of the King of Wessex, one village was required to provide 10 sheep for the royal table. But sheep meat was not eaten generally until the industrial revolution. In fact, in the time of Elizabeth I it was illegal to eat sheep unless they had died naturally – they were prized for their wool.

KNOW YOUR LAMB CHOPS

There are several cuts of lamb used for chops.

Loin chops come from the back of the lamb, known as the saddle. They have a nugget or 'eye' of meat on a small T-shaped bone with a little fat. Extremely tender, these chops are perfect for grilling or frying. The whole saddle – a double loin of up to 13 chops joined by the backbone – can also be bought as a roasting joint for a special occasion. Delicate noisettes of lamb – the 'eye' meat, taken off the bone and neatly tied – also come from loin chops.

Chump chops come from the lower back of the animal, between the end of the loin and the start of the leg. They are shaped rather like steaks, very meaty with a small round bone at the base. These chops are also tender but can be expensive, as the yield from one lamb is only 4-6 chops. Good for barbecuing.

Lamb cutlets are taken from the upper rib of the carcass. This cut is known as the best end of neck. It can also be left as a 'rack' of lamb, consisting of usually 6-8 chops. Two racks can be tied together to form a Guard of Honour or Crown roast. Both racks and cutlets are trimmed of most of the fat and the bone scraped clean for better presentation after cooking. This is called a French trim. Cutlets trimmed in this way are suitable for grilling or baking 'en croute'.

Neck chops are from the middle of the neck and have lean meat on the bone with some fat and connective tissue attached. They are not very expensive and full of flavour, but need long, slow cooking as the meat is tough. They are excellent for dishes like Irish stew.

NUTRITION

Lamb is an important source of protein containing all the essential amino acids.

As far as energy is concerned, this depends on the amount of fat in the meat – which is extremely variable. 4oz/100g of lean roast leg of lamb could contain as few as 191 calories, but the same amount of roast lamb with fat soars to 266 calories.

Lamb contains no carbohydrate except a trace of glycogen stored in the muscle tissue, and has no fibre. But it has useful amounts of minerals and B group vitamins including iron and Vitamin B12.

4oz/100g lean lamb contain:	
191 calories	17.9g protein
18.7g fat	trace of carbohydrate

SPRINGTIME STEW

Economical, tasty neck of lamb chops in a white wine gravy with tiny spring vegetables. *Serves 4*

2 tbsp oil
2 cloves garlic, crushed
12 button onions, peeled
8 neck of lamb chops, trimmed
Seasoned flour
2 glasses white wine
³/₄pt/425ml lamb stock
1 tbsp tomato purée
¹/₂ tbsp finely chopped fresh rosemary
1 tsp chopped fresh thyme
Salt and freshly ground black pepper
1 small bunch baby turnips, stalks trimmed and washed
1 small bunch baby carrots, stalks trimmed and scrubbed

Heat oil in a pan and fry the garlic and baby onions until softened. Remove with a slotted spoon and reserve. Dip chops in flour and shake off excess. Fry quickly to seal. Transfer to a large saucepan with garlic and baby onions. Pour over wine, stock and tomato purée. Add rosemary and thyme.

Bring to the boil, season and simmer covered for 1¹/₂ hours or until chops begin to tenderise. Add turnips and carrots and continue cooking for 30 minutes. Pile into a warmed dish and serve with new potatoes.

Preparation time: 20 minutes
Cooking time: 2 hours approx

Approximate nutritional values per portion:	
400 calories	20g protein
25g fat	18g carbohydrate

LAMB CUTLETS IN MINT ASPIC

Flavoursome, tender nuggets of lamb on the trimmed bone, in a minty, aspic jelly. *Serves 4*

8 lamb cutlets, trimmed of all fat and
    bones cleaned
2 tbsp oil
1 clove garlic, crushed
Salt and freshly ground black pepper
1 packet aspic jelly
6 mint sprigs
8 mint leaves

Fry cutlets in oil with garlic until brown on the outside but still pink in the centre. Season with salt and pepper. Remove with a slotted spoon and leave to cool.

Make up aspic according to instructions on the packet. Add 5 mint sprigs, reserving one to decorate. Leave to infuse. Remove mint and allow aspic to set to a syrupy consistency.

Place cutlets on a wire rack over a tray. Arrange a mint leaf on each one. Spoon over a little aspic and leave to set. Spoon over another layer and set again. Chill and serve decorated with a sprig of mint.

Preparation time: 10 minutes
Cooking time: 10 minutes approx

Approximate nutritional values per portion:	
300 calories	20g protein
10g fat	nil carbohydrate

CHAR-GRILLED CHUMP CHOPS

Meaty chump chops marinated in red wine, garlic and fresh herbs then char-grilled for a succulent smoky flavour. *Serves 4*

4 chump chops
1 wine glass red wine
2 tbsp oil
2 cloves garlic, peeled and sliced
2 sprigs fresh thyme, chopped
1 sprig fresh rosemary, chopped
Salt and freshly ground black pepper

Layer chops in a shallow dish, then mix together the red wine with the oil, garlic and herbs and pour over. Leave to marinate for about 30 minutes, turning chops over once.

Remove chops from marinade, season with salt and freshly ground black pepper. Grill on a barbecue or under a conventional grill for 5 minutes each side or until chops are cooked to preference. Baste with marinade occasionally during the cooking time. Serve with grilled tomato slices and fried slices of cooked potato.

Preparation time: 10 minutes plus marinating
Cooking time: 10 minutes

Approximate nutritional values per portion:	
350 calories	30g protein
15g fat	nil carbohydrate

LAMB IN A JACKET

This special rack of lamb joint is roasted with a herb mustard and a fresh herb coating. Serve together with sautéed new potatoes and seasonal vegetables. *Serves 4*

1 rack of lamb, trimmed
1 tbsp herb mustard
Oil for drizzling
2 tbsp finely chopped mixed fresh herbs
    like parsley, rosemary and chives
Salt and freshly ground black pepper
Cooked new potatoes, butter and rosemary sprigs
Sprig of parsley for decoration

Wipe lamb and make sure bones are clean. Brush with mustard and drizzle with oil. Sprinkle over most of chopped herbs to coat. Season with salt and pepper.

Roast at Gas 6, 400F, 200C for 20 minutes or until cooked to preference.

Sauté new potatoes in butter and toss with rosemary sprigs and salt and freshly ground black pepper. Sprinkle remaining chopped herbs on to lamb and arrange on a warmed platter with potatoes. Decorate with a sprig of parsley.

Preparation time: 10 minutes
Cooking time: 20 minutes

Approximate nutritional values per portion:	
380 calories	18g protein
15g fat	nil carbohydrate

LAMB CHOP TIPS

● Sugar-glazed loin chops are a swift and superb supper dish. Simply brush chops with mustard, sprinkle with brown sugar and drizzle with olive oil. Season with salt and freshly ground black pepper and grill for 5 minutes each side or until cooked to preference. Serve with broccoli and new potatoes.

● Freshly made mint sauce is the best. Pick sprightly leaves from fresh mint sprigs discarding the stalk and twiggy bits. Chop finely on a chopping board. Add 1 tsp of sugar and continue chopping – this produces a wonderful rich, minty juice and helps with the fine chopping. Transfer to a small bowl, add a few drops of boiling water – which also helps to enhance the mintiness. Then add malt vinegar to taste and to the desired consistency.

● Quick and delicious midweek dinner is the traditional toad-in-the-hole made with lamb cutlets, or loin chops. Make a special airy, Yorkshire pudding batter by using 2 eggs to 4oz/100g flour and ½pt/300ml milk, instead of the usual 1 egg. This guarantees the ultimate, perfect Yorkshire,

worth remembering for the next Sunday roast – it never fails. Fry chops quickly both sides and season. Heat oil in a roasting pan. Arrange chops in a roasting tin in the hot oil and pour over batter. Cook at Gas 6, 400F, 200C for 30 minutes or until pud is crisp and billowing.

● Marinate chump chops in this. Mix ¼pt/150ml runny natural yogurt with 1 puréed onion and 2 crushed cloves of garlic. Add 4 tbsp olive oil, juice of half a lemon, salt and freshly ground black pepper with ½ tbsp fresh rosemary, chopped. Grill until cooked but still pink inside.

● Lancashire Hotpot is the English contribution to gastronomic excellence as far as lamb chops are concerned. Choose lean lamb chops and layer them with lightly fried onion and potatoes, ending with a layer of potatoes overlapping roof tile fashion. Season between the layers. Pour lamb stock over the chops, onions and potatoes. Bake at Gas 4, 350F, 180C for 1½ hours, or until lamb is tender and potato is cooked and golden.

LANGOUSTINE

The langoustine is also known as the Norwegian Lobster, the Dublin Bay Prawn and Scampi. This is a very pretty, small lobster, easily recognisable by its long slender front claws.

It is widespread, found around the coast of Iceland, Norway, and down to the Mediterranean. Norway Lobster is the correct name because this is where they are most prolific. The Dublin Bay connection is simply because Norwegian fishing boats used to land there after a successful catch, and the langoustines were then sold to street traders, like Molly Malone. Langoustine comes from the French for crayfish 'langouste'.

Most of the langoustines eaten here come from Scotland, like many other varieties of fine quality shellfish. Langoustines bombarded the British restaurant business under the name scampi during the sixties (from the Italian name 'scampo'). They are still very popular in Italy and many recipes from the Adriatic include them.

Available all year round, they are at their best between April and November, sometimes fresh, though they can always be bought frozen. They range in colour from baby pink to an orangey red.

They make an attractive addition to a seafood platter, and can be used in any recipe which calls for large prawns (often referred to as gambas). They have a delicate flavour, and soft and tender flesh.

LANGOUSTINE SALAD

A simple but delicious mix of langoustine tails, avocado, melon balls and anchovy strips, lightly tossed in a refreshing ginger and onion vinaigrette. *Serves 4*

> *20 freshly cooked langoustines*
> *1 ripe Charentais melon*
> *2 ripe avocado pears*
> *Lemon juice*
> *2 anchovy fillets, rinsed and dried*
> For the dressing:
> *4 tbsp sunflower oil*
> *1 tbsp white wine vinegar*
> *1 tsp Dijon mustard*
> *2 tsp grated onion*
> *¹/₂ tsp freshly grated root ginger*
> *Freshly ground black pepper*
> *Chive batons to garnish*

Peel langoustines and place tails in a bowl. Cut up melon with a baller and add to bowl. Reserve juice and transfer to another bowl. Do the same with the avocado, but sprinkle with lemon juice before adding to the rest of the salad to prevent it from discolouring. Slice anchovies very finely and add to langoustines, melon and avocado.

Shake dressing ingredients with reserved melon juice together in a screw-top jar and pour over salad. Toss gently with your hands, then transfer to individual serving dishes. Garnish with chive batons.

Preparation time: 15 minutes
Cooking time: nil

Approximate nutritional values per portion:	
440 calories	44g protein
37g fat	8g carbohydrate

LANGOUSTINES WITH CITRUS MAYONNAISE

The best way to eat langoustines is freshly cooked and cooled, with a homemade mayonnaise. This one has the citrussy freshness of lemon and lime. *Serves 4*

> *16 medium-sized freshly cooked langoustines*
> For the mayonnaise:
> *2 fresh egg yolks*
> *1 tsp Dijon mustard*
> *2 tsp white wine vinegar*
> *2 tsp lemon juice*
> *Freshly ground white pepper*
> *¹/₄pt/150ml olive oil*
> *¹/₄pt/150ml sunflower oil*
> *Juice and zest of a lime*
> *Zest of a lemon*

Place egg yolks in a bowl with mustard, vinegar, lemon juice and freshly ground white pepper. Using an electric whisk, gradually add oils drip by drip until the mixture is visibly thickening. When this happens, add remaining oil in a thin stream, still whisking, until all oil is used.

Add lime juice and zest. Transfer to a serving pot, or a small ramekin for each person. Sprinkle with lemon zest before serving with langoustines.

Preparation time: 10 minutes
Cooking time: nil

Approximate nutritional values per portion:	
385 calories	45g protein
40g fat	2g carbohydrate

NUTRITION

Langoustines are a good source of 'complete protein', that is protein which contains all the essential amino acids, and in 4oz/100g there is 19g. However, they are low in calories, with only 90 in the same weight. They are relatively low in fat with just over 1g in 4oz/100g, but are quite high in cholesterol with around 150mg in the same weight.

On the plus side, they contain Omega-3 fatty acids which can help protect the body against heart conditions.

The main vitamin contribution is the B group. These important B vitamins contribute to the manufacture of cells needed for growth and development. The formation of red blood cells is also assisted by them, and they are necessary for maintaining a healthy nervous system.

There are also useful amounts of the minerals iodine, potassium, phosphorus, calcium and some iron, in langoustines.

4oz/100g langoustines contain:	
90 calories	19g protein
1g fat	trace of carbohydrate

BUYING AND STORING

It is important to ensure shellfish is completely fresh. Langoustines should have a sweet aroma and a certain moistness. They should not be soft and floppy – this indicates they may not be fresh. The tails should also be firm.

Buy them on the day you intend to eat them. Though they will keep for a day in the fridge, they are best eaten straight away. Frozen langoustines keep in the freezer for one month. To freeze fresh langoustines, cook them and shell them – only freeze the tails. Arrange on a flat plate to 'open freeze' with the freezer control on 'fast freeze'. When completely frozen, pack into a rigid freezer container with a lid, or a properly sealed polythene freezer bag. Make sure they are completely defrosted before using.

LANGOUSTINE ECLAIRS

Dainty little choux buns, filled with a fish-flavoured sauce. *Makes 20*

For the eclairs:
> *¹/₄pt/150ml water*
> *2oz/50g butter*
> *2¹/₂oz/65g flour*
> *Good pinch of salt*
> *2 eggs*

For the sauce:
> *1oz/25g butter*
> *1oz/25g flour*
> *¹/₄pt/150ml milk*
> *¹/₄pt/150ml fish stock*
> *Salt and freshly ground black pepper*
> *2 tbsp double cream*
> *20 prepared small langoustine tails*
> *Watercress leaves to garnish*

Place water in a pan and bring to the boil with the butter. Sift flour and salt together, then shoot all this into the pan at the same time. Beat furiously until all the flour is incorporated and the mixture forms a ball and leaves the sides of the pan clean.

Cool the mix slightly, add the eggs one at a time, beating constantly until mixture is smooth and satiny. Using two teaspoons, form small balls of choux on a greased baking sheet. Bake at Gas 5, 375F, 190C for 20 minutes. Lower heat to Gas 4, 350F, 180C until crisp. Leave to cool on a wire tray.

Meanwhile, make the sauce. Melt butter in a pan and add flour. Cook 1 minute. Remove from heat then gradually add milk and stock. Return to heat and bring to the boil, stirring until thickened. Season. Cool, then stir in cream.

Cut lids from the top of the choux buns and fill cavity with cold sauce. Tuck a langoustine tail into each one, replace lid and garnish with a watercress leaf.

Preparation time: 20 minutes
Cooking time: 40 minutes

Approximate nutritional values per eclair:	
75 calories	2g protein
6g fat	4g carbohydrate

SEAFOOD RISOTTO

A wonderful combination of shellfish cooked with rice. *Serves 4*

> *4 tbsp oil*
> *1 onion, peeled and finely chopped*
> *2 cloves garlic, peeled and crushed*
> *12oz/350g risotto rice*
> *1³/₄pt/1ltr stock*
> *2 tbsp fresh parsley, finely chopped*
> *Salt and freshly ground black pepper*
> *8oz/225g monkfish fillet, skinned*
> *12oz/350g halibut*
> *8 clams, cleaned*
> *4 whole langoustines*

Heat 2 tbsp oil in a large frying pan or paella pan and gently cook onion and garlic over gentle heat until soft but not brown. Add rice and turn over to coat. Gradually add a little stock and bring to the boil, then turn down to simmer. Sprinkle over chopped parsley and season. Gradually add remaining stock on a gentle heat until all of it is absorbed.

Meanwhile, stir the monkfish around in remaining oil in a hot pan to brown. Reserve. Lightly brown halibut in one piece, then break into chunks, removing the skin and bone. Add monkfish and clams to the rice after about 10 minutes and continue cooking until rice is just firm. Then add halibut and langoustines to the pan and cook until rice is finished, the fish is cooked through and the clams have opened. Discard any clams which remain closed. Serve.

Preparation time: 20 minutes
Cooking time: 45 minutes

Approximate nutritional values per portion:	
524 calories	65g protein
8g fat	29g carbohydrate

TIPS

● To peel fresh langoustines for salads, first pull off the head, then carefully crack the shell from the underside and peel off sideways. Remove the intestinal black thread.

● For an eat-it-with-your-fingers feast, serve a Plat de Fruits de Mer. Heap freshly cooked langoustines, crabs, prawns and raw oysters (or any available shellfish) on a bed of ice on a large platter and serve.

● Transform fish pie into a dinner party luxury. For 4: poach 8oz/225g fresh salmon fillet and 8oz/225g halibut. Discard any skin and bone and break flesh into chunks. Heat 2oz/50g butter in a pan and stir in 2oz/50g flour. Cook 1 minute. Off the heat, gradually stir in 1pt/600ml milk. Bring back to the boil and cook stirring until thickened. Add 2 tbsp white Vermouth, 2 tsp Dijon mustard and 2 tbsp freshly chopped parsley. Stir in prepared fish, 8oz/225g peeled langoustine (scampi) tails, 14oz/400g can drained quartered baby artichoke hearts. Season. Pile into an ovenproof dish and top with smooth mashed potato. Cook at Gas 5, 375F, 190C for about 20 minutes or until cooked through. Sprinkle with freshly grated Parmesan before serving.

● For a delicious first course, try Scampi Provençale. For 4: heat 2 tbsp oil in a pan and gently cook 1 finely chopped onion, ¹/₂ red pepper, chopped, and 2 cloves crushed garlic, until soft. Add 6 tomatoes, peeled and roughly chopped, 1 tbsp tomato purée, 3 tbsp dry white wine, 1 tbsp chopped mixed fresh herbs. Bring to the boil, turn down heat and reduce sauce slightly. Add 1lb/450g prepared langoustine tails and cook through. Season. Transfer to a heatproof serving dish – or 4 individual ones. Top with freshly grated Parmesan and flash under the grill to brown, just before serving.

● Langoustines are a lovely addition to barbecue kebabs. Thread them on to skewers, brushing each one with olive oil, lemon juice and ground black pepper.

LEMON SOLE

Despite their name, lemon soles are not soles – but a close relative. More accurately they are cousins of the flat-fish, dab, plaice, halibut and witch.

All flat-fish begin life swimming around like round fish. Soon, they turn sideways and the eyes, which had been on either side of the head, rearrange themselves on the top.

Lemon soles are usually around 12in/30cm long. They are brown, mottled red-brown, or grey and green. The underside is white. They are plentiful in the English Channel, North Sea and North Atlantic. Choose large soles for juicy thickness of flesh and the best flavour.

These delicious fish with an elegant taste are about a third of the price of dover soles, with a distinct character of their own.

SOLE AND SMOKED SALMON MOUSSES

Light and delicate lemon sole mousses studded with smoked salmon and served with a sunset sauce of pepper and carrot. *Serves 6*

For the mousses:
- *12oz/350g lemon sole fillets, skinned*
- *3 egg whites*
- *1/2pt/300ml double cream*
- *4oz/100g smoked salmon trimmings, chopped*
- *1 tbsp fresh dill, chopped*
- *Salt*
- *1/2 tsp cayenne pepper*
- *1 tbsp lemon juice*

For the sauce:
- *2 tbsp oil*
- *1 onion, peeled and finely chopped*
- *1 red pepper, de-seeded and diced*
- *1 small carrot, peeled and diced*
- *Wine glass dry white wine*
- *1/4pt/150ml vegetable stock*
- *2 tbsp double cream*
- *Smoked salmon roses and dill sprigs for decoration*

Whizz lemon sole fillets in a processor until smooth. Add egg whites and whizz again. Transfer to a bowl and beat in cream. Stir in smoked salmon and dill. Season with salt, cayenne pepper and lemon juice.

Spoon into oiled timbale moulds or ramekins. Cook in a bain-marie half full of boiling water at Gas 4, 350F, 180C for 20 minutes or until mousses are set.

Meanwhile make the sauce. Heat oil in a pan and fry onion, pepper and carrot until softened. Pour over wine and stock and bring to the boil. Simmer covered for 5 minutes, or until vegetables are cooked. Season. Whizz in a processor and stir in cream. Reserve.

Turn out mousses on to individual plates and serve with a puddle of red pepper sauce. Decorate with smoked salmon roses and dill sprigs.

Preparation time: 20 minutes
Cooking time: 20 minutes approx

Approximate nutritional values per portion:	
200 calories	17g protein
23g fat	4g carbohydrate

LITTLE FISH PIES

Sophisticated fish pies with a smooth parsley sauce. *Serves 4*

For the sauce:
- *2oz/50g butter*
- *1 tbsp oil*
- *1 small onion, peeled and finely chopped*
- *2 cloves garlic, peeled and crushed*
- *1oz/25g flour*
- *1/2pt/300ml milk*
- *Salt and freshly ground white pepper*
- *2 tbsp double cream*
- *Squeeze of lemon juice*
- *1 tbsp freshly chopped parsley*
- *4 large fillets of lemon sole, skinned and cut into chunks*
- *12 scallops with corals, sliced*
- *4 tbsp dry white wine*
- *2 hard-boiled eggs, shelled and quartered*
- *1 egg*
- *1lb/450g mashed potato*

First make the sauce. Melt half the butter with oil and fry onion and garlic over gentle heat until softened. Stir in flour and cook for 1 minute. Gradually add milk off the heat. Return to heat and bring to the boil to thicken, stirring. Season. Stir in cream, lemon juice and parsley. Cover with buttered greaseproof paper to prevent skin forming. Reserve.

Melt remaining butter in a frying pan. Add sole and scallops and toss around quickly until just opaque. Sprinkle over white wine. Add fish and cooking juices to the sauce with eggs.

Divide mixture between 4 individual pie dishes. Beat egg into mashed potato. Pipe rosettes around the edge of the pies using a star-shaped nozzle.

Cook in pre-heated oven at Gas 6, 400F, 200C for 15 minutes or until potatoes are golden and filling is heated through.

Preparation time: 35 minutes
Cooking time: 45 minutes

Approximate nutritional values per portion:	
450 calories	35g protein
25g fat	30g carbohydrate

NUTRITION

Lemon sole is low in calories, with only 81 in 4oz/100g. It is extremely low in fat, containing only 1g for the same weight, making this delicate fish an excellent choice for weight-watchers and the health conscious.

High in protein, lemon sole contains 17g per 4oz/100g. This protein is complete because it has all the essential amino acids required by the body for normal growth and development. Lemon sole has no carbohydrates.

A natural source of sodium, lemon sole has 120mg per 4oz/100g. This mineral is an essential part of all body cells and only 1g is required per day to meet the needs of a healthy adult. However, the usual intake is up to 12 times this amount, because salt is added to food during cooking. Excess salt intake has been associated with high blood pressure and its related problems.

Lemon sole contains 43mg of cholesterol in a 4oz/100g portion, about 20mg less than that contained in the same weight of lean beef fillet.

4oz/100g raw lemon sole fillet contain:	
81 calories	17g protein
1g fat	nil carbohydrate

BUYING AND STORING

Lemon soles are available all year round from fishmongers and supermarket fresh fish counters. They are usually sold whole and priced by the 1lb/450g. However, the fishmonger will fillet lemon soles on request and if this is the case, ask him for the bones to use in a homemade fish stock.

Choose lemon sole that are absolutely fresh. Check the eyes to see if they are bright and prod the flesh. It should feel firm and spring back immediately when the finger is lifted. Lemon sole should have an appealing fresh sea smell. Remove fish from the packaging as soon as possible after purchase. Place the fish on a clean platter and cover with film or foil. This prevents drips from the fish contaminating other foods and stops the fishy odour penetrating more delicate items. Store lemon sole in the fridge for up to a day, cooking as soon as possible after buying.

Lemon sole fillets can be bought frozen, and may be cooked without defrosting. But frozen lemon sole on the bone should be defrosted thoroughly beforehand. Never re-freeze any fish.

LEMON SOLE TIPS

● If the fishmonger fillets lemon soles for you, ask him to give you the bones. They are perfect for homemade fish stock. Wash the bones well and chop into pieces. Gently fry chopped onion, white of leek, celery and a little chopped fennel in oil until softened but not browned. Add sole bones with any trimmings and stir around to mix in. Top up with water using about 1½pt/850ml for the bones and trimmings of two large lemon sole. Bring to the boil, skimming. Simmer for 20 minutes then strain. For a more concentrated flavour, return to a clean pan and boil rapidly to reduce by about half.

● To skin a whole lemon sole, first make a small horizontal slit in the skin on one side of the sole, as close to the tail as possible. Cut into it slightly so the skin begins to lift a little. Dip fingertips in salt to get a good grip, then pull away the skin from the tail to the head end. It should come away in one piece. Repeat with other side.

● For a simple and wholesome supper treat, grill whole lemon sole with lime and herbs. Skin the fish and remove heads. Brush with a mixture of chopped fresh herbs, lime zest and juice and sunflower oil and season. Grill under a pre-heated grill for about 6 minutes each side.

● Bake skinned whole lemon sole in a paper parcel with Oriental-style flavourings. To serve 4: lay a lemon sole on each of 4 large oblongs of buttered greaseproof and season with salt and freshly ground white pepper. Sprinkle over spring onion slices, chopped fresh ginger, crushed garlic and diced chilli. Sprinkle each fish with the juice and zest of ½ lime. For an authentic taste add a star-anise, the aniseed flavoured, star-shaped Chinese spice, to each parcel. Fold up paper to enclose fish and secure edges. Bake at Gas 6, 400F, 200C for 20 minutes or until fish is cooked through. Discard the star-anise from each parcel before eating.

● Steam lemon sole fillets over a pan of boiling water to retain flavour, moisture and nutrients.

STUFFED SOLE ROLLS

Lemon sole fillets stuffed with fresh peeled prawns served in a chive and lemon butter sauce.
Serves 4

> 4 large lemon sole fillets, skinned
> Salt and freshly ground white pepper
> 4oz/100g peeled prawns
> Lemon juice
> 6 tbsp fish stock

For the sauce:
> Squeeze of lemon juice
> 6oz/175g butter, chilled and in cubes
> 3 tbsp double cream
> 1 tbsp fresh snipped chives

Cut fillets in half lengthways down the natural line in the centre. Lay 1 fillet, skinned side up, on a board and season. Place a few prawns at the wide end of the fillet and sprinkle with lemon juice. Roll up to the narrow tail end. Repeat to make 8 rolls.

Lay rolls in a shallow pan with fish stock. Cover. Poach gently over medium heat for about 6 minutes or until cooked through. Remove rolls and keep hot while making the sauce.

Add a squeeze of lemon juice to the cooking liquid and place over heat. Whisk in butter gradually, stir in cream and season. Sprinkle over chives.

Arrange rolls on a warm platter and spoon over sauce.
Preparation time: 15 minutes
Cooking time: 15 minutes

Approximate nutritional values per portion:	
495 calories	30g protein
35g fat	trace of carbohydrate

SOLE PURSES

Crackly filo pastry enclosing spiced lemon sole strips flavoured with spring onion and ginger.
Serves 4

> 2 tbsp oil
> 1 clove garlic, peeled and crushed
> 1 tbsp fresh root ginger strips
> 2 spring onions, in strips
> ½ red chilli, de-seeded and sliced
> 2 lemon sole fillets, skinned and in strips
> 1 tbsp soy sauce
> Freshly ground black pepper
> 4 sheets filo pastry
> Melted butter for brushing

Heat oil in a pan and fry garlic, ginger, spring onions and chilli for 1 minute. Add lemon sole strips and toss around quickly. Season with soy sauce and freshly ground black pepper. Cool slightly.

Lay a sheet of filo pastry on a floured worktop and cut in half. Spoon a little mixture into the centre of each half. Gather up and pinch together around the neck to make a money bag shape to enclose filling. Frill out the pastry border above the neck with the fingers. Brush with melted butter. Repeat with remaining filo and filling to make 8 purses.

Bake in a pre-heated oven Gas 6, 400F, 200C for 5-8 minutes or until pastry is crisp, crackly and brown. Decorate with lamb's lettuce.
Preparation time: 30 minutes
Cooking time: 15 minutes

Approximate nutritional values per portion:	
200 calories	18g protein
20g fat	12g carbohydrate

LIVER

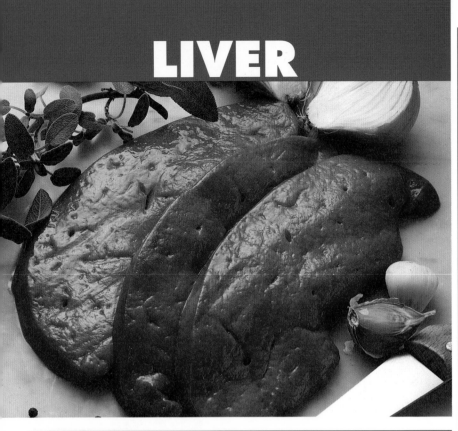

L iver is offal, a word derived from the medieval term 'off falls'. A rather unattractive title, this simply describes the parts of the animal which are left after the carcass has been butchered. This includes head and tail, tongue and cheek, the brain, tripe, feet, heart, sweetbreads, kidneys and, of course, liver.

Folklore claims that some offal caused melancholy or 'ill humours'. And some religions ban it from the diet altogether.

When man hunted with spears and traps he would cut the meat into pieces before carrying it home. The first bits to be eaten were always the liver and heart because these deteriorated quickly.

Wealthy ancient Egyptians included liver in the food parcels packed into their tombs. While in the Middle Ages liver was regarded as food for the poor because it was so cheap. During Tudor times farmers killed off their livestock during the winter months when fodder became scarce. Offal then became extremely popular as a delicacy.

Offal was given away free with prime roasting joints before the days of refrigeration because it did not keep. The famous country dish, humble pie, for example, with its filling of liver and heart was named after the word 'umbles' – or entrails. It was eaten by the servants while employers enjoyed the best cuts of meat.

SPICY LIVER GOULASH

Unusual and economical version of the favourite Hungarian stew. Slivers of lamb's liver in a paprika gravy topped with sour cream. *Serves 4*

1lb/450g lamb's liver, washed
Seasoned flour
4 tbsp oil
1 onion, peeled and finely chopped
2 cloves garlic, peeled and crushed
1½ tbsp mild paprika
2 tbsp tomato purée
1 wine glass red wine
½pt/300ml stock
Salt and freshly ground black pepper
2 tbsp sour cream
Paprika for sprinkling

Pat liver dry and trim to remove tubes. Slice into strips. Dip in seasoned flour.

Heat oil in a pan and fry onion and garlic until softened. Stir in paprika and cook for 1 minute. Add liver and stir to coat in oily mix. Stir-fry to brown. Add tomato purée, wine and stock and bring to the boil. Season with salt and pepper. Simmer until liver is cooked through and sauce is thickened.

Spoon the hot spicy liver mix into a warm dish and top with sour cream. Sprinkle with paprika before serving.

Preparation time: 20 minutes
Cooking time: 20 minutes approx

Approximate nutritional values per portion:	
250 calories	20g protein
20g fat	5g carbohydrate

LIVER SCHNITZELS

Thin slices of calf's liver in a breadcrumb coat. *Serves 4*

4 slices calf's liver
Seasoned flour
1 egg, beaten
6 tbsp fresh white breadcrumbs
Zest of 1 lemon
1oz/25g butter
2 tbsp oil
Salt and freshly ground black pepper
Lemon wedges and parsley sprigs to garnish

Wipe liver and dip in flour. Dust off excess. Dip into egg and drain. Mix crumbs with lemon zest. Coat liver. Fry in butter and oil until cooked but still slightly pink in the centre. Season.

Serve with lemon wedges and green beans, garnished with parsley.

Preparation time: 20 minutes
Cooking time: 5 minutes approx

Approximate nutritional values per portion:	
360 calories	25g protein
15g fat	25g carbohydrate

NUTRITION

Liver is highly regarded for its complete proteins, the most efficient source of vitamin A, and high amounts of iron. It is also one of the few natural sources of vitamin D. It is rich in all the B vitamins, especially B12, the vitamin which prevents or cures anaemia. Vitamin B12 is unique because it is not found in any vegetables.

High amounts of folic acid are found in liver and this vitamin works well with B12 to help cells divide. Some of this is lost during storing and cooking.

Liver also contains vitamin C and E and is high in minerals, calcium, zinc, copper, potassium, magnesium and phosphorus. Iron can be easily absorbed from liver.

Though liver is one of the most nutritious low fat foods around it should not be eaten every day because of the high level of cholesterol and vitamin A. And for this reason, as a precautionary measure, women who are, or may become pregnant are advised not to eat liver or liver products since the high levels of vitamin A may be harmful to unborn babies.

4oz/100g liver contain:	
162 calories	20g protein
8g fat	2g carbohydrate

KNOW YOUR LIVER

Ask your butcher to slice liver thinly from a whole piece, which should be smooth and glossy to denote freshness.

Calf's liver is considered the best but is the most expensive. It has a fine delicate texture and flavour and is a pale milky brown colour. It requires the minimum of cooking and is often preferred cooked just pink in the centre.

Lamb's liver is less expensive but still has a delicious flavour and texture. Any tubes or gristle must be removed before frying, grilling or casseroling. Do not choose liver which is deep brown – this will probably come from an old animal and may be tough.

Pig's liver is strong in flavour. This can be reduced if soaked in milk for a few hours before cooking. Best liver for pâtés or terrines.

Ox liver is the cheapest and is particularly coarse. Again, it may be soaked in milk to soak out the strong flavour. Stew or braise at a low temperature.

FARMHOUSE TERRINE

This moist and flavourful pâté is flavoured with red wine, oregano and fresh sage. Perfect as a first course or light lunch. *Serves 8*

> *16 rashers streaky bacon*
> *8oz/225g pig's liver*
> *4oz/100g pork, minced*
> *½ tsp oregano*
> *Few sage leaves, shredded*
> *2 tbsp oil*
> *1 onion, peeled and chopped*
> *2 cloves garlic, crushed*
> *Salt and freshly ground black pepper*
> *1 glass red wine*
> *Dash brandy*
> *1 sachet aspic jelly crystals*
> *Lemon slices, bay leaves and peppercorns*
> *for decoration*

Stretch 12 rashers with the back of a knife and line a terrine dish, leaving ends overlapping sides of dish. De-rind and chop remaining 4 rashers and reserve. Wash liver, and trim to remove tubes. Whizz in a processor until chopped but not smooth. Place in a bowl with pork, reserved bacon, oregano and sage.

Heat oil in a pan and fry onion and garlic until softened, but not browned. Cool then add to bowl. Mix and add seasoning. Pour in wine and brandy and mix. Spoon into terrine dish and smooth surface. Fold over ends of bacon rashers to enclose filling. Cover with foil and place in a roasting tray half full of boiling water. Bake at Gas 4, 350F, 180C for 1 hour. Remove terrine from roasting tray and place a board on top. Weigh down and leave to cool. Chill the terrine thoroughly.

When terrine is completely cold, turn out. Make up aspic according to instructions and leave until syrupy. Garnish top of terrine with lemon slices, bay leaves and peppercorns. Drizzle over aspic and chill until set. Serve with fresh lemon wedges.

Preparation time: 45 minutes
Cooking time: 1 hour approx

Approximate nutritional values per portion:	
250 calories	35g protein
45g fat	4g carbohydrate

FEGATO ALLA VENEZIANA

Italian treat of wafer-thin slices of calf's liver and golden onion slices scented with fresh sage.
Serves 4

> *1lb/450g calf's liver*
> *2 tbsp oil*
> *2 onions, peeled and thinly sliced*
> *Salt and freshly ground black pepper*
> *Few sage leaves, shredded*
> *2oz/50g butter*

Cut liver into paper-thin slices. Heat oil in a pan and fry onions very slowly with salt and pepper until golden and completely soft but not brown. Turn up heat to high and add liver. Quickly fry for 30 seconds, until sealed but still pink. Season again and add sage. Pile on to a warmed serving plate. Melt butter in frying pan and stir to incorporate cooking juices. Pour over liver and serve.

Preparation time: 20 minutes
Cooking time: 20 minutes

Approximate nutritional values per portion:	
235 calories	20g protein
15g fat	3g carbohydrate

LIVER TIPS

● Always remove liver from the wrapper or the pack and rinse thoroughly in cold water. Pat dry and place on a clean plate. Store covered in the fridge until required. It is best to use liver on the day of purchase.

● For a midweek mixed grill on a stick, thread chunks of liver, rolls of de-rinded bacon, tomato quarters, button mushrooms, onion chunks and cocktail sausages on to metal skewers. Mix 2 tbsp oil, good dash of Worcestershire sauce, 1 tsp English mustard, squeeze of lemon juice, salt and freshly ground black pepper. Brush liberally with mix and grill until cooked through. Serve with rice or baked potato.

● Homemade beefburgers are extra tasty if minced liver is added to the minced beef. Mix 12oz/350g lean minced beef with 4oz/100g minced lamb's liver, 2 tbsp grated onion, and ½ tsp thyme. Season with salt, freshly ground black pepper and a good dash of Tabasco. Form into 4 burger rounds and fry or grill. Serve in buns with lettuce, tomato and onion rings.

● Cook calf's and lamb's liver in a pan over a high heat to seal quickly and retain juiciness. A squeeze of lemon juice during cooking brings out the flavour.

● Ox liver is cheap and nutritious but rather coarse in texture. Best cooked slowly in a casserole for tender results.

● To mellow the flavour of ox or pig's liver, soak in milk for 2 hours before cooking.

● Try a delicious liver, bacon and mushroom pie. Fry 1 thinly sliced onion, 1 crushed clove of garlic and 1 tsp fresh chopped sage in 2 tbsp oil until softened. Add 4 rashers de-rinded chopped bacon and fry for a further 3 minutes, stirring. Add 4oz/100g wiped button mushrooms and cook together for 2 minutes. Remove from pan with a slotted spoon and place in a pie dish. Increase heat and fry strips of 8oz/225g lamb's liver dipped into seasoned flour. Seal on all sides and add to pie dish. Pour ¼pt/150ml beef stock into pan and bring to bubbling point. Add a dash of dry sherry then pour over liver mix. Top with puff pastry and brush with beaten egg. Bake at Gas 6, 400F, 200C for 20 minutes or until pastry is puffed and golden.

● For a quick supper dish, try a liver stir-fry. Cook sliced peppers, leeks and carrots in a little oil in a wok or heavy-based frying pan. Add thin strips of liver and toss around for 2 minutes until stiffened. Season with a dash of sherry, soy sauce, and freshly ground black pepper.

MACKEREL

It is extremely easy to recognise the distinctive silvery green-blue streaks on the flesh of a mackerel. Attractive in appearance, it is no surprise that the name once applied to a sartorial fellow or fop.

There are many species of mackerel in this large family including the European Spanish and the American Spanish mackerel, Cero mackerel, Frigate mackerel and Atlantic mackerel, all of them differing in size, look and taste.

Atlantic mackerel can weigh under 5lb/2.3kg or as much as 100lb/45kg. However, the fish we are familiar with is the common mackerel, found in large shoals in the North Atlantic and Mediterranean. A whole fish usually weighs about 1lb/450g, although this varies. Larger fish will serve two people adequately.

One of the oily fish family, the meaty flesh of mackerel is suited to simple cooking methods like grilling or barbecuing. An acidic fruit sauce such as gooseberry or rhubarb is a good accompaniment.

BUYING AND STORING

A row of glistening mackerel on the fishmonger's slab is a tempting sight. The first impression of these attractive and economical fish is usually a good indication of their freshness.

As with all fish, mackerel are best eaten as soon as possible after purchase. Look for bright, shining eyes and firm, undamaged flesh. When prodded with a finger, the flesh should spring back and leave no indentation. Lift up the gills to see the colour. They will be a healthy, pinky-red tone in extremely fresh mackerel, and may still be slightly bloody.

Unwrap mackerel and wash well before refrigerating.

They will keep slightly longer if they are already gutted by the fishmonger. Rinse the cavities and scrape out any blood still attached to the backbone. Lay them in a shallow dish and cover with foil or film to prevent the smell tainting other foods.

Kept like this, fresh mackerel will last for at least a day. Cover them with ice cubes to extend their keeping time. If stored too long, the natural oils in mackerel may cause a strong flavour.

NUTRITION

Mackerel is classified as an oily fish and as such it makes a valuable contribution to the diet. Extremely economical, it is a good source of protein, providing 19g per 4oz/100g raw fish, the equivalent of the same weight of rump steak, whilst containing fewer calories – 139 per 4oz/100g. There are no carbohydrates in mackerel.

Although there is more fat in mackerel than in white fish, 6g per 4oz/100g, a good proportion of this is polyunsaturated. Its fish oils are also beneficial. They contain Omega-3, which reduces cholesterol levels, prevents blood clotting in the arteries and so ultimately cuts the risk of heart disease.

Oily fish is rich in vitamin A, aiding vision, and a rare, natural source of vitamin D, usually obtained from being out in natural sunlight. This vitamin is essential for bone formation and controlling the body's calcium levels. Oily fish also contains the B complex vitamins, thiamin, riboflavin, niacin and B6. Vitamin B6 is sometimes prescribed to help relieve symptoms of premenstrual tension. Major mineral contributions include potassium, iron and phosphorus.

4oz/100g mackerel contain:	
139 calories	19g protein
6g fat	nil carbohydrate

MACKEREL TIPS

● Fresh mackerel is one of the best value catches around, a really cheap buy. It is an oily fish containing vitamin D, important to the diet. It is wise to eat fresh fish at least once a week and these two points make mackerel a perfect choice.

● Souse mackerel fillets for a simple supper treat. Buy fillets with skin and tails intact. Roll up from head end to tail and place in a shallow dish. Pour over a mixture of equal quantities of water and white wine vinegar, a few pickling spices, lemon slices, and bay leaves. Cover with foil and bake at Gas 5, 375F, 190C for 20 minutes or until cooked through. This dish is good hot, but even better served cold when the flavours have had time to infuse.

● Substitute mackerel for steak in a tasty Mackerel au Poivre. Crush mixed peppercorns and coriander seeds in a pestle and mortar, or use a plastic bag and a rolling pin. Spread on to mackerel fillets and brush with a little oil. Grill until just cooked through.

● Choose mackerel for a great barbecued fish dish. Slash the fish on both sides three times and brush with a mixture of oil, garlic, orange juice and fresh, chopped rosemary. Season with sea salt and freshly ground black pepper. Cook for 5 minutes each side until cooked through. (Or see Tandoori Mackerel recipe on next page.)

● Mackerel is a firm fish which retains its shape well when the fillets are skinned and cut into chunks. Prepare it this way for use in Mediterranean-style fish stews and soups.

● Sharp fruit sauces like rhubarb or gooseberry juice complement mackerel well. Their acidity is a good foil for the oily richness of the flesh. Cook the fruit in a little water with sugar to taste, being careful not to over sweeten. Leave slightly chunky if you like texture or purée in a blender for a smooth sauce. Serve with grilled mackerel.

● Since mackerel is a firm fish, use chunks of skinned fillet on fish kebabs. Alternate chunks with button mushrooms, green pepper chunks and onion pieces. Season, then fry kebabs on both sides.

● All fish lends itself to microwaving, and mackerel is no exception. The goodness and flavour is retained and the fish makes its own juice to pour over when serving. Sprinkle with white wine or lemon juice and seasoning before microwaving.

FAST FRIED MACKEREL WITH OYSTER SAUCE

Speedy Chinese-style supper of mackerel slivers with spring onions and fresh ginger in a rich oyster sauce. *Serves 4*

> 2 tbsp oil
> 2 bunches spring onions, trimmed and cut
>   into lengths
> 1in/2.5cm piece fresh root ginger, cut into strips
> 2 cloves garlic, peeled and crushed
> 2 yellow peppers, de-seeded and cut into strips
> 4 large mackerel fillets, skinned and cut into slivers
> ¼ wine glass dry sherry
> 4 tbsp oyster sauce
> Salt and freshly ground black pepper
> Fresh chives, in 2in/5cm lengths to decorate

Heat oil in a wok or large pan and fry spring onions, ginger, garlic and peppers until softened. Add mackerel and stir-fry quickly to seal.

Pour over sherry and oyster sauce. Gently toss to coat and season with salt and freshly ground black pepper to taste. Pile on to serving plates and decorate with fresh chives.

Preparation time: 10 minutes
Cooking time: 10 minutes approx

Approximate nutritional values per portion:	
380 calories	40g protein
15g fat	7g carbohydrate

MEDITERRANEAN MACKEREL STEW

A robust stew of mackerel and pepper chunks in red wine. *Serves 4*

> 3 tbsp oil
> 1 onion, peeled and sliced
> 2 cloves garlic, peeled and crushed
> 1 red and 1 green pepper, de-seeded and chunked
> 1 wine glass red wine
> 7oz/200g tin chopped tomatoes
> 4 ripe tomatoes, quartered
> 1 tbsp fresh oregano, chopped
> 1 bay leaf
> 4 large mackerel fillets, skinned and
>   cut into chunks
> 8 large green olives
> Salt and freshly ground black pepper

Heat oil in a pan and fry onion and garlic until softened. Add peppers and cook for a further 2 minutes. Pour over wine, add tinned and fresh tomatoes. Stir in herbs. Bring to the boil. Simmer until peppers begin to soften.

Add mackerel and bring back to boil. Cover and simmer for 10 minutes or until fish is cooked through. Stir in olives and salt and pepper. Serve immediately.

Preparation time: 20 minutes
Cooking time: 25 minutes approx

Approximate nutritional values per portion:	
320 calories	23g protein
15g fat	5g carbohydrate

TANDOORI MACKEREL

An Indian-style dish of mackerel baked in a spicy tandoori coat. *Serves 4*

> 4 mackerel, gutted and cleaned
> ½pt/300ml natural yogurt
> 3 tbsp tandoori paste
> Salt
> Juice of ½ lemon
> Salad and lemon twists to serve

Wipe fish and make three slashes on each side. Mix yogurt, tandoori paste, salt and lemon juice in a bowl. Brush one side of mackerel with mixture, rubbing well into slashes. Lay fish in a shallow dish. Pour over remaining mixture to cover. Leave for 2 hours.

Remove the mackerel from the marinade and place in a roasting tray. Bake at Gas 6, 400F, 200C for 20 minutes or until cooked through and slightly charred. Or grill for about 6 minutes each side. Serve with a crisp salad and lemon twists.

Preparation time: 10 minutes plus marinating
Cooking time: 20 minutes approx

Approximate nutritional values per portion:	
450 calories	50g protein
24g fat	5g carbohydrate

MUSTARD MACKEREL

Tasty mackerel fillets grilled with a piquant English mustard and mustard seed butter. *Serves 4*

> ½ tsp mustard seeds
> 2oz/50g unsalted butter, softened
> 2 tsp English mustard
> Squeeze of lemon juice
> 4 mackerel, filleted
> Salt and freshly ground black pepper
> Watercress sprigs to serve

Lightly crush mustard seeds in a pestle and mortar. Mix butter, mustard, mustard seeds and lemon juice very thoroughly in a bowl.

Spread most of butter mix over mackerel fillets. Season with salt and freshly ground black pepper. Grill for 10 minutes or until cooked through, dotting with remaining butter mix during cooking.

Arrange fillets on a pretty plate and decorate with watercress sprigs to serve.

Preparation time: 10 minutes
Cooking time: 10 minutes approx

Approximate nutritional values per portion:	
450 calories	45g protein
30g fat	1g carbohydrate

MINCE

Beef has been eaten for thousands of years. It was first mentioned in the Palace Records of Sumer (Babylon) in the year 2400BC, and beef ribs were found in ancient Egyptian tombs – the meat was believed to feed the dead on their journey to the other world.

Popular in this country for centuries, beef is often identified with the most typical British cookery. Until the 19th century, it was cooked on a spit, but later centuries saw the introduction of oven cooking.

Those who had no cooking facilities could take their meat to the local baker, where it was cooked for them in the bread oven as it cooled down.

Mince is a popular form of beef. It is versatile and not as expensive as other cuts. Depending on which part of the animal has been used, mince can be either lean or fatty. Most butchers will mince any cut of beef if specially asked, but best quality mince is usually taken from whatever lean beef is available. This type of mince costs more but it is better for dishes like meatloaf, meatballs and beefburgers.

Standard mince is cheaper, usually taken from the neck or flank. This contains more connective tissue with fat which melts away on cooking and can be used in stews, casseroles and shepherd's pie.

MEDICI MEATBALLS

Savoury mince meatballs with garlic, oregano and Tabasco, served with a green sauce. *Serves 4*

> 2 tbsp oil
> 1 onion, peeled and finely chopped
> 2 cloves garlic, peeled and crushed
> 1lb/450g lean mince
> 1 tsp dried oregano
> Good dash Worcestershire sauce
> Good dash Tabasco sauce
> Salt and freshly ground black pepper
> Squeeze of lemon juice
> 1 small egg, beaten to bind
> 1/2pt/300ml thick natural yogurt
> 4oz/100g frozen chopped spinach, defrosted
> 1 tbsp pesto sauce

Heat oil in a pan and fry onion and garlic until softened. Remove with a slotted spoon and cool. Mix with mince, oregano, Worcestershire and Tabasco sauces in a bowl. Season with salt, pepper and lemon juice and bind with egg. Form mixture into small balls with hands. Reserve.

For the sauce, blend yogurt, spinach and pesto in a processor. Season to taste.

Fry meatballs in a pan until browned and cooked through. Arrange in a dish and serve with warmed sauce poured over.

Preparation time: 30 minutes
Cooking time: 15 minutes approx

Approximate nutritional values per portion:	
335 calories	22g protein
25g fat	4g carbohydrate

SPICY SAMOSAS

Curried mince wrapped in little triangular crackly filo pastry parcels. *Serves 4*

> 2 tbsp oil
> 1 onion, peeled and finely chopped
> 2 cloves garlic, peeled and crushed
> 1lb/450g lean mince
> 2 tbsp mild curry paste
> 1 tbsp tomato purée
> 1 tbsp fresh parsley, finely chopped
> Salt and freshly ground black pepper
> 2 sheets filo pastry
> Melted butter for brushing
> Sprigs of parsley to decorate

Heat oil in a pan and fry onion and garlic until softened. Add mince and fry to brown. Stir in curry paste, tomato purée and parsley. Season and cool.

Lay 1 sheet of filo on a worktop, long side at the top. Cut down vertically to make 2in/5cm strips.

Take one strip and brush with melted butter.

Place a little filling near the bottom. Fold the left hand corner over to touch the right hand edge of the pastry, making a triangle shape to cover the filling. Fold the bottom right hand corner of the triangle straight up to enclose completely. Next, fold the bottom right hand corner over to touch the left hand side of the pastry strip. Repeat the folding 'flag fashion' until all the strip is used. Seal edges. Brush with melted butter again. Repeat with remaining strips, then repeat with remaining sheet.

Bake parcels at Gas 6, 400F, 200C for 10 minutes until golden and crackly. Cover with foil if pastry becomes too brown during cooking. Serve hot, decorated with parsley sprigs.

Preparation time: 45 minutes
Cooking time: 25 minutes approx

Approximate nutritional values per portion:	
450 calories	18g protein
28g fat	12g carbohydrate

NUTRITION

Best quality lean minced beef has 264 calories per 4oz/100g. Standard mince has slightly more, at 310 for the same weight.

The major vitamin contribution is the B group, especially B12, found only in animal foods. Mince also contains the minerals zinc, potassium, phosphorus, and organic iron.

Beef is one of the best sources of organic iron, which is more beneficial than the inorganic iron found in vegetables. It is always best to accompany a minced beef dish with a food high in vitamin C, to aid absorption.

4oz/100g lean minced beef contain:	
264 calories	18g protein
21g fat	nil carbohydrate

BUYING AND STORING

Mince is available fresh from butchers or you can buy it pre-packed from supermarket cold shelves, though larger supermarkets also have fresh meat counters.

There are two types of mince – 'standard', or the higher quality 'best' or 'lean' mince. Standard mince is a pinky-red colour and contains slightly more fat. Best mince is a dark red, taken from a better cut of beef with less fat and connective tissue. It is more expensive, but worth it.

The more fat in the mince, the less meat will be left after cooking, as the fat melts and drains away. Avoid pale pink mince. This means the proportion of fat to lean is high.

Choose mince which looks and smells fresh and appealing, with no sign of dark brown patches. These are caused by overexposure to the air, and may mean the meat has deteriorated. Check sell-by dates on pre-packaged mince and do not re-freeze any defrosted mince.

Pre-packed mince is usually labelled with the type of 'cut', which can be fine, medium or coarse. Butchers usually have a choice, or will mince it to specification.

Refrigerate fresh mince as soon as possible after purchase or freeze on the same day. Defrost mince before cooking for the most flavour.

SAVOURY MINCE PIE

Warming winter filler of flavourful mince with the unusual addition of anchovy fillets, topped with strips of golden crisp puff pastry. *Serves 4*

2 tbsp oil
1 onion, peeled and finely chopped
2 cloves garlic, peeled and crushed
1½lb/700g lean mince
1 wine glass red wine
1 tbsp tomato purée
¼pt/150ml beef stock
4 anchovy fillets, chopped
2 tbsp lemon juice
Salt and freshly ground black pepper
7oz/200g pack puff pastry
1 egg, beaten

Heat oil in a pan and fry onion and garlic until softened. Remove with a slotted spoon and reserve. Add mince to pan and fry to brown. Return onion mix.

Stir in wine, tomato purée, and stock. Bring to the boil and simmer until mince is tender. Stir in anchovies, lemon juice and seasoning. Cool.

Place mince in individual pie dishes. Roll out pastry on a lightly floured board and cut into ¾in/1.5cm strips. Place on top of pies, attaching edges to rim of pie dish with beaten egg. Chill for 30 minutes. Brush with beaten egg to glaze. Bake at Gas 6, 400F, 200C for 30 minutes or until pastry is risen and golden and the filling is hot. Cover with foil if top becomes too brown during cooking.

Preparation time: 45 minutes
Cooking time: 45 minutes approx

Approximate nutritional values per portion:	
600 calories	30g protein
45g fat	17g carbohydrate

PASTA WITH SPANISH MINCE

This delicious pasta dish is served with mince cooked with garlic, herbs, tomato purée, and sensuous black olive paste for added richness, topped with shavings of Parmesan cheese. *Serves 4*

2 tbsp sunflower oil
1 onion, peeled and finely chopped
2 cloves garlic, peeled and crushed
1lb/450g lean mince
3 tbsp tomato purée
4 tbsp olive oil
1 tbsp black olive paste
Salt and freshly ground black pepper
12oz/350g penne pasta
Shavings of Parmesan for topping

Heat sunflower oil in a pan and fry onion and garlic over low heat until softened but not brown. Remove with a slotted spoon and reserve.

Add mince to pan, turn up heat and cook until well browned. Return onion mix to pan and stir in tomato purée, olive oil, olive paste, salt and freshly ground black pepper. Meanwhile, cook pasta in lightly salted boiling water until just tender. Drain.

Stir mince mixture into pasta and serve immediately in a bowl topped with shavings of Parmesan cheese.

Preparation time: 20 minutes
Cooking time: 20 minutes approx

Approximate nutritional values per portion:	
500 calories	22g protein
30g fat	25g carbohydrate

MINCE TIPS

● Use a non-stick pan to fry mince with no extra oil. This allows the natural fat to 'cook out'. Calorie-counters can then drain it away, before proceeding with the recipe.

● Mince is economical and tasty and children love it – especially as shepherd's pie. Vary the topping by combining vegetables with the potato. Use puréed carrots, broccoli, leeks or tomatoes for added nutrition.

● Make your own special beefburgers with coarse-cut mince, grated onion, garlic and parsley with a little English mustard stirred in. Season well with salt and freshly ground black pepper before moulding into burgers for grilling.

● Mince and pasta were made for each other – keep the basic bolognaise sauce ingredients of tinned tomatoes, dried oregano, onions and garlic in the kitchen cupboard to produce this dish with fresh mince in less than half-an-hour.

● Add a glass of red wine or ¼pt/150ml stout to any casserole containing mince to bring out the beefy flavour and add richness.

● Perfectionists can invest in a mincer to make their own freshly prepared mince. This is especially good for the health-conscious, when leaner cuts of beef can be used and any fat removed.

● Fresh herbs add flavour and eye appeal to mince casseroles or pies. Add some fresh parsley, thyme, or oregano, during cooking, and sprinkle over a little extra to decorate.

● Transform mince into a magical supper, stuffed into green or red peppers. For 4: fry 1 peeled and finely chopped onion and 2 cloves of peeled and crushed garlic in a little oil until softened. Add 1lb/450g mince and stir until brown. Stir in ½ tsp ground cumin, 1 tsp ground coriander, pinch of chilli powder or to taste, 1 tbsp tomato purée, good dash Worcestershire sauce, 2 fresh chopped tomatoes, and ¼pt/150ml beef stock. Bring to the boil and simmer until liquid is reduced and mince is tender. Season. Cut tops from 4 green or red peppers and scoop out seeds. Fill with mince mixture and replace lids. Brush with oil and bake at Gas 6, 400F, 200C for 30 minutes or until peppers are softened. Sprinkle over grated cheese to serve.

● Keep some mince in the freezer for speedy savoury suppers. Buy it fresh in bulk and freeze it the same day, dividing it into individual 6oz/175g portions. Defrost in the microwave or overnight.

● For a spicy treat, rustle up a quick chilli con carne. Fry 1lb/450g best mince with 1 chopped onion, 2 peeled and crushed cloves garlic and one chopped red chilli. Stir in 14oz/400g tin of chopped tomatoes and kidney beans, season and bring to the boil. Simmer until mince is tender. Serve with rice.

MUSHROOMS

Mushrooms have been eaten since ancient times and have long been regarded as 'food for the gods'. Egyptian pharaohs praised them for their magical powers and the Chinese ate them to prolong life and promote good health.

The Romans also loved mushrooms and around the time of the invasion of Britain, the Emperor Claudius ate great quantities of these tasty morsels – they were his favourite food.

Mushroom cultivation is thought to have begun around the early 1600s when the first records were written. At this time, they were believed to be grown from seeds already in the ground. It was only discovered in the last century that the 'seeds' were actually spores from adult opened mushrooms that are so tiny they are invisible to the naked eye.

These days they are cultivated on a large scale. The spores are grown on nutrient jelly in a laboratory, then transplanted into the husks of sterilised rye or millet grains. These impregnated grains are then sold as mushroom spawn. The spawn is mixed with sterilised compost where it soon spreads and the mushrooms begin to grow after about 7-10 days. The crop is usually finished at the end of the sixth week and the whole process starts again.

Mushrooms are versatile vegetables. They can be eaten raw or cooked, on their own or included in recipes where they add flavour and texture to stews, pies and casseroles.

MUSHROOM AND CELERIAC SOUP

Smooth and flavourful soup cooked with white wine and flavoured with mushroom ketchup.
Serves 4

> *2 tbsp oil*
> *1 onion, peeled and finely chopped*
> *¹/₂ celeriac, peeled and finely diced*
> *12oz/350g mushrooms, chopped*
> *1³/₄pt/1ltr vegetable stock*
> *Wine glass dry white wine*
> *4 tbsp double cream*
> *2 tsp mushroom ketchup*
> *Salt and freshly ground black pepper*
> *Sliced mushrooms and dill sprigs to decorate*

Heat oil in a pan and cook onion and celeriac until soft. Stir in mushrooms and cook for 2 more minutes then add stock and wine. Bring to the boil and simmer gently for 10 minutes. Whizz in a processor until smooth.

Return to the pan and stir in cream and mushroom ketchup. Season to taste with salt and freshly ground black pepper. Pour into warmed soup bowls and decorate with fresh mushroom slices and dill.

Preparation time: 15 minutes
Cooking time: 20 minutes approx

Approximate nutritional values per portion:	
175 calories	2g protein
9g fat	4g carbohydrate

SPICED MUSHROOMS

Rich-tasting mushroom salad in a tomato and garlic sauce, spiced with paprika and allspice.
Serves 4

> *2 tbsp sunflower oil*
> *1 onion, peeled and finely chopped*
> *3 cloves garlic, peeled and crushed*
> *14oz/400g tin chopped tomatoes*
> *Wine glass dry white wine*
> *2 tsp whole allspice*
> *2 tsp paprika*
> *12oz/350g mushrooms*
> *6 tbsp olive oil*
> *1 tbsp fresh parsley, finely chopped*
> *Salt and freshly ground black pepper*

Heat oil in a pan and cook onions and garlic over gentle heat until softened. Add tomatoes, wine, allspice and paprika and cook 3 minutes more. Add mushrooms and stir well to coat in the mixture. Cook for 3 minutes. Take off the heat and cool.

Stir in oil, parsley, salt and black pepper to taste. Transfer to a serving dish and chill for at least an hour before serving – but this is best made the day before.

Preparation time: 10 minutes
Cooking time: 15 minutes approx

Approximate nutritional values per portion:	
191 calories	1g protein
28g fat	3g carbohydrate

NUTRITION

Good for dieters, raw mushrooms are low in calories, with only 13 per 4oz/100g. When they are cooked, they absorb any oil or butter they are cooked in and the calories pile up. Light cooking by poaching or grilling – or eating them raw – is best, and also helps maintain nutrients.

Mushrooms contain a small amount of protein, 1.1g per 4oz/100g, a trace of fat and no carbohydrate. Their main vitamin contribution is vitamin B2, or riboflavin. This is required for the breakdown and utilisation of proteins, fats and carbohydrates as well as for the production of energy in oxygen-using cells. Riboflavin leaches out into cooking water, but as it is not destroyed by heat, it can be retrieved by using the cooking water or liquid in an accompanying sauce or gravy.

There is some potassium in mushrooms which is helpful in controlling the body's water balance. It also contributes to the normal functioning of muscles, including the heart.

4oz/100g raw mushrooms contain:	
13 calories	1.1g protein
trace of fat	nil carbohydrate

BUYING AND STORING

Button mushrooms are available loose or pre-weighed and packed in cartons, wrapped with clear film.

Look for firm, plump, white mushrooms with smooth caps and no signs of discoloration, bruising or withering. Mushrooms which are pre-packed should have space in between for air to circulate, otherwise the surfaces may graze and lose moisture, causing them to decay quickly.

Refrigerate mushrooms after purchase until they are required, and eat them as quickly as possible for maximum freshness and taste. Wipe the skins with a damp cloth or rinse quickly in cold water and pat dry before using.

MUSHROOM TIPS

● Include even-sized, raw button mushrooms in a selection of crudités with carrot and courgette sticks, and cauliflower and broccoli florets. Serve with a savoury dip made from cream cheese, soured cream and chives.

● Fry mushrooms brown in butter with crushed garlic and season with a squeeze of lemon juice, salt and plenty of freshly ground black pepper. Sprinkle with parsley and serve as an accompaniment to grilled steak.

● Many garden centres sell a mushroom kit for enthusiasts to grow their own. Simply follow the instructions on the box for a good supply of fresh mushrooms and harvest them as required.

● The great British breakfast is not complete without a serving of mushrooms. To cook them, fry in sunflower oil or if they are large enough, grill them instead. For dieters, poach mushrooms in a little chicken stock to keep the calorie count down.

● Raw, sliced mushrooms make a wonderful first course tossed with peeled prawns in a lime vinaigrette. For 4: slice 12oz/350g wiped button mushrooms and place in a bowl with 8oz/225g peeled prawns. Shake in a screw-top jar: 4 tbsp sunflower oil with juice and zest of ¼ lime, a dash of white wine vinegar and 1 tsp mild mustard. Pour over salad and toss. Leave at least half-an-hour before serving – or overnight, if you want to make this in advance. Sprinkle with chopped dill.

● Add 4oz/100g button mushrooms to any stew or casserole 20 minutes before the end of cooking time for extra texture and taste.

● Never peel mushrooms. The nutrients and taste are in or just under the skin. Wipe them clean with damp kitchen paper and cut a thin slice from the end of the stalk.

● Mushroom pâté and crusty bread is a delicious light lunch for vegetarians and meat-eaters alike. Heat 1 tbsp oil in a pan and fry 2 peeled and finely chopped shallots with 1 peeled and crushed clove garlic until soft. Add 8oz/225g chopped mushrooms and cook for 2 minutes. Cool, then purée in a blender with 4oz/100g cream cheese and a dash of mushroom ketchup. Season with salt, freshly ground black pepper and a squeeze of lemon juice. Stir in 2 tbsp finely chopped parsley. Chill before serving.

STUFFED MUSHROOMS

Perfect button mushrooms with the stalks removed and the hole stuffed with smooth pâté, then dipped in egg and breadcrumbs and deep fried. Serve these with a simple sauce lumière of smooth red peppers, carrots and onion.
Serves 4

> 20 button mushrooms
> 10 coffee spoons smooth pâté
> 1 egg, beaten
> 4 tbsp fresh white breadcrumbs
> Oil for deep frying
> For the sauce:
> 2 tbsp oil
> 1 small red pepper, finely diced
> 1 medium carrot, finely chopped
> 1 tbsp finely chopped onion
> ¼pt/150ml vegetable stock
> Salt and freshly ground black pepper

First make the sauce. Heat oil in pan and fry pepper, carrot and onion over moderate heat until soft. Pour over stock. Bring to the boil, then cover and simmer until vegetables are tender. Whizz in a processor until vegetables are smooth. Season with salt and ground black pepper.

For the mushrooms, carefully remove stalks and fill cavities with half a coffee spoon of pâté. Dip in egg and breadcrumbs. Deep fry until golden. Drain and blot on kitchen paper. Heat sauce through and serve in a separate pot with mushrooms for dipping.

Preparation time: 20 minutes
Cooking time: 25 minutes

Approximate nutritional values per portion:	
175 calories	5g protein
12g fat	20g carbohydrate

MUSHROOM AND CRAB TARTLETS

Delicate and delicious tartlets of white crabmeat and sliced mushrooms cooked in a quiche mixture in a filo pastry case. *Serves 4*

> 4 sheets filo pastry
> Melted butter for brushing
> 3 eggs, beaten
> ¼pt/150ml double cream
> ¼pt/150ml milk
> 4oz/100g fresh white crabmeat
> 8 mushrooms, thinly sliced
> 1 tbsp freshly snipped chives
> Watercress sprigs for decoration

Cut 4 sheets of filo into 4 squares each. Butter 4 loose-bottomed tartlet tins.

To line one tartlet tin, press 4 squares of pastry one by one into the tin with the edges overlapping the sides in handkerchief points. Lay each new pastry layer on top, brushing in between with melted butter, a few degrees round so the tartlet edge has lots of points. Line the rest of the tartlet tins with remaining pastry and butter.

Beat eggs with cream and milk and season. Sprinkle base of tartlets with crabmeat and pour over quiche mix. Top with mushroom slices and chives.

Brush pastry with butter for the last time, then bake at Gas 5, 375F, 190C, for 20 minutes, or until filling is set. Cover with foil if pastry browns quickly. Remove from tartlet tins and serve decorated with watercress sprigs.

Preparation time: 30 minutes
Cooking time: 20 minutes

Approximate nutritional values per portion:	
275 calories	13g protein
14g fat	5g carbohydrate

MUSSELS

Mussels are edible shellfish found in oceans all over the world. There are several species, but the best known is the familiar blue shelled Atlantic or common mussel. The spread of these tasty morsels is thought to have been created when they attached themselves to the underside of ships travelling in waters around Europe.

Common mussels grow wild and plentiful around the coast of Great Britain, but almost all the fresh mussels available are specially cultured.

This is done by planting ropes or stakes around the shore to which the mussels cling with the 'beard' which is removed before cooking. After harvesting at low tide, they are cleaned in special tanks of purified water before being sold.

Mussel farming, or myticulture, has been practised for centuries and produces the prized, meaty specimens. They feature widely in recipes all over Europe, but the French in particular are great mussel lovers.

The famous dish of Moules Marinière – mussels cooked in white wine with garlic and parsley – originated there along with another mussel speciality, Mouclade. Very similar in style to Moules Marinière, the finished sauce is flavoured with the aniseed taste of Pernod or Ricard and thick double cream.

Mussels can also be used on fish kebabs, for pâté, fish soup or eaten cold pickled in vinegar.

MUSSEL AND TUNA PATE

A delicate dish in which the subtle taste of mussels blends well with tuna. *Serves 4*

12oz/350g cooked mussels (after shelling)
7oz/200g tuna in oil, drained
2 tbsp onion, grated
2 tsp mushroom ketchup
Juice of ½ lemon
Salt and freshly ground black pepper
1 tbsp fresh parsley, finely chopped
2oz/50g unsalted butter

Blend cooked mussels and tuna in a food processor until smooth. Add onion. Season with mushroom ketchup, lemon juice, salt and freshly ground black pepper. Stir in parsley and spoon into a pot.

Melt butter over low heat. Skim off the white solids which rise to the top leaving a clear yellow liquid which is clarified butter. Pour over pâté and chill until set.

Serve with crusty bread, or thinly-sliced toast.

Preparation time: 20 minutes
Cooking time: 2 minutes

Approximate nutritional values per portion:	
270 calories	22g protein
19g fat	1g carbohydrate

NUTRITION

A steaming bowl of freshly cooked mussels is the perfect winter supper – quick-cooking, economical and nutritious. And they are low in calories, too, with only 89 in 4oz/100g. This is because they contain no carbohydrate and have a low fat content of 2g per 4oz/100g.

Mussels are a good source of protein, needed for growth and repair of body cells – there is 12g in 4oz/100g of mussel flesh.

Mussels contain a small amount of sodium, or salt – 270mg per 4oz/100g. Some salt is essential for the body each day to maintain water balance and the best way to get it is in fresh produce which provides it naturally. An increased salt intake is believed to be linked with high blood pressure. However, salt levels can be reduced instantly by almost a third, if salt is not added to food during cooking or at the table.

Mussels also contain a little calcium, vital for healthy teeth and bones and traces of vitamin E. They also contain some cholesterol.

4oz/100g mussels contain:	
89 calories	12g protein
2g fat	nil carbohydrate

MUSSELS ROMANESQUE

A robust winter dish of mussels in a rich tomato sauce, with chilli. *Serves 4*

4lb/1.8kg mussels in the shell
3 tbsp oil
1 large onion, peeled and finely chopped
3 garlic cloves, peeled and crushed
1 red chilli, de-seeded and finely chopped
2lb/900g ripe tomatoes, chopped
3 tbsp tomato purée
2 wine glasses white wine
2 tsp paprika
Salt and freshly ground black pepper
2 tbsp fresh parsley, chopped

Prepare mussels (see Tip 2), then make the sauce. Heat oil and fry onion, garlic and chilli until softened. Add tomatoes, purée and wine. Cook until tomatoes are mushy. Add paprika.

Add mussels to the pan and cover with a lid. Turn up heat and cook for about 3 minutes, or until all mussels are opened. (Discard any that stay closed.) Season with salt and freshly ground black pepper.

Sprinkle over chopped parsley and serve in individual bowls with lots of crusty bread for the scrumptious juices.

Preparation time: 20 minutes
Cooking time: 25 minutes

Approximate nutritional values per portion:	
410 calories	30g protein
7g fat	13g carbohydrate

BUYING AND STORING

Fresh mussels are on sale in fishmongers and supermarket fish counters in the winter months. They can be bought in bags of 4¹/₂lb/2kg or 'loose' for those who require a smaller amount. Mussels are sometimes measured by the pint and 1³/₄pt/1ltr of medium sized mussels will give 6oz/175g cooked and shelled flesh – enough for one person.

It is essential that mussels are still alive when bought to ensure absolute freshness. Tightly closed shells indicate this, so if the shells are open and do not close when tapped, don't buy them.

Look for shells that are not damaged or have too many barnacles attached – this is sometimes a sign of age. Feel them too: if they are heavy in relation to their size, you may be buying just a shellful of sand.

As with all seafood, mussels are best cooked and eaten as soon as possible after buying. However, if they are cleaned and left in cold water in the fridge or a very cold place, they may keep for a day. Bags of ready-cooked and frozen mussels are available. These should be thoroughly defrosted before use. Use as for freshly cooked mussels and never refreeze.

MUSSEL TIPS

● Enjoy mussels when they are at their best in the colder months – from September to March.

● Make sure fresh mussels are tightly closed when purchased. This indicates they are alive. Clean them well by scrubbing the shells and removing the 'beards'. If there are any open mussels, tap sharply with the back of a knife and they should close. If they do not, discard them as this means they are dead. Cook cleaned mussels as stated in the recipe, and discard any that do not open after cooking.

● Strain the juice left after cooking fresh mussels to remove any sand that may have been in the shells. Pour through a fine sieve or, alternatively, let it settle for a moment and the sand will sink to the bottom of the pan. Pour off juice leaving sediment behind.

● Serve a large bowl of steamed fresh mussels as a warming winter first course. To serve 4: fry 1 peeled and finely chopped onion in a pan with 1 clove crushed garlic in 2 tbsp oil until softened. Add 4lb/1.8kg scrubbed and de-bearded mussels and stir. Pour over 1 wine glass white wine and ¹/₄pt/150ml fish stock. Cover with a lid and cook until mussels open. Season with freshly ground black pepper and spoon mussels into a large bowl with strained cooking juices poured over.

● Don't forget to give each diner an extra plate to collect empty shells and place fingerbowls of water with lemon slices in the centre of the table for cleaning hands afterwards.

● Garlic-stuffed mussels served on the half shell make great cocktail party nibbles. Steam the cleaned mussels open in a covered colander placed over a pan of boiling water. Remove the top shell from each mussel, taking care to leave the flesh intact in the bottom one. Gently fry 4 cloves crushed garlic in 1oz/25g butter until softened. Stir in 4 tbsp fresh white breadcrumbs, 1 tbsp finely chopped parsley with freshly ground black pepper. Sprinkle a little mixture over each mussel and top with freshly grated Parmesan cheese. Grill to heat through and brown before serving. (Makes enough topping for 30 mussels.)

● Use a clean empty mussel shell to tweeze and remove the meat from hot, freshly cooked mussels for ease of eating.

CREAM OF MUSSEL SOUP

A sophisticated soup with a smooth and velvety texture. *Serves 4*

3lb/1.4kg mussels, checked, scrubbed and de-bearded
1 wine glass dry white wine
3 tbsp oil
1 large onion, peeled and finely chopped
2 garlic cloves, peeled and crushed
1¹/₂pt/850ml fish stock
1 large potato, peeled and cut into chunks
4 tbsp double cream
Salt and freshly ground black pepper
Chives for decoration

Before cooking, check the mussels to make sure they are tightly closed, or do so when tapped. Then place in a pan and pour over wine. Cover with a lid and bring to the boil. Simmer until mussels open. Discard any that remain closed.

Remove opened mussels with a slotted spoon and reserve. Strain and keep the liquid. Discard sediment.

Extract mussel meat from shells and reserve. Discard shells.

Heat oil in a pan and cook onion and garlic over low heat until softened. Add reserved mussel liquid and stock. Bring to the boil and add potato. Simmer gently until potato is tender. Add mussels, reserving 8 for decoration.

Whizz soup in a food processor until smooth. Return to heat and stir in cream and seasoning. Divide between 4 warmed bowls and decorate with reserved mussels and chive batons.

Preparation time: 30 minutes
Cooking time: 35 minutes

Approximate nutritional values per portion:	
350 calories	24g protein
12g fat	13g carbohydrate

ARROZ PUERTO

Delicious and satisfying rice, cooked Spanish style with seafood and chicken. *Serves 4*

---

3 tbsp oil
1 large onion, peeled and finely chopped
2 garlic cloves, peeled and crushed
1 red pepper, de-seeded and finely chopped
10oz/275g Valencia or risotto rice
2 chicken joints, chopped
1pt/600ml chicken or fish stock
Salt and freshly ground black pepper
1lb/450g prepared mussels
8oz/225g cod or hake fillet
8oz/225g whole prawns
1 tbsp parsley, freshly chopped

Heat oil in a large pan and gently fry onion, garlic

and red pepper until softened. Add rice and stir well to coat with the onion mix.

Add chicken to pan. Pour over half stock and season. Cook over medium heat until stock is nearly all absorbed. Add mussels, white fish and prawns to the pan. Continue adding stock, and cook slowly until all of it is used, the rice is tender, and mussels have opened. Add extra stock if necessary. Discard any mussels that remain closed. Sprinkle over parsley before serving.

Preparation time: 25 minutes
Cooking time: 45 minutes approx

Approximate nutritional values per portion:	
480 calories	22g protein
4g fat	64g carbohydrate

MUSTARD

Mustard is made from seeds of plants of the Cruciferae family and there are three types of seeds – white, black and brown.

The name mustard is taken from the Latin, Mustum Ardens which means 'burning must' and probably comes from the time when it used to be mixed with grape must in France. It is often thought that all mustard is hot, when in fact many mustards are mild, herby, or even sweet. English mustard is one of the few mustards that live up to the 'hot' reputation.

Mustard has been made for thousands of years, mainly to flavour plain food. The Ancient Greeks and Romans ground the seeds to make the first mustards and introduced this condiment to Britain. France is another important centre for making mustard, especially Dijon. In 1634, Dijon was awarded the exclusive rights to make France's most famous mustard, and the recipe must always be strictly followed.

Medieval English mustard was a rough paste which was made with ground seeds mixed with water or unfermented grape juice. In the 18th century, a Mrs Clements from Durham prepared the first fine English mustard powder, which was popular with the royal court.

In London, in 1742 at Garlick Hill, the Keen family started a mustard business, hence the term 'keen as mustard'.

During the nineteenth century, the famous Colman mustard industry was founded in Norwich by Jeremiah Colman. This family firm thrives today, and the original mustard shop still exists.

POTATO GRATIN WITH MUSTARD

Layers of potato cooked with cream and mustard.
Serves 4

> *3 large potatoes, peeled and cut into slices*
> *1 clove garlic, peeled and halved*
> *Salt and freshly ground black pepper*
> *¼pt/150ml double cream*
> *2 tbsp wholegrain mustard*
> *1 egg yolk*
> *1oz/25g butter, softened*

Wash potato slices and blanch in lightly salted boiling water for 2 minutes. Drain. Rub garlic around base and sides of an ovenproof gratin dish. Layer potatoes into dish and season in between. Finish with a neat layer of potatoes.

Mix cream with mustard and egg yolk. Season and pour over the potatoes. Dot with butter. Bake at Gas 6, 400F, 200C for 40 minutes or until potatoes are tender and top is golden brown.
Preparation time: 20 minutes
Cooking time: 40 minutes approx

Approximate nutritional values per portion:	
400 calories	10g protein
30g fat	35g carbohydrate

NUTRITION

Mustard seeds are considered to contain many medicinal qualities, and are thought to be an important ingredient in natural cures for a variety of ailments.

In ancient times the flowers were used to make poultices, but today the seeds are used. Mixed with breadcrumbs and vinegar this is an old-fashioned remedy for rheumatism and sciatica. Small doses of the seeds can help as a laxative, but care must be taken. It would be advisable to ask a specialist in natural medicine for any further advice.

Because mustard is used in small quantities, it does not make a sufficient nutritional contribution in a daily diet. However, 1 tsp made mustard contains 9 calories, and minute traces of protein, fat and carbohydrate. Significant minerals are sodium, 20mg, and potassium, 10mg. There are no known vitamins in mustard.

FRAMLINGHAM RABBIT STEW

An old-fashioned country dish. *Serves 4*

> *2 tbsp oil*
> *1 onion, peeled and finely chopped*
> *2 cloves garlic, peeled and crushed*
> *1 rabbit, cut into joints*
> *Seasoned flour*
> *Good dash of dry sherry*
> *¾pt/425ml chicken stock*
> *1 tbsp Dijon mustard*
> *Salt and freshly ground black pepper*
> *2 sprigs fresh thyme*
> *4 ripe tomatoes, quartered*

Heat oil in a pan and fry onion and garlic until softened. Reserve. Wipe rabbit pieces and dip in seasoned flour. Shake off excess, add to pan and brown on all sides. Pour over sherry, return onion mix to pan and add stock and mustard. Season and add thyme. Bring to the boil, cover and simmer for 2 hours. Add tomatoes 10 minutes before end of cooking time.
Preparation time: 20 minutes
Cooking time: 2 hours 10 minutes approx

Approximate nutritional values per portion:	
600 calories	55g protein
28g fat	20g carbohydrate

KNOW YOUR MUSTARD

English mustard is a strong flavoured mustard made from a blend of ground black and white mustard seeds mixed with flour and sometimes a little turmeric. Norfolk is the home of English mustard, with Colmans blending mustard for over 170 years. Old traditional skills are still used to produce one of the world's most famous brands.

Dijon mustard is from the Burgundy region of France and is still made to the original recipe. It must follow this strictly to qualify as 'Dijon' and any mustards that do not follow the recipe exactly are labelled 'Dijon style'. It is a smooth, pale golden colour and medium hot. Perfect for French dressings and ideal for serving with any roast or grilled meats. Also good for adding flavour to sauces.

Moutarde de Meaux is made from Dijon mustard with whole black mustard seeds. Pretty hot too!

French wholegrain mustard – originally, most mustards included the seeds in the mixture, and this style of mustard is still extremely popular. The mustard is flavoured with white wine and speckled with mustard seeds to give a grainy texture to sauces and dressings. Especially good when mixed with cream to serve with steaks or pork.

English wholegrain mustard is hot and pungent and blended with allspice and black pepper.

French mustard is a mild Bordeaux mustard. Smooth and dark brown, it is often offered with English mustard as a choice when ordering steak.

American mustard is famous for complementing burgers, hotdogs, and barbecued meats. Smooth, creamy and mild, with a slight sweetness and spicy tang. Made from the white mustard seed only, blended with wine vinegar, spices and herbs.

German mustard is generally smooth and sweet, and may be dark in colour. Dusseldorf mustard is the spiciest and is great with sausages and sauerkraut.

MOSTAZOS

Wonderful homemade burgers spiked with mustard. *Makes 4*

> *1lb/450g lean minced beef*
> *1 onion, peeled and grated*
> *1 clove garlic, peeled and crushed*
> *1 tbsp finely chopped parsley*
> *2 tsp American mustard*
> *1 egg, beaten*
> *Salt and freshly ground black pepper*
> *4 burger buns*
> *Lettuce, tomato and onion slices*

Place mince in a bowl. Add onion, garlic, parsley and mustard. Mix in egg, season and form into burgers. Place under a pre-heated grill and cook 8 minutes each side or until cooked through. Serve in burger buns filled with lettuce, tomatoes and onions. Serve with extra mustard.
Preparation time: 20 minutes
Cooking time: 15 minutes approx

Approximate nutritional values per portion:	
250 calories	13g protein
10g fat	30g carbohydrate

SHERRY CHEESE RAREBIT

Usually made with beer, this version makes a delicious change. *Serves 4*

> *4 slices bread*
> *8oz/225g mature Cheddar cheese, grated*
> *1 egg, beaten*
> *2 tsp English mustard*
> *4 tbsp double cream*
> *2 tbsp dry sherry*
> *Dash of Worcestershire sauce*
> *Salt and freshly ground black pepper*
> *Watercress to decorate*

Toast bread and remove crusts. Mix cheese, egg, mustard, cream, sherry and Worcestershire sauce until almost smooth. Season and spread over toast. Cut into triangles and grill until golden. Serve with watercress.
Preparation time: 10 minutes
Cooking time: 5 minutes approx

Approximate nutritional values per portion:	
450 calories	20g protein
31g fat	20g carbohydrate

MUSTARD TIPS

● Dijon mustard is perfect for salad dressings with its smooth and peppery taste. It is one of the most famous prepared mustards and follows a strict recipe using ground black mustard seeds, spices, wine or vinegar. Place 1 tsp Dijon mustard in a screw-top jar with 6 tsp sunflower oil, 2 tbsp lemon juice, ½ tsp runny honey, ½ crushed clove of garlic, salt and freshly ground black pepper. Shake jar well to combine and pour over crisp salad ingredients a few minutes before serving.

● Perk up pork chops with a creamy wholegrain mustard sauce. Fry chops in a little oil until browned and cooked through. Remove from the pan and keep hot. Pour in a good dash of dry white wine, and ½pt/300ml pork stock. Bring to the boil and reduce slightly. Stir in 1 tbsp wholegrain mustard and 4 tbsp double cream. Bring to bubbling point and then season. Arrange the chops on a serving platter and pour over sauce. Garnish with tomato halves and watercress.

● Brush the Sunday joint of beef with a little English mustard before roasting in the normal way. Add a little extra to the roasting tray, too, to make a punchy peppery gravy.

● A mustard butter sauce turns grilled mackerel into a gourmet treat. Grill prepared fillets with a little seasoning and a squeeze of lemon juice. Meanwhile, melt 2oz/50g unsalted butter in a pan to 'foamy' stage. Stir in 1 tbsp mustard powder until it turns light brown. Place mackerel on warmed plates and drizzle over mustard butter before serving.

● Spice up a bechamel sauce with mustard of your choice. Stir in at the end of cooking time to make cauliflower cheese, pasta dishes, or vegetable gratins.

● Offer a selection of mustards when serving a cold meat platter. There are plenty to choose from including herb, honey and ginger.

● Mustard is the essential ingredient in the making of homemade mayonnaise. It gives it flavour and helps combine the mixture. Add 1 tsp of made mustard to 1 egg yolk and a little lemon juice in a bowl. Whisk until creamy then whisk in ¼pt/150ml sunflower oil drip by drip until mixture thickens. Add remaining oil in a thin stream, still whisking. Season and add extra lemon juice to taste.

● You can't beat potato salad as part of a buffet lunch, but it is even better if a little wholegrain mustard is added to the mixture. Cook small new potatoes in their skins in lightly salted boiling water. Drain and add immediately to soured cream mixed with mayonnaise and wholegrain mustard. Season and add finely chopped spring onions. Toss to coat potatoes and serve warm.

● Add a little Dijon mustard to pep up the gravy of any casserole just before serving.

NECTARINES

Nectarines, like their furry-skinned cousins peaches, were first grown in China over 3,000 years ago. Their popularity spread and they were known by the ancient Romans.

European travellers first discovered nectarines on a trip to Persia, but they were not seen in Europe until the 16th century.

These summer fruits have always been popular in France and Italy and now they are being enjoyed in Great Britain, too. They have smooth skins with a pinky-red blush, which may sometimes darken to deep red or even purple in parts. The juicy orange flesh has a good flavour, just slightly sharper than that of peaches, though the two are very similar.

Clingstone nectarines have flesh that sticks closely to the stone.

Freestone varieties are a new development in nectarine and peach growing, and these types have stones that are in fact easy to remove.

An excellent choice for fresh summer fruit salads, nectarines can be used in a variety of sweet recipes instead of peaches.

Their rich fruitiness is also a good foil for rich meats like duck or pork, either as part of a stuffing or made into a sauce or chutney.

Nectarines are also good eaten as they are with cheese.

NECTARINE CHEESECAKE

Truly delicious cheesecake with a crunchy biscuit crumb base. *Serves 6*

4oz/100g butter, melted
8oz/225g digestive biscuits, crushed
2 sachets gelatine
6 tbsp boiling water
3 eggs, separated
6oz/150g caster sugar
8oz/225g cream cheese
2 nectarines, peeled, stoned and in small chunks
1/2pt/300ml double cream, whipped
2 nectarines, stoned and thinly sliced for decoration
Lemon juice for sprinkling

Mix butter with biscuits and press into the base of a loose-bottomed 8in/20cm cake tin. Leave in the fridge while making cheesecake.

Dissolve gelatine in water and reserve. Beat yolks with sugar until light and fluffy. Beat in cream cheese and gelatine mix. Add nectarine chunks and fold in cream. Whip the egg whites stiff and carefully fold in with a metal spoon. Pour over biscuit base in cake tin. Return to fridge to set.

Sprinkle the nectarine slices with lemon juice. Arrange slices in a swirly design on top of the cheesecake and refrigerate until required.

Preparation time: 30 minutes
Cooking time: nil

Approximate nutritional values per portion:	
550 calories	44g protein
28g fat	50g carbohydrate

NUTRITION

A nectarine of average size contains around 43 calories. Nectarines have no fat and only a trace of protein. Their largest nutritional contribution to the diet is carbohydrate, with 11g in one nectarine. This carbohydrate is in the form of natural fruit sugars, which the body converts to energy.

A moderate source of fibre, nectarines contain twice as much as their fuzzy-skinned relatives, peaches. Fibre is necessary for a healthy digestive system and can prevent some serious illnesses related to this.

Nectarines have a good supply of yellow carotenoid pigment. The body converts this to vitamin A, required for good sight, especially in the dark.

Some vitamin C is present in nectarines along with a useful amount of potassium. This mineral is an essential part of muscle tissue and works alongside protein to maintain the muscular system.

1 average-size nectarine contains:	
43 calories	trace of protein
nil fat	11g carbohydrate

ICED SOUFFLES

Light mousses with a secret in the middle – tangy nectarine purée! *Serves 4*

3 nectarines
1 sachet gelatine
3 tbsp boiling water
1/2pt/300ml double cream
2 tbsp caster sugar
Juice of 1/2 lemon
3 egg whites
Whipped cream, nectarine slices and mint sprigs for decoration

First prepare the moulds. Make collars from stiff card or double thickness greaseproof to fit around 4 small ramekin dishes but about 1in/2.5cm taller. Tie in place and lightly oil.

Skin, stone and purée nectarines. Reserve. Dissolve gelatine in water and reserve. Whip cream stiff and add 3 tbsp nectarine purée, sugar and lemon juice. Add gelatine. Whip egg whites stiff and fold in with a metal spoon. Half fill each ramekin with mousse mix then add a little nectarine purée. Top with remaining mousse mix to top of collars. Place in the freezer to set.

Remove mousses from freezer about 30 minutes before serving. Carefully peel off collars. Decorate with swirls of whipped cream, sliced nectarines and mint sprigs.

Preparation time: 30 minutes
Cooking time: nil

Approximate nutritional values per portion:	
300 calories	2g protein
24g fat	10g carbohydrate

BUYING AND STORING

Nectarines are summer fruit and available in the shops from early to late season.

Choose nectarines with a yellow-gold background colour and a pinky-red tinge. The skins should be smooth, undamaged and blemish-free and the flesh should feel firm, but not hard.

Avoid buying nectarines which feel extremely soft to the touch, as these are probably over-ripe and may in fact be bruised.

Nectarines have a round shape with a seam running down one side. This is a natural indentation and should give when pressed lightly if the nectarine is ripe.

Store ripe nectarines in the fridge until required. Unripe fruits can be left in a warm place to soften for a few days. Once ready, use up the fruit as quickly as possible to avoid spoilage.

SALADE EMPRESSE

Lovely mix of flavours and textures in this summer salad of prawns with nectarine slices, spring onions, new potatoes and tomatoes. *Serves 4*

> 1lb/450g small new potatoes, scrubbed
> 2 nectarines
> Lemon juice for sprinkling
> 12oz/350g large peeled prawns
> 2 tomatoes, de-seeded and diced
> 6 spring onions, trimmed and sliced
> Chive strips for decoration

For the dressing:
> 1 tbsp lemon juice
> 1/2 tsp Dijon mustard
> 4 tbsp sunflower oil
> Dash of dill vinegar
> Salt and freshly ground black pepper

Cook potatoes in boiling salted water until tender. Drain, cool and halve. Stone and slice nectarines and sprinkle with lemon juice.

Mix the prawns, potatoes, tomatoes, nectarines and spring onions. Shake dressing ingredients in a screw-top jar and pour over. Pile into a pretty dish and decorate with chive strips.

Preparation time: 15 minutes
Cooking time: nil

Approximate nutritional values per portion:	
230 calories	16g protein
6g fat	23g carbohydrate

PORK WITH NECTARINE AND ONION CONFIT

Delightful dinner party main course of delicious tender pork fillet topped with a melting mix of caramelised onions and nectarines. *Serves 4*

> 1 1/2lb/700g pork fillet
> Wine glass dry white wine
> 1/4pt/150ml stock
> 3 tbsp double cream
> Flat parsley for decoration

For the confit:
> 1 onion, peeled and thinly sliced
> 5 tbsp oil
> 2 cloves garlic, peeled and crushed
> 2 nectarines, peeled, stoned and finely chopped
> Salt and freshly ground black pepper

Make the confit first. Thinly slice the onion and cook gently in 2 tbsp oil for about 8 minutes until soft. Add the garlic and the finely chopped nectarines and continue cooking over low heat until all has incorporated into a melting mass.

Season with salt and freshly ground black pepper according to taste. Take off the heat and reserve.

Trim the pork fillet and cut into rounds 1in/2.5cm thick. Heat remaining oil in a pan and fry pork 5 minutes each side until browned and cooked through. Remove and keep warm.

Pour wine and stock into pan and scrape up sediment. Bring to bubbling, then simmer until reduced by a third. Add cream and season. Place noisettes on a serving plate, top with confit and pour sauce around. Decorate with parsley.

Preparation time: 30 minutes
Cooking time: 35 minutes

Approximate nutritional values per portion:	
430 calories	40g protein
22g fat	4g carbohydrate

NECTARINE TIPS

● Nectarines are easy to peel. First, make a small cross in the skin with the point of a sharp knife. Next, pop them into boiling water for 30 seconds, then into cold water to refresh. The skin around the cut should have started to peel back with the heat so simply continue pulling. It will slip off easily.

● Serve whole poached nectarines with ice cream and hot chocolate sauce, as a special weekend pud. Poach 4 nectarines in water to cover, with sugar to taste and 1/2 wine glass white wine or a dash of a favourite tipple. Cook until just tender, then lift out, and remove skin. Meanwhile, melt 3oz/75g plain chocolate in a pan with 2oz/50g caster sugar, 1 level tsp cocoa powder and 1/4pt/150ml water. Stir until smooth. Add another 1/4pt/150ml water and bring to the boil. Simmer for 15 minutes or until sauce is dark and shiny. Serve nectarines in dessert dishes with ice cream scoops, drizzled with hot chocolate sauce.

● Sprinkle nectarines with a little lemon juice after slicing or chopping for decoration, to prevent the delicate flesh from discolouring.

● Nectarines make a good accompaniment to crumbly, delicate flavoured cheeses, like Wensleydale or Lancashire. Serve the cheese with a bowl of fresh, ripe nectarines after a summer dinner party, or as a light lunch with crusty bread. Remember to take the cheese from the fridge an hour before serving it to allow it to come to room temperature.

NOODLES

It is widely believed that the Chinese invented noodles – and that Marco Polo brought them to Italy on his return.

However, documents from the 13th century lodged in the museums of Genoa and Pontedassio make references to 'macceroni' and 'lagana' long before Marco Polo returned. So the controversy remains unsolved.

Noodles can be made of any grain, usually the staple of the region. They are always an important component of any Oriental meal.

Egg noodles, made from wheat flour, are available fresh or dried, sometimes round, looking like unravelled knitting, or flat, like tagliatelle. Egg noodles are quite substantial and are used in fried dishes like the exotic Singapore Noodles, or as a base for meat, fish and vegetable dishes.

Rice noodles look completely different. They are usually sold dried in packets, are fine, translucent and delicate. These are perfect for stirring into thin soups, or with shellfish dishes. And they make a brilliant side dish, deep fried, when they crisp up into delicious fragile heaps of crackly strands, in seconds.

SINGAPORE NOODLES

Chinese noodle dish, packed with prawns, pork, red and green pepper, spring onion and subtle chilli, topped with slices of omelette. *Serves 4*

> 4oz/100g pork fillet
> 4 tbsp oil
> Salt and freshly ground black pepper
> 4 spring onions, trimmed and chopped
> 1 red and 1 green pepper, de-seeded and sliced into matchsticks
> 2 cloves garlic, peeled and crushed
> 1/2in/1cm fresh root ginger, finely chopped
> 1 red chilli, de-seeded and in rings
> 12oz/350g cooked egg noodles
> 4oz/100g peeled prawns
> 2 eggs

First cook the pork fillet for 10 minutes. Heat 1 tbsp oil over high heat, then brown fillet all over and season. Turn down heat and continue cooking over medium heat until cooked through.

Heat remaining oil in a pan and fry spring onions, peppers, garlic, ginger and chilli. Add cooked noodles to pan and turn over to coat in the flavoursome mix. Season with salt and freshly ground black pepper.

Cut the pork into thin shreds and toss through mix with prawns then heat through. Meanwhile beat eggs with seasoning and make a small thin omelette. Remove from the pan and cut into strips. Strew these over the top of the noodles just before serving.

Preparation time: 10 minutes
Cooking time: 25 minutes

Approximate nutritional values per portion:	
440 calories	30g protein
15g fat	65g carbohydrate

EGG AND BACON NOODLES

Fabulous fast supper dish made from ingredients you are bound to have in the cupboard. *Serves 4*

> 4 rashers back bacon, de-rinded and chopped
> 4 tomatoes
> 10oz/275g dried egg noodles
> 1oz/25g butter
> 4 eggs
> Salt and freshly ground black pepper

Fry bacon until crisp and reserve. Drop tomatoes into boiling water, skin and dice (this takes literally a couple of minutes and is really worth it).

Cook noodles in boiling salted water for 4 minutes. Drain and add butter.

Beat eggs with salt and freshly ground black pepper. Immediately stir eggs through the noodles while they are still hot so that they scramble on to the strands. Scatter in bacon and turn over, then dot with tomato dice.

Preparation time: 5 minutes
Cooking time: 10 minutes

Approximate nutritional values per portion:	
445 calories	25g protein
17g fat	65g carbohydrate

NUTRITION

Egg noodles contain 354 calories per 4oz/100g uncooked portion. This amount when cooked, though, is a generous portion for one person or enough for a lunch snack for two, with accompaniments.

There are almost 67g of carbohydrate in 4oz/100g egg noodles, in the form of starch, which the body converts to energy. In poor countries, carbohydrates provide almost 90 per cent of the daily total calorie intake. But in richer parts of the world, where the diet is more varied, carbohydrates make up only around 40 per cent. The remainder

comes from protein and fat in the form of meat, fish and dairy products.

Egg noodles have 15g protein in a 4oz/100g uncooked portion. Protein is necessary for normal growth and development and for maintenance and repair. There is some fat in egg noodles, because of the egg content, but it is still fairly low with 3g in 4oz/100g uncooked weight.

4oz/100g uncooked egg noodles contain:	
354 calories	15g protein
3g fat	67g carbohydrate

BUYING AND STORING

There are several types of noodle available, all suitable for different styles of cooking. Egg noodles are good in stir-fried dishes and for pasta sauces, whilst the Chinese rice noodles are suited to soups and crispy noodle recipes.

Egg noodles are available both fresh and dried from good supermarkets. Dried rice noodles are also available from supermarkets, packed in cellophane in neat little nests. However, these can sometimes be bought fresh in specialist Oriental shops.

Always store dried noodles in an airtight jar or tin after opening the packet.

Fresh noodles are bought loose by weight, or pre-packed, ready weighed.

Always buy fresh noodles on the day you want to use them and keep in the fridge. Cook as soon as possible after purchase.

Fresh noodles freeze well and can be cooked straight from frozen.

CHICKEN NOODLE SOUP

Light, extremely tasty soup made substantial by rice noodles and slivers of chicken, for which you *must* make your own stock. *Serves 4*

2 chicken leg quarters
6 chicken wings (not breasts)
1 large carrot, chopped
2 sticks celery, leaves on, chopped
½ large onion, chopped, skin on
1 large leek, cleaned and chopped
3 sprigs parsley
2 wine glasses dry white wine
Salt and freshly ground black pepper
1 heaped tbsp freshly chopped parsley
Juice of ½ lemon
2oz/50g rice noodles

Put chicken leg quarters and wings in a large pan. Add carrot, celery, onion, leek and parsley sprigs. Cover with water. Bring to the boil, then simmer for 45 minutes.

At this point retrieve a leg joint and remove thigh meat. Reserve. Put remainder of leg joint into the pan and continue simmering for another hour or so, topping level up. Strain and discard vegetables and chicken debris. Leave to cool. The fat will form an easy to remove transparent 'skin' on top. Discard it.

Add wine to the pan and bring back to the boil. Turn down to simmer, until reduced by half – about 1¾pt/1ltr should be left. Season to taste, then sprinkle in chopped parsley and a squeeze of lemon juice. Add rice noodles and simmer for about 4 minutes. Shred reserved chicken thigh meat and put this in as well. Continue simmering until heated through. Serve in soup bowls.

Preparation time: 20 minutes
Cooking time: 2 hours (including stock which could be made in advance and frozen)

Approximate nutritional values per portion:	
120 calories	4g protein
1g fat	14g carbohydrate

BEEF WITH CRISPY NOODLES

This spicy beef dish is served with noodles cooked straight from the pack. *Serves 4*

2 tbsp oil
4 large spring onions, green on, chopped into 1in/2.5cm lengths
1 red pepper, de-seeded and in chunks
2 cloves garlic, crushed
1 red chilli, de-seeded and chopped
6oz/175g fillet steak in thin slivers
2 tbsp dry sherry
1 tbsp soy sauce
Salt and freshly ground black pepper
Oil for frying
2oz/50g rice noodles

Heat oil in pan and fry spring onions, pepper, garlic and chilli over gentle heat until softened. Remove with slotted spoon and reserve. Heat pan until really hot. Add beef and toss around over high heat to brown. Return vegetables. Add sherry and soy sauce and cook 2 minutes more. Season.

Heat remaining oil in a deep pan and drop dry noodles in. They will wriggle into crispness in seconds. Remove with a slotted spoon, drain on kitchen paper. Add to beef and serve.

Preparation time: 15 minutes
Cooking time: 15 minutes

Approximate nutritional values per portion:	
175 calories	18g protein
5g fat	16g carbohydrate

NOODLE TIPS

● Toss freshly cooked egg noodles in melted butter and season. Stir through finely snipped chives and serve as an accompaniment to chicken casserole, sliced duck breasts in red wine sauce or beef stew.

● This pretty presentation for egg noodles makes it easier for diners to help themselves at a supper party. For 4: cook 12oz/350g egg noodles in lightly salted boiling water until just al dente. Drain and toss through a knob of butter and season. Divide into 4 equal piles. Insert the prongs of a carving fork into the centre of a pile of noodles then twist them clockwise, just like twisting spaghetti around a table fork, so the noodles spread along the length of the prongs. Do this with each pile of noodles, laying each twirl side by side on a warmed serving dish. Top with fresh, finely chopped parsley.

● Stir-fried rice noodles with vegetables make a good vegetarian supper dish or can be served as part of a Chinese menu. For 4: soak 8oz/225g rice noodles in warm water for about 20 minutes. Drain and leave in cold water while preparing the vegetables. Soak 1oz/25g dried mushrooms in enough water to cover. De-seed 1 red and 1 green pepper and cut into matchstick strips. Thinly slice 1 onion, crush 2 cloves peeled garlic and thinly slice a de-seeded red chilli. Drain noodles well. Drain mushrooms, reserving liquid. Heat 2 tbsp oil in a large pan or wok. Fry onion, garlic and chilli until softened then add pepper strips and cook for 2 more minutes. Add noodles and mushrooms and stir-fry quickly over high heat for 2 minutes. Stir through 3 tbsp mushroom soaking liquid, 1 tbsp mushroom ketchup and a dash of dry sherry. Season with salt and freshly ground black pepper and serve immediately.

OATS

Oats are one of the oldest cereals known to man. Originating in the Middle East, they have been cultivated in Western Europe since the Iron Age.

Oats were grown for food by cave-dwellers in Switzerland before 1000BC. And the Romans and Greeks used this versatile cereal as well. In fact it was probably the Ancient Greeks who first made porridge from oats.

Oats have been a popular crop in Britain since before the 13th century, when oat cakes and cheese were a staple part of the diet of country folk. By this time oats had become well established in Scotland where the soil and climate provide the best growing conditions.

In the 18th and 19th centuries the successful Scottish varieties were developed and refined. One of the easiest and hardiest cereals to grow, it is also one of the most nutritious, satisfying and sustaining.

CHICKEN AND SMOKED HADDOCK CRUMBLE

A superb mixture of tastes, this supper dish has chunks of chicken breast with flaked smoked haddock. *Serves 4*

> *8oz/225g undyed smoked haddock fillet*
> *1/2pt/300ml chicken stock*
> *2 tbsp oil*
> *1 onion, peeled and finely chopped*
> *3 large chicken breast fillets, skinned and in chunks*
> *Seasoned flour*
> *4 tbsp double cream*
> *Salt and freshly ground black pepper*
> *1 tbsp fresh snipped chives*
> For the topping:
> *1oz/25g butter*
> *1oz/25g flour*
> *2oz/50g oats*
> *1oz/25g grated cheese*

Place fish in a large shallow pan and pour over stock. Cover and poach gently for 5 minutes. Remove and reserve liquid. Skin and break fish into chunks, removing any bones.

Heat oil in a pan and fry onion over low heat until soft. Dip chicken in seasoned flour and add to the pan. Toss around in the pan until stiffened and lightly coloured. Pour over reserved cooking liquid and bring to the boil. Simmer covered until chicken is cooked through. Mix in fish and add cream.

Season and add chives. Transfer mix to an ovenproof pie dish.

For the topping, rub butter into flour to breadcrumb stage. Add oats and cheese and season. Cover chicken and fish with this mixture in an even layer. Bake at Gas 5, 375F, 190C until topping is golden.

Preparation time: 15 minutes
Cooking time: 40 minutes

NUTRITION

Oats have been eaten in Britain for hundreds of years. They are most popular in the form of porridge, and this traditional breakfast of oats and hot milk provides a warming and satisfying start to the day. The health-conscious will appreciate its benefits too – made with water, porridge contains only 115 calories per serving – although it is just as filling and delicious.

Oats contain 452 calories per 4oz/100g with 12g protein and 2g of fat. They are high in carbohydrate – almost 85g per 4oz/100g – and provide a rich source of dietary fibre.

Dietary fibre is important for body functions. It maintains healthy bowels, combats constipation, and in some cases, helps prevent bowel cancer. The fibre in oats is soluble and known to lower the amount of cholesterol in the blood if oats are eaten regularly as part of a healthy diet.

Excess cholesterol causes arteries to become furred with a fatty deposit, slowing the blood flow and forcing the heart to work harder to pump it around the body. This means an increased chance of heart disease or other related illnesses. The type of soluble fibre in oats is known to slow down absorption of certain substances, including cholesterol, into the blood, so that levels are reduced.

Oats contain some B vitamins which help maintain the nervous system, and traces of iron for healthy blood. They also provide a natural source of salt in the form of sodium, which is an essential part of all body cells.

4oz/100g oats contain:	
452 calories	12g protein
2g fat	85g carbohydrate

Approximate nutritional values per portion:	
480 calories	40g protein
24g fat	18g carbohydrate

TRADITIONAL COUNTRY PORRIDGE

An old-fashioned, warming way to start the day – with a little extra something! Serve the porridge topped with a spoonful of thick natural yogurt and a drizzle of honey. Substitute skimmed milk or water for a lower calorie count. *Serves 2*

> 1pt/600ml milk
> 1 cinnamon stick
> Good fresh grating nutmeg
> 3oz/75g porridge oats
> 2 tsp thick natural yogurt
> 2 tsp runny honey

Bring milk almost to the boil with cinnamon stick and nutmeg. Leave to infuse for 10 minutes then discard cinnamon stick.

Stir oats into milk and return to heat. Bring to the boil, stirring. Simmer for about 5 minutes, stirring occasionally. Spoon into bowls and top with yogurt and honey. Grate over a little extra nutmeg to serve. Porridge can also be made in the microwave. Follow the instructions on the packet.

Preparation time: 10 minutes
Cooking time: 5 minutes approx

Approximate nutritional values per portion:	
350 calories	14g protein
13g fat	50g carbohydrate

HERRING IN OATS

A simple and economical dish of herrings fried with an oat coating. *Serves 4*

> 4 herrings, gutted, washed and heads removed
> Salt and freshly ground black pepper
> 2 juicy limes, halved
> 2oz/50g butter
> 4oz/100g oats
> 4 tbsp oil
> Lime twists for decoration

First fillet the herrings. They will be slit on the underside where the fishmonger has gutted them, but make sure the slit goes all the way down to the tail without cutting through it.

Place one herring, belly side down, on a chopping board with flaps opened out like a book. With the palm of the hand, press all the way down the back bone to flatten herring and open out completely. Turn over herring to flesh side up. Carefully peel out the back bone. The smaller bones should come with it. Season and squeeze over juice of half a lime. Repeat with remaining herrings. Fold herrings back to original shape.

Melt half the butter and brush over herrings on the skin side. Cover with oats, pressing well to coat. Heat remaining butter in a pan with oil and fry herrings for about 5 minutes each side, or until cooked through. Decorate with lime twists.

Preparation time: 20 minutes
Cooking time: 10 minutes approx

Approximate nutritional values per portion:	
495 calories	27g protein
32g fat	21g carbohydrate

BUYING AND STORING

Oats are widely available in packs, usually as 'porridge oats', although they may be bought loose from health food shops. Some pre-packed brands may be labelled 'original' or 'old-fashioned': the latter contains oats that are slightly thicker and coarser textured.

Oats should have a creamy appearance with a golden brown tinge. Pick out any darker coloured oats – they have been burnt in the milling process and will taste bitter. Regular in shape, fresh oats should be firm and will not disintegrate into flour when rubbed between thumb and forefinger. This may sometimes happen as a result of lengthy storage. Smell them too – they will have a nutty aroma and taste slightly sweet.

Oats have a relatively long shelf life and should last well if stored correctly. Once the pack is open, place the contents in an airtight jar and keep in a cool, dry cupboard.

OATJACKS

Not just kids' favourites – grown-ups find these biscuits irresistible, too. *Makes 18*

> 8oz/225g oats
> 8oz/225g melted butter
> 8oz/225g soft dark brown sugar

Place all ingredients in a bowl and mix well with a fork. Press evenly into a buttered swiss roll tin, smoothing the surface. Bake at Gas 4, 350F, 180C for 30 minutes, or until brown. Remove from the oven and mark into lozenge or finger shapes with the point of a sharp knife. Cool completely in the tin. Finally, break along the marked lines.

Preparation time: 10 minutes
Cooking time: 30 minutes

Approximate nutritional values per oatjack:	
180 calories	1.5g protein
10g fat	18g carbohydrate

OAT TIPS

● Toasted oats have a 'roasted nut' aroma and taste. To toast them, spread oats evenly over a baking sheet and place under a hot grill for 3 minutes, turning, until golden.

● Add toasted oats to the topping mix of a fruit crumble for extra flavour and crunch.

● Make a light 'oatcrust' pastry topping for sweet or savoury pies. Place 4oz/100g wholemeal self-raising flour in a bowl with 3oz/75g oats and a pinch of salt. Rub in 3oz/75g butter. Separate 1 egg and add the white to the mix with enough cold water to make a firm but pliable dough. Chill for 30 minutes. Roll out thinly on a floured board and use to top pies. Glaze with the remaining beaten egg yolk before baking.

● Tempt them at tea-time with rich Scottish oaty shortbread. To make 2 x 8in/20cm rounds: sift 5oz/150g plain flour into a bowl. Stir in 5oz/150g oats and 2oz/50g brown sugar. Rub in 4oz/100g butter and add enough milk to form a firm dough. Knead well and halve the dough. Roll out to 2 x 8in/20cm circles, and crimp edges to give a pretty

finish. Prick with a fork and place on greased baking sheets. Mark 8 triangles with a sharp knife and bake at Gas 4, 350F, 180C for 20 minutes or until golden. Sprinkle with sugar and cool before breaking into triangles to serve.

● Give a wholemeal loaf made from ready-mixed bread dough the homemade touch by sprinkling with oats before baking. No-one will ever guess it is not your own handiwork!

● Start the day with a bowl of muesli made from chopped hazelnuts, snipped dried apricots, little chunks of fresh apple and oats. Top with thick Greek yogurt.

● Top a midweek shepherd's pie with oats and cheese and grill to brown before serving.

● Oats come in different grades, and some are slightly thicker and larger than others. Experiment with the various styles until you find one that suits.

● Make a healthy, filling, low-fat version of porridge using water, instead of milk. The result is delicious and creamy-textured, economical and the calorie-counter's friend, too.

OLIVE OIL

The olive tree is a native of the eastern Mediterranean. They were first cultivated there 6,000 years ago. Fossilised wild olive remains have also been found from prehistoric days.

One of the oldest, most natural and healthy foods in the world, olive oil's use in cooking dates back to Ancient Egyptian times. It has been respected for its nutritive and medicinal properties, and has even been worshipped. References to olive trees are made in the Bible.

Today, olive oil is an important part of healthy eating worldwide, and in the Mediterranean countries over two million people are involved in its production.

The cultivation of olives and olive oil production is a year-round process. There are many varieties of olive trees, and the type grown depends on the climate, soil, and whether they are to be eaten or pressed for oil. Some olive trees live up to 600 years, and can grow to a height of 50ft/16m.

All olives start off green. Fully ripe olives are black, while there are intermediate shades in between which range from green to violet, then red and finally black.

Black olives are richest in oil. But for pressing, some of the best quality oil sometimes comes from olives which are not completely ripe.

Olives are usually hand-picked, although mechanical shakers have been developed and some are in use.

The olive harvest is taken to an oil mill where the fruit is sorted, washed and stored for up to three days to generate heat. This allows the moisture content to evaporate which releases the oil more easily.

Olives are crushed to a paste, complete with stones, then mixed to a uniform pulp. The pulp is then pressed to extract the oil which is then graded as Extra Virgin, or Virgin. Oils which do not match up to these qualifications are refined to remove impurities, blended with Virgin olive oils and sold labelled as 'olive oil'.

WILD MUSHROOM AND PRAWN SALAD

The best dinner party starter ever. This simple recipe is quick, easy and a real reputation-maker. *Serves 4*

    12oz/350g oyster mushrooms
    8oz/225g peeled fresh prawns
    8 quail's eggs, hard boiled
    8 spring onions, trimmed and chopped
For the dressing:
    4 tbsp olive oil
    1 tbsp white wine vinegar
    1 tsp mild French mustard
    Salt and freshly ground black pepper
    1 tbsp fresh chives, chopped

Tear mushrooms into strips and place in a large bowl. Add prawns, eggs and spring onions.

Shake dressing ingredients together in a screw-top jar and pour over salad 30 minutes before serving. Toss gently.

Serve in a bowl, or on individual plates sprinkled with chopped chives.

Preparation time: 15 minutes
Cooking time: nil

Approximate nutritional values per portion:	
130 calories	13g protein
10g fat	trace of carbohydrate

MINT RATATOUILLE

Fragrant version of this popular Mediterranean vegetable stew cooked slowly in olive oil. *Serves 4*

    6 tbsp olive oil
    1 large onion, peeled and finely chopped
    2 cloves garlic, peeled and crushed
    1 aubergine, diced
    1/2 red, 1/2 green and 1/2 yellow pepper, de-seeded
        and in squares
    2 courgettes, in chunks
    14oz/400g can chopped tomatoes
    8oz/225g ripe tomatoes, quartered
    2 sprigs fresh thyme, chopped
    Salt and freshly ground black pepper
    Few mint leaves, shredded
    Mint sprig for decoration

Heat oil in a pan and fry onions, garlic and aubergine over slow heat until soft. Stir in peppers and courgettes and cook for a further 2 minutes. Add canned and fresh tomatoes and thyme. Bring to the boil, stirring. Cover and simmer until vegetables are tender. Season and stir in mint. Decorate with mint sprig. Serve hot or cold as a side dish or as a light lunch.

Preparation time: 20 minutes
Cooking time: 30 minutes

Approximate nutritional values per portion:	
115 calories	2g protein
10g fat	12g carbohydrate

NUTRITION

One of nature's most healthy products, olive oil has a pure, fresh taste. It enhances many recipes, from salad dressings to stews and casseroles.

Olive oil contains oleic acid which is a mono-unsaturated fat. This type of fat has been shown in recent research to reduce cholesterol in the blood. In fact, in Mediterranean countries, where olive oil is used in abundance, the incidence of coronary heart disease and other cholesterol-related illness is relatively low.

Traces of vitamin E are found in olive oil. This vitamin is necessary for healthy skin and is thought to be of use in the treatment of sterility and other sexual disorders.

1 tbsp olive oil contains:	
44 calories	nil protein
5g fat	nil carbohydrate

KNOW YOUR OLIVE OIL

The country of origin, variety and ripeness, degree of pressing and purification all give character and flavour to olive oil. Here is a guideline to the different types:

Extra virgin olive oil is the best quality, and has not been purified. It meets the high standards required for aroma, colour and flavour. Usually, extra virgin oil has a clear distinct green hue and a full olive character.

This premium oil comes from the first pressing, giving a natural taste. Contains no more than 1 per cent acidity.

Virgin olive oil is made in the same way as extra virgin olive oil. This oil is slightly more piquant in taste, but contains no more than 2 per cent acidity. Over 2 per cent acidity it cannot be called extra virgin or virgin olive oil.

Olive oil is a blend of refined olive oils with extra virgin oil, making a quality oil suitable for all culinary purposes. 'Olive oil' or 'pure olive oil' is inexpensive and widely available.

OLIVE OIL TIPS

● Serve a tomato and onion salad with separate bottles of olive oil and wine vinegar so diners can sprinkle their own to personal taste – in true Mediterranean style.

● Olive oil comes in different tastes and colours ranging from full flavoured green extra virgin oil to oil which is pale yellow, light and fruity. Experiment with the different types to find one that suits you best.

● Brush cod fillets with olive oil, sprinkle with lemon juice and zest, and season with salt and freshly ground black pepper. Grill until cooked through then scatter over finely chopped parsley just before serving with extra lemon wedges.

● Marinate juicy green or black olives in a mixture of olive oil, white wine vinegar, garlic, oregano and thyme for 30 minutes. Serve as a nibble with aperitifs.

● Make a rich garlic olive oil to serve in salad dressings and for cooked meat or fish. Pour 1pt/600ml light olive oil into a clean bottle with a stopper. Add 2 cloves peeled and bruised garlic and 2 sprigs of fresh rosemary. Leave for a week in a cool place. Strain, discard flavourings and return oil to cleaned bottle with fresh garlic and rosemary. The oil is then ready to use.

● Serve a delicious onion marmalade, slowly cooked in olive oil, for an unusual accompaniment to grilled chops or sausages. Peel and slice 2lb/900g onions thinly. Heat 8 tbsp olive oil in a pan and add onions with salt and freshly ground black pepper. Fry gently for 2 minutes to soften then sprinkle over 2oz/50g brown sugar. Cover and cook for about 20 minutes, stirring occasionally. Add 6 tbsp cider vinegar, cover and continue cooking for a further 20 minutes or until the mixture has a jam-like consistency. Check seasoning and cool slightly before serving.

● Toss cooked hot new potatoes in olive oil with chopped rosemary, salt and freshly ground black pepper, for a tasty vegetable treat.

OLIVE BREAD

Sensuously tasty bread flavoured with a spiral of black olive paste. *Makes 2 loaves*

> 1¹/₂lb/700g strong plain white flour
> Pinch of salt
> 1 sachet easy mix dried yeast
> 4 tbsp olive oil
> 1 tsp sugar
> ³/₄pt/425ml tepid water
> 8 tbsp black olive paste
> 1 egg, beaten to glaze

Sift flour and salt in a large bowl. Add yeast with olive oil and sugar. Stir well. Make a well in the centre of flour and add enough water to mix to a soft, but not sticky dough. Knead on a lightly-floured board until smooth. Leave in a warm place until doubled in bulk.

Knead dough again and halve. Roll one half to a 10in/25cm square. Spread with half olive paste. Roll up, swiss-roll fashion. Repeat with remaining dough and olive paste.

Place on a baking sheet and brush liberally with beaten egg. Bake at Gas 6, 400F, 200C for 25 minutes, or until loaves sound 'hollow' when tapped.

Preparation time: 1 hour
Cooking time: 25 minutes approx

Approximate nutritional values per portion:	
220 calories	7g protein
3g fat	48g carbohydrate

CROWN ROAST WITH OLIVE MASH

Super-sophisticated roast of tender lamb stuffed with delectable mashed potato with olive oil and chopped anchovy stuffed olives. *Serves 4*

> 1 crown roast of lamb
> Olive oil for brushing
> Salt and freshly ground black pepper
> For the mash:
> 1¹/₂lb/700g peeled potatoes, in chunks
> 3 tbsp olive oil
> Freshly ground black pepper
> 3 tbsp anchovy stuffed green olives
> Extra green olives and watercress sprigs
>   for decoration

Brush lamb with olive oil and season with salt and ground black pepper.

Roast on a trivet in a roasting tray at Gas 6, 400F, 200C for 30 minutes, or to taste.

Meanwhile, boil potatoes in salted water until tender. Drain, then mash with olive oil, and lots of freshly ground black pepper. Add chopped stuffed olives and check seasoning.

Place lamb on a serving platter and pile olive mash in the centre. Decorate each bone with an olive and serve surrounded with watercress sprigs.

Preparation time: 15 minutes
Cooking time: 30 minutes approx

Approximate nutritional values per portion:	
410 calories	11g protein
22g fat	36g carbohydrate

ORANGES

The name orange is around 3,000 years old and means 'perfume within'. The wild bitter orange grew in the warm climate of the Caribbean on the island of Curaçao.

It was Edouard Cointreau's son, also named Edouard, who discovered this unique citrus fruit there while on a sales trip for his father during the 19th century.

However, the Chinese were cultivating oranges 500 years before the birth of Christ, and Confucius wrote about the provinces where they were found. Up until the 9th century, only bitter oranges were grown, which may have contributed to a general dislike of what was then a new fruit. It took four centuries before the sweet strain was developed and, from that time on, they were sought after as a much-prized delicacy. In fact it was an ostentatious sign of wealth to serve oranges at meals – or to use them in cooking.

Louis XIV of France was a great lover of oranges. He built a spectacular orangery at Versailles – which was a great attraction to visitors from the rich gentry and royalty all over the world. He loved the distinctive, heady scent of the blossom which pervaded his garden, so much, in fact, that the peel of the fruit was used in potions, perfumes and pot pourri in the palace.

The first sweet orange tree from China arrived in Spain around 1630 and gradually, and not surprisingly, became more popular than the bitter Seville. But these are still grown in Spain, mainly for the English marmalade market.

Sweet oranges imported from Spain were sold by Nell Gwynne to theatre-goers in the West End as refreshments. Although expensive, at this time, they became an extremely fashionable fruit and even started to appear in cookery books. However, it was – and is – important that it was made clear which type of orange was required in recipes – the bitter or the sweet.

CHICORY ORANGE AND WALNUT SALAD

A delicious mix of flavours and textures, this lovely, simple winter salad, which makes an interesting and light starting course, is dressed with a walnut vinaigrette. *Serves 4*

2 heads chicory, leaves separated and rinsed
4 oranges, peeled and pith removed
12 walnuts
For the dressing:
1 tbsp walnut oil
2 tbsp sunflower oil
1 tbsp white wine vinegar
½ tsp Dijon mustard
Salt and freshly ground black pepper

Drain chicory leaves and carefully pat dry on kitchen paper. Place leaves in a salad bowl. Using a sharp knife, slice oranges thinly horizontally to give even circles. Catch any juice in a bowl. Reserve to add to the dressing. Add orange slices to chicory leaves and sprinkle over walnuts.

Whisk oils together and place in a screw-top jar with remaining dressing ingredients. Add reserved juice and shake thoroughly to mix, drizzle over salad. Toss lightly to coat and serve decorated with watercress.

Preparation time: 10 minutes
Cooking time: nil

Approximate nutritional values per portion:	
135 calories	3g protein
10g fat	12g carbohydrate

ORANGE CHEESECAKE

Creamy and citrusy, this is an easy-to-make 'set' cheesecake. *Serves 6*

6oz/175g digestive biscuits
3oz/75g unsalted butter, melted
8oz/225g curd cheese
Juice of 1½ oranges
Zest of ½ orange
1 tbsp lemon juice
2 tbsp sugar
¼pt/150ml double cream
1 egg white
1 sachet gelatine
3 tbsp hot water
Orange slices and zest for decoration

Crush biscuits with a rolling pin, stir in butter and press base mixture firmly into the bottom of a loose-bottomed flan tin. Chill thoroughly.

Mix cheese with juices, orange zest and sugar and beat until smooth. Whip cream until it forms soft peaks and stir into cheese mixture. Whisk egg white until stiff and fold in. Dissolve gelatine in water and melt over a pan of simmering water. Allow it to cool and quickly stir into cheesecake mixture. Pour into flan tin and smooth surface. Chill until the cheesecake is firmly set. Decorate with orange slices cut into triangles and strips of orange zest.

Preparation time: 40 minutes
Cooking time: nil

Approximate nutritional values per portion:	
350 calories	3g protein
30g fat	20g carbohydrate

KNOW YOUR ORANGES

Oranges may look similar, but each one has its own distinctive characteristics. Readily available varieties are:

Navels have a smooth thin peel. At one end there is a circular break in the skin – hence the name.

Seville are the best for making marmalade. These Spanish oranges are slightly more bitter, with a sharp tasting yellowy flesh and quite a few pips. Available for a few weeks in January and February.

Valencia are not, as the name suggests, from Valencia in Spain but are grown in California and Australia. They are sweet, thin-skinned, juicy and almost seedless.

Blood oranges, mainly grown in Italy, are named because of the reddish flush of their skin and flesh. They also give blood red juice.

Mandarin oranges, named after their Chinese origin, are small and the loose skin is easy to peel, leaving behind juicy little segments.

SEVILLE ORANGE MARMALADE WITH WHISKY

Seville oranges are available in January and early February and are best for making marmalade.
Makes 8 jars approx

3lb/1.4kg Seville oranges
Juice of 2 lemons
6pt/3.5ltr water
6lb/2.8kg preserving sugar
¼pt/150ml whisky

Clean oranges and with a potato peeler, pare off peel, leaving pith. Cut peel into shreds and reserve.

Remove pith from oranges with a sharp knife and set aside. Halve oranges and squeeze out as much juice as possible into a bowl. Pick out pips and reserve. Place orange pith and pips in a muslin bag and tie securely with string or cotton.

The reason for adding this to the mixture is because high quantities of pectin, the natural setting agent, are found here.

Roughly chop orange flesh and place in a large, heavy-based pan with the shreds of peel and muslin bag. Pour in orange juice, add lemon juice and water. Slowly bring to the boil then simmer uncovered for 2 hours or until reduced by half.

Discard muslin bag and stir in sugar until dissolved. Add whisky and bring back to the boil and cook until setting point is reached, about 20 minutes. Test by spooning a little of the mixture on to a cold saucer. It should wrinkle when pushed gently with a finger. Skim marmalade and leave to cool for 30 minutes. Pack into prepared jars, seal and label.

Preparation time: 45 minutes
Cooking time: 2 hours approx

Approximate nutritional values per tbsp:	
55 calories	nil protein
nil fat	15g carbohydrate

NUTRITION

Oranges are packed with vitamin C – approximately 50mg per 4oz/100g flesh. They also contribute a great deal to cooking, both as an ingredient and as a flavouring. Most of the vitamin C is concentrated in the white layer of pith under the skin. One orange contains twice the UK recommended daily intake of vitamin C.

Oranges are often sprayed with waxes and chemicals to prevent mould, dehydration and to protect them against damage in transit. Always wash and dry oranges thoroughly, if using the rind or zest in recipes.

To choose oranges, look for smooth, thin-skinned varieties which feel heavy in the hand.

4oz/100g of oranges contain:	
47 calories	1g protein
nil fat	12g carbohydrate

PORK AND ORANGES

Orange sauce is a great foil for rich meats like duck and pork. This sauce is flamed with brandy for a special taste. *Serves 4*

1½lb/700g pork loin, fat trimmed
2 tbsp oil
1 clove garlic, crushed
Salt and freshly ground black pepper
4 tbsp brandy
Juice of 2 oranges
Zest of 1 orange, cut into strips
½pt/300ml chicken stock
2 level tsp arrowroot
½oz/15g butter
Orange segments for decoration

Cut pork into even slices about ½in/1cm thick. Fry in hot oil with garlic until browned and cooked through. Season with salt and pepper.

Pour over brandy, then carefully tilt the pan downwards so the alcohol ignites. Wait until the flames have died down, then remove pork from pan and keep warm. Add orange juice and zest to pan and pour over stock. Bring to the boil, stirring well to incorporate cooking juices. In a small bowl, mix the arrowroot to a thin paste with a little water, then stir into the sauce stirring until sauce thickens. Season again and stir in butter.

Either arrange pork slices on a warmed serving platter and serve the sauce separately with garnish, or place separate slices on warmed plates and drizzle a little sauce and zest over each.

Preparation time: 20 minutes
Cooking time: 20 minutes

Approximate nutritional values per portion:	
300 calories	45g protein
15g fat	12g carbohydrate

ORANGE TIPS

● Serve a sorbet or savoury starter in scooped-out orange halves. Cut a large orange in half and loosen flesh from the peel with a sharp knife, or serrated grapefruit knife. Reserve flesh for use in the recipe. Chill shells before use.

● Oranges are the basis of the most popular sauce served with duck. After roasting, remove duck from tray and pour off excess fat. Stir in 1 tbsp flour to the cooking juices and cook for 1 minute over low heat. Gradually add the juice of 2 oranges and ½pt/300ml duck or chicken stock. Bring to the boil and add a dash of sherry or port. Season well and strain into a warmed sauce boat.

● Caramelised oranges make a super light and refreshing dessert. For 4: peel, remove pith from and segment 4 oranges. Collect juice over a bowl to use in the sauce. Slice oranges thinly horizontally and arrange in a pretty bowl. Drizzle over reserved juice. Dissolve 4 tbsp sugar in a pan with ¼pt/150ml water over low heat, then bring to the boil and bubble until the mixture turns a light golden colour. Pour over orange slices and juice and leave to cool. Chill before serving and decorate with strips of blanched orange zest.

● Add a pinch of orange zest to a jar of sugar to infuse it with a citrus aroma and tang.

PAPRIKA

Paprika is made from red peppers, or capsicums. Hungary produces the best known paprika, made in different strengths from hot to sweet. This subtle, attractive spice is most famous in the Hungarian dish of goulash. But Spain also supplies and uses paprika and it is included in the Spanish Romesco sauce for fish, vegetables or grilled meat.

The peppers used to make paprika have a mild sweetness, unlike those grown for chilli powder. The central core and seeds, which have the hot taste, are removed before drying. After this, the dried pepper pieces are very finely ground.

The resulting bright red powder has a mild flavour and even the strongest style of paprika does not give a hot taste to recipes, but rather just a piquant sweetness.

With its vibrant red appearance, paprika is a good garnish sprinkled on to creamy soups, egg and cheese dishes and sauces.

And a pinch of paprika gives not just colour but also adds a subtle flavour to a hearty meat casserole or homemade tomato soup.

BAKED EGGS WITH SERRANO HAM

Easy first course or lunch dish, these appetising eggs are baked with paprika- sprinkled cream on a bed of Serrano ham. *Serves 4*

2oz/50g Serrano ham
4 fresh eggs
Salt and freshly ground black pepper
4 tbsp double cream
2 tsp paprika

Shred ham and divide between 4 buttered ramekins. Carefully break an egg into each one, and season with salt and pepper. Top with cream and sprinkle with paprika.

Bake in a pre-heated overn Gas 6, 400F, 200C, for 10 minutes, or until eggs are set. Serve immediately.

Preparation time: 5 minutes
Cooking time: 10 minutes

Approximate nutritional values per portion:	
120 calories	12g protein
15g fat	nil carbohydrate

NUTRITION

Paprika is used merely as a flavouring and to add colour to stews, casseroles and soups. As such, this spice makes no contribution to the diet on a daily basis so that nutritional values are irrelevant.

However, in Hungary, where the spice is produced and used widely, it is believed that paprika can cure a variety of complaints.

It is boiled with other flavourings in water and given as a medicine for any number of illnesses from the common cold to a tummy upset.

BUYING AND STORING

There are two sorts of paprika available, Spanish and Hungarian. Of the two Hungarian paprika is probably the better known and has a variety of strengths.

This spice is sold in supermarkets and delicatessens in packs labelled 'hot' or 'sweet', but there is only a subtle difference between the two. Hot paprika has a little more spiciness for adding to hearty beef goulashes and stews. Use the sweeter style in fresh tomato sauce to accompany pasta or in a chicken casserole.

Keep paprika in an airtight jar in a cool, dry place out of direct sunlight to ensure maximum freshness and taste. A damp atmosphere will create lumps in the spice. Overstorage of paprika causes both colour and flavour to fade.

MARMITE MARSEILLAISE

Spicy fish stew. Chunks of cod, scallop, and prawns are cooked in an aromatic sauce.
Serves 4

3 tbsp oil
1 onion, peeled and sliced
2 cloves garlic, peeled and crushed
2 tbsp paprika
1½lb/700g cod fillet, skinned and in chunks
8 shelled scallops with corals
4oz/100g whole prawns
Wine glass dry white wine
¼pt/150ml fish stock
1 tbsp tomato purée
Salt and freshly ground black pepper
1 tbsp freshly chopped parsley
Lime slice
Flat parsley for garnish

Heat oil in a pan and fry onion and garlic over gentle heat until soft. Stir in paprika and cook 1 minute more.

Add cod, scallops and prawns and stir well to coat in the mix. Cook 2 minutes until stiffened.

Pour over wine. Mix fish stock with tomato purée and stir in. Add seasoning and chopped parsley. Bring to the boil, then turn down and simmer for 15 minutes. Serve sprinkled with chopped parsley, a lime slice and flat parsley.

Preparation time: 15 minutes
Cooking time: 20 minutes

Approximate nutritional values per portion:	
318 calories	40g protein
10g fat	3g carbohydrate

PAPRIKA TIPS

● The attractive colour of paprika makes it a perfect decoration for pale dishes like parsnip soup, macaroni cheese or egg mayonnaise.

● Often quite large amounts of paprika – 2 or 3 tbsp, for example – are needed in recipes. Add half of the amount at the beginning of cooking the dish, when the onions and garlic and other flavourings are being softened, and the rest 15 minutes before the end.

● Paprika cheese straws are crisply irresistible. Roll out 13oz/375g packet of defrosted puff pastry to a rectangle ¼in/0.5cm thick. Sprinkle one half with 2oz/50g grated Cheddar cheese. Fold other half over to enclose. Roll out again thinly to the same size as before and cut into thin strips. Twist some, barley-sugar style, paint with beaten egg and sprinkle with paprika. Place on a greased baking sheet and bake for 10 minutes at Gas 6, 400F, 200C.

● Blend 4 tsp hot paprika, a good grinding of black pepper and a little sea salt into 4oz/100g butter. Roll up into a sausage shape in foil and chill until cold. Use as pats to top baked potatoes in their jackets.

● Give subtle spiciness to a homemade tomato soup by adding 1 level tbsp sweet paprika. Gently fry 1 chopped onion and 2 crushed cloves garlic with paprika. Add 2lb/900g chopped tomatoes, 1 tbsp tomato purée, with a few shredded basil leaves. Add 2pt/1.1ltr vegetable or chicken stock. Bring to the boil then simmer for 20 minutes. Whizz in the blender, then strain and season. Serve immediately with croutons.

● For an interesting and stylish first course marinate overnight 4 slices of goats' cheese in a mix of sunflower oil and paprika. Remove with a slotted spoon, then grill and serve on slices of toasted French bread with a green salad.

● For a cold buffet, grill chicken drumsticks sprinkled with a mixture of paprika, ground coriander and black pepper for a spicy, tasty coating.

PAPRIKA SCONES WITH TOMATO BUTTER

Light and airy savoury cheese buns flavoured with paprika and filled with tomato butter – delicious for tea – or make tiny ones to serve with drinks.
Makes 12 medium-sized scones

> 8oz/225g self-raising flour
> 1½ tsp baking powder
> 2 tbsp paprika
> Pinch of salt
> 4oz/100g butter, softened
> 3oz/75g Cheddar cheese, grated
> 8 tbsp milk
> Watercress for garnish

For the tomato butter:
> 1 tbsp tomato purée
> 4oz/100g butter, softened
> Freshly ground black pepper
> Dash Worcestershire sauce
> Squeeze of lemon juice

Sift flour, baking powder, paprika and salt together into a large bowl. Rub in butter to breadcrumb stage, then stir in cheese.

Add milk and gather the mix together with the hands. Turn out and knead lightly on a floured surface. Wrap in film and chill in the fridge for 20 minutes.

Roll out on a floured work surface and cut into rounds the size you prefer. (This mix makes 12 2in/5cm scones.) Place on a greased baking sheet and brush beaten egg to glaze. Bake at Gas 7, 425F, 220C, for 12 minutes or until risen and golden brown. Remove from oven and cool on a wire rack.

Meanwhile, make the tomato butter. Beat tomato purée into butter with freshly ground black pepper, a dash of Worcestershire sauce and squeeze of lemon juice. Chill slightly then use to fill split scones.

Preparation time: 20 minutes
Cooking time: 12 minutes approx

Approximate nutritional values per scone:	
170 calories	4g protein
16g fat	18g carbohydrate

HUNGARIAN GOULASH

Rich and flavourful stew of lean chuck steak.
Serves 4

> 5 tbsp oil
> 1 large onion, chopped
> 3 cloves garlic, crushed
> 2lb/900g chuck steak, cubed
> Seasoned flour
> 2 x 14oz/400g tins chopped tomatoes
> 2 tbsp tomato purée
> 2 tbsp paprika
> 1 tsp caraway seeds
> Salt and freshly ground black pepper
> 2 tbsp white wine vinegar
> 2 tbsp soured cream
> Snipped chives

Heat 2 tbsp oil in a deep pan and fry onion and garlic over gentle heat until softened. Remove with a slotted spoon.

Coat the steak cubes in seasoned flour then shake off excess. Add remaining oil to pan and fry steak in batches to brown all over. Do not crowd the pan. Return all meat, onion and garlic and pour over tomatoes. Add tomato purée, paprika, caraway seeds, salt and pepper. Bring to boil, then turn down to simmer, covered for about 1½ hours, or until meat is tender. Add vinegar 10 minutes before the end of cooking time. Transfer to a serving dish and drizzle over soured cream. Sprinkle with chopped chives.

Preparation time: 20 minutes
Cooking time: 1 hour 45 minutes approx

Approximate nutritional values per portion:	
350 calories	25g protein
15g fat	7g carbohydrate

PARSLEY

Mostly known as the ever popular culinary herb, parsley has been cultivated since medieval times, more often than not for medicinal uses and especially noted for dealing with digestive problems.

Everyone knows parsley and even nervous cooks who rarely experiment with other herbs feel quite safe using a sprinkling of this herb as a decoration, or a few sprigs in a casserole or soup to liven up the flavour.

The tight-headed curly parsley has a delicate taste and looks good as a decoration. But the continental flat-leafed variety is becoming more popular with its elegant, flat leaves and stronger flavour. This is perfect for use in sauces and omelettes where the flavour needs to show through.

PARSLEY TIPS

● Store washed sprigs of parsley in an airtight container in the salad drawer of the fridge. This way they will stay green and sprightly for several days.

● Don't throw away parsley stalks – they are full of flavour and good for using in homemade meat, fish, chicken or vegetable stocks. Tie the stalks in a bundle with thyme sprigs and a bay leaf, using a long string. Attach the end of the string to the pan handle so the herbs dangle in the stock. This makes it easier to pick them out.

● Add plenty of freshly chopped parsley to a simple white sauce for fish. For 4: melt 1oz/25g butter in a pan and stir in 1oz/25g flour. Cook for 1 minute. Remove from heat and gradually add 1pt/600ml milk. Return to heat and bring to the boil, stirring continuously, until thickened. Season with salt, freshly ground white pepper and freshly grated nutmeg. Stir in the grated zest of ½ lemon and 3 tbsp finely chopped parsley. Add a squeeze of lemon juice to taste and serve with grilled or poached white fish.

● Make a parsley butter to melt over plain grilled steak. Soften 4oz/100g unsalted butter and stir in 2 tbsp finely chopped parsley, 1 tbsp lemon juice, salt and freshly ground black pepper. Form into a roll using non-PVC clingfilm. Chill until set and serve in pats.

● Slice leftover boiled potatoes and shallow fry in melted butter and oil until golden. Season with salt and freshly ground black pepper and toss through some fresh finely chopped parsley. Serve with chops or sausages for a fast midweek supper dish.

● Keep a terracotta pot of growing parsley on a sunny windowsill in the kitchen or on the patio by the kitchen door. Water frequently and simply snip off sprigs when required.

● Turn a plain omelette into a gastronomic treat with a sprinkling of chopped fresh mixed herbs like chervil, chives and parsley. Cook the omelette in the usual way and sprinkle in half the herbs before folding. Flip over and turn out on to a plate, then sprinkle over the remaining herbs before serving.

BUYING AND STORING

Parsley is best bought fresh. Greengrocers sell it by weight or bunches, and most supermarkets in small packets.

Only buy sprightly looking sprigs. And check for any shrivelling or brown patches on the leaves. If it is packaged, avoid any packs with visible droplets of water as this could indicate deterioration.

Put fresh parsley bunches in cold water as soon as possible. This will keep them fresh for at least 24 hours. Or wash them, blot dry on kitchen paper and keep in a polythene bag in the fridge.

Leftover chopped parsley can be stored in an ice-cube tray and dropped into gravies, soups and sauces as needed.

Parsley can also be frozen in polythene bags in sprigs. Chop these before they are totally defrosted before use. Dried parsley will do, but it does not have the same leafy freshness.

NUTRITION

Since parsley is used mainly as a flavouring or garnish, it contributes little to the diet on a recognisable basis. Nevertheless, it is a good source of vitamins, particularly C, and minerals.

There is no carbohydrate in this herb - but 1 sprig contains 0.1g protein, no fat and no calories. The soup in the recipe opposite would contain about 5g protein and a worthwhile quantity of minerals.

4oz/100g has 150ml vitamin C, essential for growth and maintenance of healthy teeth, gums and blood vessels. Vitamin A is also present – about 11.5mg in the same amount. This helps development of healthy cells.

Calcium makes up a large proportion of the bones and teeth, and is also essential for proper functioning of the muscles. Parsley is rich in this.

4oz/100g parsley contain:	
nil calories	5g protein
nil fat	nil carbohydrate

TAGLIATELLE WITH ZESTO

A super pasta dish with a herby sauce of parsley, ground almonds and Gorgonzola mixed with olive oil. *Serves 4*

2oz/50g Gorgonzola
3 tbsp finely chopped fresh flat parsley
3 tbsp ground almonds
3 cloves garlic, peeled and crushed
4 tbsp olive oil
Salt and freshly ground black pepper
12oz/350g tagliatelle

Mash Gorgonzola in a bowl. Add finely chopped parsley, almonds and garlic and blend smooth with a fork. Gradually incorporate oil drop by drop until the mixture has the consistency of a thick sauce. Season with salt and freshly ground black pepper.

Cook pasta in boiling salted water until just tender and drain. Drizzle with a little olive oil to stop it sticking.

Toss zesto through tagliatelle and serve immediately on hot plates with grated Parmesan to taste. Garnish with a flat parsley sprig.

Preparation time: 20 minutes
Cooking time: 12 minutes

Approximate nutritional values per portion:	
412 calories	7g protein
12g fat	54g carbohydrate

LAMB WITH PARSLEY GRAVY

Tender trimmed lamb cutlets cooked with garlic and parsley and served with a delicious rich gravy flavoured with finely chopped fresh parsley. *Serves 4*

4 tbsp freshly chopped parsley
2 cloves garlic, peeled and crushed
12 lamb cutlets, trimmed
Salt and freshly ground black pepper
2 tbsp oil
Wine glass red wine
1/4pt/150ml lamb stock or beef stock
New potatoes and green beans to serve

Mash half the parsley in a mortar with garlic. Reserve.

Season cutlets with plenty of freshly ground black pepper. Then cook in a little oil according to preference. Remove from pan and keep warm.

Remove excess fat from the pan, keeping the meat juices. Pour red wine into pan scraping up all the sediment. Bring to bubbling point, then add remaining parsley and stock. Simmer until reduced by a third. Season to taste.

Arrange cutlets on warmed plates and top each cutlet with a little parsley and garlic mix. Pour the gravy around cutlets. Serve together with new potatoes and green beans.

Preparation time: 15 minutes
Cooking time: 15 minutes

Approximate nutritional values per portion:	
350 calories	36g protein
30g fat	1g carbohydrate

PARSLEY AND POTATO SOUP

An intensely coloured and rich parsley soup. A deliciously different taste. *Serves 4*

1 large bunch parsley, washed
1oz/25g butter
1 onion, peeled and finely chopped
2 cloves garlic, peeled and crushed
2pt/1.1ltr vegetable or chicken stock
1 large potato, peeled and cubed
2 slices white bread, crusts removed
Oil for frying
4 tbsp double cream
Salt and freshly ground black pepper

Remove stalks from parsley and chop roughly.

Melt butter in a pan and cook onion and garlic until softened. Stir in parsley and pour over stock. Add potato. Bring to the boil and simmer, covered, until potato is tender.

Meanwhile, make the croutons. Fry cubed bread in hot oil until golden and crisp. Remove with a slotted spoon and drain on kitchen paper. Reserve.

Whizz soup in a blender until smooth. Return to a clean pan and stir in cream, season with salt and freshly ground black pepper to taste.

Finally, to serve, pour into warmed bowls and sprinkle with croutons.

Preparation time: 15 minutes
Cooking time: 15 minutes

Approximate nutritional values per portion:	
230 calories	5g protein
15g fat	22g carbohydrate

TROUT WITH PARSLEY AND HORSERADISH MAYONNAISE

Poached rainbow trout served cold with a delicately flavoured mayonnaise. *Serves 4*

4 rainbow trout, cleaned
1/2pt/300ml fish stock
For the mayonnaise:
2 egg yolks
1 tsp English mustard
1/2pt/300ml sunflower oil
3 tbsp finely chopped parsley
2 tsp finely grated horseradish
Salt and freshly ground black pepper
Squeeze of lemon juice
Watercress sprigs for garnish

Poach trout in fish stock in a large shallow pan. Remove to a rack and allow to cool slightly. Carefully peel away skin and discard. Leave trout to cool completely.

For the mayonnaise, whisk yolks in a bowl with mustard. Gradually incorporate oil, drop by drop with an electric whisk until mix begins to thicken. Then continue adding oil in a thin stream until all is added. Stir in parsley, horseradish and season with salt and freshly ground black pepper. Add a squeeze of lemon juice to taste.

Transfer trout to individual serving plates. Serve with parsley and horseradish mayonnaise, piped along the edge for a pretty decoration. Add a flourish of watercress sprigs.

Preparation time: 30 minutes
Cooking time: 15 minutes

Approximate nutritional values per portion:	
425 calories	44g protein
22g fat	nil carbohydrate

PARSNIPS

Parsnips are native to Europe and have been cultivated since Roman times. The Romans thought them a great luxury and the Emperor Tiberius ate them cooked in honey and wine which emphasised their natural sweetness.

In fact, before sugar became widely available, parsnips were used in cakes and puddings, mixed with eggs and spices. In the Middle Ages, 'parsnebbs', 'pasnepis' or 'pasternaks' were served with roasts before the advent of potatoes.

Parsnips were also thought to have medicinal qualities, curing coughs, colds, stomach ache and snake bites.

Though parsnips are available all the year round, they are mostly regarded as winter vegetables. They were a traditional food of fast days when it was forbidden to eat meat.

BUYING AND STORING

Parsnips are sold pre-packed in supermarkets or loose from the greengrocer. Packaged supermarket vegetables have been scrubbed and graded for even size, but often have less flavour than 'loose' parsnips from the greengrocer. These can be quite knobbly and whiskery, and have been stored longer, giving a sweeter taste.

If your greengrocer is the 'serve yourself' type, choose small, creamy-coloured, even-sized parsnips with as few blemishes as possible. Otherwise, you have to take pot luck. Remember, though, that large parsnips may be woody and coarse.

Never buy packed or loose parsnips with soft brown patches on the skin. And inspect packed parsnips carefully to make sure there is no moisture under the packaging.

Keep parsnips cold in the salad tray in the fridge.

PARSNIP AND MUSHROOM LASAGNE

A lovely vegetarian treat. *Serves 4*

4 tbsp oil
1 onion, finely chopped
2 cloves garlic, peeled and crushed
12oz/350g field mushrooms, sliced
1lb/450g button mushrooms, sliced
1 tbsp fresh parsley, finely chopped
Juice of 1 lemon
Salt and freshly ground black pepper
2 parsnips, peeled, parboiled, in rounds
For the sauce:
2oz/50g butter
2oz/50g flour
1pt/600ml milk
2oz/50g Cheddar cheese, grated
1 tsp English mustard
9 sheets 'no pre-cook' lasagne verde
Extra chopped parsley for decoration

Fry onion and garlic in 2 tbsp oil until soft. Remove from pan. Reserve.

Add button mushrooms to pan and cook to soften. Remove and reserve. Add remaining oil to pan and cook the field mushrooms until browned. Reserve.

Add parsley and lemon juice to button mushrooms and onion mix to field mushrooms. Season both.

For the sauce, melt butter in a pan and stir in flour. Cook 1 minute. Remove from heat and gradually add milk. Return to the heat and bring to the boil, stirring until thickened. Add cheese, mustard and seasoning. Stir to melt cheese.

Butter a lasagne dish and arrange a layer of pasta in the base. Top with button mushroom mix, then another layer of pasta. Spread field mushroom mix over this, and place another layer of pasta on top. Arrange parsnips neatly on top and pour over cheese sauce. Bake at Gas 5, 375F, 190C for about 45 minutes or until pasta is cooked when tested with the point of a knife. Serve sprinkled with chopped parsley.

Preparation time: 45 minutes
Cooking time: 1 hour 15 minutes

Approximate nutritional values per portion:	
550 calories	16g protein
30g fat	36g carbohydrate

NUTRITION

Parsnips are low in calories, with around 60 in 4oz/100g flesh. They have a small amount of protein, about 2g, in the same weight and no fat.

High in starchy carbohydrate, parsnips have 16g in 4oz/100g which is broken down into glucose by the body. It is interesting to note, though, that the longer the vegetables are kept, more of their starch turns to sugar. This gives them their familiar sweet taste and makes them caramelise when roasted.

Parsnips are a moderate source of vitamin C. In fact, a 4oz/100g portion has 10mg of this vitamin, which is a third of the recommended daily amount for a health adult.

There is a useful amount of potassium in parsnips, which makes up the body's muscle tissue. A little calcium is also present, for healthy teeth and bones.

4oz/100g parsnips contain:	
60 calories	2g protein
nil fat	16g carbohydrate

PARSNIP ROSTI

Super accompaniment to roasts and grills. *Serves 4*

1 large carrot
2 large parsnips
1 onion
1 large potato
2 eggs, beaten
Salt and freshly ground black pepper
Oil for frying
Parsley to decorate

Peel and grate carrot, parsnips, onion and potato. Mix together with beaten egg and seasoning.

Heat oil in a large shallow pan. Place tablespoons of rosti mixture carefully in the pan and press down lightly to make round cakes. Fry until golden, then turn over and cook the other side. Cook in batches. Decorate with parsley.

Preparation time: 20 minutes
Cooking time: 20 minutes

Approximate nutritional values per portion:	
150 calories	5g protein
8g fat	22g carbohydrate

PARSNIP TIPS

● The sweet taste of caramelised roast parsnips is a good accompaniment to roast lamb, duck or pork. For 4: peel and cut 4 parsnips into big chunks. Melt 2oz/50g butter in a pan with 1 tbsp oil. Add parsnip chunks and turn in melted butter mix until lightly golden. Transfer to the meat roasting tray and cook around the joint for 45 minutes or until crisp and browned. Season with salt and freshly ground black pepper.

● Overcooked parsnips? Mash them to a purée with a dash of double cream. Season with salt and plenty of freshly ground black pepper. Spoon into a flameproof dish and grate a little Cheddar cheese on top. Grill until golden and bubbling.

● Add chunked parsnip to a beef stew with carrots, celery, onion and leeks. They add a delicate sweetness to the gravy.

● Older parsnips have tough cores that are best removed before cooking. Cut the peeled parsnips in half lengthways then into quarters. Cut out the core with a sharp knife and discard. Chop parsnips and proceed with chosen recipe.

● Young parsnips are good grated into a salad. Choose small, tender parsnips and scrub well, peel thinly then grate.

● Add parsnip matchsticks to an Oriental stir-fry with carrots, peppers, spring onion, ginger and garlic. Season with sherry and soy sauce.

● For vegetarians a parsnip and cheese omelette makes an unusual lunch or supper dish. For 1: beat 2 eggs with 1 tbsp water. Season with salt and freshly ground black pepper. Melt a knob of butter in an omelette pan and pour in egg mix. Stir rapidly with a fork so the uncooked mixture runs underneath. Spoon in 2 tbsp parsnip purée and 1 tbsp grated Cheddar cheese. Flip over omelette to enclose and cook 1 minute more to melt cheese. Slide on to a plate and serve immediately.

GUINEA FOWL WITH PARSNIP RIBBONS

The bird is cooked with a honey, soy and garlic baste which enhances the gaminess of the flesh. Serve with parsnip ribbons for a superb match.
Serves 4

3¹/₂lb/1.6kg oven-ready guinea fowl
For the baste:
1 tbsp runny honey
2 tbsp soy sauce
3 tbsp sunflower oil
2 cloves garlic, crushed
1 tbsp tomato purée
Salt and freshly ground black pepper
For the ribbons:
8 small young parsnips
Oil for frying
Watercress sprigs for decoration

Mix together baste ingredients and brush liberally over bird. Roast at Gas 5, 375F, 190C for 1¹/₂ hours, or until juices run clear when the thigh is pierced with a skewer. Baste during cooking time, but cover with foil if the bird becomes too brown.

For the ribbons, peel and thinly slice parsnips on a mandolin or grater. Shallow fry in batches in hot oil until golden and crisp. Drain and season. Serve guinea fowl surrounded with ribbons and decorated with watercress.

Preparation time: 20 minutes
Cooking time: 1 hour 30 minutes

Approximate nutritional values per portion:	
450 calories	30g protein
33g fat	18g carbohydrate

CURRIED PARSNIP SOUP

A delightful, subtle soup. *Serves 4*

2 tbsp oil
1 onion, peeled and finely chopped
2 cloves garlic, peeled and crushed
2 large parsnips, peeled, cored and chopped
2 tsp curry paste
2¹/₂pt/1.4ltr vegetable stock
Salt and freshly ground black pepper
3 tbsp double cream
Extra cream for swirling
Finely chopped coriander for decoration

Heat oil in a pan and fry onion and garlic until softened. Add parsnips and fry 2 more minutes, gently. Stir in curry paste and pour over stock. Bring to the boil, cover, then gently simmer until parsnips are tender. Whizz in a blender until smooth. Return to a clean pan, season and stir in cream.

Decorate with swirls of cream and chopped coriander.

Preparation time: 15 minutes
Cooking time: 40 minutes

Approximate nutritional values per portion:	
125 calories	1g protein
18g fat	10g carbohydrate

PEACHES

Peaches have been favoured by royalty over the centuries. Louis XIV was presented with a basket of the fruit which had been grown by a gardener who lived near Versailles. They became a royal passion.

Yellow is the most common colour, although white fleshed peaches are thought to have the finest flavour. A red blush does not indicate ripeness.

The peach is a member of the Prunus genus, which means that it can be identified by a central woody stone, soft pulpy flesh and a thin skin.

The two major peach types are the clingstone, whose flesh sticks closely to the stone, and the freestone, whose stone separates easily from the flesh. Clingstone peaches are often canned, as they hold their shape when cooked. Freestone peaches are sold fresh, and need careful handling, as they are easily bruised when ripe.

Peaches are in season early to late summer. They are excellent accompaniments to meat, game and poultry dishes, as well as being used in countless desserts.

PEACHES IN WHITE WINE

A quick to make, yet sophisticated dessert of peaches poached in syrup, which turns a delightful crimson colour. *Serves 4*

1 bottle sweet white wine
1 cinnamon stick
1 tbsp sugar
4 peaches
Clotted cream to serve

Put the wine, cinnamon stick and sugar into a pan. Simmer over a low heat until the sugar has been dissolved. Gently add peaches to the pan and poach for about 20 minutes, turning occasionally.

Remove the peaches and reserve liquid, discarding cinnamon stick. Skin peaches – the skin will slip off easily. Arrange in a dish, and pour the syrup over the top. Serve with clotted cream.

Preparation time: 5 minutes
Cooking time: 20 minutes

Approximate nutritional values per portion:	
210 calories	nil protein
nil fat	20g carbohydrate

BUYING AND STORING

Choose peaches with an even-coloured creamy or yellow skin. The red pigmentation is not an indication of ripeness. Make sure the skin is not damaged and there are no bruise marks. Never squeeze peaches, as the flesh is very delicate and deterioration happens quickly due to cell damage. Hold them in the palm of the hand – they should feel firm.

When ripe, peaches have an intensely fruity aroma. Unripe peaches have little fragrance – they also have a bitter taste due to the phenol content which disappears as the fruit ripens.

Avoid buying unripe peaches as they do not continue to ripen after picking – they simply get softer. The longer the fruit is left on the tree, the sweeter it will be.

If peaches are not needed immediately, keep them at room temperature until they are soft enough. Then store them in the refrigerator until required. Refrigeration halts the enzyme action which softens the fruit.

NUTRITION

Peaches are perfect for weight watchers, as they contain only 37 calories per 100g. There is a little dietary fibre present, a trace of protein and hardly any fat.

Peaches are rich in vitamin A, which is obtained from the yellow carotenoid pigments which give the fruit its bright shade. Vitamin A is essential for normal growth, vision and healthy cell structure. It is also necessary for fertility in both sexes.

Vitamin C can be found in moderate amounts.

Peaches are a good source of potassium which controls the body's water balance, conduction of nerve impulses, and the maintenance of a normal heart rhythm.

4oz/100g peach contain:	
37 calories	0.6g protein
trace of fat	9.1g carbohydrate

SUMMER PEACH AND AMARETTO TRIFLE

A creamy, refreshing pudding of peaches, nectarines and custard, delicately flavoured with Amaretto liqueur. *Serves 6*

1 packet boudoir biscuits
2 tbsp Amaretto liqueur
6 peaches
2 nectarines
1 packet instant custard
¼pt/150ml double cream
1pt/600ml whipping cream

Line the bottom of a trifle bowl with biscuits, cut to fit. Pour over liqueur.

Chop two of the peaches and spoon them into the middle of the dish. Slice the rest of the peaches, and one of the nectarines and arrange them around the inside of the dish, so that the skin shows outwards through the glass.

This is cheat's custard. Make up the instant custard with half the quantity of water stated on the packet. Allow it to cool, then stir in the double cream. Carefully pour the custard over the peaches in the dish. Leave to cool completely and set in the fridge. Meanwhile, whip the cream, reserving a little for piping.

Spoon the cream on top and smooth over. Pipe 5 swirls around the edge of the dish. Slice the remaining nectarine and place a slice of nectarine on to each swirl.

Preparation time: 40 minutes
Cooking time: nil

Approximate nutritional values per portion:	
350 calories	10g protein
20g fat	26g carbohydrate

PEACH TIPS

● To skin a ripe peach, simply plunge it into simmering water for about 15 seconds. Remove carefully with a slotted spoon, and the skin will slip off easily.

● A simple and delicious pudding: stone and slice fresh peaches into a bowl, pour over sweet white wine and serve with double cream.

● Peaches and apricots make a good base for a crumble: add brown sugar and cinnamon to the crumble topping mix.

● Treat yourself to Peach Melba. This is a delightful pud of halved peaches, poached in vanilla syrup and coated with raspberry purée.

● Serve up a yellow summer fruit salad based on peaches with their richly-coloured flesh. Include nectarines, ogen melons, bananas, papaya, and mangoes. Pour over a glass of chilled Cointreau and scatter with mint before serving.

● Use sliced peaches as a crudité with a cream cheese dip sweetened with apricot brandy.

● Don't throw peach stones away – plant them. They grow into beautiful, free house plants.

● Halve ripe peaches, remove stones, and place a rum truffle in the cavity. Replace other half of peach and serve with a little white rum poured over.

PEACH TARTLETS

A summery combination of melt in the mouth pastry and refreshing peaches with cream. *Serves 6*

8oz/225g shortcrust pastry
¼pt/150ml whipping cream
2 tbsp Cointreau
5 peaches
Apricot jam to glaze

Roll out pastry and line 4 small tartlet tins, then chill in the fridge for about 30 minutes.

Bake blind in the oven at Gas 6, 400F, 200C for approximately 15 minutes.

Softly whip the cream, then stir in the Cointreau. Slice the peaches.

Spoon some cream into the bottom of the tartlets, then arrange peaches in a swirl on top.

Gently heat some apricot jam in a pan. Carefully brush this over the peaches and leave to set before serving.

Preparation time: 30 minutes
Cooking time: 15 minutes

Approximate nutritional values per portion:	
310 calories	1.5g protein
25g fat	25g carbohydrate

DUCK WITH PEACHES AND SPRING ONIONS

An elegant dinner party dish of roast duck cooked with quartered peaches and spring onions. *Serves 4*

4lb/1.8kg Barbary duck
Salt and freshly ground black pepper
4 peaches
1 large bunch spring onions, topped and tailed
New potatoes and a green vegetable to serve

Truss the duck with small skewers or string and place on a rack in a roasting tin. Season with salt and prick the skin with a fork.

Cook for about 2 hours at Gas 4, 350F, 180C, then add the quartered peaches and the onions.

Continue cooking for about 10 minutes, or until the juices run clear when the thigh is pierced with a skewer. Carefully turn peaches over.

Transfer to a serving dish, and arrange the peaches and onions around the duck. Serve with new potatoes and a green vegetable.

Preparation time: 10 minutes
Cooking time: 2 hours 10 minutes

Approximate nutritional values per portion:	
850 calories	70g protein
30g fat	10g carbohydrate

PEARS

Pears have been grown for over 3,000 years and have always been considered a 'gift of the gods'. They were found growing in the garden of Alcinous, King of the Phaeacians, according to Homer's poem, *The Odyssey*. Around 200BC, Cato mentioned six pear varieties in a work on farming.

Ancient Greeks and Romans consecrated pears to Venus, and because of this they were thought to have aphrodisiac powers. But the Romans also grew pears for medicinal reasons. They were considered good for the stomach, and a useful antidote to eating poisonous fungi.

Although the first pears were introduced here before the Roman Conquest, there are no written records until the 13th century, when they were favoured by Henry III and Edward I.

In 14th century England, the Warden pear was talked of and became famous for pies. In fact, Warden pies appear in *The Winter's Tale* by Shakespeare. By the middle of the 1600s, there were 64 varieties of pear known and new strains introduced from Belgium in the 18th century rapidly increased this number.

Conference pears were introduced to England by Thomas Rivers in the late 1800s. He had been growing them for 20 years from the pips of a cooking variety called Leon Le Clerc de Laval. His carefully nurtured fruits were entered at the International Pear Conference in Chiswick in 1885 and won a first class certificate. The judging committee specially asked for them to be called 'Conference' to mark the occasion.

The other popular variety here is the Comice, which came from France. The original Comice pear tree was in the first seed bed in the fruit garden of Comice Horticole in Angers. The first pears picked in 1849 were called 'Doyenne du Comice' but now the name is shortened.

PEAR AND GORGONZOLA SALAD

Delightful mix of little pear chunks, sliced celery and spring onions with crumbled Gorgonzola tossed in a herb and lemon dressing. *Serves 4*

4 ripe pears
Lemon juice
4 sticks celery, washed and chopped
8 spring onions, trimmed and chopped
3oz/75g Gorgonzola
For the dressing:
4 tbsp sunflower oil
Juice of ½ lemon
1 tsp Dijon mustard
Salt and freshly ground black pepper
1 tbsp chopped fresh herbs (chives, parsley, chervil)
Flat parsley sprigs for garnish

Quarter pears, remove cores and chop into small chunks. Sprinkle mixing well. Then add in the chopped celery and spring onions. Crumble in Gorgonzola.

Shake dressing ingredients in a screw-top jar. Drizzle over salad. Garnish with a sprig of flat parsley to serve.

Preparation time: 15 minutes
Cooking time: nil

Approximate nutritional values per portion:	
400 calories	5g protein
22g fat	10g carbohydrate

NUTRITION

Fresh pears have 59 calories per 4oz/100g flesh, and a whole pear weighing 4oz/100g with skin and core contains around 40. There is a trace of protein in pears and no fat.

Pears have 15g of carbohydrate in 4oz/100g of flesh. This is in the form of natural fruit sugars which are converted by the body to energy.

Vitamin A is present. This is important for good vision. Vitamin A is stored in the liver, so deficiency is rare in this hemisphere.

There is also some vitamin C in pears, for healthy skin and to aid healing.

Pears are moderately high in fibre, with about 3g in 4oz/100g weight. Most of the fibre is in the peel. Fibre is required for a healthy digestive system. Low fibre intake has been linked with bowel cancer and heart disease.

4oz/100g pear flesh contain:	
59 calories	trace of protein
nil fat	15g carbohydrate

KNOW YOUR PEARS

There are several varieties of pear available in the UK, all with their own characteristics. These three are perhaps the most well known.
Comice pears (pictured) have a full rounded shape with green peel and browny-russet spots. Tender and juicy, they have a full, aromatic flavour and creamy white flesh.
Conference pears have a slim, tapering shape with yellow-green peel, covered with large patches of russet. They have tender but quite coarse flesh and are extremely juicy with a very sweet flavour.
William's pears have yellow skin with a deep red glow. Soft and juicy with a sweet taste.

All pears bruise easily and should be handled carefully. Choose pears which are not fully ripe and ripen them at home in a warm, draught-free place. They go from hard and inedible to soft and juicy very quickly, so keep an eye on them and move pears which are ready to eat to a cooler place to avoid over-ripening.

DUCK WITH PEARS

Super dinner party dish of duck cooked with pear slices in white wine flavoured and thickened with ground almonds. A great blend of tastes and textures. *Serves 4*

2 tbsp oil
1 onion, peeled and finely chopped
3 cloves garlic, peeled and crushed
4lb/1.8kg oven-ready duck, in 8 pieces
Wine glass dry white wine
³/₄pt/425ml duck or chicken stock
1 tsp fresh thyme, chopped
Salt and freshly ground black pepper
2 pears, peeled, cored and sliced thickly
1oz/25g unsalted butter
3 tbsp ground almonds
Freshly chopped parsley to garnish

Heat oil in a pan and fry onion and garlic until softened. Remove with a slotted spoon and reserve. Add duck pieces to pan and fry briskly to brown. Return onion mix and pour over wine and stock. Add thyme. Bring to the boil and season. Cover and simmer for 1¹/₂ hours or until duck is tender.

Meanwhile, fry pears gently in butter for 3 minutes to caramelise. Remove with a slotted spoon and reserve. About 15 minutes before end of cooking time, stir ground almonds into duck stew. Add pears and gently mix in. Check seasoning.

Spoon stew into a serving dish and sprinkle with chopped parsley to garnish.

Preparation time: 20 minutes
Cooking time: 2 hours approx

Approximate nutritional values per portion:	
900 calories	57g protein
32g fat	8g carbohydrate

TIPS

● Sprinkle peeled or sliced pears with a little lemon juice to prevent them from discolouring.

● Pears and blue cheese are the perfect partners. For a quick first course, serve peeled and sliced pears with a blue cheese sauce. To serve 4: carefully peel 2 large pears and halve lengthways. Scoop out pips and core, without damaging pear shape. Drizzle with lemon juice. For the sauce, mash smooth 3oz/75g blue cheese then beat in ¹/₄pt/150ml single cream. Add a dash of port and season with plenty of freshly ground black pepper. Slice pears into a fan shape and serve on 4 individual plates. Spoon a puddle of sauce around each one and garnish with sprigs of watercress.

● Roasting a duck or a pork joint? About 20 minutes before end of cooking time, add peeled pear halves to the roasting pan and baste with pan juices. Return to oven to finish cooking the meat, basting pears frequently. Serve meat on a platter surrounded with pear halves. Cooked this way, they make a wonderful fruity garnish for the richness of the meat.

PEARS WITH CHOCOLATE SAUCE

Pears poached with cinnamon and served with a sophisticated shiny dark chocolate sauce – a grand finale. *Serves 4*

4 ripe pears
¹/₂ wine glass white wine
Water to cover
1 cinnamon stick
For the sauce:
¹/₂pt/300ml water
2oz/50g caster sugar
1 tsp cocoa powder
3oz/75g plain chocolate

Peel pears carefully, leaving stalks intact. Place in a pan with white wine and water. Add cinnamon stick. Bring to just bubbling. Lower heat, cover pan and gently poach until pears are tender.

Meanwhile, make the sauce. Heat half the water with sugar, cocoa and chocolate until chocolate has melted. Stir and heat gently until smooth.

Stir in remaining water and bring to the boil. Lower heat and simmer for 15 minutes or until mixture is dark brown and shiny.

Remove pears from poaching liquid with a slotted spoon. Drain and place on plates. Spoon a little chocolate sauce over each pear to serve.

Preparation time: 10 minutes
Cooking time: 15 minutes approx

Approximate nutritional values per portion:	
235 calories	1g protein
7g fat	45g carbohydrate

CRACKLY PEAR TARTS

Crisp sweet pastry cases filled with pastry cream and sliced pears, topped with crackly caramel. Sweet shortcrust pastry is now available ready made. *Serves 4*

13oz/375g pack sweet shortcrust pastry
4 whole peeled pears, poached
For the pastry cream:
2 eggs
2oz/50g caster sugar
1oz/25g plain flour
¹/₂pt/300ml milk
Few drops vanilla essence
For the caramel:
4oz/100g sugar
¹/₄pt/150ml water

Roll out pastry on a lightly-floured board. Line 4 individual loose-bottomed fluted tart tins. Chill for 30 minutes. Bake blind for 15 minutes at Gas 6, 400F, 200C until pastry is set and crisp. Remove from oven and cool.

For the pastry cream, whisk eggs and sugar until light and creamy. Whisk in flour. Bring milk up to bubbling point and gradually whisk into egg mixture. Add vanilla essence. Return to a clean pan and stir over low heat until thickened. Do not allow to boil. Remove from heat. Cover surface with buttered greaseproof paper to prevent a skin forming. Cool.

Fill cases with pastry cream. Cut pears in half and slice lengthways. Arrange slices on top of each tart in a fan shape.

For the crackly caramel topping, dissolve sugar in water over low heat. Boil rapidly until just golden. Spoon over tarts and leave to cool and set.

Preparation time: 30 minutes
Cooking time: 20 minutes approx

Approximate nutritional values per portion:	
400 calories	10g protein
25g fat	3g carbohydrate

PEAS

Peas used to be called 'pise', 'pease', 'peasons', 'pisons' and other sound-alike variations.

One of the earliest cultivated vegetables, evidence of pea eating goes back to 9750BC. This was found near the Burmese border with Thailand. Other remains have been discovered in Stone Age camps in Switzerland, and Bronze and Iron Age dwellings in England and France.

There have been periods of history when peas have been regarded as a luxury. In Elizabethan times, for example, peas were expensively imported from Holland and were described as 'fit and daintie for ladies'. Just over a hundred years before, during the reign of Henry VI they were so plentiful and cheap, they were sold on street corners.

During the Middle Ages, dried peas were an important part of the diet. They provided sustenance during winter months and complemented preserved meats which had been salted and cured to last through the lean months.

These days, peas are frozen to preserve the nation's most popular green vegetable. A packet of frozen peas will keep for 12 months or more in the freezer and the peas will be as fresh and flavoursome as the day they were picked.

The annual pea harvest in July is a race against time. Peas are picked, blanched, frozen and packed in an amazingly rapid 90 minutes. Taste, nutrients and colour are stopped in time. No additives are used.

SQUID WITH PEAS

Robust and tasty dish of squid rings, cooked slowly in white wine with peas and tomatoes. *Serves 4*

2 tbsp oil
1 onion, peeled and sliced
4 cloves garlic, peeled and crushed
6 prepared squid, medium size
1lb/450g peas
2 wine glasses dry white wine
Salt and freshly ground black pepper
8 medium tomatoes, quartered

Heat oil in a pan and fry onion and garlic until soft but not brown. Cut squid into thick rings and add. Toss around with the onion mix for a minute. Add peas and wine and season with salt and freshly ground black pepper. Cover and cook over low heat for about 45 minutes, or until squid is tender.

Fifteen minutes before the end of cooking time add tomatoes. Cover and continue cooking.

Preparation time: 15 minutes
Cooking time: 50 minutes

Approximate nutritional values per portion:	
190 calories	15g protein
3g fat	12.5g carbohydrate

NUTRITION

Peas are low in calories with only 67 calories per 4oz/100g. They are good news for slimmers on a calorie-controlled diet. They contain an appreciable amount of protein, 5.8g in 4oz/100g, 10.6g carbohydrate and are low in fat, only 0.4g in the same weight. They are also cholesterol free.

Also present are useful amounts of dietary fibre, mineral salts and trace elements. Peas are an excellent source of vitamin A, with vitamin C and B1, too.

Vitamin A is essential for good growth and strong bones and teeth. It is necessary for normal vision and healthy cell structure.

Vitamin C is vital for the growth of healthy bones, teeth, gums, ligaments and blood vessels. It is also required for the absorption of iron, and can be found in small amounts in peas.

High amounts of potassium are present in peas. Potassium controls the conduction of nerve impulses, and maintenance of a healthy heart rhythm. It is essential for the storage of carbohydrate and its breakdown for energy.

Vitamin B1 helps the breakdown of carbohydrates, maintains a healthy nervous system, and normal heart function.

Always keep the cooking liquid from peas and use in gravies or sauces. It contains the water soluble B vitamins which leak out during cooking.

4oz/100g peas contain:	
67 calories	5.8g protein
0.4g fat	10.6g carbohydrate

GUINEA FOWL STUFFED WITH PEAS AND HAM

Roast guinea fowl with an unusual green stuffing based on puréed peas with chopped ham and onion. *Serves 4*

3lb/1.6kg guinea fowl
A little oil
For the stuffing:
3 tbsp peas
3 tbsp fine white breadcrumbs
3 tbsp finely diced ham
1 tbsp grated onion
1 clove garlic, peeled and crushed
Salt and freshly ground black pepper

First make the stuffing. Purée peas in a processor. Transfer to a mixing bowl. Add breadcrumbs, ham, grated onion, garlic, salt and freshly ground black pepper.

Spoon into neck cavity of guinea fowl and secure skin flap underneath with a cocktail stick.

Brush with oil and season skin. Roast in a pre-heated oven Gas 6, 400F, 200C for 1 hour 10 minutes or until the juices run clear when a thick part such as the thigh is pierced with a skewer.

Preparation time: 20 minutes
Cooking time: 1 hour 10 minutes

Approximate nutritional values per portion:	
373 calories	36g protein
20g fat	12g carbohydrate

KNOW YOUR PEAS

Garden peas or **shelling peas** available from June to October, and peak in July.

Petit pois are a tiny variety cultivated to remain particularly sweet after picking.

Mangetout or **snow peas** have a flat pod with immature peas inside. These are eaten pod and all. Usually available in spring.

Sugar snaps have a crisp stringless pod with peas which swell inside. The pod remains tender and is edible. Usually available in spring.

Frozen peas are grown specifically for freezing from a selection of 30 varieties.

PEAS TIPS

● For an extra-tasty pea dish, cook them the French way. Place 2oz/50g butter and 1lb/450g shelled peas in a pan on top of a few lettuce leaves. Scatter over a few chopped spring onions, a little chopped parsley, salt and freshly ground black pepper. Cover with foil and a tight fitting lid and cook over gentle heat for 20 minutes.

● Peas cook quickly in the microwave. 8oz/225g shelled fresh peas in 2 tbsp water and a pinch of salt take 8 minutes, covered, on high. Cook frozen ones in 5 minutes. Stir half way through cooking time and leave to stand 3 minutes before serving.

● Home-grown garden peas are available from June to October, and peak during July. However, 92 per cent of all peas consumed are frozen.

● Spanish Tortilla is a thick, cake-like omelette. The traditional filling is sliced, cooked potatoes, onions and peas. Layer these in an omelette pan, pour over 4 beaten eggs and season. Cook over medium heat until the underneath is cooked. Turn over and cook other side.

● Use cooked cold peas in a cold cooked chunky vegetable salad. Include sliced courgettes, thin French green beans, and broccoli florets. Toss lightly in a lemon vinaigrette.

● Purée peas and mash with potatoes for a pretty topping for shepherd's pie. Sprinkle with grated cheese and grill before serving.

● Children like peas. Make your own baby food with freshly cooked free-range chicken breast meat, puréed with cooked peas.

● For a super vegetarian quiche, line a flan tin with shortcrust pastry and bake blind. Sprinkle strips of sautéed red, green and yellow peppers over the base with 8oz/225g peas. Pour over savoury custard mix in the proportion 3 eggs to ½pt/300ml seasoned cream. Cook for 35 minutes at Gas 5, 375F, 190C until just set.

● Risi e Bisi is a dish of rice and peas from Venice, easiest made with frozen peas. To serve 4: fry a chopped rasher of streaky bacon and a chopped onion in a little oil and a knob of butter. Add 1¾pt/1ltr chicken or vegetable stock and bring to the boil. Add 6oz/175g Arborio rice. Season, then cook over low heat until rice is tender, adding extra stock if necessary. Stir in 1oz/25g butter, 1 tbsp fresh chopped parsley and lots of freshly grated Parmesan.

PEA AND MINT SOUP

Vibrant green soup speckled with mint and topped with a swirl of soured cream and mint. *Serves 4*

> 1 tbsp oil
> ½ onion, peeled and finely chopped
> 1 large potato, peeled and chopped
> 1lb/450g peas
> 2 tbsp mint leaves
> 2pt/1.1ltr chicken or vegetable stock
> Salt and freshly ground black pepper
> 4 tbsp soured cream
> Mint sprigs for decoration

Heat oil in a saucepan and gently fry onion until soft but not brown. Add potato, peas, mint, stock and seasoning. Bring to the boil, then turn down heat to simmer and cook for 15 minutes.

Whizz in a processor until smooth. Pour into 4 soup bowls, top with a swirl of cream and decorate with mint sprigs.

Preparation time: 10 minutes
Cooking time: 20 minutes

Approximate nutritional values per portion:	
135 calories	10g protein
1.5g fat	17g carbohydrate

GREEN PEA SALAD

Fresh tasting summer salad of rice, spring onion, chopped green pepper and peas. *Serves 4*

> 12oz/350g cooked rice
> 6 spring onions, trimmed and chopped
> 1 green pepper, de-seeded and diced
> 8oz/225g cooked peas
> 1 tbsp freshly chopped parsley
> For the vinaigrette:
> 6 tbsp olive oil
> 2 tbsp white wine vinegar
> Zest of ½ lemon
> 1 clove garlic, peeled and crushed
> Salt and freshly ground black pepper

Heap rice in a salad bowl. Add vegetables and parsley. Shake dressing ingredients together in a screw-top jar and pour over. Toss lightly.

Preparation time: 10 minutes
Cooking time: nil

Approximate nutritional values per portion:	
180 calories	5g protein
7g fat	17g carbohydrate

PEPPERS

There are more than 100 varieties of peppers, but the most commonly seen in the greengrocers are red, green, yellow and orange. Peppers vary in shape from bell-shaped to squat and chunky. Known as capsicums or sweet peppers, and grown in the warmer parts of the world, they were first discovered by the Spaniards in Mexico during the early 16th century. In Victorian times they intermittently appeared in recipes, but after World War II their popularity grew.

Originally from tropical America and the West Indies, some peppers are home-grown in glasshouses, but most are imported from Spain, Holland, Canary Islands, Italy and Israel. Green peppers have a slightly bitter taste, but if allowed to ripen and turn red, when they are fully matured, the taste is much sweeter. Orange and yellow peppers are sweet and quite similar in taste. Their main attribute is their versatility in cooking. Eaten raw or cooked, they also bring colour to the finished dish.

GOOD IDEA

For a Hallowe'en treat, cut out eyes and mouth in red, yellow or green peppers to make a pretty pepper lantern. Place on a table for decoration or hang up by the stalk with a little string.

CHICKEN-STUFFED PEPPERS

Juicy halves of sweet red peppers packed with chicken and rice. *Serves 4*

> 3oz/75g wild rice, cooked
> 3oz/75g white rice, cooked
> 2 tbsp oil
> 8 spring onions, chopped
> 1 clove garlic, crushed
> 2 chicken breast fillets, skinned and chopped
> 2 tomatoes, peeled, de-seeded and finely chopped
> 1/2pt/300ml chicken stock
> Salt and freshly ground black pepper
> 1 tbsp finely chopped parsley
> 2 large red peppers, halved and de-seeded
> Oil for brushing

Heat oil in a pan and fry spring onions and garlic until softened. Remove with a slotted spoon and reserve. Add chicken to pan and fry to seal. Return vegetables to pan and add rice. Stir. Add tomatoes and pour over stock. Season and bring to the boil. Cover and simmer until chicken is cooked. Sprinkle in parsley.

Brush peppers with oil. Season. Fill with rice mixture. Cover and bake at Gas 6, 400F, 200C for 15 minutes. Serve with salad.

Preparation time: 20 minutes
Cooking time: 45 minutes

Approximate nutritional values per portion:	
150 calories	20g protein
5g fat	20g carbohydrate

PIPERADE

Mix of peppers, onion, garlic and tomatoes with scrambled egg. *Serves 4*

> 2 tbsp olive oil
> 1 onion, peeled and finely sliced
> 2 cloves garlic, peeled and crushed
> 2 large red, green and yellow peppers, de-seeded and roughly chopped
> 1 sprig thyme, chopped
> 4 tomatoes, chopped
> Salt and freshly ground black pepper
> 4 eggs, beaten
> 2 tbsp cream

Heat oil in a pan and cook onion and garlic until softened. Add peppers and thyme and cook for a further 5 minutes. Stir in tomatoes and season. Mix eggs with cream and add to pan. Cook, stirring until egg is just set. Re-season and serve immediately with warm crusty bread.

Preparation time: 20 minutes
Cooking time: 15 minutes

Approximate nutritional values per portion:	
260 calories	15g protein
10g fat	2g carbohydrate

NUTRITION

Botanists regard peppers as fruits, but in cooking they are used like vegetables. Grown in warmer climates, they feature strongly in Mediterranean dishes, adding colour and sweetness to salads, stews and sauces.

All sweet peppers are green before ripening, which is why green peppers are slightly bitter. Peppers have a high vitamin C content, around 80mg per 4oz/100g and the riper they are the more nutritious. Extremely low in calories – around 25 per pepper – they have no fat or cholesterol. Being sweeter, red peppers contain a few more calories than less ripe peppers.

Peppers are rich in minerals and other vitamins.

One pepper contains 7.2mg calcium, 20mg phosphorus which works with calcium phosphates in the body.

The skins on red, yellow and purple peppers are fairly thick and may be removed to make them more digestible.

1 red pepper contains approximately:	
25 calories	1g protein
nil fat	5g carbohydrate
7.2mg calcium	3mg sodium

SOLE WITH TWO-PEPPER SAUCE

Spectacular dish, perfect for a special dinner party. Delicate sole fillets served with two sauces, spicy red pepper and tangy yellow pepper. *Serves 4*

For the red pepper sauce:
> 2 tbsp oil
> 1 large red pepper, peeled, de-seeded and
>   finely chopped
> 1 clove garlic, peeled and crushed
> 2 shallots, finely chopped
> Pinch of chilli powder
> Salt
> Pinch of cayenne pepper
> 2 tbsp dry sherry
> ½pt/300ml vegetable stock

For the yellow pepper sauce:
> 2 tbsp oil
> 1 large yellow pepper, de-seeded and
>   finely chopped
> 1 clove garlic, crushed
> 2 shallots, finely chopped
> Squeeze of lemon juice
> Salt and freshly ground black pepper
> 2 tbsp dry sherry
> ½pt/300ml vegetable stock

To finish:
> 8 sole fillets, trimmed
> Salt and freshly ground black pepper
> 4 parsley sprigs to decorate

For the red pepper sauce, heat oil in a pan and cook pepper, garlic and shallots until softened. Stir in chilli, salt and cayenne and cook for a further 30 seconds. Pour over liquids and bring to the boil. Simmer until slightly reduced. Pour into a blender and whizz until smooth. Strain through a fine sieve and pour into a clean pan. Reserve.

For yellow pepper sauce, repeat method using yellow pepper sauce ingredients. Strain into a clean pan and reserve.

Wipe sole fillets and season with salt and pepper. Neatly roll them up. Steam until cooked through. Meanwhile reheat the two pepper sauces.

To serve, pour a little red and yellow pepper sauce on to 4 warmed serving plates. Arrange 2 sole curls in the middle of each plate and top with a sprig of parsley. Serve with new potatoes and crisp green beans.

Preparation time: 30 minutes
Cooking time: 30 minutes

Approximate nutritional values per portion:	
250 calories	40g protein
5g fat	2g carbohydrate

PAN-ROASTED PEPPER SALAD

Colourful mix of red, yellow and green peppers, scorched in olive oil with garlic and rosemary. *Serves 4*

> 2 large red, 2 large green and 2 large yellow peppers
> 4 tbsp olive oil
> 2 cloves of garlic, peeled and cut into slivers
> 2 sprigs rosemary, broken
> Salt and freshly ground black pepper

Remove stalks from peppers and carefully de-seed. Cut into thick strips. Heat oil in pan and fry garlic until softened. Add peppers and fry over high heat to soften and scorch the skins. Stir in rosemary sprigs and season with salt and ground black pepper. Pile on to a serving plate and serve with warm crusty bread.

Preparation time: 10 minutes
Cooking time: 15 minutes

Approximate nutritional values per portion:	
80 calories	1g protein
6g fat	5g carbohydrate

PEPPER TIPS

● The skins on peppers are often removed before grilling or baking as they may become a little tough or indigestible. There are two methods for removing the skins. Either roast the peppers under a grill, turning until the skin blisters and chars. This takes about 12 minutes. Or hold the pepper with a two-pronged fork over a gas flame until charred. Place in a cloth or a plastic bag to help loosen the skin. Peel off skin with a knife.

● To remove the seeds and stalk from a pepper, cut around the core, twist and pull out stalk. Halve pepper lengthways and scrape out seeds with a knife. Remove any coarse inner parts.

● Stuffed peppers make a wholesome, appetising and colourful supper dish. Cut in half lengthways or remove the top to form a lid. Fill with a cooked savoury mixture and top with cheese. Bake for 30 minutes at Gas 4, 350F, 180C.

● Finely chopped peppers added to a savoury stuffing give a pretty jewelled effect and crunchy bite.

● Pepper chunks are great threaded on to metal skewers with chunks of pork, chicken or fish. Drizzle over some olive oil and season well before cooking.

● Apart from adding peppers raw to salads, peppers are perfect for flavouring rich beefy stews. Add chunks of peppers about 15 minutes before end of cooking time.

● Ratatouille is a wonderful dish of fried peppers, with onion, tomato, aubergine and courgettes. Add a dash of Tabasco to pep it up.

PORK CHOPS

Pork was first eaten by man in the Near East around 9,000 years ago. Later the Chinese kept domestic pigs for meat and had a particular preference for smaller breeds. About 2,000 years ago roast suckling pig was considered a delicacy and was given as a mark of respect to old people.

The Ancient Greeks also ate pork, even at a time when meat was not popular. And rich Romans had their chefs carve pork into fancy shapes and patterns just before it was served, to revive their jaded palates. The poorer people, who had no cooking facilities, bought pork ready cooked from local shops.

In London during the 14th century, poor agricultural workers paid up to three days' wages for a ready roasted whole pig.

Pork has been popular in this country for hundreds of years. Peasants used to graze pigs on common land, then fatten them up in winter by feeding them on acorns. They were then slaughtered in November.

Modern methods of farming combine a healthy environment, correct feeding and cross-breeding to produce a good supply of tender and reasonably priced pork.

CRUSTY GLAZED PORK CHOPS

Loin chops grilled with a spicy baste of wholegrain mustard, honey and lemon. *Serves 4*

4 loin pork chops
For the baste:
2 tbsp oil
1 tbsp wholegrain mustard
1/2 tbsp honey
Juice of 1 lemon
1 tbsp Worcestershire sauce
Good dash Tabasco
Salt and freshly ground black pepper

First mix the baste. Combine oil, mustard, honey, lemon juice, Worcestershire sauce and Tabasco. Season. Trim chops and brush generously on both sides with the baste. Cook under a pre-heated grill for 6 minutes each side or until chops are cooked through, basting with any remaining mixture during cooking. The chops will take on a wonderful dark, caramelised crust. Serve with lemon wedges and parsley sprigs for decoration.
Preparation time: 10 minutes
Cooking time: 12 minutes

Approximate nutritional values per portion:	
340 calories	43g protein
21g fat	2g carbohydrate

NUTRITION

Pork is a fatty meat, and as such it is reasonably high in calories. One grilled lean pork chop weighing about 5oz/150g has 305, with 14g of fat in the same weight. For the calorie-and-health-conscious, however, fat intake can be slightly reduced by choosing a loin chop and removing all the rind and the excess fat layer. And an even bigger saving is made by grilling the chop as it is, without adding any oil.

A good source of 'complete' proteins, pork chops provide all the essential amino acids for a healthy diet. There are 43g of protein in a 5oz/150g chop with no carbohydrate.

Other major nutritional contributions in pork are vitamin B1 or thiamin, B3 or niacin and vitamin B6. The vitamin B group is required for maintaining a healthy nervous system and is responsible for the breakdown of carbohydrate in the body. Vitamin B6 in particular is also thought to be of help to women suffering from premenstrual tension.

Pork contains iron, essential for healthy blood, and also potassium, which works with protein to build up muscle tissues.

1 grilled 5oz/150g pork chop contains:	
305 calories	43g protein
14g fat	nil carbohydrate

WILTSHIRE HOT POT

A wonderful country dish of slowly cooked spare rib chops, with pork kidney, salami and butter beans in a spicy tomato sauce. *Serves 4*

2 tbsp oil
1 onion, finely chopped
2 cloves garlic, crushed
4 spare rib chops
1 pork kidney, in chunks
2 tbsp seasoned flour
2oz/50g salami slices
2 x 14oz/400g cans butter beans, drained
1/2pt/300ml pork stock
3 tbsp tomato purée
1 level tbsp paprika
1 tsp dried thyme
Salt and freshly ground black pepper
Chopped parsley for decoration

Heat oil in a pan and fry onion and garlic until soft, but not brown. Remove with a slotted spoon and transfer to a flameproof casserole. Dip the chops and kidney in seasoned flour and fry to brown. Add to casserole with salami.

Add beans, stock, tomato purée and paprika and bring to the boil. Stir in thyme and seasoning and simmer for 1¾ hours, or until chops are tender. Sprinkle with chopped parsley before serving.
Preparation time: 20 minutes
Cooking time: 2 hours approx

Approximate nutritional values per portion:	
650 calories	68g protein
28g fat	41g carbohydrate

KNOW YOUR CHOPS

There are several types of pork chop available, from different parts of the pig; some leaner and more expensive than others.

Loin chop. There are two sorts of loin chop. One is from the foreloin joint, with a long thin bone similar to a lamb cutlet. The other is from the middle loin, and is usually thicker with only a small bone at the bottom. This loin chop will sometimes also provide noisettes, the trimmed medallions of pork.

Chump chop. These come from the back of the animal towards the rear. They are large chops with no bone.

Spare rib chop. Located on the underside of the pig, these chops are large and fleshy with a marbling of fat. They are cheaper than loin or chump chops and benefit from longer, moist cooking in a sauce or gravy for the best results.

PORK CHOP TIPS

● A delectable cream and wholegrain mustard sauce brings a simple meal of pork chops into the realms of luxury. For 4: fry 4 lean loin chops in a little oil with a clove of crushed garlic and seasoning until cooked through. Remove with a slotted spoon and keep hot. Pour off excess fat from the pan and stir a glass of white wine into the meat juices. Add ¼pt/150ml stock and bubble rapidly to reduce slightly. Stir in 1 tbsp wholegrain mustard and 4 tbsp double cream. Season with salt and freshly ground black pepper and pour over chops to serve.

● For posh presentation, ask the butcher to remove rind and fat from loin chops and tie them to make little pork 'medallions'. Fry them on both sides and then make a pan-juice gravy by pouring a glass of red or white wine and ¼pt/150ml stock into the frying pan. Bring to the boil to reduce slightly and enrich with a nugget of unsalted butter. Sprinkle in freshly chopped herbs and season with salt and freshly ground black pepper. Serve the medallions in a puddle of sauce, decorated with parsley sprigs.

● Choose the more robust fresh herbs to enhance the flavour of pork. Rosemary, sage, thyme and parsley are all good accompaniments.

● Pork chops do well with a fruity sauce accompaniment. The classic sauce for pork is apple, but the more adventurous can choose gooseberry, cranberry or even apricot by way of a change. Almost any fruit with a brush of acidity is a good foil for the rich fattiness of pork.

● Choose the less expensive spare rib pork chops for a warming casserole. These are slightly more fatty and the meat requires longer cooking in a flavourful sauce to give an economical dish of tender chops.

● Only 2 chops and 4 guests? Trim off the fat and thinly sliver the meat then use in a stir-fry with matchstick vegetables with ginger, garlic and spring onions.

PORK WITH APPLE SAGE AND REDCURRANT

Noisettes of pork cut from the loin and served with an apple and sage sauce, flavoured with redcurrant jelly. *Serves 4*

> 1 large cooking apple
> 1 wine glass dry white wine
> 1½ tbsp redcurrant jelly
> Salt and freshly ground black pepper
> Few fresh sage leaves, shredded
> 4 noisettes of pork loin chops
> 2 cloves garlic, peeled and halved
> New potatoes and green beans to serve

For the sauce, peel, core and chop apple and place in a pan over a gentle heat with the wine. Cook until apple is mushy. Beat to purée with a wooden spoon. Stir in redcurrant jelly over heat and season. Add sage.

Rub noisettes with garlic and fry in oil to brown on both sides. Turn down heat and continue frying gently until cooked through. Season to taste with salt and freshly ground black pepper and then transfer to serving plates and spoon a little sauce over the top. Pour pan juices around. Serve with roasted baby new potatoes and thin green beans.

Preparation time: 15 minutes
Cooking time: 25 minutes approx

Approximate nutritional values per portion:	
325 calories	35g protein
17g fat	6g carbohydrate

PIGGY IN THE MIDDLE

Pork chops cooked with sliced onions in Yorkshire pudding batter. *Serves 4*

> 4 tbsp oil
> 4 loin chops, trimmed
> 1 onion, peeled and sliced in rings
> 4oz/100g plain flour
> Salt and freshly ground black pepper
> 2 eggs
> ½pt/300ml milk
> Tomato slices for decoration

First heat 2 tbsp oil and brown the chops on both sides. Remove from pan and reserve. Next gently fry onion rings in the same pan to soften and brown slightly.

Meanwhile make the batter. Sift flour and salt into a bowl. Beat in eggs with half the milk. Stir in remaining milk to make a creamy batter. Season.

Pour remaining oil into a roasting tray and place in a pre-heated oven Gas 6, 400F, 200C until oil smokes. Arrange chops and onions in the tray. Season. Pour batter around and return to the oven.

Cook for 35 minutes, or until batter is golden and chops cooked through. Decorate with tomato.

Preparation time: 15 minutes
Cooking time: 40 minutes

Approximate nutritional values per portion:	
550 calories	50g protein
35g fat	28g carbohydrate

PRAWNS

These small members of the crustacean family are highly valued for their nuggets of tender and tasty flesh in the tail. The attractive pretty pink shells add to their appeal, especially for buffet centrepieces, arranged in a cascade over ice.

Most prawns are fished from the cold waters of the North Atlantic, and are considered to have a better flavour than those from the warmer Pacific or Indian oceans. About 2in/5cm long and a delicate grey when caught, it is only heat in the cooking process which changes the shell to pink.

Prawns live on the sea bed close to the shore, and feed by scanning the ocean floor with large black eyes and antennae and the legs behind to scrape up fine morsels of food. They are often described as 'scavengers of the sea'.

Americans refer to all small prawns as 'shrimps' and this may lead to confusion. In this country shrimps are the smallest crustaceans measuring about 1in/2.5cm and with a brown or grey shell.

Most prawns are sold cooked, either peeled or whole with the shells on. When buying frozen prawns it is advisable to check the ice content of the pack, as this contributes to the weight, which means fewer prawns and more water. All frozen prawns must be thawed naturally and thoroughly, then drained of excess water. If time allows, buy whole prawns and peel as needed. These are usually more flavourful and do not contain as much water as frozen.

FISKAJA

Smooth and velvety cod mousse spiked with nuggets of prawn. This is easy to prepare and is ideal as a starter or light lunch. *Serves 10*

> *2lb/900g cod fillet, skinned*
> *4 egg whites*
> *³/₄pt/450ml double cream*
> *Salt*
> *Pinch of cayenne pepper*
> *1 tbsp fresh dill, finely chopped*
> *6oz/175g peeled prawns, chopped*
> *Few whole prawns for decoration*

Wipe fish and whizz in a blender until smooth. Beat in egg whites and cream. Season and fold in dill and prawns. Spoon mixture into a lightly oiled terrine dish and smooth surface. Place in a roasting tray half full of boiling water and cover surface with buttered foil. Bake at Gas 5, 375F, 190C for 40 minutes or until set. Leave to cool. Chill the terrine thoroughly in the fridge.

Turn out terrine onto a serving platter and garnish with whole prawns and dill sprigs.

Serve cut into medium-sized slices.

Preparation time: 15 minutes
Cooking time: 40 minutes approx

Approximate nutritional values per portion:	
200 calories	20g protein
15g fat	1g carbohydrate

BUYING AND STORING

Prawns are available whole with shells on or ready-peeled and are either fresh or frozen.

Fishmongers may sell prawns by the pint and each pint usually contains about 40 whole prawns, or 120 peeled.

Fresh whole prawns should have sharp 'stiff' feelers – bendy feelers indicate lack of freshness. Always eat fresh prawns on the day of purchase.

Eat prawns as soon as possible after defrosting them and always check freezer storage details on pre-frozen packets.

NUTRITION

Prawns are an excellent source of protein, low in calories and high in iodine, potassium, phosphorus, iron and calcium. They are also low in fat, but unlike other types of seafood are high in cholesterol – 4oz/100g of peeled prawns contain 200mg while the same weight of cod fillet contains 50mg. Enough necessary cholesterol is produced by the body but sometimes there is an excess which accumulates in the blood. Together with a high animal fat diet, this may cause health problems.

The sodium level is high, and certain low-salt diets may exclude prawns – 4oz/100g will contain 1,590mg.

Shellfish are one of the best sources of iodine which is an essential part of the hormones that are produced in the thyroid gland.

4oz/100g prawns contain:	
107 calories	22g protein
1.8g fat	nil carbohydrate

HOT CHILLI PRAWNS

Colourful Mediterranean dish of chilli-fried whole prawns in a peppery garlic butter and olive oil.
Serves 4

1 tbsp olive oil
2oz/50g butter
2 medium cloves garlic, peeled and crushed
1 small red and 1 small green chilli, de-seeded and
cut into thin rings
1¼lb/700g whole prawns
Plenty of freshly ground black pepper

Heat oil and butter in a skillet. Add garlic and chilli and fry for 1 minute. Add prawns and stir to coat in buttery mix. Season with freshly ground black pepper.

Toss around over high heat until prawns are heated through. Serve with warm crusty French bread to mop up the juices.

Preparation time: 10 minutes
Cooking time: 5 minutes

Approximate nutritional values per portion:	
270 calories	30g protein
15g fat	nil carbohydrate

PRAWN AND MUSHROOM SALAD

Use large plump peeled prawns or peel your own for this simple but delicious first course of marinated prawns with sliced button mushrooms all tossed in a tangy lime vinaigrette. *Serves 4*

1lb/450g peeled prawns
6oz/175g button mushrooms, wiped and sliced thinly
For the chive dressing:
1 tbsp white wine vinegar
1 heaped tsp Dijon mustard
Squeeze of lime juice
1 medium clove garlic, peeled and crushed
4 tbsp sunflower oil
Salt and freshly ground black pepper
1 tsp snipped chives
1 head chicory, leaves separated and rinsed
Chive batons for garnish

Place prawns and mushrooms in a large bowl. Mix vinegar, Dijon mustard, lime juice and garlic in a bowl and gradually whisk in oil to form an emulsion. Season and stir in chives.

Pour dressing over prawns and mushrooms and toss to coat. Cover and chill for 2 hours in order to marinate.

Arrange chicory leaves in a serving bowl and pile prawn mix in the centre. Sprinkle over chive batons before serving.

Preparation time: 10 minutes
Cooking time: nil

Approximate nutritional values per portion:	
160 calories	25g protein
2g fat	1g carbohydrate

PRAWN AND DILL QUICHE

This attractive mix of pink prawns and feathery dill in savoury egg custard encased in crisp pastry has a subtle, unbeatable flavour.
Serves 6

8oz/225g shortcrust pastry
3 eggs
½pt/300ml milk
¼pt/150ml double cream
Salt and freshly ground black pepper
12oz/350g peeled prawns
1 bunch spring onions, trimmed and finely sliced
1 tbsp fresh dill, chopped

Roll out the shortcrust pastry to line an 8in/20cm fluted flan dish. Chill for 30 minutes in the fridge. Bake blind using greaseproof paper to line the pastry base, weighed with kidney beans (remember the beans cannot be used for cooking afterwards) at Gas 6, 400F, 200C for 10 minutes. Allow quiche base to cool slightly.

For the filling, beat eggs, milk and cream together and season with salt and freshly ground black pepper. Evenly scatter prawns and sliced spring onions into base of pastry case and sprinkle over the chopped dill. Pour over egg mix. Lower heat to Gas 5, 375F, 190C and bake for 40 minutes or until the egg mixture sets.

Serve warm or cold with a crisp green salad such as fresh spinach, or tomato and basil salad.

Preparation time: 20 minutes
Cooking time: 50 minutes approx

Approximate nutritional values per portion:	
350 calories	15g protein
20g fat	15g carbohydrate

PRAWN TIPS

● Make a Thai prawn and coconut curry for a quick, spicy supper dish. Heat 2 tbsp oil in a large pan and fry 1 peeled and finely chopped onion, 2 crushed cloves garlic and 1 tsp fresh chopped root ginger with ½ tsp chilli powder until softened. Stir in 1lb/450g peeled prawns, and 2oz/50g creamed coconut. Pour over ¼pt/150ml fish stock and season with salt and freshly ground black pepper. Bring just to the boil to heat through, being careful not to overcook prawns as they will become hard. Serve this curry dish immediately.

● When buying whole prawns, allow 6oz/175g per person. Once peeled, this will yield about 4oz/100g, enough for a single portion.

● Everybody loves a prawn cocktail, best with a homemade cocktail sauce. For ¼pt/150ml sauce, place an egg yolk in a bowl with ½ tsp Dijon mustard and the juice of ½ lemon. Whisk until combined.

Gradually whisk in ¼pt/150ml sunflower oil drip by drip until the mixture thickens. Continue adding oil in a thin stream, whisking continuously until combined. Stir in 1 tbsp tomato purée, a dash of Worcestershire sauce and a dash of Tabasco sauce. Season with salt and pepper.

● Reserve prawn shells and heads to make a quick shellfish stock. Simmer with fish stock, sliced onion, parsley, bay leaves and peppercorns for 15 minutes. Strain and discard shells and flavourings. Use in fish sauces and soups.

● Whole prawns are easy to peel and the flesh is plump and flavourful. To peel, twist off head then peel off body shell and legs with fingertips. Avoid over rinsing.

● Add a few peeled prawns to a fish pie of cod or coley for a little taste of luxury.

RASPBERRIES

Raspberries came originally from Eastern Asia. The wild fruit grew on Mount Ida in Asia Minor and were often referred to as 'Ideas'.

Though this delicious summer fruit has been known in Europe for centuries, it was not until the 1600s that market gardeners and horticulturalists regarded it as a serious fruit. But by the 18th century, cookery writers were including it in dessert recipes, savoury recipes, and wines and vinegars.

Golden raspberries are considered superior by some, and make an unusual ingredient in a yellow summer pudding using apricots and peaches, instead of the more common red berries. Less widely available are black and even purple raspberries.

All soft berries, which include strawberries, raspberries, blackberries and loganberries, are best eaten raw as soon as possible – they deteriorate quickly. A good way to get round this problem is to make raspberry jam, a perfect way to use up a summer home-grown glut.

BUYING AND STORING

Raspberries are a super summer treat which should be enjoyed as soon as possible after buying. Look for plump fruit with no sign of bruising or damage. Sometimes larger punnets may have squashed berries at the bottom so inspect these carefully. Also check for any mould on the fruit.

Store fresh raspberries in the fridge until ready for use for up to 24 hours as they deteriorate extremely quickly. Do not wash raspberries unless absolutely necessary as water collecting in the crevices may cause mould. Freeze an excess of home-grown raspberries in single layers in freezer-proof containers. Defrost at room temperature.

SALADE CARLTON

Slivers of lamb fillet, tossed with pretty leaves, fresh raspberries and raspberry vinaigrette. *Serves 4*

> 1 tbsp oil
> 1 lamb fillet
> Salt and freshly ground black pepper
> Pretty salad leaves like treviso and rocket
> 1 punnet fresh raspberries
> For the dressing:
> 1 tbsp raspberry vinegar
> ½ tsp Dijon mustard
> 3 tbsp sunflower oil

Heat oil in a frying pan and fry lamb fillet until browned on the outside and pink in the centre. Season and remove from the pan.

Shake dressing ingredients in a screw-top jar with seasoning. Cut cooked fillet into thin slices and place in a bowl with leaves and raspberries. Drizzle over dressing, toss and coat to serve.

Preparation time: 15 minutes
Cooking time: 15 minutes approx

Approximate nutritional values per portion:	
170 calories	15g protein
10g fat	6g carbohydrate

OLD-FASHIONED RASPBERRY ICE CREAM

Raspberries are the star attraction in this refreshing, ripply dairy ice cream. *Serves 6*

> ½pt/300ml single cream
> 4 egg yolks
> 4oz/100g caster sugar
> ½pt/300ml double cream
> 4fl oz/100ml fresh raspberry purée
> ½ punnet fresh raspberries
> Extra fresh raspberries for decoration

Bring single cream to the boil in a pan. Whisk egg yolks and sugar together in a bowl. Add hot cream gradually to egg mixture, stirring continuously. Return mixture to pan and heat to thicken, stirring. Do not boil or the mixture will curdle. Pour into a basin and leave to cool completely.

Stir occasionally to prevent a skin forming on the surface.

Whip double cream until thick. Fold into custard mixture. Spoon into a freezer container and freeze until almost set. Remove from freezer and stir thoroughly. Add raspberry purée and chopped fresh raspberries, mixing lightly to produce a ripple effect. Return to freezer until firm. Serve in scoops topped with fresh raspberries.

Preparation time: 30 minutes
Cooking time: nil

Approximate nutritional values per portion:	
200 calories	4g protein
7g fat	30g carbohydrate

NUTRITION

The most nutritious way to eat raspberries is whilst fresh and raw. 4oz/100g of raw fruit contain only 28 calories, making them good for dieters.

The same weight contains 1.3g protein and 6.4g carbohydrate. There is a little fibre in them and no cholesterol.

Raspberries contain appreciable amounts of vitamins C and E. Vitamin C is vital for the healthy growth of teeth, gums and blood vessels. Vitamin C also helps normal immunity to infection and the healing of wounds. Vitamin E helps healthy cell structure and the formation of red blood cells. Cooking the fruit destroys some of the vitamin C and will allow the valuable water soluble B vitamins to leach out.

The important minerals in raspberries are calcium, 30.7mg in 4oz/100g, for healthy teeth and bones, and potassium, 165mg, which works with sodium to balance the water content in the body, and aids the proper function of nerve impulses.

4oz/100g raspberries contain:	
28 calories	1.3g protein
trace of fat	6.4g carbohydrate

RASPBERRY TIPS

● Add a few fresh raspberries to a morning bowl of cereal for a refreshing start to the day.

● Whizz up a fruity raspberry milkshake. Purée a scoop of vanilla ice cream with ½pt/300ml chilled fresh milk and a good dash of raspberry syrup. Add 1 tbsp fresh raspberries and whizz again. Serve in tall glasses.

● Raspberries freeze very well. Place them in a single layer in a freezer-proof container. Do not pile them up or they will become mushy when defrosted. Allow to defrost at room temperature. Use as fresh.

● Raspberry Brulée is a chic and stylish fruity dessert. Place a few fresh raspberries in the bottom of 6 ramekins and top with a beaten mixture of ½pt/300ml double cream, 2 egg yolks and 2 tbsp caster sugar or to taste. Bake in a bain marie at Gas 4, 350F, 180C for 30 minutes or until just setting. Cool and sprinkle with extra caster sugar. Grill until crackly.

● Make your own raspberry vinegar. Place whole raspberries in a bowl of white wine vinegar. Cover and refrigerate for about a month. Strain through a fine nylon sieve and pour into a clean bottle. Label and use for sauces and dressings.

● Stir fresh raspberries into thick Greek yogurt with shredded fresh mint for a fast and healthy dessert.

● Most rich meats such as duck and pork are well accompanied by a fruity sauce. Fry a finely chopped shallot in a little butter in a small pan. Pour off excess fat from meat roasting tray and add shallot. Stir in 3 tbsp fresh raspberries, 2 sage leaves and 2 wine glasses dry white wine. Stir to combine and bring to the boil. Blend in a processor and season. Strain into a sauce boat and serve with the meat.

CHILLED RASPBERRY SOUFFLES

Light and airy pink pudding with the flavour of fresh raspberries. *Serves 4*

8oz/225g raspberries
½pt/300ml double cream
3 tbsp caster sugar
1 sachet gelatine
3 tbsp boiling water
2 egg whites
Whipped cream, fresh raspberries and mint sprigs for decoration

Purée raspberries in a processor. Whip cream in a large bowl. Add raspberry purée and sugar. Dissolve gelatine in boiling water and leave until syrupy. Whip egg whites until stiff and fold into cream mixture with a metal spoon.

Stir in gelatine and pour into ramekins. Chill to set. Decorate with swirls of whipped cream, raspberries and mint sprigs.
Preparation time: 20 minutes
Cooking time: nil

Approximate nutritional values per portion:	
320 calories	1g protein
26g fat	16g carbohydrate

FRESH RASPBERRY TART

A crisp pastry case filled with Amaretto cream, ground almonds and fresh raspberries. *Serves 6*

8oz/225g shortcrust pastry
½pt/300ml double cream, whipped
1 tbsp caster sugar
3 tbsp Amaretto
1 tbsp ground almonds
2 punnets raspberries

Roll out pastry on a lightly floured board and line an 8in/20cm flan case. Bake blind at Gas 6, 400F, 200C for 20 minutes or until set and crisp. Remove and leave to cool.

Mix together cream, sugar, Amaretto and ground almonds. Fill pastry case with cream mixture. Arrange raspberries on top. Keep in a cool place until it is needed.
Preparation time: 15 minutes
Cooking time: 20 minutes approx

Approximate nutritional values per portion:	
340 calories	3g protein
11g fat	16g carbohydrate

RHUBARB

Rhubarb has been known since ancient times and originated in China, India, Siberia and Mongolia. Its healing qualities were highly praised by the Chinese and later the Greeks and Romans.

In the 14th century, European monks cultivated rhubarb for strictly medicinal purposes. Later it was grown by the Germans and Italians, who produced a massive prize plant in the botanical gardens in Padua.

This acidic plant rose in popularity in England in the late 1700s, and was cooked with sugar for puddings and pies. It is said that even Queen Victoria enjoyed it, and a number of varieties were named after her.

Early or 'forced' rhubarb is grown in special houses in the dark so that the sticks remain pink and is picked by candlelight . In these conditions it grows almost 2in/5cm per day, and it is said that it can be heard squeaking as it pushes up through the soil.

Rhubarb today is treated mainly as a dessert and its pleasant acidity enhances many puddings and mousses. Rhubarb can also be used in savoury dishes. The tart flavour is a good foil for fatty meats such as pork, or for oily fish.

CHILLED RHUBARB MOUSSE

Delicately pale pink, creamy dessert. *Serves 4*

> 6 sticks rhubarb, chopped
> 4 tbsp caster sugar
> 4 tbsp water
> 2 eggs
> 1 egg yolk
> 4fl oz/100ml double cream, whipped
> 1 sachet gelatine dissolved in
> 3 tbsp boiling water
> 1 egg white

For the rhubarb sauce:

> 2 sticks rhubarb, chopped
> 1 tbsp sugar
> 1 wine glass sweet white wine
> Mint sprigs for decoration

Poach rhubarb with 2 tbsp sugar in water. Bring to the boil and simmer until soft. Whizz in a blender to purée. Cool.

Whisk eggs and yolk in a bowl with remaining sugar over a pan of simmering water until the mixture is thick and frothy and leaves a trail when the whisk is lifted out. Remove from heat and stir in rhubarb purée. Fold in cream. Stir in gelatine. Whip egg white stiff and fold in. Pour into oiled mould. Chill.

For the sauce, poach rhubarb with sugar in wine until soft. Purée and cool. Pour sauce onto serving plate. Unmould mousse on top, and decorate with mint.

Preparation time: 30 minutes
Cooking time: 15 minutes

Approximate nutritional values per portion:	
260 calories	5g protein
15g fat	30g carbohydrate

MACKEREL WITH RHUBARB, ORANGE AND SAGE

A lovely mixture of tastes and textures, this mackerel dish is a delight, with the rhubarb a perfect contrast to the rich-tasting fish. *Serves 4*

> 4 large mackerel fillets, skin on
> Oil for brushing
> Salt and freshly ground black pepper
> 2 sticks rhubarb
> 1 wine glass orange juice
> ¼pt/150ml fish stock
> Few sage leaves, shredded

Cut mackerel fillets diagonally in half. Slash each skin with a sharp knife. Brush with oil and season. Roast at Gas 6, 400F, 200C for 10 minutes. Poach rhubarb in orange juice until soft. Purée. Add stock, seasoning and sage. Return to heat and bring to the boil. Reduce slightly. Arrange fish on 4 warmed plates. Drizzle a little sauce around each and decorate with a sage sprig.

Preparation time: 10 minutes
Cooking time: 15 minutes approx

Approximate nutritional values per portion:	
200 calories	20g protein
12g fat	3g carbohydrate

NUTRITION

The leaves of the rhubarb plant are poisonous, and were used as an old-fashioned form of insecticide – shredded and mixed with water for spraying over plants and bushes. Always remove the leaves before cooking, and discard.

Rhubarb only provides a little fibre, and is extremely low in calories. The main nutritional contribution is vitamin C – around 7mg per 4oz/100g, and potassium, around 600mg.

Rhubarb contains astringent tannins and phenols which cause the initial acidic taste.

4oz/100g rhubarb contain:	
6 calories	0.6g protein
trace of fat	1g carbohydrate

BUYING AND STORING

Early forced rhubarb: This should be firm, pale pink and have absolutely no signs of damage or deterioration. Thin sticks are often called pipe cleaners, and usually do not need to be peeled. Peak season is early spring. This type is ideal for crumbles, pies, sauces and for bottling. It should not be overcooked as it breaks up and purées quickly.

Outdoor-grown: Sometimes called green-top, this takes over when the forced rhubarb season finishes. Cawood Delight is a red variety and is good for jams and preserves because it keeps its shape when cooked. Also good for home-brewing.

To freeze: Wash and trim. Pack into rigid freezerproof containers. For older, thicker sticks, blanch for 45 seconds. Drain well and pack into freezer containers. Seal and store for about 3 months.

RHUBARB TIPS

● To prepare rhubarb, snip off root ends and remove leaves. Wash in plenty of cold water and pare off any tough strips. Chop into 1in/2.5cm lengths.

● No need to add water when cooking rhubarb – it produces plenty of juice itself. Sugar should be added to offset the tartness.

● To make a luxury rhubarb and ginger crumble, prepare 2lb/900g rhubarb and cut into 1in/2.5cm pieces. Place in an ovenproof dish and sprinkle over the juice of 1 orange and 3 tbsp caster sugar. Add 1 tbsp chopped stem ginger in syrup and mix in. For the topping, rub 3oz/75g butter into 6oz/175g plain flour to breadcrumb stage. Mix in 3 tbsp caster sugar and 2 tbsp finely chopped hazelnuts. Pile on top of rhubarb and smooth over. Bake at Gas 6, 400F, 200C for 35 minutes or until golden on top. Cover if top becomes too brown. Serve the crumble with lashings of whipped cream or creamy custard.

● Next time you make trifle, use rhubarb. This adds a refreshing and zippy dimension to an old favourite. Place a trifle sponge in the base of 4 pretty dessert glasses. Drizzle over sherry. Spoon a layer of poached rhubarb on to each sponge. Make up a sachet of instant custard mix with ½pt/300ml boiling water, cool and fold in ¼pt/150ml whipped double cream. Spoon over rhubarb, chill and leave to set. Top with piped swirls of whipped cream and a sprinkling of toasted almonds.

● The fruity tang of rhubarb teams well with roast meats, and a rhubarb and apple sauce is perfect with a roast loin of pork. Place 4 prepared and chopped rhubarb sticks in a pan with 1 peeled, cored and chopped dessert apple. Add a squeeze of orange juice and sugar to taste, and a knob of butter. Cover and cook over a low heat until fruit is softened. Serve separately either as it is, or puréed.

● Use older rhubarb for making jams and chutneys and younger thinner stalks for delicate dishes and desserts.

● Perk up limp rhubarb by soaking upright in cold water for about 1 hour.

TARTE ST AUBIN

Delicious tart with vanilla base. *Serves 6*

> 8oz/225g sweet or shortcrust pastry
> 2 eggs
> 2oz/50g sugar
> 1oz/25g plain flour
> ½pt/300ml milk
> 1 vanilla pod
> 4 sticks rhubarb, chopped and poached with sugar
> 3 tbsp redcurrant jelly
> Squeeze of lemon juice

Roll out pastry on a lightly floured surface. Line a 7in/18cm oiled fluted flan ring on a greased baking sheet with pastry. Trim. Chill for 30 minutes. Bake blind for 20 minutes. Cool. Whisk eggs and sugar. Stir in flour. Bring milk and vanilla almost to the boil. Remove vanilla pod. Cool. Whisk into egg mix. Return to a clean pan. Stir over a low heat to thicken. Do not boil. Remove from heat, cover with buttered greaseproof and cool.

Spread over base of pastry case. Arrange rhubarb on top. Melt redcurrant jelly with lemon juice. Cool and spoon over rhubarb to glaze.

Preparation time: 40 minutes plus chilling
Cooking time: 30 minutes

Approximate nutritional values per portion:	
450 calories	10g protein
20g fat	40g carbohydrate

PORK AND RHUBARB PIES

Old English shiny glazed hot water crust pies, filled with chopped pork and bacon, and layered with rhubarb. *Makes 2 pies*

For the hot water crust:
> 1lb/450g plain flour
> 2 tsp salt
> 6oz/175g lard
> 8fl oz/225ml water
> 1 egg, beaten, for glaze

For the pork and rhubarb filling:
> 1lb/450g belly pork, finely chopped
> 8oz/225g lean pork, finely chopped
> 8 rashers streaky bacon, de-rinded and snipped
> 1 onion, peeled and grated
> 1 clove garlic, peeled and crushed
> 2 tsp fresh thyme
> 2 tsp fresh sage, shredded
> Salt and freshly ground black pepper
> 6 sticks rhubarb, washed, trimmed and chopped
> 1 tbsp sugar
> 1 packet aspic, made up to instructions
> Parsley sprigs for decoration

Sift flour and salt into a large bowl. Melt lard with water and bring to the boil. Pour over flour and gradually work in, adding extra hot water if the dough is too dry. Cover and cool slightly.

Halve dough. Cut a third from each half for the two lids. Mould pastry around lightly-oiled round jam jars, pressing upwards to make cases. Roll remaining dough into 2 circles for the lids. Chill until firm. Carefully remove pastry cases from jars.

Mix meats with onion, garlic, herbs and seasoning. Poach rhubarb in sugar and 2 tbsp water until tender. Drain and cool.

Fill pastry cases with half the pork mixture, the rhubarb, then the rest of the pork. Dampen top edges of pastry cases then attach lids. Seal well. Glaze with beaten egg. Tie a double strip of greased greaseproof around each pie. Cut slits in the tops. Bake at Gas 4, 350F, 180C for 1 hour. Twenty minutes before the end of cooking time, remove the greaseproof. Re-glaze.

Cool pies. Carefully pour aspic into pies. Chill.

Preparation time: 45 minutes
Cooking time: 1 hour 20 minutes

Approximate nutritional values per portion:	
450 calories	40g protein
33g fat	20g carbohydrate

ROOT GINGER

Root ginger is the bulbous root-like stem of the ginger plant and is one of the most versatile of the hot spices. Originally from South East Asia, this peppery seasoning is an essential ingredient in Middle and Far Eastern cookery.

Southern European cuisine also includes root ginger, but the West took a little longer to accept this ugly-looking, knobbly flavouring.

Root ginger, known in Latin as *Zingiber officinale*, is often cooked with fish, shellfish, poultry and stronger meats such as duck.

During cooking, root ginger releases its pungent aroma and flavour, and marinades with a little added chopped root ginger infuse a delicate piquancy.

Fresh root ginger must be peeled before using and grated, chopped or sliced according to the recipe. This should not be confused with either the crystallised stem ginger or the powdered ginger.

All these come from the root, even though crystallised root ginger is often called 'stem'.

HAPPY SOUP

Clear chicken soup with strips of breast meat, mangetout, broccoli florets, and sliced button mushrooms flavoured with ginger and chilli.
Serves 4

> 1in/2.5cm piece of root ginger
> ½ fresh red chilli
> 1 bunch spring onions, trimmed
> 2 chicken fillets, skinned
> 2oz/50g mangetout, washed and stalks removed
> 2 pt/1.1ltr homemade chicken stock
> 1 clove garlic, crushed
> 2oz/50g broccoli florets
> 2oz/50g button mushrooms, wiped and
>   thinly sliced
> Salt and freshly ground black pepper

Peel root ginger and cut into fine strips. De-seed chilli and slice thinly. Cut spring onions on the slant into rings. Cut chicken into strips and the mangetout into diamonds.

Place chicken stock in a pan and add garlic, root ginger, chilli and spring onions. Bring to the boil. Add chicken strips and simmer until just cooked through. Add remaining vegetables and simmer for a further minute. Season with salt and pepper and serve in warmed bowls.

Preparation time: 30 minutes
Cooking time: 10 minutes

Approximate nutritional values per portion:	
280 calories	30g protein
20g fat	5g carbohydrate

NUTRITION

Root ginger is not consumed in any great quantity. Just 1 tsp of freshly chopped root ginger added to a stir-fry to serve 4 gives plenty of spiciness and flavour to the dish but unfortunately adds no significant nutritional value.

However, root ginger has known medicinal uses. There is scientific proof that it thins blood and lowers blood cholesterol.

The Japanese use small quantities to relieve pain, reduce blood pressure and stimulate the heart – perhaps the origin of the term 'to ginger things up'.

Nutritionally, root ginger contains a little carbohydrate, some fibre, protein and fat, and traces of sodium, zinc and iron.

4oz/100g root ginger contain:	
347 calories	9g protein
6g fat	71g carbohydrate

PORK AND GINGER STEW WITH PRUNES

The flavour of ginger complements pork well. This stew is fragrant and flavourful. *Serves 6*

> 1½lb/700g lean pork, cubed
> Seasoned flour
> 2 tbsp oil
> 8 shallots, peeled
> 2 tsp root ginger, chopped
> 2 cloves garlic, crushed
> ½ wine glass dry vermouth
> 1 tbsp tomato purée
> 1pt/600ml chicken stock
> Sprig of thyme, finely chopped
> 16 no-soak pitted prunes
> Salt and freshly ground black pepper
> 4 tomatoes, quartered
> 1 tbsp fresh coriander, chopped

Dip pork in seasoned flour and shake off excess. Fry in oil until browned. Remove with a slotted spoon and transfer to an ovenproof casserole. Add shallots, ginger and garlic to pan. Cook until softened.

Add vermouth, tomato purée, chicken stock and thyme. Bring to the boil and pour into casserole. Add prunes and seasoning. Cover and cook at Gas 4, 350F, 180C for 1½ hours. Add tomatoes 15 minutes before end of cooking time. Sprinkle over coriander just before serving.

Preparation time: 20 minutes
Cooking time: 1 hour 45 minutes

Approximate nutritional values per portion:	
650 calories	45g protein
30g fat	15g carbohydrate

GOOD IDEA

Homemade ginger beer is a refreshing fizzy drink. To make about 9 pt/5 ltr, place rind of a large juicy lemon, 5 tsp cream of tartar and 1lb/450g sugar in a large bowl. Peel 1oz/25g root ginger and crush it using a flat knife blade and add to bowl.

Pour over 4 pt/2.3 ltr boiling water and stir until the sugar begins to dissolve. Add a further 4 pt/2.3 ltr of cold water and the lemon juice.

Spread ¹/₂oz/15g fresh yeast on a piece of toast and float on top of the mixture. Cover and leave in a warm place for 24 hours.

Spoon off any scum from the mixture, and discard toast. Strain and funnel the beer into prepared bottles stoppered with corks – not screw-tops as this might cause the bottles to burst if fermentation goes on too long. Cork and leave for about 3 days in a cool place before drinking. Be sure to drink within three days for the best flavour.

ROOT GINGER TIPS

● The versatile root ginger is available fresh from greengrocers and supermarkets. Use for flavouring meat, fish, vegetables, stir-fries, casseroles and drinks.

● Root ginger is a rhizome and easily recognised by its unique and somewhat ugly, twisted knobbly appearance. The best root ginger must not be withered or shrivelled. Cut off the required amount and carefully peel away the tough skin. About a 1in/2.5cm piece is enough for a stir-fry to serve 4. Slice thinly into strips, then into small dice if preferred.

● Some recipes suggest using root ginger juice to give a more subtle flavour. Squash finely chopped root ginger in a garlic press, or place in a clean piece of muslin and squeeze well into a small saucer or bowl.

● Root ginger is indispensable in all Oriental cooking. It adds an essential spicy scent that is peppery, pungent and flavoursome. Fry peeled and chopped ginger gently in a little flavoured oil such as sesame with garlic and chopped spring onions before making a stir-fry.

● Root ginger is now available prepared, chopped and puréed in small glass jars and squeezable tubes. Available from major supermarkets or delicatessens.

● Everyone loves spicy spare ribs. To serve 4: trim 2lb/900g pork ribs. Roast in a shallow baking tin for 20 minutes at Gas 6, 400F, 200C. Remove from oven and pour off most of the fat. Meanwhile, mix 2 tbsp tomato purée, 2 tbsp soft brown sugar, 1 tbsp Worcestershire sauce, 1 tbsp soy sauce, 1 tbsp grated root ginger, 1 crushed clove of garlic, 1 small sliced onion and ¹/₄pt/150ml water. Pour over ribs and continue cooking for a further 45 minutes at Gas 4, 350F, 180C. Baste throughout cooking until sauce thickens. Serve with jacket potatoes.

● For a speedy marinade for 4 chicken pieces, mix ¹/₄pt/150ml white wine, 2 tbsp oil, 2 crushed cloves garlic, 1 tbsp chopped parsley, 2 tsp grated root ginger, zest and juice of ¹/₂ orange, salt and pepper. Soak for at least an hour before cooking.

DRAGON TAIL PRAWNS

Colourful and appetising healthy dish using uncooked prawn tails with strips of pepper and spring onions. *Serves 4*

> 2 tbsp oil
> 2 cloves garlic, peeled and crushed
> 2 tsp peeled and chopped root ginger
> 1lb/450g raw prawn tails, peeled
> 2 red and 2 green peppers, de-seeded and cut into strips
> 1 bunch spring onions, trimmed and halved
> Dash of soy sauce
> Dash of lemon juice
> Salt and freshly ground black pepper

Heat oil and fry garlic and root ginger until softened. Add prawns and stir-fry quickly until they turn pink and are cooked through. Remove with a slotted spoon and keep hot. Add peppers and spring onions to pan and fry for 2 minutes. Return prawns and season with soy sauce, lemon juice, salt and black pepper. Serve immediately.

Preparation time: 20 minutes
Cooking time: 10 minutes approx

Approximate nutritional values per portion:	
260 calories	30g protein
8g fat	15g carbohydrate

SOLE WITH GINGER AND LIME

Rolled fillets of sole delicately flavoured with root ginger juice and lime. *Serves 4*

> 2 Dover soles, filleted
> Bay leaves
> Lime twists and fresh dill for decoration
> For the ginger marinade:
> 1 tsp root ginger juice
> 1 tsp finely chopped root ginger
> Zest and juice of ¹/₂ lime
> 2 tbsp sunflower oil
> 1 tsp finely chopped dill
> Salt and freshly ground black pepper

Cut each sole fillet in half down the centre. Then cut each strip in half. Neatly roll up and thread 4 rolls onto metal kebab skewers with bay leaves.

Mix marinade ingredients and brush over fish. Chill for 10 minutes. Lightly grill until cooked through basting with any leftover marinade. Decorate the sole fillets with lime twists and dill fronds.

Preparation time: 25 minutes
Cooking time: 5 minutes approx

Approximate nutritional values per portion:	
180 calories	40g protein
8g fat	trace of carbohydrate

SAFFRON

Saffron is a fragrant, golden-coloured spice which comes from the stigmas of a specially cultivated saffron crocus that is native to the Mediterranean, Asia Minor and Iran.

The ancient Assyrians knew this spice, using it in medicinal potions, and in the year 1552BC it was mentioned in the medical papyrus of Thebes. Saffron was also believed to have grown in the gardens of King Solomon.

The Romans were saffron-lovers, too. They crushed the threads in water to dye special garments, or spread them on the floors of their private rooms to scent the air before celebrations.

Introduced to Spain by the Arabs, saffron takes its name from the Arabic word za'faran which means yellow. Today, most saffron is grown is Spain, and the best quality comes from the region of La Mancha.

Saffron is the most expensive spice in the world because the careful harvesting and preparation is carried out by hand. The crocus blossoms are collected at dawn and the petals are picked away to reveal the saffron stigmas. Each flower yields only three of these, and it takes 225,000 stigmas to produce 1lb/450g of saffron. After harvesting, the stigmas are dried immediately, and the whole process must take place the same day to avoid any risk of spoilage.

SAFFRON RICE WITH SQUID

A delightfully fragrant, pale yellow rice dish cooked with fresh squid rings, prawns, green peppers and peas. *Serves 4*

Pinch of saffron threads
1¹/₂pt/850ml fish stock
4 tbsp oil
1 onion, peeled and finely chopped
2 cloves garlic, peeled and crushed
1 green pepper, de-seeded and finely chopped
8oz/225g risotto rice
8oz/225g squid rings
4oz/100g peas
8oz/225g peeled prawns
Salt and freshly ground black pepper
Watercress sprigs to decorate

Infuse saffron in hot fish stock.

Heat oil in a pan and gently fry onion, garlic and green pepper over a low heat until soft. Add rice and stir to coat in the mixture.

Gradually add half the fish stock with the saffron in it, cooking over a gentle heat. Add squid and a little more fish stock and cook for about 10 minutes, or until stock is completely absorbed.

Add the peas and prawns and remaining stock and continue cooking until rice is tender. Season with salt and freshly ground black pepper. Serve decorated with watercress.

Preparation time: 15 minutes
Cooking time: 45 minutes

Approximate nutritional values per portion:	
350 calories	23g protein
6g fat	48g carbohydrate

SAFFRON THINS

These crisp little biscuits, chewy on the inside and scented with saffron are perfect for petits fours. *Makes about 20*

4oz/100g plain flour
Pinch of salt
1 tsp baking powder
1 tsp bicarbonate of soda
1 tsp ground ginger
1 tsp mixed spice
2oz/50g butter
2 tbsp sugar
¹/₂ tsp powdered saffron
Finely grated zest of 2 large lemons
3 tbsp golden syrup
Few saffron threads to decorate

Sift flour, salt, baking powder, bicarbonate of soda, ginger and mixed spice into a bowl. Rub in butter to breadcrumb stage. Stir in sugar, saffron, lemon zest and golden syrup.

Grease a baking sheet and place tiny balls of mixture on it, spacing well apart. Sprinkle 2 or 3 saffron threads on each one. Bake at Gas 5, 375F, 190C for 15 minutes or until crisp and golden. Remove and cool on a wire rack. Store in an airtight tin to retain crispness.

Preparation time: 15 minutes
Cooking time: 15 minutes approx

Approximate nutritional values per biscuit:	
55 calories	0.5g protein
2g fat	10g carbohydrate

NUTRITION

Saffron is used for flavouring and colouring dishes, adding an exotic touch to many sweet and savoury recipes.

This spice has long been linked with good health. The ancient Assyrians used saffron for medicinal purposes and it was also mentioned in the medical papyrus of Thebes, written in 1552BC.

Latter-day herbalists believed saffron to be useful in treating some epidemics, including smallpox and measles. It was also prescribed for illnesses relating to the chest and lungs and to aid breathing difficulties. Women who suffered pain during the menstrual cycle took an infusion of saffron in boiling water.

Calorie contents and nutritive values are irrelevant to this spice, because it is used purely for its taste and colour and only in very small amounts. It makes no contribution to the diet on a daily basis.

Hello! Good Cooking

MONKFISH STEAKS WITH MUSSELS IN SAFFRON SAUCE

A stylish dish of thick monkfish slices and fresh mussels cooked in a scented saffron sauce. *Serves 4*

2lb/900g white fish bones (turbot, sole or other)
1 tbsp oil
½oz/15g butter
1 onion, peeled and roughly chopped
1 leek, trimmed, washed and chopped
2pt/1.1ltr cold water
1 fresh bouquet garni
6 black peppercorns

For the sauce:

1oz/25g butter
1 onion, peeled and finely chopped
2 cloves garlic, peeled and crushed
½ wine glass dry white wine
½ tsp saffron threads (or to taste)
12 thick slices monkfish, cut across the tail
12 mussels, tightly closed, scrubbed and de-bearded
4 tbsp semi-whipped double cream
Salt and freshly ground black pepper
2 tomatoes, peeled, de-seeded and diced
Flat continental parsley sprigs to decorate

First make the fish stock. Chop fish bones and wash thoroughly under cold running water to remove any traces of blood. Heat oil and butter in a pan and gently sweat onion and leek until soft, but not browned. Add fish bones and stir around for a minute. Top up with water to cover. Add bouquet garni and peppercorns. Bring to the boil and simmer for 20 minutes, skimming off froth occasionally. Strain and reserve stock, discarding debris.

Melt butter in a pan and fry onion and garlic until soft. Add reserved stock, white wine and saffron and boil rapidly to reduce by half. Add monkfish in batches and poach until cooked through. Add mussels and cook, covered, until opened.

Discard any that do not open. Reserve fish and mussels, covered, and keep hot.

Whisk cream into sauce and season with salt and freshly ground black pepper. Sprinkle in tomato dice. Arrange monkfish and mussels on individual plates and spoon over a little sauce to serve. Decorate with continental parsley sprigs.

Preparation time: 30 minutes
Cooking time: 45 minutes

Approximate nutritional values per portion:	
375 calories	40g protein
21g fat	5g carbohydrate

BUYING AND STORING

Saffron threads are available from supermarkets and also delicatessens. They are expensive, but a little goes a long way. If too much is used in a recipe, this intensely flavoured, fragrant spice can be overpowering.

Sachets of powdered saffron are cheaper and may be substituted in any recipe which calls for threads. This does not need infusing in water first as the threads do – simply add straight from the sachet to the dish.

Always store saffron in an airtight dark glass jar or tin, away from heat and sunlight which affect the flavour and colour of the delicate threads. Place container in a dry larder or cupboard to preserve the saffron.

RABBIT WITH SAFFRON

A great mix of flavours in this robust stew of rabbit flavoured with bacon, garlic and saffron. *Serves 4*

6 tbsp oil
4 rashers streaky bacon
4oz/100g small button mushrooms, wiped
1 oven-ready rabbit in 8 joints
Seasoned flour
8 shallots, peeled
½ onion, peeled and finely chopped
4 cloves garlic, peeled and crushed
  (add more to taste if you like it)
½pt/300ml dry white wine
¼pt/150ml chicken stock
Pinch saffron threads
Good squeeze of lemon
Salt and freshly ground black pepper

In 2 tbsp oil, cook bacon and mushrooms until bacon is crisp. Remove with a slotted spoon and transfer to a flameproof casserole.

Dip rabbit joints in seasoned flour and fry in remaining oil on all sides until brown. Remove from pan and add to casserole.

Add shallots, onion and garlic to the pan and cook over gentle heat until golden and soft, but not brown. Add to other ingredients.

Pour over white wine and stock. Add saffron threads. Bring to bubbling point, then turn down to simmer for 1 hour, or until rabbit is almost cooked. Add lemon juice, season, and continue cooking until rabbit is tender.

Preparation time: 20 minutes
Cooking time: 1½ hours approx

Approximate nutritional values per portion:	
400 calories	35g protein
18g fat	10g carbohydrate

SAFFRON TIPS

● Soak saffron threads in a little water before using in cooking. Place them in a small bowl, pour over hot water and leave for 15 minutes. This brings out the flavour and colour. Use both threads and the liquid in the recipe.

● Saffron is a fragrant spice best used in small quantities because it has a strong flowery aroma and pungent flavour. It is better to use it on its own in a recipe, as it does not blend well with conflicting herbs or spices.

● Saffron risotto is the traditional accompaniment to the Italian dish Osso Buco, a slowly cooked stew of shin of veal. It goes well with other meaty stews too. For 4: soak ½ tsp saffron threads (or to taste) in a little hot water for 15 minutes.

Meanwhile, heat 2 tbsp oil in a pan and fry 1 onion with 2 crushed cloves garlic until softened but not brown. Stir in 8oz/225g risotto rice to coat.

Add saffron threads and liquid and some chicken or vegetable stock from 1½pt/850ml. Bring to the boil and simmer until all liquid is absorbed. Gradually add more stock, waiting until the last lot has soaked in before adding more. Cook until rice is tender. Stir in 2 tbsp freshly grated Parmesan cheese. Season with salt and freshly ground black pepper. Sprinkle with extra grated Parmesan cheese to serve.

● Add a pinch of saffron threads to a chicken casserole to give a lovely yellow colour and exotic taste to the sauce.

● Saffron mashed potatoes are a great match with grilled lamb or steak. Infuse a few strands of saffron for 2 minutes in melted butter. Gradually beat the saffron butter into mashed potato, with a little salt and lots of freshly ground black pepper.

SCALLOPS

Scallops are popular molluscs, highly sought after for specialities worldwide. Both the delicate white flesh and the pretty pink roe or 'coral' are used in many shellfish recipes.

It is because of the fluted or 'scalloped' shell that these tender delicacies are connected with the birth of Venus. She was reputed to have ridden in a half shell. The pilgrims of St James were also associated with scallops. They wore the shells as badges on their hats. In France scallops are known as Coquilles St Jacques, taken from the English name James.

Scallops can propel themselves through the water by opening and closing their shells. Some are lazy and anchor themselves to rocks. Found in many oceans including the Pacific, north Atlantic and Mediterranean, they are caught by trawling or dredging. When caught they are either stored in seawater to keep them alive and at the peak of freshness, or they are completely prepared and cleaned at sea. They are then sold frozen.

An increase in their popularity in restaurants and hotels the world over has forced the price of scallops into the luxury bracket. However, since there is little waste and they add a touch of sophistication to seafood dishes, it is worth spending the extra. They are best cooked for a short time in delicate flavourings and go well with creamy or buttery sauces.

PANG'S SCALLOPS

Delicate stir-fry of thinly slivered scallops flavoured with ginger, sherry and soy sauce and cooked with matchstick strips of carrot and leek – a fast and tasty first course. *Serves 4*

2 tbsp oil
1oz/25g butter
1 clove garlic, crushed
1 carrot, peeled and cut into thin sticks
1 leek, trimmed, cut into thin strips and washed
4 spring onions, trimmed and cut into sticks
1in/2.5cm root ginger, peeled and cut into strips
8 scallops with corals, sliced
Dash of soy sauce
Dash of dry sherry
Freshly ground black pepper

Heat oil and butter in a large pan. Add garlic, carrot, leek, spring onions and root ginger. Stir-fry over a high heat for 4 minutes. Remove with a slotted spoon and keep hot. Add scallops to the pan and cook for 30 seconds to seal. Add soy sauce, sherry and return vegetables to pan. Season with black pepper. Stir to mix then pile onto warmed serving dishes. Garnish with coriander sprigs.

Preparation time: 20 minutes
Cooking time: 5 minutes approx

Approximate nutritional values per portion:	
220 calories	28g protein
10g fat	5g carbohydrate

SCALLOP CHOWDER

A truly exquisite soup. *Serves 4*

2 tbsp oil
1 onion, peeled and finely chopped
4 sticks celery, washed and sliced
2pt/1.1ltr fish stock
2lb/900g potatoes, peeled and cut into chunks
7oz/200g tin sweetcorn kernels
¼pt/150ml double cream
12 shelled scallops with corals
Few chopped chives

Heat oil and fry onion and celery over low heat until softened.

Pour in stock. Add potatoes. Bring to the boil and simmer until potatoes are tender. Add sweetcorn, cream and scallops with corals. Cook gently until scallops are just cooked. Sprinkle with chives.

Preparation time: 15 minutes
Cooking time: 20 minutes

Approximate nutritional values per portion:	
425 calories	44g protein
18g fat	28g carbohydrate

NUTRITION

Scallops are hermaphrodite molluscs prized for their sweet, creamy white flesh known as the 'nut' and the pale orange roe called the 'coral'. Scallops must always be fresh and a sweet smell indicates this, but they do not have to be 'alive' prior to cooking. Live scallops removed from shells will store for up to 24 hours. Fresh scallops are often sold already opened and cleaned, with beards and muscle tissue removed.

Per 4oz/100g scallop meat contains approximately 90 calories, 17g protein, 1g fat, 3g carbohydrate, 87mg sodium, and 36mg cholesterol.

4oz/100g scallops contain:	
90 calories	17g protein
1g fat	3g carbohydrate

SCALLOP SHELLS

Use scallop shells to make these pretty pastry cases. *Serves 4*

8 scallop shells, 4 'top' and 4 'base'
Butter for brushing
1lb/450g shortcrust pastry
1 egg, beaten
1oz/25g butter
2 shallots, peeled and chopped
4oz/100g button mushrooms, wiped and sliced
8 scallops with corals, sliced
Good dash of dry white wine
1/4pt/150ml double cream
Salt and freshly ground black pepper

Check shells for any cracks, and dry thoroughly. Lightly butter the insides of each shell. Roll out pastry thinly on a lightly floured board and use to line inside of the shells. Trim edges and firmly press pastry into the shells. Chill for 30 minutes. Bake at Gas 6, 400F, 200C for 15 minutes or until golden. Cool slightly and remove shell from pastry. Brush egg over outside of 4 'top' shells and return to oven for 5 minutes to become glossy. Remove and cool.

Melt butter and fry shallots and mushrooms until softened. Remove with a slotted spoon and reserve. Add scallops and corals to pan and quickly fry to seal. Return mushroom mixture and stir in wine, cream, salt and pepper. Bring to bubbling point. Remove from heat.

Place 4 'base' shells on 4 individual plates and fill with mixture. Place lid on top and decorate with frisée. Pour cream sauce around each shell.

Preparation time: 45 minutes
Cooking time: 25 minutes approx

Approximate nutritional values per portion:	
750 calories	40g protein
45g fat	95g carbohydrate

BROCHETTES OF SCALLOP

Luxury kebabs for all fish lovers. Brushed with this special lemon baste this makes a perfect dinner party dish very original and simply wonderful. *Makes 4*

8 scallops with corals
12oz/350g monkfish, boned and cut into
    neat chunks
4 bay leaves

For the lemon and garlic baste:
2 tbsp oil
2 cloves garlic, peeled and sliced
Zest of 1/2 lemon
1 tbsp finely chopped parsley
Salt and freshly ground black pepper

Thread scallops, corals, monkfish and bay leaves on to 4 metal skewers. Mix baste ingredients and spoon over kebabs. Grill until just cooked through, turning and basting occasionally. Serve with lettuce and lemon twist.

Preparation time: 25 minutes
Cooking time: 5 minutes approx

Approximate nutritional values per portion:	
250 calories	45g protein
8g fat	nil carbohydrate

SCALLOP TIPS

● To prise open fresh scallops firstly pick over and rinse mud or any dirt from the shells. Hold the scallop flat side down in a cloth in the palm of one hand. Using an oyster knife, gently lever between the two shells to separate. Cut through the muscle and discard the top shell. Gently scoop out white flesh and coral of the scallop in one piece if possible, leaving the darker pieces and the 'frilly' membrane behind. Remove the crescent-shaped muscle from the scallop before reserving. Always open scallops over a bowl to catch the juices.

● Coquilles St Jacques is a delicious dinner party starter. To serve 4: remove 4 scallops from the shells, reserving shells for serving. Separate white meat from the orange 'coral' and slice thinly. Poach gently for 1 minute with 1/4pt/150ml dry white wine and 1/2pt/300ml fish stock until just cooked. Remove and reserve. Make a white sauce using reserved poaching liquid and enrich with 2 tbsp double cream and 1 egg yolk. Do not boil. Pile mixture into 4 cleaned shell halves. Pipe a ring of hot mashed potato around each one and grill until potato browns. Sprinkle over finely chopped parsley.

● To make sophisticated party nibbles, fill vol-au-vents with sliced scallops in a creamy sauce. First poach prepared scallops in a little fish stock and dry white wine for 1 minute or until just cooked. Remove with a slotted spoon and reserve liquid. To make the sauce, melt 1/2oz/15g butter in a pan. Add 1/2oz/15g flour and stir for 1 minute. Gradually add reserved cooking liquid, made up to 1/4pt/150ml with extra fish stock. Stir, bring to the boil until thickened. Season and stir in 2 tbsp double cream and a little finely chopped dill. Mix scallops with sauce and spoon into cooked vol-au-vent cases.

SMOKED HADDOCK

Haddock is a member of the cod family, and is a round fish which usually grows to around 32in/80cm.

The outstanding features of haddock are the dark grey smudges found on both sides of the fish behind the fins which look like thumb prints. It was believed that St Peter picked up the fish and the indentations from his hands remained on the skin. Haddock are a glossy steel green-grey, with a clear black line running along the length.

Smoking fish is an ancient method of preserving, and there are two ways to do this. 'Cold smoking' means the fish is cured by smoking at a temperature of around 92F/33C. This does not cook the flesh of the fish, but imparts the distinctive smoky flavour. Fish smoked this way must be cooked before consumption. Finnan haddock, named after the village of Findon in Scotland, are split and cold smoked, not usually dyed and must be cooked before eating. These may also be known as Finnan Haddie. Smoked salmon is the exception to this rule, and is eaten straight from the cold smoking. Glasgow Pales are smaller haddock prepared the same way as Finnans.

Hot smoking means the fish is smoked at a higher temperature, which cooks the fish. Arbroath Smokies are small haddock which are beheaded, left whole and then hot smoked in pairs. These should be heated before serving with a brush of butter to moisten the flesh.

Smoked haddock is available all year round and can be poached, grilled or baked.

SMOKED HADDOCK FLORENTINE

Substantial supper dish packed with protein and vitamins. *Serves 2*

8oz/225g smoked haddock fillet
1½oz/40g butter
4oz/100g cooked leaf spinach
Salt and freshly ground black pepper
Grated nutmeg
1 tbsp flour
½pt/300ml milk
1oz/25g grated Cheddar
2 eggs

Poach haddock in a little water until cooked through. Discard water. Keep fish hot.

Melt ½oz/15g butter in a pan and add spinach. Toss to coat and heat through. Add salt, pepper and nutmeg. Pile into a warmed gratin dish. Place the fish on top, cover and keep hot while making the sauce.

Melt remaining butter in a pan and stir in flour. Cook for 1 minute. Gradually add milk, stirring, and bring to the boil until thickened. Add cheese and stir until melted. Season and pour over fish. Place under a hot grill to brown. Meanwhile soft poach eggs and place on top of haddock before serving.

Preparation time: 20 minutes
Cooking time: 30 minutes

Approximate nutritional values per portion:	
400 calories	35g protein
16g fat	10g carbohydrate

NUTRITION

The process of smoking a haddock causes no significant changes in its nutrients. A light smoking gives a mild flavour, and when no artificial dyes are used, the haddock is a delicate pale straw colour. Check with the fishmonger which process has been used or, if the fish is pre-packed, from the label.

Fish is one of the healthiest foods in the diet. Regions of the world where fish is on the menu at least twice a week have less incidence of heart disease.

White fish is also a rich source of minerals. One fillet around 4oz/100g contains 87mg calcium, 1.5mg iron, 0.6mg zinc, 435mg potassium, 37.5mg magnesium and 375mg phosphorus. When poached or baked without extra oil the calorie count is around 150.

Haddock is cold smoked which means the fish is cured by smoking at an air temperature of around 92F/33C. This means the fish doesn't cook, but absorbs a delicate smoky aroma. It does require cooking afterwards.

4oz/100g smoked haddock contain:	
150 calories	35g protein
1g fat	nil carbohydrate

SMOKED HADDOCK AND SWEETCORN QUICHE

Sunshine yellow quiche packed with smoked haddock flakes and sweetcorn kernels. *Serves 6*

8oz/225g shortcrust pastry
1lb/450g smoked haddock fillet, poached
4 tbsp sweetcorn kernels
3 eggs
4 tbsp double cream
¼pt/150ml milk
Freshly ground black pepper

Roll out pastry on a lightly floured board. Line an 8in/20cm flan dish. Chill for 30 minutes, then bake blind at Gas 6, 400F, 200C for 10 minutes. Cool.

Flake poached haddock and remove bones. Sprinkle into pastry case with sweetcorn. Whisk eggs, cream and milk together with black pepper and pour over. Return to oven and bake at Gas 6, 400F, 200C for 30 minutes or until it has set.

Preparation time: 20 minutes
Cooking time: 45 minutes approx

Approximate nutritional values per portion:	
420 calories	25g protein
25g fat	20g carbohydrate

Kedgeree was once a favourite Victorian breakfast of smoked haddock, rice and eggs. Although still a breakfast treat, these days it has become a lunch, supper or chic buffet party dish, too.

For 2: fry 1 chopped onion in 2oz/50g butter until softened. Add ½ tsp curry paste. Add 8oz/225g cooked long grain rice and stir. Poach 1lb/450g smoked haddock in milk until cooked through. Skin, flake and remove bones, then add to rice to heat through. Add 2 chopped hard-boiled eggs, and season.

SMOKED HADDOCK TIPS

● Smoked fish should have a delicate smoked aroma, with a bright smooth surface and firm texture. The colour of smoked fish varies between regions because of different smoking techniques. However, smoked haddock which has not been artificially dyed is a delicate pale straw colour, while dyed fish is an unattractive deep golden yellow.

● Finnan haddock is a whole haddock smoked on the bone, split along the length and sold opened out flat. It is considered to be the best quality haddock.

Arbroath Smokies are delicious too. These are smaller haddock with heads removed, cleaned but left whole before being hot smoked to a rich deep brown colour. These are ready to eat as bought but even more delicious grilled or baked with a light brushing of butter.

● Mix smoked haddock with cream cheese for a fishy stuffing for tartlets, canapés or profiteroles, or to serve with toast.

Place 8oz/225g smoked haddock in a pan with a little milk flavoured with half an onion and a few black peppercorns. Poach until cooked through, and remove from liquid. Mash with a fork and cool. Mix with 8oz/225g cream cheese adding a little milk if necessary and some grated onion. Season well with plenty of freshly ground black pepper.

● One of the most famous dishes using smoked haddock is Omelette Arnold Bennett, an omelette with a rich filling of haddock and cheese.

Mix 2oz/50g cooked flaked Finnan haddock with ½ tbsp freshly grated Parmesan cheese. Pour the mixture for a 2-egg omelette into a hot buttered omelette pan and stir briskly with a fork, dragging the sides to the middle. When the egg has almost set, scatter over fish and cheese. Spoon over a little double cream. Remove from heat and place under a hot grill until bubbling and golden. Season with freshly ground black pepper and slide on to a warmed plate. Serves 1.

● Mix smoked haddock with white fish for a tasty fish pie. Top with piped mashed potato sprinkled with grated cheese and flash under the grill for a golden finish.

● When poaching smoked haddock always keep the liquid to make a flavoursome sauce.

● Fancy fish for breakfast? Smoked haddock served with a poached egg on top makes a delicious and healthy alternative.

SMOKED HADDOCK PATE

Sophisticated, subtly flavoured fish pâté perfect for a dinner party starter or a lunch or supper snack. *Serves 6*

12oz/350g smoked haddock fillet
¼pt/150ml milk
4oz/100g curd cheese
1 tbsp grated onion
4 tbsp double cream
2 tbsp freshly chopped dill
Freshly ground white pepper
½ sachet aspic powder
Frond of dill, peppercorns and bay leaves
for decoration

Poach haddock in milk until it is cooked through.

Cool, remove skin and flake. Pick out any bones. Place in processor with cheese and whizz until blended. Add onion, cream, dill and season with pepper. Spoon into a pot. Make up aspic according to instructions.

Place a frond of dill, a few peppercorns and bay leaves in a pretty pattern on top of pâté. When aspic is syrupy, pour a thin layer over pâté and refrigerate until set. Serve with fresh crusty bread.

Preparation time: 15 minutes
Cooking time: 10 minutes

Approximate nutritional values per portion:	
270 calories	15g protein
30g fat	8g carbohydrate

CULLEN SKINK

Based on a traditional soup from Scotland, this is a delectable mixture of haddock, onions and mashed potato. *Serves 4*

1lb/450g smoked haddock fillet
½pt/300ml water
1 onion, peeled and sliced
1½pt/850ml milk
2 potatoes, peeled, cooked and mashed
2 tbsp finely chopped parsley
Salt and freshly ground black pepper
Chopped parsley for decoration

Poach haddock in water with onion until cooked

through. Remove and reserve liquid and onion slices. Remove skin from fish, flake and pick out bones.

Add milk to fish cooking liquid and stir in potatoes and parsley. Bring to the boil to thicken and add fish flakes. Season and bring back to just bubbling. Spoon into bowls and sprinkle with parsley to decorate.

Preparation time: 20 minutes
Cooking time: 20 minutes

Approximate nutritional values per portion:	
250 calories	15g protein
5g fat	10g carbohydrate

SMOKED SALMON

Often regarded as the king of smoked fish, the best smoked salmon is said to come from Scotland. But it is also produced elsewhere in the British Isles, such as Wales, and Northern Ireland. Cures differ between regions and smokehouses, but the basic principle is the same.

First the fish is filleted into 'sides'. Next it is soaked in salt – either dry or in the form of brine, usually for 24 hours. The recipe for the brine is often the secret which gives the finished smoked salmon different flavours. It might be juniper berries, herbs, rum, Drambuie, even molasses, or other ingredients.

The next stage is the cold smoking of the fish. Cold smoking is the process usually given to fish which need to be cooked before eating. The smoking is only hot enough to flavour it – not to cook it as well – as with kippers. Smoked salmon is, of course, eaten raw, and cold smoking gives it the delicate flavour of the wood used – often from whisky casks plus other wood chips.

A new method of rearing salmon organically has been developed over the last 12 months off the coast of Northern Ireland. No chemicals are used in the feed or to combat diseases. These Glenarm fish are split, then dry salted in the traditional way. The process is finished with smoking at the Severn and Wye Smokery in Gloucester over oak chips to give a smoked salmon with a refined and sophisticated flavour and texture.

SMOKED SALMON PATE

This smoked salmon pâté is served in scoops. Made with curd cheese, low in fat, it is then flavoured with lemon, Tabasco and grated onion.
Serves 4

4oz/100g smoked salmon scraps
4oz/100g curd cheese
2 tbsp double cream
1 tbsp grated onion
Juice of ½ lemon
Dash of Tabasco sauce
Freshly ground black pepper
Dill fronds, smoked salmon knots and lemon
  triangles for decoration

Roughly chop the smoked salmon and whizz in the blender until very fine. Add curd cheese and whizz again until all is incorporated and it becomes an even coral pink colour. Add cream and blend to soften the consistency. Stir in grated onion, lemon juice, and Tabasco and whizz again for 10 seconds. Season with plenty of black pepper.

Transfer to a bowl since this makes it easier to serve with an ice cream scoop. Scoop out a portion for each person and unmould on to a bed of dill fronds. Decorate each with a knotted strip of smoked salmon and a peeled triangle of lemon. Serve with crisp Melba toast.
Preparation time: 15 minutes
Cooking time: nil

Approximate nutritional values per portion:	
115 calories	11g protein
7g fat	1g carbohydrate

NUTRITION

For most people, smoked salmon is a luxury food eaten as a special treat rather than an everyday item, simply because of its high price. So although this delicacy has valuable nutrients, they don't make a significant contribution to the average diet.

Two slices of smoked salmon weighing about 4oz/100g contain 160 calories, about a third less than ordinary raw salmon fillet.

Smoked salmon is a good source of protein.

There are important minerals in smoked salmon.Calcium, for healthy teeth and bones, potassium, for the make-up of muscle tissue, and phosphorus, needed for cell replacement, are all present.

4oz/100g smoked salmon contain:	
160 calories	28g protein
5g fat	nil carbohydrate

BUYING AND STORING

Best smoked salmon is reddish-pink with a firm texture – although the colour is no real indication of quality. Slices should be just opaque, with a waxy look.

Smoked salmon can be bought sliced to order, or pre-packed. Fresh sliced salmon should be kept wrapped in the fridge to keep it from drying out. Eat within a week.

A side of smoked salmon, however, will keep well in the fridge for around three weeks, wrapped well, once it has been cut. If you eat smoked salmon often, it is well worth buying a whole side since these are much cheaper than already sliced. Vacuum packed will also keep for two to three weeks.

To prolong the life further, these packs can be successfully frozen with no impairment of flavour for up to six months.

SMOKED SALMON RITZIES

Irresistible bites of smoked salmon whirls on croutons topped with lumpfish roe and a slice of hard-boiled quail's egg. *Makes 12*

> *3 slices white bread*
> *1oz/25g butter for spreading*
> *4oz/100g smoked salmon slices, cut in long strips*
> *1oz/25g black lumpfish roe*
> *4 hard-boiled quail's eggs, shelled*
> *Sprigs of parsley*
> *Lemon twists for decoration*

Cut out 12 rounds from the bread. Toast and butter.

Cut smoked salmon lengthways into ½in/1cm strips. Roll up into coils. Place on the croutons buttered side up. Spread a little lumpfish roe on top. Finish with a slice of hard-boiled quail's egg, a small sprig of parsley, and a twist of lemon.

Preparation time: 20 minutes
Cooking time: 3 minutes

Approximate nutritional values per portion – 3 ritzies:	
163 calories	10g protein
10g fat	15g carbohydrate

SMOKED SALMON AND ASPARAGUS TARTS

Crisp tartlets filled with asparagus tips and smoked salmon strips. *Serves 4*

For the pastry:
> *4oz/100g butter, in cubes*
> *6oz/175g plain flour, sifted*
> *Pinch of salt*
> *1 egg, beaten*

For the filling:
> *2 eggs*
> *5 tbsp double cream*
> *Salt and freshly ground black pepper*
> *14oz/400g tin asparagus tips, drained*
> *4oz/100g smoked salmon slices, in strips*

For the pastry, rub butter into flour and salt to breadcrumb stage. Add a whole beaten egg, and work this into the mixture by hand until smooth. Turn out on to a floured worktop and knead lightly. Wrap in non-PVC film or foil and chill for 30 minutes.

Roll out pastry on a lightly floured board to line 4 individual loose-bottomed fluted tartlet tins. Bake blind at Gas 6, 400F, 200C for 5 minutes or until set. Remove from the oven. For the filling, beat eggs and cream together and season. Arrange asparagus in parallel lines over base of tins leaving spaces in between. Pour filling over. Lay smoked salmon strips in the spaces between asparagus. Return to oven at Gas 4, 350F, 180C for 15 minutes or until set. Serve hot, warm or cold.

Preparation time: 30 minutes
Cooking time: 20 minutes

Approximate nutritional values per portion:	
485 calories	21g protein
50g fat	35g carbohydrate

NOODLES WITH SMOKED SALMON AND SALMON CAVIAR

An appealing dish of fresh egg noodles tossed in cream with strips of smoked salmon. Salmon eggs are available in small jars from delicatessens and fish shops. *Serves 4*

> *12oz/350g fresh egg noodles*
> *4 tbsp double cream*
> *2 tbsp fresh chives, chopped*
> *8oz/225g smoked salmon, in thin strips*
> *2oz/50g jar salmon eggs*
> *Salt and freshly ground white pepper*

Cook noodles in boiling, lightly salted water for 3 minutes or until just tender. Drain. Return to pan and pour over cream and sprinkle in chives. Add smoked salmon strips and salmon eggs and turn over gently. Season.

Divide between 4 warmed pasta bowls and serve immediately.

Preparation time: 5 minutes
Cooking time: 5 minutes approx

Approximate nutritional values per portion:	
240 calories	21g protein
21g fat	20g carbohydrate

SMOKED SALMON TIPS

● It's cheaper to buy a whole side of smoked salmon on the skin and slice it when required. The bones have to be removed before slicing though, otherwise they will tear through the flesh as you cut, and spoil the slices. Pare away the top surface of dried flesh and cut off the fins and any visible large bones at the head end. Next, run an index finger down the centre to feel any small bones sticking out. Pick them out with clean tweezers or a small pair of pliers.

● Save smoked salmon trimmings left over after slicing to make mousse or smoked salmon pâté.

● To keep the remaining unsliced flesh on the salmon moist, fold over the exposed skin at the tail end. Wrap the fish in non-PVC film or foil and store in the fridge.

● For a super luxury breakfast, mix strips of smoked salmon with soft scrambled eggs and season with freshly ground black pepper. Serve with brown toast and a glass of chilled Champagne!

● A side of smoked salmon is easy to slice after the bones have been removed. Starting about one third of the way along, slice the flesh thinly at a slight angle towards the tail end. Proceed in this way along the salmon, moving the knife a little further up the fish with each slice. As you slice, the angle will become steeper and eventually the knife blade will come into contact with the skin. Do not cut right through.

● Include smoked salmon pieces in a luxury fish pie. For 4: cut 1½lb/700g skinned cod fillet into chunks and poach in a little fish stock. Drain and reserve. Melt 1oz/25g butter in a pan and sweat 2 tbsp finely chopped onion. Stir in 1oz/25g flour. Cook for 1 minute. Gradually add 1pt/600ml milk, stirring continuously. Bring to the boil to thicken. Season with salt and freshly ground white pepper and a squeeze of lemon juice. Stir 8oz/225g peeled prawns, 4oz/100g cooked shelled mussels and 2oz/50g smoked salmon, in strips, plus reserved cod chunks. Add 2 quartered hard-boiled eggs and 1 tbsp chopped parsley. Stir gently to heat fish through. Spoon into a pie dish and top with swirls of mashed potato. Bake at Gas 6, 400F, 200C for 30 minutes or until filling is hot and potato is golden.

SPINACH

Spinach is thought to have its origins in Asia. It has long been known as a cultivated plant, grown by the Graeco-Roman civilisations in Persia. It is believed to have reached Europe via Dutch travellers who introduced it in the 16th century.

At this time spinach was referred to as 'spynnage' and was termed a herb or 'salat-herbe', as one English writer described it.

Almost 100 years later, spinach was still considered best used in salads, and another journal reported spinach as being good for the stomach.

Supposedly, it was the Dutch who taught the English their method of cooking spinach – in a pot with no water added. These days, this way is still very popular, cooking the spinach to absolute perfection without actually ruining its flavour or destroying its vitamin content.

This leafy green vegetable was made famous in the thirties by the American cartoon character Popeye. Its valuable nutrients fortified him and gave him strength, energy and large muscles to fight his rival for the attentions of his leading lady, Olive Oyl.

Far from being just a salad leaf, spinach can be used in a variety of recipes. Spinach soup is a good dish for older, tougher leaves, while younger more tender spinach can be wilted in hot oil and tossed with slivers of avocado and crispy bacon for a quick first course or light lunch.

Eggs Florentine is one of the most famous spinach dishes. This consists of poached eggs nestling on a bed of buttered spinach topped with a creamy bechamel sauce.

SPINACH ROLLOS

Crackly filo pastry encases a filling of spinach and curd cheese flavoured with nutmeg, garlic and grated onion. *Serves 4, makes 8*

2 tbsp oil
1 onion, peeled and finely chopped
2 cloves garlic, peeled and crushed
1lb/450g fresh spinach, cleaned and trimmed
6oz/175g curd cheese
Salt and freshly ground black pepper
Freshly grated nutmeg
2 sheets filo pastry
Melted butter

Heat oil in a pan and fry onion and garlic until soft. Remove with a slotted spoon and reserve. Cool. Blanch spinach and chop roughly. Squeeze out excess water. Mix in a bowl with onion, garlic and curd cheese. Season with salt, freshly ground black pepper and nutmeg.

Cut each sheet of filo pastry into 4 squares. Brush with melted butter. Spoon mixture onto the pastry. Fold the sides inwards to enclose. Roll up to make a pastry cigar.

Brush with more melted butter. Bake in a pre-heated oven Gas 6, 400F, 200C for about 15 minutes or until pastry is crackly and golden. Cool on a wire rack.

Preparation time: 30 minutes
Cooking time: 15 minutes

Approximate nutritional values per rollo:	
55 calories	3g protein
3g fat	1g carbohydrate

BUYING AND STORING

Home-grown spinach is in the shops from May to June, and September to October. Imported varieties from Italy, France, Belgium, Spain and Cyprus are available at other times of the year.

Greengrocers usually sell spinach 'loose' and this makes it easy to check for freshness. Look for relatively clean leaves with a good green colour. Pick out any dead, yellow or damaged leaves and avoid those with hard stalks or flowering shoots. These indicate that the spinach is past its best.

Supermarkets stock pre-weighed bags of spinach wrapped in plastic. This may cause sweating of the leaves and will eventually lead to rot. Inspect bags carefully and check sell-by dates.

Spinach should be purchased and eaten as fresh as possible. Store it in the fridge and eat within 2 days.

When fresh spinach is not available, it may be bought frozen or canned instead.

NUTRITION

Spinach is low in calories, with only 30 in a 4oz/100g cooked portion. The same weight has 5g of protein, necessary for normal growth and development and 1.4g of carbohydrate, for energy. There is only a trace of fat in spinach.

High in vitamin C, 4oz/100g fresh raw spinach provides 80 per cent of the recommended daily amount for a healthy adult. Its deep green colour indicates a very good supply of yellow carotenes, which the body converts to vitamin A.

Spinach leaves are rich in vitamin B2, or riboflavin. This vitamin is not as easily destroyed by cooking as other vitamins, but because it is water soluble, some will leak out into the cooking liquid.

To retain lost nutrients, it is best to include the water in any accompanying sauce or gravy.

To gain the benefit of all the valuable vitamins and minerals in spinach, it is best eaten fresh and raw or very lightly cooked by steaming or wilting in hot oil.

Calcium, required for healthy teeth and bones, is present in spinach. There is also a useful amount of iron, for healthy blood.

4oz/100g cooked spinach contain:	
30 calories	5g protein
0.5g fat	1.4g carbohydrate

SOLE WITH CRISP-FRIED SPINACH

Oriental-style dish of sole strips served on a bed of crisp ribbons of spinach. *Serves 4*

1lb/450g fresh spinach
Oil for frying
Salt and freshly ground black pepper
Pinch of cayenne
1in/2.5cm fresh root ginger, peeled and in strips
2 cloves garlic, peeled and crushed
1 red and 1 yellow pepper, de-seeded and in strips
4 spring onions, sliced
4 sole fillets, in strips
1 tbsp soy sauce
2 tbsp dry sherry
Juice of ½ lemon

Wash spinach and pat dry. Trim stalks and cut leaves into ½in/1cm ribbons. Shallow fry in batches until crisp. Remove with a slotted spoon and drain on kitchen paper. Season with salt, pepper and cayenne.

Heat 2 tbsp oil in a pan and fry ginger, garlic, peppers and spring onions gently until soft. Remove with a slotted spoon. Stir-fry sole strips quickly to seal. Return vegetables to pan and sprinkle over soy, sherry and lemon. Cook 2 minutes more and season.

Arrange spinach on a platter and heap sole mixture on top.

Preparation time: 20 minutes
Cooking time: 25 minutes

Approximate nutritional values per portion:	
150 calories	20g protein
3g fat	5g carbohydrate

SMOKED DUCK WITH SPINACH

Smoked duck served with wilted spinach and papaya purée. *Serves 4*

2 papayas
2 tbsp dry white wine
Salt and freshly ground black pepper
Juice of ½ lime
1lb/450g fresh spinach, trimmed
Little oil
2 cloves garlic, crushed
1 tsp grated fresh root ginger
2 smoked duck breasts, ready to serve

Peel and de-seed papayas and purée with white wine. Season with salt and freshly ground black pepper, plus a dash of lime juice.

Wilt the spinach by tossing in a large heavy bottomed pan with a little oil, garlic and grated ginger.

Neatly slice duck breasts and arrange on a serving platter. Surround with wilted spinach and drizzle over sauce.

Preparation time: 10 minutes
Cooking time: 10 minutes

Approximate nutritional values per portion:	
320 calories	32g protein
15g fat	10g carbohydrate

QUAILS EGGS FLORENTINE

Delightful first course of lightly poached quails' eggs resting on a bed of buttered spinach topped with cheese sauce and paprika. *Serves 4*

12oz/350g fresh spinach, washed and trimmed
Melted butter
Salt and freshly ground black pepper
12 quail's eggs
For the sauce:
1oz/25g butter
1 tbsp flour
½pt/300ml milk
2oz/50g Gruyère, grated
Extra cheese for decoration and paprika
  for topping

Cook spinach in lightly salted boiling water for 2 minutes. Drain and squeeze out excess water. Stir through butter and season to taste, then place spinach in the base of 4 ramekins.

Next, make the sauce. Melt butter in a pan and stir in flour. Cook 1 minute. Remove from heat and gradually add milk. Stir to incorporate. Return to heat and bring to the boil, stirring all the time to thicken. Add cheese and stir until melted. Season. Remove from heat and cover with buttered greaseproof.

Poach 12 quail's eggs and trim with a small round cutter to remove excess white. Sit on top of spinach. Top with sauce and extra grated cheese. Grill until golden and serve sprinkled with paprika.

Preparation time: 30 minutes
Cooking time: 30 minutes

Approximate nutritional values per portion:	
280 calories	15g protein
20g fat	5g carbohydrate

SPINACH TIPS

● Spinach produces a lot of liquid during cooking. Drain it, then squeeze out excess by placing the spinach between two plates and pressing hard over a bowl to catch juices. Save the liquid that runs out and add to a sauce or gravy to retain lost nutrients. After squeezing, toss the spinach in butter and season with salt and freshly ground black pepper.

● Freshly grated nutmeg enhances the flavour of plain buttered spinach. Grate a little over whilst tossing in melted butter, then add seasoning.

● Spinach needs thorough washing in lots of cold water before cooking to remove any grit and dirt stuck to the leaves. Change the water several times to ensure the leaves are clean. Drain them well in a colander or put them into a salad spinner.

● After trimming, remove stalks. Cooking spinach reduces its bulk dramatically. Always allow 8oz/225g fresh raw spinach per person when buying to make certain of enough for everyone.

● Toss young and tender, de-stalked raw spinach with other pretty leaves to make a tumbly summer salad. Mix spinach with rocket, frisée, radicchio or any other combination and dress in a nutty vinaigrette dressing. Shake 3 tbsp sunflower and 1 tbsp walnut oil in a jar with ½ tsp Dijon mustard, 1 tbsp sherry vinegar, salt and freshly ground black pepper. Drizzle over leaves before serving in a pretty glass bowl.

● Spiced spinach is often served with curry dishes. For a quick homemade version, fry 1 peeled and finely sliced onion in 2 tbsp oil with 1 clove crushed garlic. Stir in 2 tbsp mild curry paste and cook for 1 minute. Add 1lb/450g cooked chopped spinach and toss in oily mixture. Add 2 peeled and de-seeded chopped tomatoes and cook until softened. Season with salt and freshly ground black pepper.

● Spinach gratin makes a good accompaniment to roast lamb or beef. Cook 2lb/900g cleaned and prepared chopped spinach in a covered pan with no extra water until tender. Heat ¼pt/150ml double cream in a separate pan and add cooked spinach. Season with salt, freshly ground black pepper and a little grated nutmeg. Place in a flameproof dish and sprinkle over 3 tbsp grated Parmesan or Gruyère. Brown under a hot grill and serve.

STILTON

The 'king of English cheeses', blue Stilton, can only be made in three counties – Leicestershire, Derbyshire and Nottinghamshire. The name is patented and the cheese must be made to the original old-established methods.

It was never actually produced in Stilton, a village in Cambridgeshire.

The first records of the cheese go back to the 18th century. It was made by Mrs Paulet, a farmer's wife who lived near Melton Mowbray. Her brother-in-law ran the Bell Inn in Stilton, a coaching house on the Great North Road, and it was here that the cheese was first served to travellers en route for London, York and Edinburgh. Its reputation soon spread.

The secret recipe was passed from mother to daughter – but soon similar recipes were being used in the surrounding villages, a threat to the true identity of the cheese.

In 1910, the main producers defined the region where it was allowed to be made – the Vale of Belvoir – and also the character of the cheese. In 1969 it became law that no cheese made outside this area could be described as Stilton.

It takes a gallon of milk to make a pound of Stilton. The milk is pumped into a vat and a starter culture and rennet are stirred through.

When curds form they are cut with knives to break them up. Next day the curds are cut again and ground into small pieces, seasoned, packed into moulds and left for seven days to develop. The cheeses are removed from the moulds and prepared for the rind to form.

At six weeks old, the cheeses are pierced with skewer-sized stainless steel rods which let in air and activate the harmless penicillium mould. The blue veins start to develop soon afterwards.

STILTON CHEESECAKE

This is a sensational light and airy textured baked cheesecake, packed with flavour. A wonderful savoury mix of blue Stilton and cream cheese on a cracker crumb base. *Serves 10*

For the base:
- *6oz/175g wholemeal crackers*
- *3oz/75g melted butter*

For the filling:
- *4 eggs, separated*
- *5fl oz/150ml sour cream*
- *2 tbsp plain flour*
- *8oz/225g cream cheese*
- *8oz/225g blue Stilton, mashed*
- *Salt and freshly ground black pepper*

Crumble crackers in a processor and whizz to crumb. Add butter. Press into the base of a loose-bottomed buttered 7in/18cm cake tin. Chill.

Whisk egg yolks until pale and thick. Fold in sour cream and sifted flour. Beat in cream cheese. Mix in mashed blue Stilton with a fork.

Whisk egg whites stiff and fold in with a metal spoon. Season with salt and freshly ground black pepper. Spoon mixture on to crumb base and smooth top. Bake at Gas 4, 350F, 180C for 1 hour, or until risen and golden, and firm to the touch. Cover with foil if top browns too soon. Remove from oven and cool on a wire rack. Chill before serving.

Preparation time: 20 minutes
Cooking time: 1 hour approx

Approximate nutritional values per portion:	
360 calories	10g protein
30g fat	15g carbohydrate

PASTA SALAD WITH PEAR AND STILTON

Pasta, crumbled blue Stilton and diced William's pears make a great flavour mix. *Serves 4*

- *12oz/350g pasta bows*
- *2 ripe William's pears*
- *Good squeeze of lemon juice*
- *4oz/100g blue Stilton*

For the dressing:
- *4 tbsp sunflower oil*
- *1 tbsp white wine vinegar*
- *1 tsp Dijon mustard*
- *1 tbsp snipped fresh chives*
- *Salt and freshly ground black pepper*

Cook pasta in boiling salted water according to instructions on the packet. Drain and refresh in cold water. Drain again.

Place in a bowl. Leaving the skin on, core and chop pears into small chunks and sprinkle with lemon juice to prevent discoloration. Add to pasta, and crumble in blue Stilton.

Shake dressing ingredients together in a screw-top jar. Pour over salad and toss lightly to mix. Sprinkle over extra snipped chives for decoration.

Preparation time: 15 minutes
Cooking time: 10 minutes approx

Approximate nutritional values per portion:	
466 calories	15g protein
15g fat	70g carbohydrate

NUTRITION

Blue Stilton, like all other English and Welsh cheeses, is an excellent source of essential nutrients. Most of these are retained from the milk during making and in fact cheese-making is one of the oldest ways of preserving these.

There are 23g of protein in 4oz/100g blue Stilton. The same weight contains 411 calories, but a normal portion is probably only 1oz/25g. There are 35g of fat in 4oz/100g blue Stilton and a trace of carbohydrate.

Blue Stilton provides generous amounts of calcium, required for healthy bone formation. There is a good quantity of vitamin A present, for healthy vision, along with some B vitamins for the maintenance of the nervous system, and traces of vitamins D and E.

There is a useful amount of folic acid in blue Stilton, which is needed for healthy blood. Other minerals include phosphorus, potassium, zinc and magnesium.

4oz/100g blue Stilton contain:	
411 calories	23g protein
35g fat	trace of carbohydrate

Hello! Good Cooking

WARM POTATO AND EGG SALAD IN STILTON VINAIGRETTE

This scrumptious chunky warm salad has the most delectable blue Stilton dressing. *Serves 4*

> *4 eggs*
> *1lb/450g small new potatoes, scrubbed*
> *2 medium courgettes, washed and in chunks*
> For the dressing:
> *2 tsp Dijon mustard*
> *1 tbsp white wine vinegar*
> *4 tbsp sunflower oil*
> *2 tbsp sour cream*
> *2oz/50g blue Stilton, mashed*
> *Salt and freshly ground black pepper*
> *Good squeeze lemon juice*

First make the dressing. Whisk together mustard and vinegar. Gradually add oil, drip by drip to combine evenly. Beat in sour cream and blue Stilton. Season with salt and freshly ground black pepper and lemon juice.

Hard boil eggs. Cook potatoes in lightly salted boiling water. Drain. Blanch courgettes and drain. Peel and quarter eggs. Place in a bowl.

Pour over dressing and carefully toss to coat while vegetables and eggs are still warm. Decorate with watercress.

Preparation time: 15 minutes
Cooking time: 15 minutes

Approximate nutritional values per portion:	
300 calories	12g protein
18g fat	23g carbohydrate

STILTON TIPS

● Potted blue Stilton makes a wonderful snack lunch. For a small pot, mash 8oz/225g blue Stilton with 2 tbsp port and a squeeze of lemon juice. Season with freshly ground black pepper. Spoon into a pretty pot and smooth surface. Chill and serve with crackers or brown toast.

● Add blue Stilton to a plain omelette for a rich and savoury creaminess. For 1: beat 2 eggs and season with salt and freshly ground black pepper. Heat oil in an omelette pan and add eggs, stir with a fork, bringing eggs in from sides to centre of pan. When the omelette has set on the bottom, but is still soft on top, crumble in 1oz/25g blue Stilton. Flip over one side of omelette to enclose and slide on to a warmed plate. Serve immediately.

● Stilton and celery make a classic soup. For 4: melt 2oz/50g butter in a large pan. Add 1 small onion, peeled and finely chopped and 2 sticks celery, chopped (including leaves) and fry gently to soften. Stir in 2 tbsp flour and cook 1 minute. Gradually pour over 1½pt/850ml chicken or vegetable stock. Bring to the boil, stirring until thickened. Simmer gently, covered, until celery is tender. Whizz smooth in the blender. Return to heat and crumble in 6oz/175g blue Stilton. Add 2 tbsp double cream and seasoning. Stir until cheese has melted.

BUYING AND STORING

Blue Stilton is a semi-hard, unpressed cheese, with a rich and creamy texture and the characteristic marbling of blue veins. It is often chosen as an after-dinner cheese with a glass of port. But its versatility, unique tangy flavour and salty piquancy makes it a perfect choice in many savoury dishes.

Best quality blue Stilton is creamy-white in colour with evenly distributed veining coming from the middle of the cheese. Whether bought loose, or pre-packed, the quality remains the same.

Always check vacuum-packed wedges for signs of sweating or discoloration.

After purchase wrap it in clean greaseproof paper and store in an airtight snap-top box in the fridge. Unwrap and leave for one hour before serving, to allow the flavour to develop.

BEEF PIES IN STILTON CRUST

Stilton pastry is perfect for savoury dishes like these little beef and mushroom pies. *Serves 4*

> For the pastry:
> *6oz/175g plain flour*
> *2oz/50g butter*
> *2oz/50g blue Stilton, crumbled*
> *½ tsp mustard powder*
> *1 egg*
> *Beaten egg to glaze*
> For the filling:
> *1½lb/700g chuck steak in chunks*
> *Seasoned flour*
> *3 tbsp oil*
> *1 onion, peeled and finely chopped*
> *2 cloves garlic, peeled and crushed*
> *1 tbsp fresh parsley, finely chopped*
> *½pt/300ml beef stock*
> *¼pt/150ml red wine*
> *6oz/175g button mushrooms, quartered*
> *Salt and freshly ground black pepper*

First make the pastry. Place flour, butter, blue Stilton, mustard and the egg in a processor and whizz until the mix makes a ball. Knead lightly on a floured surface, then wrap in film and chill.

For the filling, dip meat in seasoned flour and shake off excess. Heat oil in a pan and fry onion and garlic over low heat until soft. Remove with a slotted spoon and place in a large flameproof casserole. Turn up heat and fry coated chunks of chuck in batches to brown all over. Add to casserole. Sprinkle over parsley.

Add beef stock and wine. Bring to the boil, cover and simmer for 1¼ hours or until beef is tender. Add mushrooms and cook 10 minutes more. Taste for seasoning and adjust.

Spoon filling into individual pie dishes.

Roll out pastry on a lightly floured board and cut out lids, slightly larger than the dishes. Dampen edges of the pie dishes and sit lids on top of the meat, overhanging the edges. Press down on the rims of the dishes to seal. Use trimmings to make pastry strips for decoration. Brush with beaten egg to glaze.

Bake at Gas 6, 400F, 200C for 20 minutes or until pastry is golden brown and crisp.

Preparation time: 30 minutes
Cooking time: 1¼ hours

Approximate nutritional values per portion:	
765 calories	62g protein
89g fat	64g carbohydrate

STRAWBERRIES

The name strawberry originates from the Anglo-Saxon word 'streawberige' which proves they have been grown here for centuries. Oddly, the name has nothing to do with the fact that they are sometimes grown on straw. It probably refers to the plants' straying runners – 'streaw' could mean 'stray'.

There have been various spellings over the years. In 1000AD they were 'streaberize' later 'straubery' and even 'strewbery'.

The great traditional English summer treat of strawberries and cream was allegedly invented by Cardinal Wolsey when he served them at a feast in 1509. He probably chose the dish because the strawberry is the symbol of the Virgin Mary – and also John the Baptist. This is due to the fact that not only is the fruit sweet and soft, it has no stone, nor does it come from a plant with thorns.

Because of these high credentials, the leaves of the strawberry have been used in designs of crests for European nobility. Eight are intertwined for a duke or an earl, and four for a marquis.

In the Middle Ages, strains from Chile arrived here. Strawberries had been grown there for centuries previously. These were then crossed with French varieties. By the middle of the 19th century, the forerunner of today's fruit was being widely cultivated.

During the First World War, only strawberries picked on a Saturday could be sold to the public. The rest of the harvest was made into jam for the army. Today, as fruit is imported or grown in greenhouse conditions, strawberries can be bought almost all year round.

BUYING AND STORING

English strawberries are one of the highlights of the British summer. Even on the wettest days at the Wimbledon Tennis Tournament or Henley Regatta, spectators can be seen enjoying strawberries and cream under umbrellas.

The season for outdoor-grown English strawberries starts in the month of May and lasts until October. At this time, they are plentiful in greengrocers and supermarkets.

Pick Your Own farms are a popular way to buy these delicate and delicious soft fruits. They are often cheaper this way with the added bonus of giving the family a day out in the sunshine.

Strawberries should have the leafy stalk attached when buying, as this maintains freshness after picking. Choose firm, dry fruit of even colour – wet fruit or that displayed in rain will turn mouldy quickly. Cheaper strawberries sold 'loose' by the pound can be a good buy for cooking, but jam needs berries that are still firm and slightly under-ripe.

Strawberries do freeze, but not totally successfully. They lose their texture and shape when thawed. They are suitable for pies, purées and sauces. Defrost in the fridge for the best results.

NUTRITION

Strawberries are low in calories, with only 26 per 4oz/100g. These delicious summer berries are an excellent weight-watcher's pud either served as they come or with thick low-fat yogurt. The calorie count soars if they are served with double cream or ice cream.

Fresh, ripe strawberries contain as much vitamin C as the same weight of fresh oranges. They are a good source of this vitamin, required for a healthy skin and healing wounds. Some believe that large doses of vitamin C can assist cold sufferers, though this has not been reliably proved. Vitamin C cannot be stored by the body, so there is no need to worry about taking too much.

Strawberries contain some fibre, about 2g per 4oz/100g, necessary for a healthy digestive system. Most of this fibre is lignin, which is a non-carbohydrate fibre found in the seeds. They also have some iron, for healthy blood cells, and potassium, which plays an important part in the make-up of the body's muscle tissue.

4oz/100g strawberries contain:	
26 calories	trace of protein
trace of fat	8g carbohydrate

FRAISES REGINE TATHAM

Simple but sophisticated dinner party salad of strawberries doused in Marc de Champagne, the distilled residue left after pressing the grapes for Champagne. The juice of this is incredible! Marc de Champagne is available from wine shops.
Serves 4

1½lb/700g firm, ripe strawberries
Sifted icing sugar to taste
Marc de Champagne to taste
Mint sprig to decorate

Rinse, hull and carefully slice strawberries. Make a layer of strawberry slices in the base of a pretty glass bowl. Sprinkle liberally with sifted icing sugar, then drizzle with Marc. Continue making layers, sprinkling with icing sugar and Marc in between the fruit.

Leave the strawberries in the fridge for at least 1 hour, occasionally tilting the bowl and basting with juices. Decorate with a whole strawberry and mint sprig before serving.
Preparation time: 15 minutes
Cooking time: nil

Approximate nutritional values per portion:	
120 calories	1g protein
nil fat	17g carbohydrate

STRAWBERRY RIPPLE FOOL

Utterly scrumptious fool with fresh strawberry purée folded in. *Serves 4*

4oz/100g hulled strawberries
2 pieces preserved stem ginger, chopped
Sugar to taste
½pt/300ml double cream
¼pt/150ml thick Greek yogurt
Small strawberries for decoration

Purée hulled strawberries with chopped ginger and sugar. Reserve.

Whip cream to soft peaks and stir in yogurt. Gently fold in strawberry and ginger purée to create a rippled effect. Spoon into glass dishes to serve. Chill before serving decorated with small whole strawberries.

Preparation time: 15 minutes
Cooking time: nil

Approximate nutritional values per portion:	
265 calories	3g protein
25g fat	6g carbohydrate

STRAWBERRY GATEAU

Superb summer gateau filled and topped with whipped cream and strawberries. The light and airy sponge is made in one go in a processor using a plastic blade. *Serves 6*

4oz/100g self-raising flour
1 tsp baking powder
4oz/100g caster sugar
4oz/100g softened butter
2 eggs
2 tbsp strawberry liqueur
¾pt/425ml whipping cream
1 punnet strawberries
Mint leaves to decorate

For the sponge, sift flour and baking powder into the bowl of a processor. Add sugar, butter and eggs and whizz until blended and smooth. Spoon into 2 greased and lined non-stick 7in/18cm sandwich tins.

Bake in a pre-heated oven at Gas 6, 400F, 200C for 20 minutes or until risen, golden and firm to the touch. Turn out on to a wire rack to cool.

Sprinkle bases of sponges with strawberry liqueur to moisten.

Whip cream to peaks and use half to spread on one sponge on the liqueur side. Halve strawberries, reserving a few whole ones for decoration, and layer on to cream. Sit remaining sponge on top, liqueur side down. Spread top with cream, saving some for decoration.

Pipe remaining cream into swirls with a piping bag fitted with a fluted nozzle and top with whole strawberries and mint leaves. Chill until required.

Preparation time: 40 minutes
Cooking time: 20 minutes

Approximate nutritional values per portion:	
275 calories	5g protein
120g fat	40g carbohydrate

SUMMER PUDDINGS

Delicious fresh-tasting mix of strawberries and orange chunks. *Serves 4*

Oil for greasing
14 slices white bread, crusts removed
4 oranges, peeled
1 punnet strawberries, hulled
4 tbsp orange liqueur

Lightly oil 4 individual ramekin dishes. Cut 8 circles from bread slices to fit bases of the dishes and to make lids. Reserve.

With the remaining bread, cut oblongs the same height as the dishes to line the sides. Fit them in, roof tile style, overlapping them as you go. The edges of the bread will stick together when fruit is pressed in, sealing the sides.

Segment oranges over a bowl to catch juice.

Squeeze pith after segmenting to extract any remaining juice. Reserve the juice.

Chop the orange flesh and strawberries into small equal-sized chunks. Mix the orange juice with the orange liqueur. Pile the fruit into the bread-lined ramekin dishes, pressing well down. Pour over juice mix. Place remaining lid bread circles on top to seal. Place plates with weights on dishes. Leave in fridge overnight.

To serve, turn puddings out and decorate with strawberry slices.

Preparation time: 20 minutes
Cooking time: nil

Approximate nutritional values per portion:	
430 calories	15g protein
5g fat	75g carbohydrate

STRAWBERRY TIPS

● The leafy stalks make a pretty decoration on strawberries to be served whole or as part of a selection of fruit crudités. Wash the strawberries well, leaving stalks intact, and pat dry. Arrange on a platter with other fruits like orange segments, sliced fresh peaches, apple wedges, and some dessert biscuits. For the dip, beat 8oz/225g curd cheese smooth then stir in ¼pt/150ml double cream. Add 1 tbsp runny honey, grated zest of 1 orange and 2 tbsp orange liqueur or juice. Beat well and spoon into a pot. Serve with fruit and biscuits for a help-yourself dessert.

● Make a delicious chilled fresh strawberry milk shake. For 2: whizz 1pt/600ml ice cold milk in a blender with 2 scoops of strawberry ice cream and 4oz/100g fresh hulled and washed strawberries until smooth. Pour into glasses.

● Fresh strawberries make an excellent fruity sauce to serve with bought ice cream for a quick midweek pud. Whizz up 8oz/225g washed and hulled strawberries in a processor with sugar to taste and a dash of white wine or other favourite tipple. Pour

over scoops of vanilla dairy ice cream and serve with a few extra fresh strawberries to decorate.

● For an afternoon tea-time treat serve homemade scones filled with clotted cream and sliced fresh strawberries. Sift 8oz/225g self-raising flour into a bowl with 2 tsp baking powder and a pinch of salt. Rub in 2oz/50g butter to breadcrumb stage then mix to a soft dough with ¼pt/150ml milk. Knead lightly then roll out to ⅜in/1.5cm thick. Cut into rounds with a 2in/5cm plain cutter and place on a greased baking sheet. Brush tops with milk to glaze and bake at Gas 6, 400F, 200C for 15 minutes or until risen and golden. Cover with foil if tops become too brown during cooking. Cool and halve. Fill with clotted or whipped double cream and sliced strawberries.

● Fresh ripe strawberries are a delicious accompaniment with soft cheeses like Brie, Camembert and Chèvre. Take the cheeses from the fridge 1 hour before required.

● Use softer strawberries for purées, fruit sauces or baking in tarts and puddings.

TOMATOES

The Spanish probably brought tomato seeds to Europe from South America. But the first records of the plant in Britain are dated around the mid-16th century – although how it came to be here is not known.

Tomatoes were originally prized for their leaves – people were uncertain about eating the fruit. They are fruits, and not vegetables and in fact are related to the potato and also Deadly Nightshade.

Some thought tomatoes harmful but they also had a certain reputation as an aphrodisiac. The nickname 'love-apple' probably originated from this. But they were also called 'pomo di Mori' (apple of the Moors) by the Italians. The French may well have corrupted this to 'pommes d'amour' or 'apples of love'.

The Italians were the first to exploit tomatoes with enormous gastronomic success, and it was several centuries before they became equally popular in the rest of Europe.

Most supermarkets now stock a range of tomatoes from the minute cherry tomatoes to big beef tomatoes.

TOMATO AND ONION BREAD

Little rolls flavoured with fresh tomatoes and fried onion. *Makes 30 approx*

> 2 tbsp oil
> 1 onion, peeled and finely chopped
> 1lb/450g tomatoes, peeled
> 1½lb/700g strong plain flour
> Pinch of salt
> 1oz/25g lard
> 1 sachet fast action dried yeast
> 1 tbsp tomato purée
> ¼pt/150ml approx hand hot water
> 1 egg, beaten
> Poppy seeds for decoration

Heat oil in a pan and fry onion until softened but not browned. Remove with a slotted spoon and cool. Purée tomatoes in blender and reserve.

Sift flour into a bowl with salt. Rub in lard. Stir in dried yeast, and the fried onion. Add blended tomatoes, with tomato purée and enough water to make a dough of soft consistency. Turn on to a floured board and knead smooth. Return to a clean bowl, cover, and leave in a warm place to rise, approx 40 minutes.

Knead dough on a floured surface. Nip off large marble-sized balls and roll smooth. Place on a greased baking sheet. Brush tops with beaten egg and sprinkle with poppy seeds.

Bake rolls at Gas 7, 425F, 220C for 15 minutes or until they sound 'hollow' when tapped underneath.

Preparation time: 20 minutes
Cooking time: 20 minutes approx

Approximate nutritional values per roll:	
95 calories	3g protein
3g fat	10g carbohydrate

BUYING AND STORING

Tomatoes are usually graded in two classes according to EC regulations. Class I must be as near perfect as possible with few visible defects. Class II may have minor defects, such as a slight variation in colour, shape or size, or with a small blemish.

Choose tomatoes which are firm. They should have a good rounded shape and bright colour with a matt skin and delicate bloom. Fresh ripe tomatoes ready for eating will have a faintly aromatic smell and sprightly stalks which should not be dry or withered. They will be juicy with a savoury sweetness.

Some shops and supermarkets sell cheaper, over-ripe tomatoes which can be used for making fresh tomato sauce, or juice, or added to casseroles and stews.

Smaller or cherry tomatoes are now popular for salads and are sold in 8oz/225g plastic packs. But these should not be confused with the smallest size of ordinary tomatoes, sometimes called 'mini' tomatoes. These have a more intense flavour than larger varieties. Inspect pre-packaged tomatoes closely and check for damaged or mouldy specimens which will rot the others.

The largest tomatoes are known as 'beef' tomatoes and these are usually featured in Greek salads and other Mediterranean dishes. These are also the best for stuffing with rice or savoury mince as a main course dish.

NUTRITION

Tomatoes are low in calories with only 14 in 4oz/100g raw weight. This increases to 69 when fried in oil as a breakfast or mixed grill accompaniment.

Vitamin C is the most important nutritional contribution in tomatoes. They are an excellent source, and most of it is found in the jelly-like substance which encloses the seeds. There is 25mg of vitamin C in 4oz/100g fresh tomatoes, which makes up 80 per cent of the recommended daily amount for a healthy adult. Outdoor-grown tomatoes contain twice the amount of vitamin C as hot house varieties.

There is some calcium present, essential for healthy teeth and bones, along with a useful amount of potassium, which is vitally important in the make-up of muscle tissue.

4oz/100g tomatoes contain:	
14 calories	1g protein
nil fat	2.8g carbohydrate

TOMATO UPSIDE DOWN POTATO CAKE

Layers of potato, tomato and onion baked with eggs and cream. *Serves 6*

1½lb/700g medium-sized potatoes, peeled and sliced
1lb/450g firm tomatoes
2 tbsp oil
1 onion, peeled and finely chopped
3 eggs
½pt/300ml single cream
Salt and freshly ground black pepper
Melted butter for brushing
Basil leaves, shredded
Basil sprig for decoration

First parboil the potatoes, drain, pat dry. Slice tomatoes and reserve.

Heat oil in a pan and fry onion until soft but not brown. Beat eggs, cream and seasoning in a bowl.

Butter a 7in/18cm non-stick sandwich tin and line the base with a circle of greaseproof paper.

Arrange a layer of tomatoes in a swirling roof tile pattern over the base. Sprinkle over some onion, some shredded basil, and black pepper. Next add a layer of potatoes. Pour over a little egg mixture. Continue like this until the ingredients are used up.

Bake at Gas 5, 375F, 190C for 45 minutes, or until potatoes are tender and egg is set. Leave to cool slightly, then turn out on to a serving plate. Peel off greaseproof and decorate with a basil sprig.

Preparation time: 30 minutes
Cooking time: 50 minutes

Approximate nutritional values per portion:	
245 calories	7g protein
15g fat	23g carbohydrate

FRESH TOMATO CHUTNEY

A delightful crisp and piquant pickle of tomatoes and chunky courgettes. *Serves 10*

1lb/450g tomatoes
2 tbsp oil
1 onion, peeled and finely chopped
2 cloves garlic, peeled and crushed
1 red chilli, de-seeded and in rings
1 large courgette, in chunks
1 tbsp sugar
2 tbsp white wine vinegar
Salt and freshly ground black pepper

Wipe and quarter tomatoes and reserve. Heat oil in a pan and fry onion, garlic and chilli until just soft but not browned. Stir in courgette and cook for a further minute. Add tomatoes with sugar and vinegar and season. Bring to the boil and simmer for 5 minutes, covered. Remove pickle mixture from heat.

Spoon pickle into a pot and leave to cool completely. Eat within two days, with cold ham, cheese or cold sliced chicken.

Preparation time: 15 minutes
Cooking time: 10 minutes approx

Approximate nutritional values per portion:	
24 calories	0.3g protein
1g fat	4g carbohydrate

PENNE ARRABIATTA

Italian dish of pasta quills tossed in a hot and spicy tomato sauce. *Serves 4*

4 tbsp oil
1 large onion, peeled and finely chopped
4 cloves garlic, peeled and crushed
1 red chilli pepper, de-seeded and chopped
 (or more to taste)
2 tsp paprika
14oz/400g tin chopped tomatoes
2 tbsp tomato purée
1lb/450g fresh tomatoes, skinned and chopped
Salt and freshly ground black pepper
12oz/350g penne pasta
Freshly grated Parmesan and parsley sprigs
 for decoration

For the sauce, heat the oil in a pan and cook onion and garlic over gentle heat until softened but not browned. Add chilli and paprika and cook for a further minute. Stir in canned tomatoes. Bring to the boil. Simmer for 10 minutes, or until slightly reduced.

Stir in tomato purée and fresh tomatoes and cook for a further 5 minutes, or until sauce is mushy and thickened. Season.

Meanwhile, cook pasta in plenty of boiling salted water until just tender. Drain. Pour over tomato sauce and toss through. Serve with grated Parmesan cheese and a sprig of parsley.

Preparation time: 20 minutes
Cooking time: 20 minutes approx

Approximate nutritional values per portion:	
425 calories	7g protein
16g fat	76g carbohydrate

TOMATO TIPS

● To skin a tomato, first make a small cross with the point of a sharp knife on the top of the tomato, opposite the stalk end. Dip into boiling water for about 30 seconds, or until the skin around the cross starts to peel back. Remove with a slotted spoon and plunge tomato into cold water immediately. Drain and pull off skin with finger tips. It will come away easily.

● Little cherry tomatoes make pretty additions to kebabs, speared with other colourful vegetables like green and yellow peppers, courgettes, aubergines and wedges of onion. Brush with a mixture of olive oil, crushed garlic, lemon juice, finely chopped rosemary, and seasoning. Place over hot barbecue coals or grill in the conventional way, until the vegetables are just tender, basting with oil mixed with white wine or lemon juice all the time.

● Make a warm tomato vinaigrette to serve over grilled fish. Peel and de-seed 2 tomatoes, then dice flesh finely. Shake 4 tbsp oil with 1 tbsp white wine vinegar, 1 tsp mild mustard, salt and freshly ground black pepper in a screw-top jar. Pour into a bowl and place over a pan of boiling water. Heat gently, whisking until just warm. Add tomato dice and 1 tbsp fresh snipped chives and pour over grilled cod or haddock steaks. Serve with a green salad and new potatoes or crusty bread.

● Use a glut of unripened home-grown tomatoes to make green tomato chutney. Peel, core and finely chop 1 large onion and slice 3lb/1.4kg de-stalked green tomatoes. Place these in a heavy-bottomed pan with 8oz/225g soft brown sugar, 6oz/175g large sultanas, 1 tsp salt, ¾pt/425ml malt vinegar, 2 tsp finely chopped fresh root ginger, 1 crushed clove garlic, 1 tsp mustard powder and plenty of black pepper. Bring to the boil and turn down heat. Simmer gently until the liquid is almost absorbed and the mixture thickened. Stir during cooking. Spoon into clean jars and seal with vinegar-proof caps.

● Stuff tiny baby tomatoes with a mixture of fresh breadcrumbs, crushed garlic and finely chopped fresh parsley and grill until browned on top. Serve with drinks.

TROUT

Originating from the lakes of North America, the rainbow trout is an attractive fish with a gleaming silvery skin flecked with pink. The flesh is pink, tender and succulently smooth with a delicate flavour.

Trout are found naturally in lakes, but increasingly they are being reared on farms with no detriment to the taste or texture of the flesh.

A versatile fish, it is probably one of the least expensive forms of protein. The flesh is meaty, but tender and lends itself to plain grilling and baking.

But for those who are averse to whole fish complete with head and tail, skinned fillets are available – either from supermarkets, or the fishmonger.

This way they can take the place of any white fish in fish cakes, pies, curries, stews and soups.

Cold smoked trout is similar to smoked salmon. The larger trout are split and brined, then slowly smoked over oak chippings.

The consumption of British trout has doubled over the last 10 years. With the nation's diet moving away from high consumption of red meat, trout has become a very popular alternative. It is inexpensive, packed with protein, tastes good and is always quick to cook.

POACHED TROUT WITH HORSERADISH MAYONNAISE

Delicious cold summer dish, either a first course or a light main course served with potato salad. The fish is cooked in a microwave. *Serves 1*

1 cucumber
Salt
1 trout, cleaned, head and tail removed
2 tbsp mayonnaise
2 tsp horseradish mustard
For the vinaigrette:
1 tsp Dijon mustard
1 tbsp white wine vinegar
3 tbsp olive oil
Salt and freshly ground black pepper

Prepare the cucumber salad first. Peel and thinly slice cucumber. Place in a colander over a bowl and sprinkle salt over the cucumber. Leave to drain.

Place trout in a microwave dish and cover with film. Cook for 3 minutes in the microwave on high, or until fish is cooked (don't overcook). Remove from microwave and leave for 3 minutes. Peel off the skin and fins. Cool completely. Mix mayonnaise with the horseradish mustard.

Rinse and blot cucumber. Shake dressing ingredients together in a screw-top jar. Pour over cucumber and toss. Serve trout with sauce and the cucumber salad as an accompaniment.

Preparation time: 15 minutes
Cooking time: 3 minutes approx

Approximate nutritional values per portion:	
330 calories	42g protein
15g fat	15g carbohydrate

TROUT CUTLETS WITH MUSHROOMS

Lovely way to serve trout minus the head and tail. Simply cut across into cutlets for this sophisticated supper dish. *Serves 4*

1 tbsp oil
1 onion, peeled and finely chopped
12 trout cutlets
2 wine glasses white wine
1/4pt/150ml fish stock
8oz/225g sliced mushrooms
Few sprigs tarragon
Salt and freshly ground black pepper

Heat oil in a flameproof dish and fry onion until soft but not brown. Place the cutlets on top. Pour over wine and fish stock.

Scatter around the mushrooms and tarragon and then season to taste with salt and freshly ground black pepper.

Cover with foil and simmer over low heat for about 15 minutes, or until the trout cutlets are opaque and cooked through. To serve, decorate each cutlet with a tarragon leaf.

Preparation time: 15 minutes
Cooking time: 20 minutes

Approximate nutritional values per portion:	
310 calories	42g protein
9g fat	2g carbohydrate

NUTRITION

The delicate trout makes a great contribution to a healthy lifestyle containing only 100g calories per 4oz/100g. A whole trout grilled is around 180 calories.

The protein content is high at 28g for 4oz/100g. There is no carbohydrate or fibre.

Useful amounts of Vitamins A, B1, B2, C and D are there. But trout is low in saturated fats and sodium.

Trout is also rich in dietary fish oil which is a valuable aid to health. In trout the oils are three times more concentrated than in many white fish.

Calcium is present at 42mg per 4oz/100g. It also contains 444mg potassium for regulating the water balance of the body and for healthy muscles and nerves.

4oz/100g trout contain:	
100 calories	28g protein
5.2g fat	nil carbohydrate

BUYING AND STORING

Like all fresh fish, trout should have bright eyes and a glossy sheen to the skin. If the skin shows no shine, or the eyes are sunken, the fish has seen better days and is not fresh.

Trout is best eaten on the day of purchase. Unwrap the fish before storing in the refrigerator. Place in a single layer on a plate and cover with film, greaseproof paper or foil until needed – but use within two days.

Fresh trout can be stored in the freezer. It must first be gutted, washed under cold running water and dried. Each fish should be individually wrapped in freezer film or plastic bags, then wrapped together in a large plastic bag which should be sealed, or placed in a small box.

For the best results, defrost before cooking.

TROUT TIPS

● Trout is a fish which cooks perfectly in the microwave. It can be poached in wine, fish stock, cider, or brushed with lemon juice or melted butter. Remember to cover the dish with some film. An 8oz/225g trout will take about 3-4 minutes.

● One of the best ways to cook trout is to bake it in foil in the oven. Gut 4 whole trout, and wash thoroughly. Grease a piece of foil with a knob of butter. Insert 2 slices of lemon and 1 bay leaf in the belly. Season well. Bring up the ends and sides of the foil to form an open envelope. Pour in about 5 tbsp white wine. Seal the foil, and place on a baking tray. Bake at Gas 6, 400F, 200C for 15-20 minutes.

● If you don't own a fish kettle you can cook a large trout just as effectively in a large square of butter muslin in the base of a large pan. When cooked the fish can be lifted out on the muslin just as easily as on the trivet of a kettle.

● The easiest way of skinning a raw fish is to make an incision at the tail end, and then pull off the skin from the tail up. It can be made easier by wetting your fingers and then dipping them in salt to get a good grip. But if you have a friendly fishmonger he will do it for you.

● Fried trout with almonds make a quick and easy supper or lunch dish. Clean, wash and dry 4 trout. Dip them in seasoned flour, and fry them in 3oz/75g butter for about 10 minutes until lightly browned. Add some lemon juice to the pan and pour over the fish. Fry 2oz/50g flaked almonds in some butter until lightly browned. Scatter over the trout, and garnish with lemon twists.

● A chic first course is the now widely-available smoked trout – rather like smoked salmon – though some say it has a superior flavour. Serve thin slices with lemon wedges and freshly ground black pepper.

● To give a plain grilled trout extra flavour marinade it first. Blend together 1 crushed clove garlic, a few rosemary leaves, 2 tbsp dry white wine, 4 tbsp olive oil, salt and freshly ground black pepper. Soak the slashed fish for 15 minutes before grilling and baste with the marinade during cooking.

TROUT FILLETS WITH PRAWNS

Luxury dish of whole filleted trout stuffed with chopped prawns. *Serves 4*

> *4oz/100g fresh shelled prawns*
> *4 trout fillets*
> *2 wine glasses white wine*
> *1 tbsp oil*
> *1 small onion, peeled and finely chopped*
> *4 tbsp soured cream*
> *Few sprigs dill, chopped*
> *Salt and freshly ground black pepper*
> *4 shell-on prawns for decoration*

Roughly chop prawns in a blender. Place about 1 tbsp of prawns on each fillet, and then roll up. Transfer to an ovenproof dish. Pour over white wine. Season. Cover with foil. Cook at Gas 6, 400F, 200C for 12 minutes.

Remove from oven and strain off liquid. Heat a little oil in a pan and cook onion for a couple of minutes over low heat. Add cooking juices and boil until reduced by one third. Stir in the soured cream and dill and season.

Pour around fillets and serve immediately garnished with unpeeled prawns, accompanied by new potatoes and thin green beans.

Preparation time: 10 minutes
Cooking time: 20 minutes

Approximate nutritional values per portion:	
250 calories	25g protein
14g fat	nil carbohydrate

BARBECUED TROUT

Don't forget trout for the barbecue for non-meat-eaters. The flesh is succulent and tasty and the skin crisps beautifully. *Serves 4*

> *2 tbsp finely chopped parsley*
> *2 cloves garlic, finely chopped*
> *Juice and grated zest of ¹/₂ lime*
> *2oz/50g butter, softened*
> *4 trout, cleaned*
> *Olive oil*
> *Salt and freshly ground black pepper*
> *Melted butter*
> *Lime slices and lamb's tongue lettuce*
>   *for decoration*

First make the parsley and garlic butter. Work half the parsley and garlic with lime juice and zest into the butter until well blended. Roll into a cylinder in a piece of foil and leave in the freezer to firm up while you cook the fish.

Stuff the cavity of each trout with remaining parsley and garlic. Brush the fish with oil and then season well.

Cook on the barbecue or under the grill – about 5 minutes each side depending on size. Serve with a slice of herb butter tucked inside.

Preparation time: 15 minutes
Cooking time: 12 minutes

Approximate nutritional values per portion:	
350 calories	40g protein
20g fat	nil carbohydrate

TUNA

T una is an impressive gunmetal-colour fish which can often grow to 10ft/3m in length. It is unusual in being warm-blooded, which means it needs large amounts of oxygen. It achieves this by swimming at high speeds, often at around 30mph, so its gills are continuously vigorously bathed with water.

This constant activity means that this is a muscular fish, whose flesh is firm and dense, but it has a remarkable, unusual taste and texture, not unlike veal.

Fresh tuna is now widely available, and the best meat comes from the belly, or 'ventresca'. So look out for this word on imported tinned tuna.

Tuna steaks are juicy, flavourful and tender and can be cooked in the same way as any beef steak dish. Thinly sliced escalopes of tuna make a delicate alternative to veal.

Large 'joints' of fresh tuna can be roasted, cooked en croute, or braised. Cut into chunks, tuna makes a tender meaty stew when cooked with potatoes or other vegetables such as tomatoes and peppers. Marinated, the chunks are perfect for threading on kebabs and charcoal grilling. Alternate with prawns, scallops or other firm fish.

TUNA DIANNE

Thin slices of tuna quickly pan fried in a sauce of chopped shallots, brandy and cream with a dash of Worcestershire sauce and lemon juice.
Serves 4

> *4oz/100g butter*
> *4 shallots, peeled and finely chopped*
> *8 thin slices fresh tuna*
> *Juice and grated zest of ¹/₂ lemon*
> *Good dash of Worcestershire sauce*
> *3 tbsp brandy*
> *4 tbsp cream*
> *1 tbsp fresh parsley, finely chopped*
> *Salt and freshly ground black pepper*

Heat half the butter in a pan and fry shallots until soft. Remove with a slotted spoon and reserve. Add remaining butter to pan and fry tuna steaks quickly over high heat until cooked through. Remove and keep hot.

Return shallots to pan and stir in the lemon juice and zest, Worcestershire sauce and brandy. Tilt pan to ignite. When the flames have died down, stir in cream and parsley and season with salt and freshly ground black pepper. Pour sauce over steaks to serve. Decorate with parsley sprigs.
Preparation time: 10 minutes
Cooking time: 15 minutes

Approximate nutritional values per portion:	
380 calories	10g protein
32g fat	3g carbohydrate

TUNA AND SCALLOP KEBABS

Basted chunky tuna and sliced scallops, skewered with button mushrooms and served on a bed of rice. **Serves 4**

> *1lb/450g fresh tuna*
> *4 large scallops*
> *8 button mushrooms*
> *4 bay leaves*
> For the baste:
> *4 tbsp oil*
> *1 tsp mustard*
> *1 tbsp soy sauce*
> *2 cloves garlic, peeled and crushed*
> *Juice and zest of ¹/₂ lemon*
> *1 tbsp fresh parsley, finely chopped*
> *Salt and freshly ground black pepper*

Cut the tuna into large chunks.

Separate corals from scallops and slice the scallops. Wipe and trim mushrooms. Thread neatly on to kebab skewers with bay leaves.

Mix baste ingredients together and brush over kebabs.

Grill or barbecue, turning frequently until cooked, basting all the time with juices.

Serve kebabs on a bed of rice.
Preparation time: 20 minutes
Cooking time: 10 minutes

Approximate nutritional values per portion (without rice):	
230 calories	25g protein
15g fat	1g carbohydrate

NUTRITION

Fresh tuna is an oily fish rich in valuable nutrients. It is surprisingly low in calories, with only 144 in 4oz/100g raw weight, compared with 256 in the same amount of tinned tuna in oil.

An excellent source of protein, required for growth and development, fresh tuna has 23g per 4oz/100g. It has only 5g of fat and no carbohydrates.

All fish are rich in the B vitamins, particularly nicotinic acid. This vitamin is not destroyed by heat, but it is water soluble. To avoid loss, use even the smallest amount of tuna cooking liquid in the sauce or dressing to accompany the finished dish.

Oily fish are one of the few natural sources of vitamin D, called the 'sunshine vitamin' because most is produced when the skin is exposed to sunlight.

Required for normal bone formation, vitamin D also controls the amount of calcium in the blood. A deficiency of vitamin D can cause joint problems in old age or in very young children. And expectant mothers should have a good supply. Babies form a reserve of vitamin D before they are born.

One of the most important nutrients in fish is the Omega-3 fatty acids. They have been linked with lowering blood cholesterol levels, because they appear to reduce the molecules that carry cholesterol into the blood and increase the molecules that carry it away from the body.

4oz/100g raw fresh tuna contain:	
144 calories	23g protein
5g fat	nil carbohydrate

Hello! Good Cooking

BUYING AND STORING

Tuna is a large fish usually sold in steaks or joints. The flesh should be moist and have a fresh smell. The colour is light red – but dark patches near the skin can indicate bruising, although there is always some variation in colour near the bone.

Although it is firm and pale when cooked, the raw flesh is soft and easy to slice extremely thinly. The Japanese use it raw in sushi and sashimi because it has exactly the right texture for these.

The skin is quite tough and hard to cut, so ask the fishmonger to remove this for you.

Store tuna covered on a plate in the fridge before use, to ensure freshness and to stop it being tainted by the aromas of other foods. Although it will keep for up to 2 days, it is best used within 24 hours. So it is better to buy it on the day you need it.

Fresh tuna will freeze – but the texture becomes softer when defrosted. This is no problem if the meat is being used in a stew, but it impairs the final result if used for grilling, kebabs, or Japanese raw fish dishes.

TUNA FISHCAKES

Absolute favourite for anyone who loves fishcakes, these are fantastic. Made from fresh tuna, grated onion, parsley and dill, they're served with a tomato sauce. Use more tuna and less potato if you like a sturdier fishcake. *Serves 4*

1lb/450g fresh tuna
1lb/450g potatoes mashed with butter
2 tbsp grated onion
1 tbsp fresh parsley, finely chopped
1 tbsp dill, finely chopped
Salt and freshly ground black pepper
Seasoned flour
Oil for frying
For the sauce:
2 tbsp oil
1 medium onion, peeled and finely chopped
1 small red pepper, de-seeded and chopped
2 cloves garlic, peeled and crushed
7oz/200g tin chopped tomatoes
1 tbsp tomato purée
1 tbsp fresh parsley, finely chopped
Lemon twists and watercress sprigs for decoration

Cook tuna by grilling, poaching or in the microwave. Cool and flake flesh. Stir into mashed potatoes with grated onion, parsley, dill, salt and freshly ground black pepper.

Next make the sauce. Heat oil in a pan and fry onion, pepper and garlic until soft but not brown. Add tinned tomatoes, tomato purée, parsley, salt and freshly ground black pepper. Bring to bubbling and cook until reduced slightly. Blend until smooth, or sieve. Keep warm.

Shape tuna mix into rounds. Coat in seasoned flour and fry gently on both sides until browned and cooked through.

Serve on a puddle of sauce and decorate with lemon twists and watercress sprigs.

Preparation time: 30 minutes
Cooking time: 25 minutes

Approximate nutritional values per portion:	
350 calories	25g protein
15g fat	35g carbohydrate

TUNA PIE

A large flat fresh tuna pie in crisp egg pastry, served warm or cold, cut into squares. A good lunch, supper or snack dish. **Makes 12 pieces**

For the pastry:
8oz/225g butter
12oz/350g plain flour, sifted
Pinch of salt
2 eggs
For the filling:
1lb/450g fresh tuna
2 tbsp oil
1 onion, peeled and finely chopped
3 cloves garlic, peeled and crushed
14oz/400g tin chopped tomatoes
2 tbsp fresh parsley, finely chopped
2 tbsp tomato purée
Zest and juice of 1 lemon
Salt and freshly ground black pepper
1 egg, beaten to glaze

First make the pastry – this is a food processor pastry. Cut butter into small pieces and add to blender with flour, salt and eggs. Whizz until a ball of pastry is formed. Remove, wrap in cling film and chill for at least 30 minutes.

Meanwhile make the filling. Poach, grill or microwave the tuna and leave to cool. Heat oil in pan and fry onion and garlic until softened. Add tomatoes, parsley, tomato purée, zest and juice of lemon, salt and freshly ground black pepper. Add finely flaked tuna and turn over to mix thoroughly. Cool.

Halve pastry and roll out one half to line the base of a buttered swiss roll tin. Heap filling on top and smooth out. Roll out remaining pastry and place on top, sealing edges with water. Trim. Roll out pastry trimmings and cut out shapes to decorate the top. Brush with beaten egg to glaze. Bake at Gas 6, 400F, 200C for 20 minutes, or until pastry is shiny and golden brown.

Cut into squares to serve.

Preparation time: 35 minutes
Cooking time: 35 minutes

Approximate nutritional values per piece:	
335 calories	16g protein
20g fat	25g carbohydrate

TUNA TIPS

● Fresh tuna is a flavourful fish, perfect for a summer barbecue. Brush it with a little sunflower oil and season with crushed garlic, salt and freshly ground black pepper. Squeeze over some fresh orange juice and cook over hot coals for about 5 minutes each side or until cooked through.

● Tuna makes a hearty stew, cooked with red wine. For 4: heat 2 tbsp oil in a large pan and fry 1 finely chopped onion with 2 crushed cloves garlic. Remove with a slotted spoon and reserve. Dust 2lb/900g chunked tuna in seasoned flour. Fry to brown and seal. Return onion mix and pour over 1 wine glass red wine with ¼pt/150ml fish stock. Bring to the boil and add 14oz/400g tin chopped tomatoes. Sprinkle in 1 tsp chopped thyme and 1 tsp dried oregano. Season. Cook until fish is cooked through. Stir in 1 tbsp fresh finely chopped parsley, 8 quartered black olives and a squeeze of lemon juice.

● Make a delicious Niçoise with leftover cooked tuna. Toss with finely sliced onion rings, cooked thin French beans, sliced new potatoes, black olives, quartered hard-boiled eggs and anchovy fillets. Dress with vinaigrette and serve on a bed of crisp iceberg.

● Serve a joint of tuna as the alternative Sunday roast. Ask the fishmonger for a skinned 3lb/1.4kg middle cut of tuna. Cover with streaky bacon rashers to keep it moist then brush with oil and season with freshly ground black pepper and lemon juice. Spread with crushed garlic and roast at Gas 5, 375F, 190C for approximately 45 minutes.

SEASONAL PLANNER

JANUARY

FISH AND SHELLFISH

Bass, brill, clams, cod, coley, conger eel, crabs, dabs, Dover Sole, grey mullet, gurnard, haddock, hake, halibut, herring, langoustine, lemon sole, lobster, mackerel, monkfish, mussels, oysters, plaice, prawns, scallops, shrimps, skate, sprats, squid, rainbow trout, turbot, whiting, winkles

MEAT, GAME AND POULTRY

Beef, chicken, duck, goose, guinea fowl, hare, lamb, partridge, pheasant, pigeon, pork, rabbit, turkey, venison

VEGETABLES AND SALAD

Aubergine, avocado, beetroot, broccoli, Brussels sprouts, cabbage, carrots, cauliflower, celeriac, celery, chicory, courgette, cucumber, endive, fennel, French beans, garlic, globe artichokes, herbs, horseradish, Jerusalem artichokes, kale, kohl rabi, leeks, lettuce, mushrooms, onions, parsnips, peppers, potatoes, radishes, salsify, Savoy cabbage, shallots, spinach, spring greens, spring onions, swede, sweet potatoes, tomatoes, turnips, watercress

FRUIT

Apples, bananas, clementines, cranberries, dates, grapefruit, grapes, lemons, lychees, mandarins, mangoes, melons, nectarines, oranges, pears, pineapples, plums, pomegranates, rhubarb (early), satsumas, Seville oranges, tangerines

NUTS

Almonds, Brazils, chestnuts, walnuts

FEBRUARY

FISH AND SHELLFISH

Bass, bream, brill, clams, cod, coley, crabs, Dover Sole, grey mullet, gurnard, haddock, hake, halibut, herring, John Dory, langoustine, lemon sole, lobster, mackerel, monkfish, mussels, oysters, plaice, prawns, salmon, scallops, shrimps, skate, sprats, squid, rainbow trout, swordfish, tuna, turbot, whitebait

MEAT, GAME AND POULTRY

Beef, chicken, duck, guinea fowl, hare, lamb, pheasant, pigeon, pork, rabbit, turkey, venison, wild duck

VEGETABLES AND SALAD

Aubergine, avocado, beetroot, broccoli, Brussels sprouts, cabbage, carrots, cauliflower, celeriac, celery, chicory, courgette, cucumber, endive, fennel, French beans, garlic, globe artichokes, herbs, horseradish, Jerusalem artichokes, kale, kohl rabi, leeks, lettuce, mushrooms, onions, parsnips, peppers, potatoes, radishes, salsify, Savoy cabbage, shallots, spinach, spring greens, spring onions, swede, sweet potatoes, tomatoes, turnips, watercress

FRUIT

Apples, bananas, clementines, cranberries, dates, grapefruit, grapes, lemons, lychees, mandarins, mangoes, melons, nectarines, oranges, pears, pineapples, plums, rhubarb (early), satsumas, Seville oranges, tangerines

NUTS

Almonds

MARCH

FISH AND SHELLFISH

Bass, brill, clams, cod, coley, conger eel, crabs, Dover Sole, grey mullet, gurnard, haddock, hake, halibut, herring, huss, John Dory, langoustine, lemon sole, lobster, mackerel, monkfish, mussels, oysters, plaice, prawns, rainbow trout, salmon, salmon trout, scallops, shrimps, skate, squid, swordfish, tuna, turbot, whitebait, whiting

MEAT, GAME AND POULTRY

Beef, chicken, ducklings, English lamb, guinea fowl, hare, pigeon, pork, rabbit, turkey, venison

VEGETABLES AND SALAD

Aubergine, avocado, beetroot, broccoli, Brussels sprouts, cabbage, carrots (baby), cauliflower, celeriac, celery, chicory, courgettes, cucumber, fennel, French beans, garlic, globe artichokes, herbs, horseradish, Jerusalem artichokes, kale, kohl rabi, leeks, lettuce, mushrooms, onions, parsnips, peppers, potatoes, radishes, Savoy cabbage, spinach, spring greens, spring onions, swede, sweet potatoes, tomatoes, turnips (baby), watercress

FRUIT

Apples, bananas, dates, grapefruit, grapes, kumquats, lemons, limes, mandarins, mangoes, melon, oranges, ortaniques, passion fruit, pears, pineapples, plums, rhubarb (early), satsumas, tangerines

APRIL

FISH AND SHELLFISH

Bass, brill, clams, cod, coley, conger eel, crabs, dabs, Dover Sole, gurnard, haddock, hake, halibut, herring, huss, John Dory, langoustine, lemon sole, lobster, mackerel, monkfish, mussels, oysters, plaice, prawns, rainbow trout, red mullet, salmon, salmon trout, scallops, shrimps, skate, squid, swordfish, tuna, turbot, whitebait, whiting

MEAT, GAME AND POULTRY

Beef, chicken, duck, English lamb, guinea fowl, pigeon, pork, quails, rabbit, turkey, venison

VEGETABLES AND SALAD

Aubergine, avocado, beetroot, broad beans, broccoli, Brussels sprouts, cabbage, carrots (baby), cauliflower, celeriac, celery, chicory, chillies, courgettes, cucumber, endive, fennel, French beans, garlic, globe artichokes, herbs, kohl rabi, leeks, lettuce, mushrooms, onions, parsnips, peas, peppers, potatoes, radishes, salsify, spinach, spring greens, spring onions, swede, sweet potatoes, tomatoes, turnips (baby), watercress

FRUIT

Apples, bananas, dates, grapefruit, grapes, kiwis, kumquats, lemons, limes, mangoes, melons, oranges, ortaniques, passion fruit, peaches, pears, pineapples, plums, rhubarb, strawberries

MAY

FISH AND SHELLFISH

Brill, clams, cod, coley, conger eel, crabs, dabs, Dover Sole, haddock, hake, halibut, herring, huss, langoustine, lemon sole, lobster, mackerel, monkfish, plaice, prawns, rainbow trout, red mullet, salmon, salmon trout, shrimps, skate, squid, swordfish, tuna, turbot, whitebait, whiting

MEAT, GAME AND POULTRY

Beef, chicken, duck, English lamb, guinea fowl, pigeon, pork, quails, rabbit, turkey, venison

VEGETABLES AND SALAD

Asparagus, avocado, beetroot, broad beans, broccoli, cabbage, carrots, cauliflower, celery, chicory, chillies, courgettes, cucumber, endive, fennel, French beans, garlic, globe artichokes, herbs, leeks, lettuce, mangetouts, mushrooms, new potatoes, onions, peas, peppers, radishes, salsify, spinach, spring greens, spring onions, swede, sweet potatoes, tomatoes, turnips (baby), watercress

FRUIT

Apples, bananas, dates, grapefruit, grapes, kiwis, kumquats, lemons, limes, mangoes, melons, oranges, peaches, pears, pineapples, plums, rhubarb, strawberries

JUNE

FISH AND SHELLFISH

Bass, bream, brill, clams, cockles, cod, coley, conger eel, crabs, dabs, Dover Sole, haddock, hake, herring, huss, langoustine, lemon sole, mackerel, monkfish, plaice, prawns, rainbow trout, red mullet, salmon, salmon trout, shrimps, skate, squid, swordfish, tuna, turbot, whitebait, whiting

MEAT, GAME AND POULTRY

Beef, chicken, duck, guinea fowl, lamb, pigeon, pork, quails, rabbit, turkey, venison

VEGETABLES AND SALAD

Asparagus, aubergine, avocado, beetroot, broad beans, broccoli, cabbage, carrots, cauliflower, celery, chicory, chillies, courgettes, cucumber, endive, fennel, French beans, garlic, globe artichokes, herbs, leeks, lettuce, mangetouts, mushrooms, new potatoes, okra, onions, peas, peppers, radishes, runner beans, salsify, shallots, spinach, spring greens, spring onions, swede, sweet potatoes, tomatoes, turnips, watercress

FRUIT

Apples, apricots, bananas, blackcurrants, cherries, gooseberries, grapefruit, grapes, kiwis, kumquats, lemons, limes, mangoes, melons, oranges, peaches, pears, pineapples, plums, raspberries, redcurrants, rhubarb, strawberries

Hello! Good Cooking

JULY

FISH AND SHELLFISH
Bream, brill, clams, cockles, cod, coley, conger eel, crabs, dabs, Dover Sole, grey mullet, gurnard, haddock, hake, halibut, herring, huss, langoustine, lemon sole, lobster, mackerel, monkfish, plaice, prawns, rainbow trout, red mullet, salmon, salmon trout, shrimps, skate, squid, swordfish, tuna, turbot, whitebait, whiting

MEAT, GAME AND POULTRY
Beef, chicken, duck, guinea fowl, lamb, pigeon, pork, quails, rabbit, turkey, venison

VEGETABLES AND SALAD
Asparagus, aubergine, avocado, beetroot, broad beans, cabbage, carrots, cauliflower, celery, chillies, corn on the cob, courgettes, cucumber, fennel, French beans, garlic, globe artichokes, herbs, leeks, lettuce, mangetouts, marrow, mushrooms, new potatoes, okra, onions, peas, peppers, radishes, runner beans, salsify, shallots, spinach, spring onions, sugar peas, swede, sweet potatoes, tomatoes, turnips, watercress

FRUIT
Apples, apricots, bananas, blackberries, blackcurrants, cherries, dates, figs, gooseberries, grapefruit, grapes, kiwis, lemons, limes, loganberries, mangoes, melons, nectarines, oranges, passion fruit, peaches, pears, persimmons, pineapples, plums, raspberries, redcurrants, rhubarb, strawberries

AUGUST

FISH AND SHELLFISH
Bream, brill, clams, cockles, cod, coley, conger eel, crabs, dabs, Dover Sole, grey mullet, gurnard, haddock, hake, halibut, herring, huss, langoustine, lemon sole, lobster, mackerel, monkfish, plaice, prawns, rainbow trout, red mullet, salmon, salmon trout, shrimps, skate, squid, swordfish, tuna, turbot, whiting

MEAT, GAME AND POULTRY
Beef, chicken, duck, grouse, guinea fowl, hare, lamb, pigeon, pork, quails, rabbit, turkey, venison

VEGETABLES AND SALAD
Asparagus, aubergine, avocados, beetroot, broad beans, cabbage, calabrese, carrots, cauliflower, celery, chillies, corn on the cob, courgettes, cucumber, endive, fennel, French beans, garlic, globe artichokes, herbs, leeks, lettuce, mangetouts, marrow, mushrooms, new potatoes, okra, onions, peas, peppers, radishes, runner beans, shallots, spinach, spring onions, swede, sweet potatoes, tomatoes, turnips, watercress

FRUIT
Apples, apricots, bananas, blackberries, blackcurrants, cherries, damsons, dates, figs, gooseberries, grapefruit, grapes, greengages, kiwis, lemons, limes, loganberries, mangoes, melons, mulberries, nectarines, oranges, passion fruit, peaches, pears, persimmons, pineapples, plums, raspberries, redcurrants, strawberries, watermelons, white currants

NUTS
Walnuts

SEPTEMBER

FISH AND SHELLFISH
Bass, bream, brill, clams, cockles, cod, coley, conger eel, crabs, dabs, Dover Sole, grey mullet, gurnard, haddock, hake, halibut, herring, huss, langoustine, lemon sole, lobster, mackerel, monkfish, mussels, oysters, plaice, prawns, rainbow trout, red mullet, salmon, shrimps, skate, squid, swordfish, tuna, turbot, whiting

MEAT, GAME AND POULTRY
Beef, chicken, duck, goose, grouse, guinea fowl, hare, lamb, partridge, pigeon, pork, quails, rabbit, turkey, venison, wild duck

VEGETABLES AND SALAD
Aubergine, avocado, beetroot, broccoli, Brussels sprouts, cabbage, calabrese, carrots, cauliflower, celery, chicory, chillies, corn on the cob, courgettes, cucumber, endive, fennel, French beans, garlic, globe artichokes, herbs, horseradish, leeks, lettuce, mangetouts, marrow, mushrooms, new potatoes, okra, onions, parsnips, peas, peppers, radishes, runner beans, shallots, spinach, spring onions, swede, sweet potatoes, tomatoes, turnips, watercress

FRUIT
Apples, apricots, bananas, bilberries, blackberries, blackcurrants, blueberries, damsons, dates, figs, grapefruit, grapes, greengages, kiwis, lemons, limes, mangoes, melons, oranges, peaches, pears, pineapples, plums, pomegranates, pumpkins, quince, raspberries, strawberries, watermelons

OCTOBER

FISH AND SHELLFISH
Bass, bream, brill, clams, cockles, cod, coley, conger eel, crabs, dabs, Dover Sole, grey mullet, gurnard, haddock, hake, halibut, herring, huss, langoustine, lemon sole, lobster, mackerel, monkfish, mussels, oysters, plaice, prawns, rainbow trout, salmon, scallops, shrimps, skate, sprats, squid, swordfish, tuna, turbot, whiting, winkles

MEAT, GAME AND POULTRY
Beef, chicken, duck, goose, grouse, guinea fowl, hare, lamb, partridge, pigeon, pork, quails, rabbit, turkey, venison, wild duck, woodcock

VEGETABLES AND SALAD
Aubergine, avocado, beetroot, broccoli, Brussels sprouts, cabbage, calabrese, carrots, cauliflower, celery, chicory, chillies, corn on the cob, courgettes, cucumber, endive, fennel, French beans, garlic, globe artichokes, herbs, horseradish, Jerusalem artichokes, leeks, lettuce, mangetouts, marrow, mushrooms, potatoes, okra, onions, parsnips, peas, peppers, radishes, runner beans, shallots, spinach, spring onions, swede, sweet potatoes, tomatoes, turnips, watercress

FRUIT
Apples, apricots, bananas, blackberries, blueberries, cranberries, damsons, dates, figs, grapefruit, grapes, kiwis, lemons, limes, mangoes, melons, nectarines, oranges, papaya, peaches, pears, pineapples, plums, pomegranates, pumpkins, quince, satsumas, strawberries

NUTS
Chestnuts, coconuts, filberts, walnuts

NOVEMBER

FISH AND SHELLFISH
Bass, bream, brill, clams, cockles, cod, coley, conger eel, crabs, dabs, Dover Sole, grey mullet, gurnard, haddock, hake, halibut, herring, huss, langoustine, lemon sole, lobster, mackerel, monkfish, mussels, oysters, plaice, prawns, rainbow trout, scallops, shrimps, skate, sprats, squid, swordfish, tuna, turbot, whiting, winkles

MEAT, GAME AND POULTRY
Beef, chicken, duck, goose, grouse, guinea fowl, hare, lamb, partridge, pheasant, pigeon, pork, quails, rabbit, turkey, venison, wild duck, woodcock

VEGETABLES AND SALAD
Aubergine, avocado, beetroot, broccoli, Brussels sprouts, cabbage, carrots, cauliflower, celery, chicory, chillies, courgettes, cucumber, fennel, French beans, garlic, herbs, horseradish, Jerusalem artichokes, kale, kohl rabi, leeks, lettuce, mangetouts, marrow, mushrooms, okra, onions, parsnips, peppers, potatoes, radishes, runner beans, salsify, Savoy cabbage, spinach, spring onions, swede, sweet potatoes, tomatoes, turnips, watercress

FRUIT
Apples, bananas, cranberries, dates, figs, grapefruit, grapes, kiwis, lemons, limes, mandarins, mangoes, medlars, melons, nectarines, oranges, papaya, peaches, pears, pineapples, pomegranates, pumpkins, satsumas, tangerines, ugli fruit

NUTS
Almonds, Brazils, chestnuts, coconuts, filberts, walnuts

DECEMBER

FISH AND SHELLFISH
Bass, bream, brill, clams, cockles, cod, coley, crabs, dabs, Dover Sole, eels, grey mullet, gurnard, haddock, hake, halibut, herring, huss, langoustine, lemon sole, lobster, mackerel, monkfish, mussels, oysters, plaice, prawns, rainbow trout, scallops, shrimps, skate, sprats, squid, swordfish, tuna, turbot, whiting, winkles

MEAT, GAME AND POULTRY
Beef, chicken, duck, goose, grouse, guinea fowl, hare, lamb, partridge, pheasant, pigeon, pork, quails, rabbit, turkey, venison, wild duck, woodcock

VEGETABLES AND SALAD
Aubergine, avocado, beetroot, broccoli, Brussels sprouts and tops, cabbage, carrots, cauliflower, celeriac, celery, chicory, chillies, courgettes, cucumber, endive, fennel, French beans, garlic, herbs, horseradish, Jerusalem artichokes, kale, leeks, lettuce, mangetouts, mushrooms, potatoes, okra, onions, parsnips, peppers, radishes, runner beans, salsify, Savoy cabbage, shallots, spinach, spring onions, swede, sweet potatoes, tomatoes, turnips, watercress

FRUIT
Apples, bananas, clementines, cranberries, dates, figs, grapefruit, grapes, kiwis, lemons, limes, mandarins, mangoes, melons, nectarines, oranges, papaya, peaches, pears, pineapples, pomegranates, satsumas, sharon fruit, tangerines, ugli fruit

NUTS
Almonds, Brazils, chestnuts, coconuts, walnuts

WINES

Drinking wine is one of life's great pleasures. But choosing wine to go with food can sometimes be bewildering when you look at the vast range available on the shelves of wine shops and supermarkets.

Most wine retailers have helpful information in the form of shelf-talkers and back labels, which offer advice on the style of the wine and the kind of dish it best accompanies. But this is of necessity rather general. Some have qualified assistants who are more than willing to help. But if they haven't and you are on your own, there are one or two points worth following.

The general advice on serving red wine with red meat and white with chicken and fish is a reasonable rule of thumb – but remember, rules are meant to be broken. What you like best and feel confident about is the most important point. But it still remains that some combinations make happier matches than others.

If the style of the dish is light, say a salad, cold chicken, quiche, or some vegetarian dishes, the wine needs to be light as well. Robust and hearty stews need correspondingly sturdy wines, and so on. Otherwise, either the dish or the wine will overpower, or even walk off in the opposite direction.

A wine which is high in acidity will help balance the richness in some oily dishes. And though white wine is often the general choice with spicy dishes, for example curry, a spicy red would probably be a more compatible partner.

Sometimes, odd combinations are a surprisingly good mix. Sauternes, the sweet white wine from Bordeaux, is quite perfect with foie gras. And one of the best matches with Stilton, the king of English cheeses, is Monbazillac, another luscious sweet white. Just try it and see. And if it seems logical to drink white wine with fish because it has such a delicate flavour, don't rule out light reds like Beaujolais, served chilled, especially good with grilled fish such as salmon.

Any wine served with a dessert must be sweeter than the pudding – otherwise the wine will taste dry.

WHICH WINE?

This is a general chart, matching food with wine using as examples a selection of dishes in the book. You usually decide on the food first, then choose the wine to go with it. The suggestions following are, of course, only to be regarded as a guide. Always be prepared to experiment – you may come up with a winner.

APERITIFS

The ultimate aperitif and perfect ice-breaker is a glass of fizz. This might be Champagne, Cava from Spain or any number of great value sparklers from Australia, New Zealand, Italy, or even India.

CANAPES

Dry white wines, fresh fino sherries or Montillas and not forgetting chilled sparkling wines are all great with canapés which are usually light and tiny bites.

Cucumber and Salmon Egg. A dry sparkling white wine such as a Cava, a light still wine from Italy like Frascati.

Angels on Horseback. Aperitif style dry white wine, a fresh fino sherry, or a dry Montilla are all good matches with this.

SOUPS

Vegetable soups such as Fennel and Tomato or Pea and Mint. A fino sherry.

Fish soups such as Cream of Mussel or Cullen Skink. Fino – or perhaps Manzanilla which has a salty brush of the sea about it.

COLD FIRST COURSES

These range from light salads and tartlets to pâtés and terrines.

Langoustine Salad with melon balls and avocados in an Oriental dressing. A crisp dry white such as Sancerre.

Smoked Salmon and Asparagus tarts. A fruity dry wine from Penedés in northern Spain.

Luxury Chicken Liver Pâté. A smooth red such as a spicy Rhone, or Tempanillo, from northern Spain. Or for a change perhaps Galestro from Tuscany.

The elegant Asparagus Terrine. A dry sparkling wine.

HOT FIRST COURSES

Hot Chilli Prawns. A light red such as Beaujolais.

Avocado and Prawn Soufflé. This glamorous dinner party starter needs a South African Chenin Blanc, or New Zealand Sauvignon Blanc.

MAIN COURSES

MEAT

Meaty dishes such as the robust Braised Beef with Olives. A full-bodied, rich red like an Italian Barolo.

Wiltshire Hot Pot with butter beans – pork spare rib chops in a piquant tomato sauce. A spicy country red wine from Provence.

Spicy Liver Goulash. A full-bodied red like a Cabernet Sauvignon from Chile.

A gutsy plate of Medici Meatballs with a spinach and pesto sauce. A Chianti.

Filet de Boeuf en Croûte. A special wine such as a mature Hermitage, Châteauneuf-du-Pape, or Gran Reserva Rioja.

POULTRY

Crispy Duck with pancakes. Australian Chardonnay where the full-bodied richness is a great match.

Chicken and Tarragon Kiev has a subtle mix of garlic and herbs in the butter filling. Try an oaked Chardonnay with this. Or an Alsace Riesling, Pinot Blanc, or a Bergerac Blanc.

Chicken Farah with Cous Cous. These kebabs need something simple like a French Country white wine.

Chicken with 40 Cloves of Garlic, a richly flavoured dish from Provence. An Australian Sauvignon Blanc.

FISH

Mediterranean Mackerel Stew is rich and chunky. A rosado from northern Spain or a light red from southern France.

Tuna Fishcakes, flavourful and herby. The crispness of an Australian Sauvignon Blanc.

Seafood Risotto with langoustine tails, monkfish, halibut and clams. A Muscadet sur Lie or an Italian Chardonnay.

Prawn and Dill Quiche could be a light lunch or dinner party dish. A New Zealand Sauvignon Blanc.

Creamy Cod Curry is delicately spiced with ginger and chilli. A chilled Pinot Noir from Romania.

CHEESE

Beef Pies in Stilton Crust is a robust dish with a delightful tang in the pastry. A Californian Zinfandel or Cabernet Shiraz from Australia, or a Dão from Portugal.

Stilton Cheesecake is a wonderful dish. A red Reserva from Penedés.

Cheddar and Tuna Soufflé, light and airy. A fruity dry white like a Semillon Chardonnay from Australia.

VEGETARIAN

Cheese and Tomato Pie. Full flavoured with sun-dried tomatoes and fresh tomatoes in the ingredients. A red Corbières with this.

Penne Arrabiatta – pasta quills with an exceedingly spicy sauce. A robust red wine such as a Bulgarian Cabernet Sauvignon.

Parsnip and Mushroom Lasagne – a great vegetarian treat. A dry white wine such as Vinho Verde from Portugal with its slight petillance.

Avocado and Courgette Risotto is sultry and creamy. A buttery un-oaked Chardonnay, perhaps from northern Spain.

DESSERTS

Summer Pudding. An inexpensive luscious Moscatel de Valencia.

Fig Tart. A chilled Late Harvest Muscat from Australia with this.

Nectarine Cheesecake. A Sauternes or Loupiac with this rich pudding.

SERVING WINE

White wines and rosés are generally served chilled and reds at room temperature. However, it is possible to chill the flavour and aromas right out of white wine – it should not be too cold. One hour in the fridge is quite enough.

Full-bodied whites and sparklers can take more chilling than light whites. Serve all whites and rosés in an ice bucket of water with some ice added. A bucket packed only with ice will reduce the temperature too much.

'Room temperature' when applied to reds, refers to the temperature of rooms in the days before central heating. It doesn't actually mean warm. In fact quite often light reds such as Beaujolais taste better slightly chilled – it brings out the fruit. So keep an open mind on this point – and experiment.

It is usual to open full-bodied reds at least an hour before serving.

OPENING BOTTLES

The reason sparkling wines often open with an explosion is because they are bottled under pressure. Without care while opening, the cork will shoot out at great speed – and worse, will be followed by a large quantity of wine, something to be avoided at all cost.

Chilling the bottle first helps to subdue some of the liveliness. Remove the foil covering the top of the bottle, then, keeping your thumb over the cork, remove the wire cage. (Corks sometimes have a will of their own and simply shoot out the moment the cage is removed. This could injure someone.)

Hold the bottle at 45 degrees, still keeping the cork in place with your hand. Hold the body of the bottle with your other hand. Hold the cork steady, and turn the bottle, not the cork. As you feel the pressure being released, press slightly on the cork so when it finally comes out of the bottle it does it with a discreet hiss, not an ear-splitting pop.

If you have a tough cork which is impossible to budge, there are special grippers which will do the trick.

GLASSES

Some people think there is a lot of nonsense talked about 'proper' wine glasses. But behind the general advice, there is basic common sense. As an experiment, just try drinking wine out of a mug. Then compare it with sipping from an elegant glass and you will see the logic.

A basic glass for general use should be clear, so you can see the colour of the wine, and goblet shaped, so the aroma can be trapped in the glass. Sometimes white wines are served in smaller size glasses than reds, on the assumption that reds have more aroma. This is not necessarily so. The same size will do for both.

Sparkling wine should always be served in tall flutes, not in 'saucers'. The reason for this is so there is less surface of the wine for the bubbles to escape. Tulip-shaped flutes again trap the fragrance and keep the fizz in longer. The reverse happens with 'saucers'.

After sampling the wine, fill the glass up to no more than two-thirds, so the aroma can be appreciated.

WINE REGIONS

Wine is produced in more than twenty countries in the world, which means there is quite a choice. This is a thumbnail directory of what is available and from where.

FRANCE

France is the world's largest producer of high quality wines, which most of the rest of the world respects and tries to match.

Champagne, the most famous sparkling wine in the world, is made in a small region of this country. It has no equal.

The classic reds of Bordeaux and Burgundy are legendary. And the sweet wines of Bordeaux are luscious and renowned worldwide.

The Loire region is noted for its juicy, crisp dry whites, perfect with fish and shellfish. And from the sunny Rhone come spicy peppery reds.

Alsace whites have elegance and sophistication.

In short, France does just about everything the rest of the world would like to do.

ITALY

Italy makes more wine than any other country in the world. Much of this is made from indigenous grape varieties, but French grapes are now being grown with great success.

Some of the most famous wines like fragrantly fruity Chianti and truffly Barolo are made from native grapes – Chianti from Sangiovese and Barolo from Nebbiolo.

Whites include Frascati, Soave and Verdicchio. Popular inexpensive light reds like Valpolicella and Bardolino are perfect for everyday drinking.

SPAIN

A country of great diversity. Over the past few decades the Spanish wine business has dramatically changed its image and now makes wines to rival and often beat the best in the world. Great value for money, quality wines are now being made in the modern style which have enormous international appeal.

As well as fresh and fruity styles of wine made by up-to-date methods, Rioja still produces wine in the time-honoured traditional way with bags of oak. So take your choice.

Navarra, next door to Rioja, makes stunning dry rosés, reds from Tempranillo and kernelly whites.

The cultivation of French grape varieties started in Penedés. These are now blended with local grapes to make excellent wines. This region too, is famous for Cava, Spanish sparkling wine made exactly like Champagne, sometimes with their own grapes – and sometimes with the French ones.

Other good value wines come from Valdepeñas, La Mancha and Valencia.

Jerez in the south is the home of sherry.

PORTUGAL

Many good wines from here in recent years – particularly suitable for drinking with food of the robust kind.

Vinho Verde is one of the most famous dry whites which has a lively spritz. Another well-known wine is a medium dry rosé in a flask bottle.

But Portugal is best known for Port.

GERMANY

Light floral, medium dry wines, low in alcohol, represent the general image of Germany. Quality wines range upwards in sweetness from Kabinett, medium dry; Spätlese, late-picked; and Auslese, made from very ripe grapes. After this comes Beerenauslese made from selected grapes affected by Noble Rot, and then Trockenbeerenauslese from shrivelled Botrytised grapes. Eiswein is made from frozen shrivelled grapes and needless to say is the sweetest and most expensive.

In recent years two new styles have been introduced to appeal to drier palates. Trocken is dry and Halbtrocken, medium dry.

ENGLAND

Due to the vagaries of the British climate with little reliable sunshine, grapes have a hard time ripening, so English wines are usually dry, and crisp, sometimes low in alcohol.

EASTERN EUROPE

Good value quality reds from Bulgaria made from Cabernet Sauvignon, Merlot and Pinot Noir have been popular and affordable choices for everyday drinking. Whites from Chardonnay have also been successful. Romania is making very acceptable Pinot Noirs.

AUSTRALIA

Australia produces wines to suit all tastes. Almost every conceivable grape variety is grown. The best reds are made from minty Cabernet Sauvignon and spicy, peppery Shiraz.

The whites range from crisp and fresh Sauvignon Blancs which can sometimes be matured in wood for extra depth, Chardonnays, which may be light and elegant or rounded and buttery, and classy Semillons which can be youthful or sophisticated.

Sparkling wines made in the Méthode Champenoise are excellent value for money.

Australia's special contribution to the drinking world is fortified liqueur muscats – superb luscious sweeties for sipping after dinner.

NEW ZEALAND

Excellent grassy gooseberry Sauvignon Blancs from here with refreshing juiciness. Elegant Chardonnays as well. Reds include dry Cabernet Sauvignons, and there are some richer versions too.

Other varieties include Pinot Noir and Gewürztraminer.

CALIFORNIA

Famous for varietal wines – that is wines made from a single grape variety. In the past often big wines, now they are more subdued and in an elegant European style.

Rich blackcurrant Cabernets and blends of this grape are excellent. There are some very good Pinot Noirs. The native Zinfandel makes a characterful red – and also the fashionable blush. Good sparklers from here, too.

CHILE

Full and voluptuous deep-coloured wines from Cabernet Sauvignon are popular brushed with herbs and spice. Fresh and fruity whites come from Chardonnay and Sauvignon Blanc, or Semillon which can be either simple or sophisticated.

SOUTH AFRICA

Many good wines from here, particularly Chenin Blanc and their own Pinotage, a cross between Pinot Noir and Hermitage.

Lots of good value inexpensive wines too using Sauvignon Blanc, Chardonnay and Cabernet Sauvignon.

INDEX